ENDGAME

ENDGAME

THE BETRAYAL
AND FALL OF SREBRENICA,
EUROPE'S WORST MASSACRE
SINCE WORLD WAR II

DAVID ROHDE

Westview Press
A Member of the Perseus Books Group

Copyright © 1997 by David Rohde
Maps copyright © 1997 by David Herring

This edition published in 1998 in the United States of America by Westview Press, A Member of the Perseus Books Group, 5500 Central Avenue, Boulder, Colorado 80301-2877

First published in hardcover in 1997 by Farrar, Straus and Giroux and in Canada by HarperCollins*CanadaLtd*

Designed by Abby Kagan
Jacket design by Michael Ian Kaye

Library of Congress Cataloging-in-Publication Data
Rohde, David S., 1967-
   Endgame : the betrayal and fall of Srebrenica, Europe's worst
massacre since World War II / David S. Rohde.
       p. cm.
   "First published in hardcover in 1997 by Farrar, Straus & Giroux
and in Canada by HarperCollins "Canada Ltd."—CIP t.p. verso.
   Includes bibliographical references and index.
   ISBN 0-8133-3533-7 (pbk.)
   1. Yugoslav War, 1991– —Campaigns—Bosnia and Hercegovina—
Srebrenica. 2. Yugoslav War, 1991– —Atrocities. 3. Srebrenica
(Bosnia and Hercegovina)—History, Military. I. Title.
DR1313.32.S68R64   1998
949.703—dc21   98-26127
                                                                          CIP

The paper used in this publication meets the requirements of the American National Standard for Permanence of Paper for Printed Library Materials Z39.48-1984.

10   9   8   7   6   5   4   3   2   1

To the people of Srebrenica
and to my family

CONTENTS

MAPS

PREFACE

In August 1995, while covering the war in Bosnia for *The Christian Science Monitor,* I heard about suspected mass graves U.S. spy planes had located near Srebrenica in eastern Bosnia. The surrounded Muslim town had fallen to the Bosnian Serbs a month earlier. Survivors reported mass executions.

On August 16, I received permission from the Bosnian Serbs to enter their territory and drive straight to Pale—their self-declared capital. With a faxed copy of the satellite photo of the suspected graves in hand, I headed in the direction of Pale but stopped instead in Nova Kasaba—the village where the suspected graves were spotted. After searching for two hours, I found four swaths of fresh digging, two empty ammunition boxes, notes from a Srebrenica town meeting, an elementary school diploma with a Muslim name, and finally, a decomposed human leg.

I then spent two weeks in September searching refugee camps on the other side of the front line for survivors of mass executions. I found nine survivors who told credible stories of thousands of unarmed Muslim prisoners being shot. Soldiers who survived the trek from Srebrenica led me to the brother of the man whose elementary school diploma I'd found twenty-five feet from a suspected grave in Nova Kasaba. When I showed the diploma to him, his face went blank and he turned and disappeared into a crowd of soldiers. His twenty-one-year-old brother Murat had been missing since Srebrenica fell.

In October, I reentered Serb territory without permission and found two more execution sites. At the first were three canes and a stack of civilian clothes one hundred yards from what looked like two freshly dug mass graves, corroborating survivors' stories of old men and civilians being killed. At the second, human bones lay next to an earthen dam, again confirming survivor accounts of executions. Just before I took photos of the bones, a Bosnian Serb watchman arrested me.

I was convicted of illegal entry, jailed for ten days and threatened with an espionage charge that carried a sentence of ten years to death. After twelve members of my family and two of my editors at *The Christian Science Monitor* flew to ongoing Bosnia peace talks in Dayton, Ohio, the Clinton administration pressured the Serbs into freeing me.

At that time, I believed Srebrenica's fall to be a simple tale of victim and perpetrator. But the town's fall has proven far more complex, convoluted and darker than I expected.

The fall of Srebrenica has emerged as one of the great controversies—and mysteries—of the war in Bosnia. Countless conspiracy theories, some dubious and some plausible, revolve around the tragedy.

The truth in the former Yugoslavia—a region that has been dominated by authoritarian regimes for centuries—is a nebulous concept. Exaggeration and manipulation of the facts are well-accepted tools for survival and propaganda is the norm. All sides in the brutal war—including many Western and UN officials—have resolutely convinced themselves that they are blameless and the other side is guilty.

United Nations, Dutch, French, American and Bosnian officials lied about, downplayed or covered up their own roles in the tragedy and blamed others for the enclave's fall. Survivors and people from Srebrenica exaggerated, openly lied or presented a sanitized version of their actions and decision making. Many Bosnian Serb authorities refused to speak and intimidated those who did.

This book focuses primarily on the experiences of seven people—three Muslims, two Dutch, a Serb and a Croat.[1] They were chosen because of what they lived through and because I found them to be highly credible. The account that follows, which includes individuals' detailed thoughts and recollections, is a description of events as related to me by these individuals and characterized in documents and press reports. Central characters were allowed to review the portions of the book they appear in for accuracy. I took this unusual step to avoid misinterpretation and to give the book immediacy. Every event or atrocity that occurred may not be here, but I believe this is an accurate portrayal of the dynamic at work in Srebrenica and Bosnia at the time.

Notes have been used to explain the source of information and to discuss allegations. Conversations have been reconstructed on the basis of interviews with participants or from reports written at the time. Where I am unsure of what occurred I say so, or explain why in a note. I apologize for any inaccuracies, distortions or omissions. I have tried to make this as accurate as possible. All errors in judgment are mine.

This book should be considered only an inital account of the fall of Srebrenica, not the final word. My hope is that it will spark further investigation. Propaganda, mistrust and rumor sparked and fueled the war in Bosnia and played an insidious role in Srebrenica. The goal of this book is to help break that dynamic, not feed it.

Bosnia's Muslims, Serbs and Croats are racially identical. All three groups are white Eastern European Slavs. "Yugoslavia" means "land of the South Slavs." All three groups speak Serbo-Croatian with a Bosnian accent. The difference between Bosnia's Muslims, Serbs and Croats is their religious faith. The only way a Serb, Croat or Muslim can distinguish one another is by their first or last names.

Bosnia-Herzegovina is slightly larger than the state of West Virginia. When war broke out in April 1992, the picturesque country of 4.3 million was 44 percent Muslim, 31 percent Serb, 17 percent Croat, and 8 percent "Yugoslav" or people who chose to describe themselves as part of no nationality. It was the most ethnically integrated of Yugoslavia's six republics and intermarriage between Serbs, Croats and Muslims was common in cities and larger towns.

Bosnia is one of the world's great crossroads. For centuries, civilizations, armies and empires have met and overlapped here. The country's long occupation by great empires is what divided its people into roughly three groups. Those who converted to Catholicism under the rule of the Catholic Holy Roman Empire became known as Bosnian Croats. Those who converted to Orthodox Christianity under the rule of the Eastern Orthodox Byzantine Empire became known as Bosnian Serbs. Those who converted to Islam under the rule of the Muslim Ottoman Turks became known as Bosnian Muslims.

After the death in May 1980 of Yugoslavia's founder and dictator, Josip Broz Tito, politicians playing on nationalism rose to power across the country.[2] In Serbia, Slobodan Milošević used state-controlled television to whip up nationalism and play on people's fears that past Serb suffering might be repeated. On the June 1989 anniversary of the defeat that led to the Ottoman Turks' brutal, 500-year occupation of Serbia, Milošević told a rally of roughly one million Serbs: "Six centuries later, again we are in battles and quarrels. They are not armed battles, though such things should not be excluded yet."[3]

On June 25, 1991, both Croatia and Slovenia declared independence. Fighting between Slovene nationalists and the mostly Serb Yugoslav National Army soon flared, but lasted for only ten days. In Croatia, bitter fighting erupted in July between Serbs and Croats and raged for six months amid frantic European peace efforts. A UN arms embargo was imposed on all of the former Yugoslavia in September 1991 to theoretically lessen fighting. But the embargo simply locked into place the huge military advantage enjoyed by the Serbs, the largest group in the former Yugoslavia, who controlled the Yugoslav National Army and its vast stockpile of ammunition.

Over 12,000 UN peacekeepers arrived in March 1992 to implement a tense cease-fire in Croatia. In six months of brutal fighting, ten thousand died and Serb nationalists seized approximately one-third of Croatia. They vowed to link their territory with Serbia and create a "Greater Serbia." Croats vowed to re-take every inch of it.

Fighting erupted in Bosnia less than a month later. Troops and ultranationalist paramilitary groups from Serbia crossed into neighboring Bosnia. They began expelling or "ethnically cleansing" hundreds of thousands of Muslims and Croats from eastern and northern Bosnia.

At the same time, Croatia, the second most powerful republic after Serbia, began funneling troops, weapons and ammunition to Croat nationalists living in Bosnia.[4] Serbian President Milo-šević and Croatian President Franjo Tudjman hoped to divide Bosnia between themselves and create a "Greater Serbia" and a "Greater Croatia." Bosnia's Muslims, trapped between the two more powerful groups, had few weapons and no outside backer.

Tucked into the mountains of eastern Bosnia, Srebrenica (pro-nounced *Srebreneetsa*) takes its name from the Serbo-Croatian word for silver, *srebro*. Srebrenica or "Silver City" has been known for its silver since the Romans mined the region twenty centuries ago. The Romans called it "Argentaria," a variation of the Latin word for silver.

The Roman garrison that once stood in the town is gone, but the ruins of a medieval castle built according to local legend by Jerina, the widow of a Serb lord, lie on a hill to the south. Ac-cording to the legend, the castle was built by slaves. Each night a different slave was brought to Jerina's bedroom. Each morn-ing, the exhausted slave was thrown to his death from the top of the castle.[5]

One mile east of town lies Crni Guber, a natural spring that produces medicinal water with large amounts of iron and a "harmonious" mixture of copper, cobalt, nickel and manganese. The spring has its own health spa; locals say drinking the water cures anemia, rheumatism, multiple sclerosis, lack of appetite, exhaustion and chronic diseases of the hair and skin.[6]

The town of Srebrenica is shaped like a long, thin finger. The quaint mining town had a prewar population of roughly 9,000. Driving from one end to the other takes only fifteen minutes. A thin strip of houses, schools and stores runs at the bottom of a two-mile-long, half-mile-wide ravine. Steep hills rise on either side of Srebrenica, giving one a sense of being sheltered—or trapped.

White houses with terra-cotta roofs line the streets and dot the surrounding hills. A dozen gray apartment buildings built for miners and factory workers by Yugoslavia's Communist government seem out of place. The hospital lies in the northern half of the town. The elementary and high schools are near the center. The border with Serbia is only ten miles away and many teenagers left town for jobs or universities in Belgrade, the capital of Serbia and Yugoslavia, instead of Sarajevo, the capital of Bosnia.

Small family-run grocery stores and cafés once enlivened the main street. A large gray Serbian Orthodox church, a mosque with a hundred-foot minaret and an open-air farmer's market comprise the town's historic center. A state-run department store, the six-story Hotel Domavija and a small shopping center make up its modern side.

After World War II, Yugoslavia's Communist government built car battery, car brake and zinc processing factories in Potočari, a village two miles north of Srebrenica. Bauxite and zinc mines to the south and northeast flourished. Nearly every miner or factory worker had an apartment, car and summer cottage. By the 1990s, most households had a TV, VCR, washing machine and a host of modern appliances. Movie theaters and supermarkets opened. Srebrenicans enjoyed a standard of living that rivaled that of the United States and Western Europe.[7]

According to the last census conducted before the war, 37,211 people lived in Srebrenica *opština* or municipality, which consisted of the town and an approximately fifty-square-mile area around it. Seventy-three percent described themselves as Muslims, 25 percent as Serbs and 2 percent as "Yugoslavs" or part of no ethnic group.

Soon after fighting broke out in April 1992, nationalist paramilitary groups from Serbia seized control of Srebrenica with the aim of expelling the town's Muslims as they had throughout Bosnia. Muslims fled to nearby forests. Three weeks later Mus-

lims led by Naser Orić, a charismatic twenty-six-year-old policeman, retook the town. The heavily armed Serbs had suffered
one of their first major defeats of the lopsided war, but they still
surrounded the town. Orić then led Muslim forces from Srebrenica to a series of stunning victories in 1992, which more
than doubled the size of the island of Muslim territory. By January 1993 the enclave was only five miles from linking with
Muslim-held central Bosnia.

But Bosnian Serbs, backed by troops, tanks and artillery from
neighboring Serbia, quickly launched a counteroffensive. With
the Serbs blocking UN food convoys, U.S. Air Force planes
dropped food into the area by parachute. Muslim-held towns
and villages continued to fall. By mid-March 1993, over 60,000
Muslim civilians packed the town of Srebrenica and a small area
around it.

Fearing the collapse of Srebrenica, the UN commander in
Bosnia, French general Philippe Morillon, set off for the teetering
enclave without the permission of his superiors in New York.
Morillon bluffed his way through Serb lines and entered Srebrenica. Surrounded by Muslim women and children when he
tried to leave a day later, Morillon made an impromptu announcement that would cost him his job and change the course
of the war.

"You are now under the protection of the United Nations,"
the fifty-seven-year-old, white-haired general with a flair for the
dramatic proclaimed from a post office window on March 12.
"I will never abandon you." The UN flag was then raised over
Srebrenica.

The Serbs allowed a few food convoys into the enclave but
just over a month later they attacked again. As the town's defenses crumbled on April 15, Srebrenica's leaders requested that
surrender negotiations begin. Under intense pressure to act, a
divided UN Security Council passed Resolution 819 and declared Srebrenica and a thirty-square-mile area around it the
world's first United Nations "safe area" on April 16.

When UN Secretary General Boutros Boutros-Ghali later requested 34,000 peacekeepers to police Srebrenica and five other
newly declared safe areas,[8] the United States and other countries

balked at sending their own troops. A second proposal, sarcastically referred to as "safe areas lite" by UN officials, was adopted and only 7,600 peacekeepers were sent to the six new safe areas.[9]

First Canadian and then Dutch peacekeepers were deployed in Srebrenica. Seven hundred and fifty lightly armed UN peacekeepers were responsible for disarming Srebrenica's Muslim defenders and "deterring" Bosnian Serb attacks against the safe area. Two years later, a Serb flag flew where the UN's once did and 7,079 Muslim men were missing.

THE FORMER YUGOSLAVIA

BOSNIA-HERZEGOVINA, JULY 1995

CROATIA

O Bihać

Banja Luka

BOSNIA-
HERZEGOVINA

Tuzla O

Serbia

Srebrenica

Žepa

O Sarajevo

Goražde

YUGOSLAVIA

Montenegro

Adriatic Sea

Serbs   Muslim- and Croat-controlled

O UN/Safe Areas

CHARACTERS

Ćamila Omanović, forty-two: Bosnian Muslim bookkeeper and housewife living in Srebrenica.

Hurem Suljić, fifty-five: crippled Bosnian Muslim carpenter living in a village near Srebrenica.

Mevludin Orić, twenty-five: Bosnian Muslim soldier living in a village near Srebrenica.

Zoran Radić, thirty: Bosnian Serb policeman participating in the attack on Srebrenica.

Dražen Erdemović, twenty-three: Bosnian Croat soldier fighting alongside Bosnian Serbs attacking Srebrenica.

Private First Class Marc Klaver, twenty-three: Dutch UN peacekeeper stationed in Srebrenica.

First Lieutenant Vincent Egbers, twenty-nine: Dutch UN peacekeeper stationed in Srebrenica.

ABBREVIATIONS

ABiH or BH: Army of Bosnia and Herzegovina—Muslim-led forces of the Bosnian government.

APC: armored personnel carrier.

BSA: Bosnian Serb Army.

CAS: Close Air Support.

FC: Force Commander—the commander of all UN forces in the former Yugoslavia.

FRY: Federal Republic of Yugoslavia. The name adopted by Serbia and Montenegro, two of the six former Yugoslav republics, after the dissolution of the country.

MRL: multiple rocket launcher.

OP: observation post.

RPG: rocket-propelled grenade.

SDA: Party of Democratic Action—the Muslim nationalist party headed by Bosnian President Alija Izetbegović.

SDS: Serbian Democratic Party—the Bosnian Serb nationalist party headed by Bosnian Serb leader Radovan Karadžić.

SRSG: Special Representative of the Secretary General. The civilian head of the UN peacekeeping missions in the former Yugoslavia.

UNHCR: United Nations High Commissioner for Refugees.

UNPF: United Nations Peace Forces—the umbrella name for the three separate UN peacekeeping missions in Bosnia, Croatia and Macedonia created in April 1995.

UNPROFOR: United Nations Protection Force—the name of the UN peacekeeping mission in the former Yugoslavia from February 1992 until April 1995. After April 1995, UNPROFOR referred only to the UN mission in Bosnia.

PRONUNCIATION KEY

č = *ch* as in charm

ć = *ch* as in rich

c = *ts* as in cats

š = *sh* as in shoe

ž = *s* as in measure

đ = *j* as in jump

dj = *g* as in forge

j = *y* as is yes

lj = *li* as in billion

nj = *ny* as in canyon

"An eye for an eye leaves everybody blind."

—Martin Luther King, Jr.

THURSDAY, JULY 6, 1995

SREBRENICA SAFE AREA, JULY 6, 1995

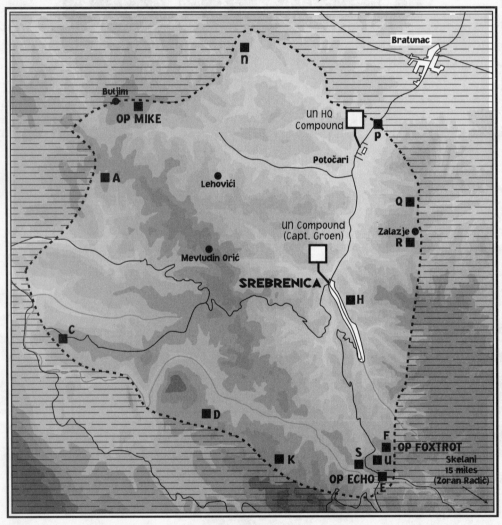

Bratunac

n

Butjim
OP MIKE

un HQ
Compound

P

Potočari

A

Lehovići

Q

Zalazje

un Compound
(Capt. Groen)

R

SREBRENICA

Mevludin Orić

H

C

D

F

OP FOXTROT

S

Skelani
15 miles
(Zoran Radić)

K

U

OP ECHO

E

Serb-controlled　　■ un observation posts　- - - - Safe Area boundary

D utch Private First Class Marc Klaver peered into the pre-dawn darkness. Perched in the watchtower of UN Observation Post Foxtrot, Klaver couldn't get his bleary eyes to focus. His mind drifted. It was just after 5 a.m. One hour into a four-hour shift, Klaver and the other peacekeeper on duty—Dutch Private First Class Raviv van Renssen—were bored.

A bright flash abruptly lit up the sky to the east. A detonation rolled across the open fields. Startled, Klaver and van Renssen instinctively turned toward the light and sound. A deafening explosion shook the tower. "Shit!" Klaver shouted as the two young soldiers dove to the plywood floor. Chunks of dirt cascaded over Biljeg, the hilltop that OP Foxtrot was perched on. Klaver and van Renssen stared at each other in disbelief.

Silence hung over the hill for a few seconds. Another flash and detonation to the east. The two young soldiers, dressed in camouflage T-shirts and shorts, pressed their chests against the floor. A shell whistled overhead. A second explosion rocked the hilltop. Klaver, twenty-three, was disoriented. Van Renssen, twenty-five, a mortar specialist, realized the first explosion was the sound of a mortar firing in front of them. The whistle was the mortar passing overhead. The second explosion was the impact behind them.

He fumbled for the radio. "Ops room, this is OP Foxtrot! Over!" van Renssen shouted.

"This is ops room. Over," a sleepy voice answered back from the operations room in the UN Bravo Company base in Srebrenica town.[1]

"This is Foxtrot. We had two detonations near the OP!" van Renssen shouted. "Mortar grenades! Fired over the OP from the Serb side!"

Klaver desperately pressed his long, thin frame against the floor and wondered if this was really happening. His ears rang. Sweat covered him. Observation Post Foxtrot had been nicknamed "OP Holiday," "OP Sun Beach" and "OP Relax," because so little happened there. Klaver and the five other peacekeepers had spent much of their time sunbathing. This was the first time Foxtrot had been shelled since their battalion arrived five months earlier.

Klaver and van Renssen scrambled down a ladder into a sandbag bunker beneath the tower. Klaver was worried. They'd heard over the radio that the Bosnian Serbs had fired six rockets over the Dutch headquarters compound in the village of Potočari at 3:15 a.m. The day before, one piece of Serb long-range artillery had abruptly appeared on a hill a mile north of the observation post. Roughly a hundred Bosnian Serb soldiers with thin white ribbons tied to their shoulders had been seen walking east. Ribbons were the primary way soldiers in Bosnia—who were physically identical and generally wore the same uniforms—could identify which side they were on. Finally, a pickup truck towing an antiaircraft gun, which the Serbs used to fire on people not airplanes, had been seen driving north.

Klaver had reported everything to the operations room in Srebrenica town, but had been told not to worry. He thought the vague answer meant his commanders didn't know what to make of the Serb troop movements either.

Set on the highest hill in the southeast corner of the enclave, OP Foxtrot was a microcosm of the confused UN mission in Bosnia.

On the one hand, Klaver and the Dutch were supposed to be neutral UN peacekeepers. They wore bright blue UN helmets, berets or baseball caps. Nearly every inch of the observation post's fifty-by-thirty-yard compound of prefabricated containers, canvas tents and sandbag bunkers was UN white. OP Foxtrot could be spotted—and shelled—from miles away. As far as Klaver, van Renssen and the other Dutch were concerned, OP Foxtrot was a great white albatross, not a defensive position.

But Klaver and his fellow peacekeepers were also expected to take sides if necessary and "deter" attacks by the Bosnian Serbs. Muslim soldiers had grudgingly turned over this and a half dozen other strategic hills to the UN when Srebrenica became a safe area. Klaver could see the jagged ridges and steep hills of eastern Bosnia rising and falling for five miles in each direction from his fifteen-foot watchtower. It was unforgiving terrain. It was almost impossible for someone to sneak up to the observation post or mount a major attack on the town without being seen. But with few weapons, blue helmets and white vehicles, the Dutch were a meager fighting force. Both confused and discouraged by their contradictory mission, Klaver and Srebrenica's Dutch peacekeepers had spent most of the last five months hoping nothing would happen.

Klaver loved being a soldier, but had felt uncomfortable as soon as he arrived in Srebrenica. A long-range rifleman, he was used to digging in and concealing himself, not painting his surroundings white. The Dutch battalion were paratroopers trained to be highly mobile. They had been taught to fire, quickly move to a new position and fire again. Firing from various locations made it difficult for the enemy to locate them or assess their strength, but in Srebrenica and all of Bosnia, UN peacekeeping doctrine was that the activities of UN soldiers should be "transparent." Peacekeepers were to go out of their way to make it easy for all sides to see what they were doing and make themselves vulnerable.

For Klaver, the safe area was a humiliating joke. The Muslims refused to be disarmed and carried out raids into Serb territory at night. Both sides occasionally sniped at the Dutch and each other. As soon as he'd seen the rugged hills and thirty-mile front line around the enclave, Klaver had known that his 750-man battalion couldn't defend Srebrenica with the limited weapons and equipment they had.

The Bosnian Serbs had blocked their resupply convoys for months. The Dutch had received no diesel fuel since February

18 and were using mules and tractors to supply most of their thirteen observation posts. They had run out of fresh food two months ago and had been eating only combat rations. Klaver hadn't had a real cigarette or a beer in four weeks. The Dutch traded food sometimes for yellow tobacco leaves grown by local Muslims. They were usually without cigarette paper, sometimes rolling the tobacco in magazine paper. Graffiti in the OP, left by past and present peacekeepers, read, "Dutchbat Victim," "Dope again" and "Come back Shitty Muslim."

After the first half hour of shelling, it started to become predictable. Klaver and van Renssen relaxed as they sat in Foxtrot's sandbag bunker and listened to the shells impacting outside. It was clear the Bosnian Serbs were not targeting the observation post. They were pulverizing the network of World War I-era trenches the Muslims had built behind the OP and on the small hills that flanked it. Klaver could hear Muslims intermittently firing AK-47 assault rifles and mortars at the Bosnian Serbs from their trenches. They fired at most a dozen mortar shells at the Bosnian Serbs. The peacekeepers were unimpressed, but still jittery.

Klaver and van Renssen climbed back up into the tower at around 7 a.m. Peering through his binoculars, Klaver saw that three tanks, two howitzer artillery pieces and a multiple rocket launcher had taken up position 1,600 yards east of the observation post. The shells and rockets flew by their watchtower trailing beautiful, long tails of fire. As the scorching July sun slowly rose, Klaver and van Renssen started to enjoy the spectacle. "Look at that one," Klaver said as a rocket flew by.

The most surreal moment of the morning came during a lull in the shelling. A bus pulled up next to the Serb artillery positions. A group of military officers stepped out. Like gawking tourists, they snapped photos of the OP and left. Klaver was again surprised by the Muslim response. No snipers appeared to shoot at the Serb officers.

At around 1 p.m., a shell abruptly tore into the front wall of the OP. The watchtower felt like it was collapsing. The sandbags over Klaver's and van Renssen's heads shook violently. Sand poured onto their helmets. Klaver felt his heart pounding in his throat. One of the Serb tanks was directly targeting them.

Four miles to the northwest, twenty-five-year-old Mevludin Orić, a Bosnian Muslim soldier, was nervously enjoying the spectacle. Standing on top of the 2,900-foot Mount Zvijezda in the center of the safe area, Mevludin, his neighbor Azem Dautović and several women were watching Serb shells career into the safe area. Mevludin had tried to walk into Srebrenica town that morning but gave up when he saw the extent of the shelling. Mevludin was confident that UN commanders in Sarajevo would soon retaliate against the Serbs.

A multiple rocket launcher in the Bosnian Serb-held town of Bratunac just north of Srebrenica was firing into the enclave. Mevludin was impressed by the thunderous sound of the rockets launching, buzzing through the air and then detonating. It was the first time the Serbs had fired them into Srebrenica since it was designated a safe area.

Mevludin had quickly decided that Srebrenica's Dutch peace-keepers were little more than greedy cowards. They had come here to make money, he thought, not to protect the safe area. While the Dutch lived like kings, hunger still haunted the over-crowded enclave's people. The Bosnian Serbs blocked UN food convoys at will. Each day, local Muslims would venture to OP Mike, the nearest UN post, and wait patiently for the Dutch to throw away their garbage. The refuse was then painstakingly searched for scraps of food. He expected the Dutch to run at the first sign of a serious attack.

But the Dutch weren't the biggest reason Mevludin Orić felt uneasy that morning, Naser was.

Naser Orić was Srebrenica's charismatic twenty-nine-year-old commander and Mevludin Orić's distant cousin. He had left the enclave two months ago. Mevludin had heard that Naser and fifteen of Srebrenica's best officers slipped out of town under cover of darkness and trekked ten miles south to Žepa, a second Muslim UN-declared safe area. From there, they had been fer-ried by helicopter to Muslim-held central Bosnia in April. The fifteen officers were supposed to be attending a short-term training course. But only two of the fifteen, the deputy commander and one brigade commander, had returned.

With Naser leading them, with his trademark .50 caliber machine gun, Srebrenica's defenders felt invulnerable. The bearded, six-foot-one-inch bodybuilder had jet-black hair and an enormous chest and powerful arms. A tough-talking former local policeman and prewar bodyguard for Serbian President Slobodan Milošević, he had spurred the Muslims on to spectacular victories in 1992. He was adored by his men and feared by his adversaries. Ambitious and ruthless, Naser had turned Srebrenica into his fiefdom. No one knew when he was coming back, but his absence hung over Mevludin Orić and Srebrenica's soldiers.

The UN's arrival in April 1993 had been a military disaster for Srebrenica's defenders. The Muslims[2] had formally disbanded their units and turned over the two tanks and the handful of artillery pieces they had captured from the Serbs—in compliance with the demilitarization agreement that was part of being a safe area. Dutch observation posts now sat on top of a half dozen of the most strategic hills along the enclave's front line. Every six months a new battalion of peacekeepers arrived. During the rotation of the UN troops, the Bosnian Serbs crept forward and took crucial high ground.

The worst case stared Mevludin in the face every day. In 1993—armed with automatic rifles and homemade guns that consisted of iron pipes filled with nails and gunpowder—the Muslims had fought desperately to hold half of Buljim, a 2,300-foot peak that loomed over the northwest corner of the enclave. Men Mevludin had known died holding that ground. The Muslims allowed the UN to set up an observation post on their half of the peak. In January 1994, the observation post was empty for several days while UN troops rotated in and out of the enclave. In the middle of the night, the Bosnian Serbs took the observation post and the hill. The Dutch complained, but as with everything else, refused to use force to get it back.

Six feet two, rail thin and wiry, Mevludin had a boyish face dotted with freckles and barely any facial hair. Constantly joking and teasing, he looked more like a teenager than a father of two. He, his wife and two children lived with his father. He made a meager living by brewing and selling *šljivovica*, or plum brandy, which enabled him to buy the precious salt, sugar and coffee his family needed. Alcohol prices fluctuated wildly in the enclave from three to fifteen dollars for a sixteen-ounce bottle, depending on the supply. There was little to do in the besieged town, so the demand was constant.

Mevludin had never expected the war. He had loved Yugoslavia and was sickened by its breakup. Once Croatia and Slovenia declared independence in June 1991, he knew Bosnia had to also. What was left of Yugoslavia would be totally dominated by Serbia, which had three times as many people as Bosnia. He was sure the Serbs would discriminate against Bosnia's Muslims. He was willing to live in Yugoslavia, not "Serboslavia," as Muslims jokingly called what was left of Tito's "land of the South Slavs."

Mevludin had grown up in Lehovići, a tiny village ten miles northwest of Srebrenica inhabited by only ten Muslim families. He'd gone to a vocational high school in Slovenia to become a mining technician. Homesick and having a difficult time understanding Slovenian, a language related to, but different from the Serbo-Croatian spoken in the rest of Yugoslavia, he dropped out of school at fifteen. In 1985, Mevludin took a job in a sugar factory in Belgrade, the capital of Serbia. For the next three years, the small-town boy had the time of his life getting drunk and chasing women in the cafés and clubs of Kalemegdan—Belgrade's old town.

He returned to Lehovići in 1990, and met his future wife, Hadzira when visiting his sister in a nearby village. Mevludin was only twenty and Hadzira only fifteen but the two married that year. Five years later, Mevludin had two daughters and spent most of his time with his twenty-four-year-old cousin and best friend, Haris. They passed the long, boring days in the enclave hunting. Their biggest treat was eating meat, or watching blurry pirated copies of Jean-Claude Van Damme movies. A makeshift waterwheel his father had built in a nearby stream barely generated enough power for a TV and VCR together. Somehow, the enclave's 40,000 people had lived without electricity or running water for three years.

A month earlier, Makso Zekić—a Serb Mevludin had feuded with years ago—had started asking around about Mevludin. In a practice that was common throughout Bosnia, Serbs and Muslims regularly talked to each other from opposing trenches. Makso had vowed that he was personally going to burn Mevludin's home to the ground. Their quarrel was over some trees Mevludin had asked Makso to haul to the lumber mill in his truck before the war. Mevludin accused Makso of cheating him. The sudden threat from Makso struck him as odd.

Relations with other Serbs were also strained. Mevludin and some men in his unit used to trade the food they had grown for salt, sugar and cigarette paper. But as the weather warmed, the Serbs talked less and shot more. Most unsettling of all, the Serbs knew Naser was gone.

"Where is your Naser now?" Serbs had shouted from their trenches, according to other Muslim soldiers. Mevludin Orić didn't have an answer.

Klaver anxiously watched the three Serb tanks on the hill 1,500 yards away. The two T-54 battle tanks—modern by Bosnia standards—appeared not to be firing at the OP. That job was left to what looked like a World War II-era Soviet-made T-34, which was so primitive that it had to come to a complete stop before it could fire a shell. But Klaver knew a direct hit could kill him just the same.

The T-34 emerged from behind some trees. A puff of thick gray smoke burst from the tank's barrel. The lookouts dove to the floor of the watchtower, fearing they might be incinerated.

Klaver, van Renssen and Jeroen Dekkers, another lookout, quickly learned the acoustics of war. Bullets and shells travel faster than sound. Hearing a shell when you are under fire is a good thing; it means the shells have already passed by or over you. You never hear the shell that kills you. The exceptions are slower-moving mortars and rockets. They can be heard shrieking through the air moments before impact.

As the tank fired, Sergeant Frans van Rossum, OP Foxtrot's twenty-seven-year-old commander, stood under the tower in direct radio contact with Captain Jelte Groen, the Dutch commander of the southern half of the enclave. Van Rossum demanded that he and his men receive Close Air Support from NATO planes or be allowed to withdraw.

"Do you see the tank? Do you see the tank?" van Rossum shouted to the lookouts in a panic. "Is the turret turning toward us?"

The T-34 nosed out from the trees every thirty to forty-five minutes and fired two or three rounds at the observation post. At 3 p.m., they figured out that the tank was firing every time they appeared in the tower. The Serbs could see their bright blue UN helmets.

Van Rossum ordered all seven of the OP's men to the bunker. The peacekeepers cowered inside the claustrophobic, ten-by-ten-foot room surrounded by sandbags. They were waiting to die. If the shells didn't kill them, the collapsing sandbag walls would smother them. There were no windows, just tiny peepholes the Dutch could barely see out of. Blind to what was happening around them, they listened helplessly as shells screeched through the air and shook the earth beneath them.

At 4 p.m., four hours after the first shell hit the OP, Captain Groen told them that NATO Close Air Support had been requested. The Dutch had been told throughout their training that when a UN post was directly targeted, peacekeepers had the right to fire back, or to call in NATO Close Air Support. If the Serbs ever threatened to take the enclave, NATO air strikes—which would involve several Serb targets being hit at once—could be requested.

Relief washed over the group. Soldiers who served in the last Dutch battalion in Srebrenica had told them how they had called in NATO planes when one of their patrols was fired on by the Serbs. Twenty minutes later, NATO jets roared over the Serb positions and dropped flares. The firing stopped immediately.

But as the torturous shelling continued Thursday afternoon, no NATO planes appeared. Captain Groen said they had been requested, but it was up to UN commanders in Sarajevo to approve the attack. The men in Foxtrot asked if they could withdraw. Captain Groen ordered them to stay.

Frustration and fear mounted. There was little enthusiasm among the Dutch peacekeepers to fire at the Serbs themselves. They had come to Bosnia to be peacekeepers, not to die in someone else's war.

Klaver had wanted to go to Bosnia. He thought he could help people as a peacekeeper. The son of a retired construction company manager and a housewife, Klaver was tall—six feet five inches—and handsome, with a broad face, short brown hair and clear blue eyes. Klaver's size and looks weren't reflected in his personality. Gentle and soft-spoken, he was modest and acted with deference toward those around him.

What he missed the most in Bosnia was his brother Tonny. At twenty-three, Klaver was by far the youngest of five boys in the family. His oldest brother was forty-four. Tonny was only nine years older than Klaver and the closest to him in age. The two had more or less grown up together. The young peacekeeper respected his older brother for his courage and loved his sense of humor. Tonny had cystic fibrosis but lived on his own and enjoyed as normal a life as possible. The Serbs had cut off most mail shipments to the enclave and Klaver was allowed only one five-minute phone call home a month. Tonny had said nothing in his letters, and his parents had said nothing on the phone. But for the last month Klaver had sensed that something was wrong. He was afraid Tonny wouldn't be there when he finally went home.

Klaver had grown up in Boekelo, a town of 5,000 in rural eastern Holland that was ten miles from the German border. He had studied business for three years and dropped out of college to join the army.

The most powerful weapon at OP Foxtrot, a highly accurate, American-made TOW antitank missile, was already useless. It was sitting on the roof. Thinking of themselves as neutral UN observers, the Dutch peacekeepers who first arrived in Srebrenica in January 1994 had mounted the missile on the roof of Foxtrot's watchtower. From there, its telescopic night vision sight could see the farthest. The sight enabled them to track Serb troop movements or Muslim raiding parties. Klaver and the other Dutch had thought nothing of the strange position of the TOW when they arrived. To operate it, one of them would have to stand in the open on the roof, load the missile, aim it, fire and guide it as the missile flew, and be vulnerable to sniper fire for at least a minute and a half.

There was another problem. Foxtrot had seven TOW missiles, but only one launcher. The TOW launchers were designed to be used in pairs because they took so long to reload. Even if they could take out a T-34 with a TOW, the two T-54 tanks would destroy the OP before they could reload.

The Serbs had allowed only six TOW launchers into the enclave when the Dutch first entered in 1994. The Dutch commanders at the time decided to place the launchers in six different locations around the enclave to maximize their observation capabilities. In essence, the launchers and their night vision sights were deployed simply as expensive binoculars, not as weapons.

The OP also had two Dragon antitank missiles. Their range was only 500 yards. They had 81 mm mortars, but against tanks a direct hit was required; basically, they were effective only against infantry. Their .50 caliber and Uzi machine guns as well as their rifles were useless against tanks and artillery. Finally, the TOW hadn't been fired since 1994 and much of the other ammunition was old. The Dutch were worried their weapons might not fire.

In the end, they decided the worst thing they could do was provoke the better-armed Serbs. They were following the logic used by many UN commanders in Bosnia: don't put a red cloth in front of a bull. The seven decided that if the Serbs came into the OP firing and it was clear they were going to die, the Dutch would fire back with everything they had. Otherwise, they would wait.

By 5 p.m., NATO planes had still not appeared. Explosions continued to rock the hilltop every fifteen to thirty minutes. The

Dutch wanted to believe that the Serbs were trying to flush them out of the OP without killing them. All the shells landed at the edges of the compound, or in the barbed wire around it. The seven knew a single random shell could destroy the bunker. The Dutch cowered and waited.

Finally at 7 p.m. Thursday, the shelling stopped. Klaver estimated that more than 200 shells had landed. The OP had been hit approximately a half dozen times. It had been three hours since Close Air Support was requested. NATO planes were nowhere to be seen.

Twenty miles south of Srebrenica in the Bosnian Serb-held town of Skelani, Bosnian Serb police officer Zoran Radić went about his duties on July 6 as if it were any other day. The thirty-year-old was unaware of the attack unleashed that morning that would change the course of the war and his life.[3]

A Bosnian Serb who grew up in Srebrenica, Radić longed for the Serbs to retake his hometown. Radić had been stunned when fighting broke out in April 1992. Like so many other people in Bosnia, he had joked with his Muslim and Croat friends as Yugoslavia disintegrated and believed that war would never come. But a book he read during 1992 in a Serb trench around Sarajevo had answered many questions for him.

Entitled *Bloody Hands of Islam,* it described atrocities carried out around Srebrenica by Muslim and Croat Fascists allied with Hitler during World War II.[4] The book had been banned by Tito's government. Forty Serbs had been executed in Zalazje, a village just outside Srebrenica. Radić could see that history was repeating itself. Roughly fifty years later, on July 12, 1992—the Serb Orthodox holiday of St. Peter's Day—Naser Orić's men killed 120 people in the same town. As time passed Radić decided the war was a good thing. The Serbs needed to live separately from the Muslims for their own protection.

Before the war, Radić had always felt that he and his family were discriminated against by the Muslim majority in Srebrenica. His father worked as a miner for twenty-five years, but never received a company-owned apartment. Muslims who worked for only five to ten years as miners got them instead. Radić had been unable to find work in town after he graduated from high school, he felt, because he was a Serb.[5]

Radić opposed Bosnia's declaration of independence. He was sure Serbs would be discriminated against even more if Bosnia became a separate country. Muslims would be the largest group; he didn't trust the Muslim politicians in Sarajevo to rule over him. Serbs had been forced to convert to Islam during the Turks' 500-year occupation of Bosnia between the fourteenth and nineteenth centuries. Serbs had also been forced to convert to Catholicism at gunpoint by Croat Fascists in World War II. Echoing the warnings of Serb nationalist politicians, he feared that the same thing would happen again in an independent Bosnia.[6]

For Radić it was simple. If the Muslims had the right to secede from Yugoslavia, ethnic Serbs should have the right to secede from Bosnia and unite with Serbia. He didn't understand why the world had created such a double standard and opposed a "Greater Serbia." Tito had divided ethnic Serbs among Serbia, Bosnia, and Croatia, he thought, in an effort to weaken Serb power. Radić thought the Bosnian Serbs, who made up only 30 percent of Bosnia's population but had won control of 70 percent of its territory, had clearly won the war. Somehow the Muslims had convinced the Americans and Europeans that they were the victims.

Srebrenica's Muslims and Naser Orić had played the United Nations beautifully in 1993. When the Serbs were on the verge of taking the town, they had tricked the West into saving them. The safe area was a joke. For two years, the UN had fed the Muslims, sold them weapons and done nothing as Naser Orić launched raids from a town that was supposed to be "demilitarized."[7] Serb villagers within thirty miles of Srebrenica lived in constant fear, waiting to hear the voices in the night and then smell smoke. Dozens of civilians had been burned alive in their homes by Orić's men. They had burned Radić's village, Obadi, to the ground in June 1992.

Radić remembered Naser Orić from before the war. Naser was athletic, but he hadn't caused much trouble. Radić's cousin had gone to school with him. Now Naser was the most hated Muslim commander in all of Bosnia. Bratunac had the second-highest casualty rate of any Serb-held community in Bosnia. Roughly 3,000 Serb soldiers and civilians had been killed around Srebrenica. Orić's men killed every prisoner they took so there would be no witnesses, it was rumored. Serb bodies had also been reportedly found with heads and ears cut off. Prisoners were allegedly skinned alive.[8]

At five feet ten inches tall with a medium build, Radić was far from intimidating. His thick brown hair, large brown eyes and easy smile combined to give his round face a soft, nonthreatening look. He had an easygoing manner that made people around him relax. Like Bosnian Muslim soldier Mevludin Orić, Radić had left Srebrenica for the big city as a teenager. Unable to find a job in Srebrenica, he studied business at a university in Sarajevo and graduated with a two-year degree in 1986. Bored with college at twenty-one, Radić started working as a cook in hotels on the scenic coast of Croatia. The next five years were the happiest of his life. He would probably still be on the coast of Croatia if the war hadn't broken out.

While he believed in the Serb cause, Radić did not believe in killing innocent people and had prided himself on treating people well throughout the war. He had spent the first two years of the war working as a guard in a combined civilian and military prison outside Sarajevo and he disliked the brutality of it. A handful of the thirty guards relished beating the Muslim prisoners of war, but Radić had never participated.[9] When the fighting flared around Sarajevo, his police unit was called up to the front line. Radić had spent long hours in the trenches surrounding a city he remembered fondly.

The fighting had been bitter at times. The Muslim and Serb trenches were only 200 yards apart. But the chatter had also been fairly constant throughout the war. Radić had known the price of cigarettes, bread and *rakija*—another kind of home-brewed brandy—in most markets in Sarajevo. If asked, one side would tell the other what time it was. One day, they serenaded each other, the Muslims singing traditional Serb songs and the Serbs singing old Muslim songs. The Muslims even invited Radić over for coffee several times, but he was never crazy enough to accept.

In March 1995, Radić had moved from Sarajevo to Skelani to be closer to his parents and two brothers living in Bratunac. He never thought he'd set foot in his hometown again, but if Srebrenica did ever fall, Radić was sure of one thing: the Serbs would treat civilians and prisoners far more humanely than Naser Orić did.

SATURDAY, JULY 8, 1995

BOSNIAN SERB ADVANCE, JULY 8, 1995

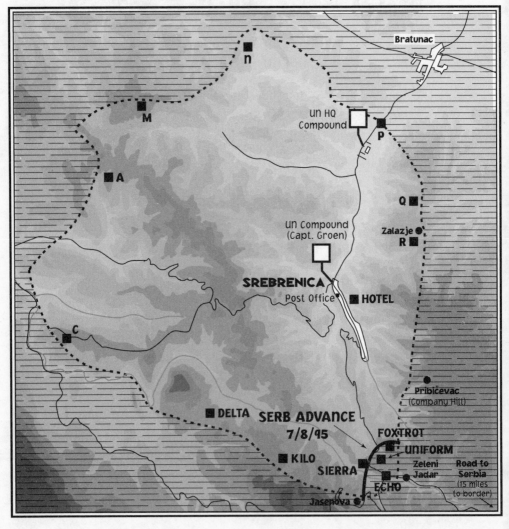

Serb-controlled ▪ UN observation posts ▪▪▪▪ Safe Area boundary

(Serb advance is approximate)

Marc Klaver began to fidget. The thick morning mist surrounding OP Foxtrot's watchtower was lifting. It always started at this time. Today would be no different.

He grabbed the radio. "Ops room, this is Foxtrot," Klaver said. "The fog is lifting."

"Foxtrot, this is Romeo One," the lieutenant[1] in command of the Srebrenica operations room answered. "Good luck."

"Foxtrot, this is OP Hotel," Sergeant Frank Struik added. "Good luck and make the best of it."

"Foxtrot, this is OP Kilo," Sergeant Werner Ceelen chimed in. "Good luck."

Good luck with what? Klaver thought to himself. The Serbs will be playing with us again soon. Klaver was furious. They all knew what was about to happen. He knew he could be dead in a few hours.

After Thursday's shelling, rain and thick mist had stilled the Serb guns on Friday. Raviv van Renssen, Klaver's fellow lookout, had even gone out and taken souvenir photos of places where the shells had landed. Klaver thought the bad weather on Friday had been a perfect opportunity for the Dutch to safely withdraw, but Captain Groen ordered them to stay. No one had given them any clear answer yet as to why no NATO planes had appeared.

As the mist slowly lifted on Saturday morning, Klaver's anger grew. He peered through his binoculars. Gradually, the Serb positions emerged at 7 a.m. Two howitzer artillery pieces, three tanks and a multiple rocket launcher. The Serbs hadn't withdrawn. The attack was continuing.

A tent had been set up next to one of the tanks. Klaver watched the tank crew wake up. The Serbs slowly packed their tent, and then warmed up the tank's engine. The minutes crawled by. At eight o'clock, no firing. At ten, nothing. Finally, at 11:25 a.m., the Serbs began methodically shelling the Muslim trenches around the OP.

Klaver didn't hear any fire being returned from the Muslims. He knew it was only a matter of time before the Serbs destroyed or stormed the OP. It was the only thing keeping them from advancing.

At around 2 p.m., the World War II-era T-34 began firing at them again. All seven men hunkered in the claustrophobic bunker, their ears ringing from deafening explosions they couldn't see. At 2:10 p.m., part of Foxtrot's sandbag defense wall was hit and collapsed, according to the men at nearby OP Kilo. The Dutch inside Foxtrot began to panic.[2]

Ten minutes later, a second, even louder explosion rocked the OP. The peacekeepers smelled something burning. Sergeant van Rossum, the commander of the OP, began screaming and cursing over the radio.

"That's it!" he shouted. "That's it for all of us!" He demanded that Captain Groen allow them to withdraw.

At 2:20 p.m., the order they had been waiting for finally arrived in the coffinlike bunker. "This is Romeo here," Captain Groen responded. "If it's safe to leave, leave. Otherwise, stay where you are."

The Dutch disabled the radio, the TOW, the mortars and other equipment they would leave behind. They waited for a lull in the shelling, then started the APC's engine and began loading it with equipment.

Van Renssen climbed into the watchtower to survey the area one last time. "There's a tank," he shouted. Klaver scrambled into the tower as van Renssen grabbed the radio.

"This is Foxtrot," van Renssen radioed at 2:30 p.m. "There's a T-54 tank that has driven one hundred yards east of us where the little house is."

The tank was trying to aim its barrel at Foxtrot, but the barrel was blocked by a row of small trees. It was only a matter of seconds before the tank would reposition itself. The Serbs would have a point-blank shot.

The Dutch in Foxtrot didn't know it, but the chief of staff of UN forces in Bosnia, Brigadier General Cees Nicolai of the Netherlands, had already turned down a request from Srebrenica to protect Foxtrot with NATO Close Air Support at 1 p.m. Nicolai had also turned down a request for NATO Close Air Support when Foxtrot was under attack on Thursday. The general told Srebrenica's UN commander, Lieutenant Colonel Thomas Karremans, that a NATO attack could disrupt a new European Union peace initiative. Nicolai was closely following a new set of guidelines issued by UN commanders on May 29.

According to the commander of all UN forces in the former Yugoslavia, Lieutenant General Bernard Janvier of France, observation posts like Foxtrot were to be abandoned when they came under attack instead of defended by peacekeepers or NATO planes.[3] The new guidelines were the latest round in a long-running dispute over how much force the UN mission in Bosnia—and peacekeepers in general in the post-Cold War era—should use to enforce Security Council resolutions.

Janvier and the civilian head of the UN mission, Special Representative of the Secretary General Yasushi Akashi, believed it was crucial that the 39,500 peacekeepers serving in Croatia, Bosnia and Macedonia stay neutral. Based in peaceful Zagreb, Akashi and Janvier considered it irresponsible to order lightly armed UN peacekeepers to engage in suicidal battles with better-armed Bosnian Serbs.

Akashi and Janvier's beliefs were in many ways diametrically opposed to those of the UN commander in Bosnia, Lieutenant General Rupert Smith of Great Britain. Smith and many UN officials in besieged Sarajevo believed that the Bosnian Serbs needed to be confronted by force. As long as they were allowed

to block UN resupply convoys, shell UN safe areas and storm
UN observation posts, the Bosnian Serbs would only be emboldened and their behavior would worsen.

Akashi, Janvier and Smith were acting out a drama with far
wider implications. Three years into the war in Bosnia, the conflict had emerged as the defining issue of the post-Cold War era.
The "New World Order" declared by U.S. President George
Bush in the wake of the Gulf War lay in tatters. The UN and
the United States, Britain and France faced a watershed. After a
series of successful post-Cold War peacekeeping missions in El
Salvador, Namibia and Cambodia, the UN had floundered badly
in Somalia and Bosnia. With the disappearance of a Soviet
threat, the United States, France and Britain were jockeying for
influence but loath to be drawn into the regional foreign conflicts
flaring around the world. But war in the former Yugoslavia—
which threatened to spread across the Balkans and destabilize
Eastern Europe—had to be contained.

At first, France and Britain saw the breakup of the former Yugoslavia as an opportunity to assert unified Europe's role as a diplomatic and military power independent of the United States. By
July 1995, 6,900 French and 4,000 British peacekeepers were in
Bosnia. The British and French contingents were the largest in the
39,500-troop UN peacekeeping mission. French and British generals commanded the largest, deadliest and at $1.6 billion most
expensive peacekeeping mission in UN history. As the war
dragged on, it became increasingly clear the fighting would not
spread. Three European peace initiatives failed between 1991 and
1994, and the former Yugoslavia was increasingly viewed as a
quagmire. The Balkans became a European "Vietnam" that
France and Britain had to contain, but not be sucked into.

Many British and French officials argued that all sides were
equally guilty and were dubious of Muslim claims that the Serbs,
who had fought with the Allies and suffered enormous casualties
in World Wars I and II, were committing large-scale atrocities.
They tended to argue that the Western media's portrayal of the
conflict as a genocidal Serb war of aggression against Bosnia's
defenseless Muslims was ahistorical, exaggerated and naive.[4]

Both British Prime Minister John Major and French President

François Mitterrand opposed lifting the UN arms embargo that Bosnia's Muslims said left them defenseless or bombing the Bosnian Serbs as a way to equalize the lopsided conflict. Sending more weapons to the region, British Foreign Secretary Douglas Hurd argued, would only "level the killing field." NATO air attacks would be largely ineffective, and would place the UN, Britain and France at war with the Serbs. "Don't add war to war," became the mantra of French President Mitterrand.[5] UN Special Representative Akashi and General Janvier, who was appointed by Mitterrand, tended to loosely reflect the "diplomacy is the only solution" European view of the conflict.

Since Yugoslavia's breakup in 1991, both George Bush and Bill Clinton talked of ending the fighting and the atrocities in the region. But their policy frequently changed. With opinion polls showing the vast majority of Americans opposing U.S. intervention in Bosnia, the overriding concern of U.S. policy from 1991 to 1995 was to keep U.S. troops out of the Balkans.[6] The UN and the Clinton administration learned a painful lesson about intervention from its politically unpopular 1993 mission in Somalia, where eighteen Americans died in a failed raid to capture Somali warlord Mohammed Farah Aidid.

After being hesitant to commit U.S. airpower earlier in the war, by 1995 the administration was urging the UN to use NATO air strikes more aggressively, but sending U.S. troops to Bosnia still remained out of the question. The American position was bitterly dismissed as "posturing" by furious French and British officials who claimed that air strikes over Bosnia would only endanger French and British soldiers who faced Serb retaliation on the ground.

The conflict over the use of airpower came to a head in May 1995. Echoing the U.S. position, General Rupert Smith believed that the Serbs would back down if confronted with overwhelming NATO air strikes. The UN mission had reached an all-time low. Bosnian Serbs were blocking 70 percent of aid convoys and the UN was unable to resupply its own peacekeepers in the surrounded Muslim enclaves of Sarajevo, Srebrenica, Žepa, Goražde and Bihać. The five enclaves, which were UN "safe areas," were routinely shelled by the Serbs in violation of UN Security Council resolutions. U.S. officials and NATO commanders complained angrily that the alliance's reputation was being ruined by the UN's hesitance to use air attacks against the Serbs.

The bitter British, French and American split over the use of airpower produced a UN-NATO "dual key" system for the approval of air attacks. If Yasushi Akashi, who generally opposed the use of force, failed to turn the UN's key, the request was blocked.[7]

After several days of the Bosnian Serbs intensely shelling Sarajevo in a blatant violation of both the city being a UN safe area and a February 1994 NATO ban on tanks and artillery being within an eight-mile-wide "exclusion zone" around Sarajevo,[8] General Smith gambled. On May 24, the reclusive UN commander issued a rare public ultimatum. If the Serbs did not begin withdrawing all their heavy weapons from around Sarajevo within twenty-four hours, they would face air strikes.

The surprise ultimatum effectively boxed in Akashi.[9] Janvier was out of town and was unable to block the request on military grounds. There was little room for Akashi to maneuver. The Serbs were grossly violating the heavy weapons exclusion zone.

With no signs the Serbs were complying, Smith chose an ammunition dump just outside of Pale as his target. The Bosnian Serbs had declared the town the capital of their newly independent state. It was Smith's way of sending a direct message to the Bosnian Serb leaders, President Radovan Karadžić and army commander General Ratko Mladić.

NATO planes struck early on May 25. Within hours, the Bosnian Serbs began shelling all six safe areas in Bosnia, including Srebrenica, in retaliation. In the safe area of Tuzla that night a shell careened into a square packed with high school students enjoying the spring weather. Seventy-one people—most of whom were under twenty-five—were killed and 250 were wounded in what would be the worst single shelling attack of the war. Smith didn't blink and ordered a second air strike carried out on the following day. Akashi, after consulting with Boutros-Ghali, again approved Smith's request.

Within hours of the second strike, the Serbs began to take more than 350 UN peacekeepers hostage. The Serbs declared them "human shields," and vowed that the peacekeepers would not be released until they received assurances of no further NATO air strikes. Images of a Canadian peacekeeper handcuffed to a Bosnian Serb ammunition dump and French soldiers surrendering with white flags were broadcast worldwide.

In a stunning surprise attack the following morning, Serb soldiers dressed in stolen French uniforms stormed a strategic UN checkpoint on the Vrbanja Bridge in Sarajevo on May 27, seizing twelve more French hostages. Smith urged French general Hervé Gobilliard, the UN commander in Sarajevo, to retake the position. In the first ever offensive UN military action in Bosnia, French commandos stormed the checkpoint that afternoon. Four Serb soldiers were captured but two French died.

Smith lost his short-lived game of brinkmanship. France, Britain, Canada and other nations with peacekeepers who had been taken hostage immediately blocked further air strikes. Believing the Serb threats of retaliation and fearful of soldiers returning home in body bags, Western leaders capitulated and began a series of secret negotiations to win the release of the hostages.

The boldness of the Bosnian Serbs surprised Smith, but he had achieved his goal of trying to "break the box" and force a change in the paralyzed UN mission. At first, approving the air strikes was a victory for Akashi. In a May 28 staff meeting, Akashi said he believed Smith's bombings had "finally shown the ineffectiveness of air strikes" as a way to confront the Serbs. The cautious UN diplomat's nonconfrontational approach had received a huge boost. The bombing-oriented approach, which the Americans now backed, appeared to have been totally discredited.

On May 29, Janvier issued the new guidelines on the use of airpower. UN headquarters in New York removed the authority to approve large-scale NATO air strikes from UN officials in the former Yugoslavia. UN Secretary General Boutros Boutros-Ghali now had to personally turn the UN key for any request for air strikes. The peacekeepers' most powerful tool for deterring the

Serbs would now need the approval of the UN—a process that could take days.

General Smith was stripped of the authority to approve Close Air Support by NATO planes. Now, all requests for Close Air Support would first have to be approved by the more conservative Janvier. Close Air Support was to be used "as a last resort." Even having NATO planes drop flares over hostile positions firing on the UN—a commonly used tactic—was cautioned against.

The priority of nations with peacekeepers on the ground in Bosnia was also made starkly clear in the guidelines: "The execution of the mandate is secondary to the security of UN personnel." Simply put, it was more important that UN peacekeepers save their own lives than carry out their mission.

After two days, the Serbs showed no signs of releasing the hostages. On June 2, they shot down U.S. pilot Scott O'Grady's F-16 fighter. Stories predicting the collapse and withdrawal of the humiliated UN mission filled the press. European governments scrambled for a response. On June 3, French, British and Dutch leaders, meeting in Paris, announced the creation of a new 12,000-soldier Rapid Reaction Force to bolster the beleaguered UN forces in Bosnia. The primary mission of the Rapid Reaction Force, which would be armed with tanks, heavy artillery and attack helicopters, was to protect peacekeepers in Bosnia. With the collapse of the UN mission looming, NATO defense officials also knew that the force could be used to aid in a UN pullout.

On June 4, Janvier held a secret meeting in the town of Zvornik with Yugoslav Army chief of staff Momcilo Perišić and Bosnian Serb commander Ratko Mladić and 111 peacekeepers were released three days later. On June 9, Akashi announced the UN would abide by "strictly peacekeeping principles"—or stay neutral—and 118 more hostages were freed four days later. Under pressure from Serbian President Milošević, the Bosnian Serbs released the remaining hostages on June 18. Bosnian Serbs said Milošević had received assurances of no more NATO air strikes, but French and UN officials denied that Janvier or other officials cut a deal in the secret talks.

A UN pullout still appeared possible. It would be both dangerous and humiliating and would involve 60,000 NATO troops—including 20,000 Americans. President Clinton had promised the British and French that U.S. troops would aid in a pullout. The NATO withdrawal plan assigned helicopter-equipped U.S. troops the most hazardous duty—extricating UN troops from the surrounded Muslim enclaves of Srebrenica, Žepa and Goražde.

The prospect of Muslim women and children begging American soldiers not to abandon them, U.S. helicopters being shot down and Serb and Muslim soldiers sniping at retreating American and UN troops was increasingly real for Bosnia planners in Washington. On a Saturday in late June, National Security Adviser Anthony Lake gathered senior aides to discuss alternatives to a pullout.[10] Lake and his aides began searching for an American "endgame strategy" for the war in Bosnia.

Two weeks later, as the Serb tank slowly repositioned itself to get a clear shot at OP Foxtrot, Klaver and van Renssen panicked. Twenty heavily armed Serb soldiers were walking toward their hilltop compound. Some of them were dressed in the trademark black uniforms of the Arkan Tigers. Klaver and van Renssen had heard stories from Muslims about the paramilitary group. They were based in neighboring Serbia and led by a Serb ultranationalist whose real name[11] they couldn't remember but whose nom de guerre was "Arkan." The group was accused of committing war crimes across Bosnia and Croatia. They were infamous for their brutality. The Serbs in regular camouflage uniforms could be Drina Wolves, Klaver thought. Local Muslims had told him they were Bosnian Serbs who had friends and parents killed during the war. Klaver waited for the Serbs to start shooting. If he was lucky, they'd be taken hostage.

The Serbs saw Klaver and van Renssen's bright blue helmets in the watchtower and a curious thing happened. They smiled and waved. Klaver was stunned. The Serbs waved again at the Dutch and flashed the three-fingered Serb salute. The two Dutch peacekeepers waved nervously back. Klaver was surprised at how relaxed and confident the Serbs were. There must be no Muslims left in the area, he thought. The Serbs were walking in the open, unconcerned about snipers.

Foxtrot's commander, Sergeant van Rossum, radioed for permission to meet the Serbs outside the front gate. Captain Groen told him he could speak with them only at the OP's perimeter. A young Serb officer and several Serb soldiers quickly reached the gate and stopped. One of the soldiers made a hand gesture as if to ask whether he could come into the OP. Klaver motioned back that his sergeant would meet them. The Serbs waited. Inside the OP, van Renssen, Klaver's fellow lookout, volunteered to go speak with them.

Van Renssen never stopped. He was constantly tinkering in the OP, finding ways to fix it. He never complained about the lack of supplies, he just dealt with it. Van Renssen fixed whatever needed to be repaired in the OP, or built things from scratch without the most rudimentary of materials—like nails or screws. Van Renssen had built the OP's makeshift chicken coop.

Twenty-five years old, van Renssen was slightly shorter and thinner than Klaver. He was handsome, with dark hair and bright blue eyes. Both of them loved the military but were unsure whether they wanted to make a career of it. Van Renssen, like Klaver, had grown up in a small town in Holland. The son of a designer and sculptor, van Renssen had somehow developed a fascination with the military. As a teenager, he joined a local club that collected military regalia from World War II. He devoured books about history, the military and espionage. He tested himself by camping outside in the dead of winter and going on weekend survivalist trips with friends in neighboring Belgium. Like Klaver, he was the only one in his family interested in the military, and he was intensely proud to be a paratrooper.

Bosnia had changed van Renssen. In March, he was in the last group of Dutch peacekeepers who were allowed back in the enclave after a two-week holiday. He was quiet and subdued on his vacation in Holland, troubled by the misery he found in Srebrenica. He had made friends with several local Muslims; when he spoke to them they asked him whether they should just end their lives now.

As Klaver and the other peacekeepers watched nervously from the OP, van Renssen and the sergeant met the Serbs. The gate, a piece of wood with barbed wire wrapped around it, had been blown ajar by a random shell. The Serb officer smiled and shook hands with the OP commander. He offered cigarettes. In broken English, he assured the Dutch they had nothing to fear. In the watchtower, Klaver radioed the Serbs' every movement to the operations room in Srebrenica. Corporal Jeffrey Schijndel, the OP's medic, secretly snapped souvenir photos of the moment. Between fifteen and twenty Serbs slowly gathered at the gate.

They looked different from the Bosnian Serbs the Dutch had seen before. Most of them wore matching uniforms, in contrast to the usual hodgepodge. All of them wore flak jackets and two even had helmets—things most soldiers in the ragtag war could only hope for. Klaver wondered whether they were soldiers from neighboring Serbia or local Bosnian Serbs.

The conversation was pleasant at first. The young Serb officer said he was a captain and assured Sergeant van Rossum that the Serbs only wanted to take the southern half of the enclave. But after five minutes, the Serb officer demanded that his men be allowed to enter the compound. Klaver was sure they'd be robbed and taken hostage.

The Serbs swarmed the OP, curious to see what was inside, and eager to get the most valuable items for themselves. Walkmans were immediately stolen. Three heavily armed Serbs began searching the armored personnel carrier (APC). Six entered the observation post itself. Two of them climbed onto the roof of the watchtower and examined the TOW missile.

Inside the OP, a fierce-looking Serb, armed with a Soviet-made Dragunov sniper rifle with a telescopic sight and long barrel Klaver recognized, walked up to him. He motioned toward the rifle Klaver was holding. The peacekeeper quickly handed it over. Klaver was convinced that resisting would only lead to his getting hurt. Other Serbs were friendlier, offering Klaver the first cigarettes he'd had in weeks. Despite the warm greetings, Klaver was still certain the Dutch were going to be taken hostage.

The Serbs searching the APC found the TOW parts and mortar sights and their demeanor changed abruptly. They rifled through bags of personal belongings, and shouted happily when they found an Uzi machine gun and a Glock 9 mm pistol. The parts and manuals for the TOW and mortars were also seized. Intimidated and disarmed, the Dutch stayed out of their way.

After forty-five minutes, the Serb officer told the Dutch they should get in the APC and leave. "I cannot control the situation," the officer said. "You should go."

Klaver was astonished. It was clear the officer was having a difficult time controlling his troops. He kept trying to get his men out of the APC. "Bratunac, Bratunac," the Serb repeated, referring to the Serb-held town just north of Srebrenica. Van Rossum wasn't sure what the Serb meant, but he didn't want to go to Bratunac. The Dutch were going to Srebrenica, he said. The Serb captain agreed and then demanded that the Dutch hand over their helmets and flak jackets. Van Rossum persuaded him to let the peacekeepers keep them.

The seven Dutch piled into the APC. Raviv van Renssen, as usual, was the first one in. He climbed into the gunner's hatch even though he wasn't the APC's regular gunner. Steven Mungra, the driver, started the engine. Van Rossum sat in the APC's third hatch—the commander's position. "Romeo, this is Foxtrot," the sergeant radioed Srebrenica. "We have to leave now. They want us out of here. We are coming back."

At 3 p.m., the Dutch set off. Van Rossum was convinced the Serbs were going to incinerate the APC. "They're going to shoot at us," he said. "Watch what's happening around the APC. Make sure you don't see anyone with an RPG." Sitting inside the APC, Klaver peered through a peephole, but, unlike van Rossum, he didn't expect the Serbs to shoot. If the Serbs had wanted to kill them, they would have done it by now.

The five-ton vehicle rocked wildly as it wound its way down the deeply rutted dirt track. Once they were out of sight of the

OP, Klaver slowly started to believe he was going to live. The mood in the APC eased. It's over, Klaver thought, we're going back.

The Dutch departure set off a panic in a Muslim trench 500 yards away from OP Foxtrot. The Muslims had dug into trenches across three small hills, known as the "three tits," that lay just west of the large hill where the OP was positioned. The Bosnians' flank was now completely exposed. From OP Foxtrot, the Serb tanks would be able to fire down on the Muslims at will.

Ibro Dudić, the commander of the "brigade" of Muslim troops responsible for the enclave's southeast corner, radioed the Bosnian Army command post in Srebrenica town. Using code names, he reported that the Serbs had taken the OP and Biljeg, the crucial hill it sat on.

"We're pulling out," Dudić said. The situation was hopeless. His "brigade" consisted of roughly 1,200 men, only 200 of whom had guns.[12]

In Srebrenica town, Major Ramiz Bećirović, Naser Orić's chief of staff and Srebrenica's acting commander, was furious about the Dutch pullout. He and the Dutch commander, Lieutenant Colonel Thomas Karremans, had made an informal agreement in the beginning of June.[13]

Karremans and Bećirović agreed that the Muslims could take up positions just behind the observation posts and openly carry guns—two things that were forbidden in the original safe area demilitarization agreement. The plan was that if the Dutch withdrew from an OP, the Muslims would quickly move forward and defend the strategic positions themselves. But there had been no warning from the Dutch at all. They'd given up one of the enclave's most strategic hills without firing a shot.

"Hold your position," Bećirović radioed back to Dudić, using his code name. "I'm sending you help. I forbid you to leave."

There was no answer.

Bećirović was worried. The section of line that was breaking near OP Foxtrot was the same section that buckled when the

town nearly fell in 1993. The Serbs were again pressing the enclave where it was most vulnerable, but that could be a diversion for an attack from the north.

Increased Serb troop movements around the enclave had been sighted for the last twenty days. But more recently, the movements had been centralized in three places. Soldiers were seen arriving in Zeleni Jadar, due south of Srebrenica, on Wednesday, the day before the attack began. In addition, the Dutch spotted two tanks moving toward the village of Jasenova, which was also just south of Srebrenica, and half a dozen APCs and a tank moving to the Gujnaći bauxite mine southwest of the enclave. A group of 200 soldiers was seen arriving in Zalazje, northeast of Srebrenica, on Wednesday.[14]

Desperate to slow the Serb advance, Bećirović sent a soldier into the next room with a walkie-talkie.

"Ibro, this is Ramiz," Bećirović said, without using code names. "Ibro, this is Ramiz. Do you hear me?"

"Yes," the soldier in the next room said, without using code names. "This is Ibro."

"Circle around Biljeg and get behind the Serbs," Bećirović said. "Circle around them and try to capture the tanks."

"I'll do it," the man answered.

Bećirović hoped the Serbs were listening.

The armored personnel carrier from OP Foxtrot screeched to a halt. It had reached the point where the dirt road from the OP meets the main paved road leading into Srebrenica town. A middle-aged Muslim farmer with a gun slung over his shoulder had placed branches across the road with the help of two women and two teenage boys. Another farmer was sawing a tree, angling the cut so that the tree would fall across the road. Inside the APC, Marc Klaver grew nervous.

"Romeo, this is Foxtrot," Sergeant van Rossum radioed. "A group of Muslims are blocking the road."

Back in Srebrenica town, Captain Groen tensed. This was exactly the scenario he had feared. For the last month Muslim soldiers had warned the Dutch that they would kill any peacekeepers who abandoned one of the strategic observation posts. Many of the Dutch were already more frightened of the Muslims they were supposed to be protecting than of the Serbs who surrounded the enclave.

On June 3, Groen himself had been held at gunpoint by Muslim soldiers after Observation Post Echo—the southernmost UN post in the enclave—had been attacked by the Serbs. Seventy-five heavily armed Arkan Tigers from Serbia had opened fire with machine guns and grenades. The Dutch withdrew from OP Echo in a panic, amazed that no one was hurt.

When Groen returned to the area with two APCs to scout for a new observation post position later that day, he was surrounded by a dozen Muslims armed with several rocket-propelled grenades. They demanded that the Dutch retake OP Echo from the Serbs. One Muslim pulled out a sniper rifle. Another lobbed some kind of grenade at a bunker. Two Serbs came running out. Standing ten feet from Groen, the Muslim calmly raised his sniper rifle and killed the two Serbs with two shots. He had made his point.

At first the Dutch worried that the June 3 attack would continue, but the enclave was calm the next few weeks. The Dutch assumed the Serbs took the OP to gain control of the road running through the southeast corner of the enclave. Two makeshift observation posts consisting of APCs and dirt berms—OP Uniform and OP Sierra—were set up to the north of the fallen OP Echo. Faced with the fall of another OP one month later, Groen didn't want the men from OP Foxtrot taken hostage. They could be used as human shields by the Muslims.

"This is Romeo. Do you see any antitank weapons?" Groen asked.

"Do you see any RPGs?" van Rossum asked Klaver and the other Dutch around the APC. Klaver anxiously peered through a small gunsight in the back of the APC. One rocket-propelled grenade (RPG) could easily penetrate the vehicle's armor, killing all of them instantly. Klaver saw only the empty dirt road behind them. "No," he said. One by one, the other peacekeepers told van Rossum they saw no RPGs.

"Negative," van Rossum radioed to Srebrenica.

"This is Romeo," Groen said. "If you're sure there are no RPGs, leave as soon as possible before it gets any worse."

Van Rossum ordered Mungra, the APC's driver, and van Renssen, the gunner, to go "below armor," or get inside the APC and close their hatches. As the APC rolled forward, a muffled bang was heard outside. Klaver tensed, expecting RPG shrapnel to burst through the wall of the APC. Nothing happened.

Raviv van Renssen abruptly collapsed into the arms of one of his best friends, Joeren Yak, the OP's antitank missile operator. Blood gushed from van Renssen's head.

"This is Foxtrot! They opened fire on us!" van Rossum screamed into the radio. "Someone is wounded!"

"Assholes!" Klaver shouted as he peered out of the small gunsight on the back of the APC. "Assholes!" The Muslim farmer was shooting at them. Klaver wished he had a gun to shoot back.

"Should someone take his place?" Klaver asked. He wanted to fire on the Muslims with the .50 caliber machine gun.

"No," van Rossum said. "I don't want anyone else hurt."

Van Renssen's blood gushed across the floor of the APC. The OP's medic, Corporal Schijndel, pressed field dressings against the wound, but blood gushed through each one.

"Someone is hurt!" van Rossum kept screaming into the radio. "Someone is hurt!"

The APC was on an open radio channel. Van Rossum's panicked cries echoed through Dutch radio rooms in the southern half of the enclave. In OP Kilo, Sergeant Werner Ceelen, who had monitored the torturous bombardment of Foxtrot for two days, felt a chill go down his spine.

Inside the APC, Schijndel quickly took van Renssen's vital signs. Sergeant van Rossum shouted them over the radio to an ambulance that was rushing from Srebrenica town to meet them. Van Renssen's helmet had been blown off by whatever hit him. The headset he used to communicate with the APC's driver and commander was in shards. Blood continued to pour from his wound.

"Where is the first-aid kit?" Schijndel shouted. "Where is that goddamn kit?"

The Dutch started handing Schijndel the field dressings each had in his personal first-aid kit, but they were as useless as the others. Blood gushed through them. The Serbs had torn the APC apart during their search. Bags were scattered everywhere. The three peacekeepers inside the APC frantically searched for the medical kit. The medic kept screaming for someone to find the first-aid kit. There was a large hole in van Renssen's skull behind his left ear.

Corporal Mungra, the driver, pushed the vehicle as hard as he could. Van Renssen's pulse began to slow. Schijndel was desperate. "Find that fucking kit!" he screamed. They rounded several turns. The first-aid kit was gone. The bleeding continued.

"There's no pulse!" Schijndel shouted. "He stopped breathing!"

Schijndel started to sob. Klaver felt rage welling up inside him. The Dutch had come to Srebrenica to help these people. Again he wished he'd had a gun to kill the bastard farmer.

They met the ambulance and quickly laid van Renssen on the road. Schijndel found the first-aid kit. It had been underneath van Renssen the entire time. The two new medics performed CPR and gave van Renssen a heart stimulant. He started to breathe again. They said that if van Renssen was operated on quickly enough he would survive. The Dutch snapped a photo of the wounded peacekeeper, figuring he might want it as a souvenir. The fallen soldier was loaded into the ambulance, which sped off to the main Dutch base in Potočari.

In shock, OP Foxtrot's survivors slowly drove back to the UN compound in Srebrenica. Van Renssen's crimson blood covered the floor of the APC. Klaver stared at it in disbelief. If the grenade hadn't hit Raviv, it would have tumbled down the hatch and into the APC itself. They all could've been killed.

Once back in Srebrenica, they washed the blood out of the vehicle, and changed out of their blood-soaked uniforms. Convinced van Renssen would live, they had coffee with Captain Groen. They told him about the shelling, about waiting for the NATO jets and about the old farmer and two teenagers. Groen explained that NATO jets had finally flown over the enclave to intimidate the Serbs. The planes had arrived at 4 p.m.—an hour after the Serbs took the OP.

The group headed for the compound's showers. Due to the battalion's shortage of diesel oil, only one had hot water. Klaver was shaving when Captain Groen walked into the bathroom. "Come with me to the main building," he said. The six quickly dressed and followed him.

They walked into an empty room. Groen turned. "What we never expected to happen, happened," Groen said. Raviv van Renssen was dead. An X ray had found thirty ball bearings from a hand grenade lodged in his brain.

Klaver cursed the Muslims. Why? he thought. Why? Rage smoldered inside him. He was angry at the Muslims, at the UN, at everyone. Van Renssen was ingenious. He fixed things without tools. He devoured books. He felt sorry for the Muslims and was constantly talking with them and trading with them around the OP. The Dutch were risking their lives here to help these people and this was what they got in return. Van Renssen had died in vain, for nothing. Any sense of duty Klaver felt toward Srebrenica's Muslims was gone. They had betrayed him.

After word of the attack on the APC reached Srebrenica, Dutch liaison officer Major Piet Booring went to the town post office, where Srebrenica's military and civilian leaders had set up a command post. He met with Ramiz Bećirović and described the fall of OP Foxtrot and the subsequent Muslim attack.[15] He accused the Muslims in the enclave of restricting the UN's movement and therefore the UN's ability to do its job. He warned Bećirović that the attack would be reported internationally.

Bećirović apologized for his troops' behavior. "They may have reacted that way out of fear," he said. "We have no way of fighting back against the Bosnian Serbs. Abandoning the OP leaves them exposed to the Serb advance. We rely on you for protection."

"The problem is that the situation is getting worse. We've

reported it to higher authorities," Booring answered. "But we've received no response yet. It's very important that you allow us to do our job our way."

Bećirović listened as the Dutch officer outlined the Dutch plans to keep track of and, if possible, stop the Serb advance. Bećirović wasn't impressed.

"Do you have any antitank weapons?" Bećirović asked.

"Yes."

"Why don't you shoot back at the Serbs when they shoot at you?" Bećirović asked.

"We don't shoot back because Bosnian soldiers are near our positions," Booring said. "If we shoot at the Serbs, it will affect the Bosnians also."

Bećirović started lecturing Booring. "Both UNPROFOR and the entire population of Srebrenica are at the mercy of the Bosnian Serbs," he said, referring to the Dutch. "The UN's reaction to this attack has been shameful."

Booring asked Bećirović what he thought the Serb objective was, but Bećirović danced around the question. "Whatever the Serb objectives are is not relevant now, because they have already entered the enclave and what is more important is to find a way to prevent a total massacre."

"Do you think it's possible to negotiate with the Serbs to stop the attack?" Booring asked. "We're willing to arrange a meeting if you'll attend."

"I am personally willing to attend such a meeting, but I'll have to get approval from my high command," Bećirović replied. "I doubt any good will come of it. We've talked to them so many times before."

Bećirović took a parting shot at Booring. "You're doing nothing to stop this carnage," he said. "You've given in to Serb pressure."

At 5 p.m., two Dutch APCs left the UN compound and gradually climbed up out of the valley in which nestled Srebrenica. They drove slowly, afraid of both Muslim hand grenades and Serb tanks. Lieutenant Vincent Egbers and the other APC commander opened their hatches and rode outside their vehicles so they could see what was happening around them. They wore light blue UN helmets. The roar of the engine and clanking of the APC's metal tracks could be heard a half mile away. They were easy targets.

Egbers had been ordered to drive an APC from the battalion's Quick Reaction Force from Potočari to Srebrenica. When he arrived, he was joined by another APC. Since OP Foxtrot had fallen, Captain Groen had been unsure of how far the Serbs had advanced into the enclave. He ordered Egbers to head south with the two APCs until they found the enclave's new front line.

Egbers was the second-in command of the battalion's Quick Reaction Force, which consisted of four armored personnel carriers outfitted with two short-range antitank missiles and .50 caliber machine guns. Unless they got close enough the missiles would disable a Serb T-54 tank, not destroy it.

After they reached the ridge overlooking the southern half of town, Egbers ordered the drivers to slow down. There was nothing complicated about what he was doing. They would drive south until someone shot at them. Then he would know where the front line was.

A mile south of Srebrenica the APCs abruptly halted. A group of Muslim soldiers were pulling tree limbs across the road. Even more could be hiding in the woods with rocket-propelled grenades, Egbers thought. This could be the same group that attacked the men from OP Foxtrot. Egbers radioed Captain Groen in Srebrenica.

"Romeo, this is Bravo One," Egbers said, using his code name. "There are a dozen BH soldiers setting up a barricade in front of us."

"Bravo One, this is Romeo," Groen said. "Do you see any antitank weapons?"

The Muslims were eyeing the Dutch APCs and talking among themselves. They were armed with rifles, possibly hand grenades.

"Romeo, this is Bravo One," Egbers said. "Not that I can see."

Groen, afraid they'd be taken hostage, ordered the APCs to abandon their mission and return to the base in Srebrenica.

The APCs began to turn around slowly. Two grenades abruptly exploded between the UN vehicles. Shrapnel pinged off the side of one of them.

"Romeo, this is Bravo One!" Egbers shouted. "They're throwing hand grenades!"

"Bravo One, this is Romeo," Groen shouted. "Return to base!"

Egbers knew he had to remain calm. His driver was jittery. The last thing they wanted was to get stuck and be taken hostage by the Muslims. He slowly climbed out of his APC and guided the drivers through the laborious process of turning the massive vehicles around. He couldn't show the Muslims he was scared. The Muslim soldiers watched silently. Egbers slowly climbed back into the APC. His heart was pounding.

The two APCs sped back to the Dutch base in Srebrenica. The grenades were designed more to frighten than kill, but the inevitable still crossed Egbers' mind. Van Renssen probably never saw it coming. Egbers had earned a reputation among the Dutch for remaining calm under fire in Srebrenica. It was being sorely tested.

At 6:30 p.m. panicked voices filled the radio room in the UN compound in Srebrenica. Observation Post Uniform, located a half mile west of OP Foxtrot, was surrounded by Serb soldiers.

"Romeo, this is Uniform. They're telling us we have a choice between going to Srebrenica or going to Bratunac. Over," Sergeant Alvin van Eck, the OP commander, radioed to Groen.

"Uniform, this is Romeo," Groen said. "What is your preference?" Groen thought driving back to Srebrenica past Muslim soldiers could be more dangerous for the Dutch than being held hostage in Serb-controlled Bratunac.

"Romeo, this is Uniform. I'd rather not come back," van Eck said. A few days before, van Eck had seen a group of Muslim soldiers with five RPGs stacked in a foxhole. They had made it clear that they'd shoot if the Dutch tried to retreat.

Groen told van Eck that they were free to go to the Serb-held town and wished them luck. About twenty minutes later, he was shocked to hear van Eck's voice again. The Serbs had not disabled the radio in the APC. As they were escorted to Bratunac, the crew of OP Uniform was getting a guided tour of the Serb side of the front along the enclave's eastern border. It was valuable information for possible NATO air strikes.

About fifty Serb soldiers were busily working around a fire base they had set up near the Serb-held village of Pribičevac southeast of Srebrenica. Approximately ten 81 mm light mortars were firing into the enclave. A World War II-era T-34 tank was also firing, and a multiple rocket launcher and a howitzer sat on hilltops.

After leaving town van Eck saw three buses full of Serb soldiers, 150 to 200 in all. They were different from any he'd seen before. They were crack combat troops.

Van Eck's report stunned the officers in the radio room in Srebrenica. Groen felt the knot in his stomach tighten. For the first time in three days, he had a sense of what he was up against. The Serbs had more than they needed for a limited operation. Groen was convinced the Serbs wanted more than the southern half of the safe area. They wanted all of it.

He couldn't believe no one had warned the Dutch of the buildup earlier. U.S. spy satellites or NATO planes should have been tracking Serb troop movements. Once van Eck and the other Dutch peacekeepers reached Bratunac, their radio went dead. The Dutch had seen no other Serb artillery or tanks along the road.

Groen turned his attention to his crumbling front line of observation posts. With OP Foxtrot and OP Uniform gone, Captain Groen was now essentially blind to what was happening in the southeast corner of the safe area.

He had ordered one of the battalion's specially trained Forward Air Controllers—men who guided NATO jets to exactly where they should drop their bombs—to drive to a high bluff west of town. It would be an excellent observation point. The Dutch Forward Air Controller, Sergeant Voskamp, could monitor the Serb advance from there and avoid running into Muslim soldiers. But the driver of Sergeant Voskamp's APC forgot to take a cloth cover off of its engine and the APC overheated before they reached the bluff. At 9 p.m., under Captain Groen's orders, Lieutenant Egbers and his two APCs left to spend the night on the bluff. In the morning, Groen would no longer be blind.

In the main Dutch battalion in Potočari that night, the UN commander in the enclave, Lieutenant Colonel Karremans, assessed the situation. The enclave and especially Srebrenica town had been shelled all day. UN Military Observers counted over 60 impacts in Srebrenica and Potočari each. After Friday's slight lull, the shelling was again approaching Thursday's level—when 150 shells hit the enclave. Seven people had died since the attack had begun three days ago. The Serbs now had six Dutch hostages and were in complete control of the southeast corner of the enclave. The Muslims were putting up little to no resistance.

Almost no ground had changed hands in Bosnia over the last two years. The Serbs, handicapped by a lack of manpower, and the Muslims, handicapped by a lack of tanks and artillery, appeared to have fought to a stalemate. A mid-June Muslim offensive to break the siege of Sarajevo had failed miserably. The attack on Srebrenica was probably an attempt by the Serbs to punish the Bosnian government for their mid-June offensive around Sarajevo or for a Muslim raid that burned the village of Višnjica and killed three Serbs on June 22.

Karremans concluded that the Serbs were only interested in taking control of the southern half of the enclave.[16] He expected the Serbs to move west on Sunday, not north toward Srebrenica town. By taking OP Foxtrot and OP Uniform, the Serbs were securing hills that overlooked the strategic road which ran along the southern edge of the enclave. By securing the road, they could open a new route to their main provider of weapons and supplies—Serbia. There were also several bauxite, or aluminum ore, mines on the road the Serbs might be trying to reopen.

UN commanders outside Srebrenica agreed with Karremans' assessment. In Tuzla, Dutch colonel Charles Brantz, the acting commander of the UN's Sector Northeast—which was responsible for Srebrenica—considered the attack a limited one. In Sarajevo, the UN's chief of staff in Bosnia, Dutch general Cees Nicolai, also agreed with Karremans. In Zagreb, Dutch and other UN officers concurred.

Simply shrinking the safe area made sense according to Western military strategy and it fit a recent pattern of limited Serb attacks on the safe areas of Goražde and Bihać. It would be illogical for the Serbs to take the entire safe area and risk facing the wrath of the international community. But most of all, taking Srebrenica would involve bitter house-to-house fighting, something the Bosnian Serbs, short of manpower, had avoided throughout the war. If the Serbs attacked, UN officials were sure that Srebrenica's Muslims, with nowhere to retreat, would put up stiff resistance.

That night, Ramiz Bećirović, Srebrenica's Bosnian Army commander, was worried but not panicked. He also thought the Serbs only wanted to take control of the road south of Srebrenica. He was confident the UN would protect the safe area if the Serbs tried to take all of it, but was surprised that the international community had let the southeast corner of the enclave fall so quickly. Still, he was certain the UN would save the town, as French UN general Philippe Morillon had in 1993. Thousands of Muslims had packed the streets. A small, white-haired man in a blue beret had electrified the desperate enclave.

But the creation of the safe area had been more haphazard and random than most Srebrenicans or Dutch realized.

Two months before Morillon's arrival, Srebrenica had been at the zenith of its power. On January 7, 1993—Orthodox Christmas—Naser Orić and his men had taken the Serb-held village of Kravica in a surprise early-morning attack. Hundreds of hungry civilians from Srebrenica pillaged Serb farms and villages, enraging local Serbs. Seventy Serb civilians were killed; what was left of Serb villages was burned. With one bold attack, Orić had linked Srebrenica with the surrounded Muslim-held towns of Čerska and Konjević Polje to the northwest.[17] The long-awaited linking of Srebrenica with Muslim-held central Bosnia appeared to be at hand. After the Serb counterattack led by General Ratko Mladić swept through Čerska and Konjević Polje and retook Kravica, one group of civilians slipped through Serb lines and survived the dangerous trek to Sarajevo.[18] They met with Deputy Prime Minister Zlatko Lagumdžija and complained that while Sarajevo was the focus of attention Srebrenica and the eastern enclaves were suffering far more. They demanded that a Serb be arrested and executed in Sarajevo for every Muslim killed in eastern Bosnia. Lagumdžija dismissed the suggestion but announced that the UN airlift to Sarajevo and UN road convoys there would be stopped until the 200,000 Muslims under siege in Srebrenica, Žepa and Goražde in eastern Bosnia received aid.

In early March the Serbs pressed their attack on Srebrenica again. Despite secret helicopter flights from central Bosnia, Naser Orić and his men were on the verge of running out of ammunition. The Bosnian Army commander in Sarajevo, Sefer Halilović, warned Morillon that the town was on the verge of falling.[19] A British doctor with the World Health Organization who had trekked into Srebrenica through the mountains got word out that refugees were living in the streets; the poorest were beginning to die of starvation. The reports were true. Over 60,000 people packed a town that had a prewar population of 9,000.

Morillon had no permission to go to Srebrenica from his superiors, who feared making more UN promises that peacekeepers couldn't keep. He had no permission from the Bosnian Serbs to enter the town. At the last checkpoint, a Serb soldier directed the French UN commander down a mined road.[20] One of the trucks in Morillon's convoy hit a mine on the way, but no one was hurt. Arriving in the dead of night, Morillon and his group were not prepared for what they encountered. Even after all the reports they were genuinely stunned by the misery they found.

The UN commander's original goal was to stay in the town for one day only and leave, but when he tried he was encircled by women and children. Surrounding his car had been far from spontaneous. Murat Efendić, Srebrenica's representative in Sa-

rajevo, had secretly ordered Naser Orić and the town's leaders
to prevent Morillon from leaving, but to do it in a "civilized
way."[21]

That night, the UN commander in Bosnia then tried to sneak
out under cover of darkness. He tried to walk out of town alone
at 2 a.m., but his drivers were discovered when they tried to
meet him. Morillon's superiors in the UN were furious. The UN
was being humiliated.

The following day, when Morillon made his famous declaration from the post office window—"You are now under the
protection of the United Nations . . . I will never abandon
you"—his aides burst out laughing. They knew Morillon did not
have permission to make the desperate promise and he had no
way to keep it. Morillon saw his promise as temporary—under
the Vance-Owen peace plan being proposed by the UN, Srebrenica would stay in Muslim hands.[22]

The next day, the French general had walked the streets of
Srebrenica with bouquets of flowers in his hands and been
greeted like a conquering hero. But his superiors in New York
and Paris were furious. The United States and Europe were now
under tremendous pressure to protect Srebrenica—something
they were not eager to do.

After he left and met with Serbian President Milošević, Morillon succeeded in getting the Serbs to allow UN aid convoys
into Srebrenica. After the food was taken off the trucks, women
and children who were desperate to leave swarmed the vehicles.
Six children were crushed to death during the evacuation of
5,000 people to Tuzla. The UN was then criticized for aiding
the Serbs in removing Muslims, by "ethnically cleansing" Srebrenica.[23]

In April, the Serbs again pressed their attack and demanded
an immediate surrender. Pressure on the UN Security Council
again increased. One journalist was helping to keep Srebrenica
in the headlines. Tony Birtley, a freelance British reporter who
worked for the American television network ABC, had flown
into the enclave on a secret Bosnian Army helicopter flight. Birtley filed stories daily describing misery among Srebrenica's civilians and predicting the surrounded town's imminent collapse.

After the Serbs issued an ultimatum in early April that Srebrenica had forty-eight hours to surrender, Morillon—whose superiors and aides saw him as dangerously obsessed with
Srebrenica—again tried to return to the town. He was detained
for seven hours by a local commander twenty-five miles outside
of Sarajevo. Three of the five cars in his convoy were turned
back. When Morillon finally was within fifteen miles of Srebrenica his car was stoned and spray-painted "Morillon-Hitler" by
a group of 300 angry Serb civilians. The humiliated UN general
limped back to Tuzla.[24]

With the Bosnian Serbs rejecting the Vance-Owen peace plan
and the U.S. State Department pushing for a debate on the lifting
of the UN arms embargo, the UN Security Council ordered 120
Canadian peacekeepers to be sent to Srebrenica to facilitate the
arrival of UN aid. General Ratko Mladić, the Bosnian Serb commander, boldly refused to let them in. It was one of the clearest
examples to date of the UN's growing powerlessness.

UN officials in Belgrade then invited Mladić for talks. After
UN officials reported "progress," an intense artillery attack on
April 12 left fifty-six people dead in Srebrenica. Fourteen chil-
dren were found dead in the town's schoolyard.

Without the enclave's people knowing it, images of the carnage shot by Birtley again made a crucial difference and put
pressure on the West to act. Out of ammunition, Srebrenica's
leaders then sent a secret message via UN officials requesting that
surrender negotiations begin. On the night of April 14, Serbs
pushed through the Muslim lines and took Zeleni Jadar, just
south of Srebrenica.

The following day, news of the secret surrender request
leaked to the press.

Sensing he had finally taken the town, General Mladić allowed the 120 Canadians to enter Srebrenica the following day.
Morillon convened talks between Mladić and Bosnian Army
commander Sefer Halilović at the Sarajevo airport on the same
day. Ammunition was so low in Srebrenica that Halilović had
to secretly check throughout the day on whether the Serbs had
taken the town yet. Morillon urged him to accept Mladić's surrender terms. Finally, at 2 a.m. Sarajevo time, after sixteen hours

of negotiations, Morillon announced a "cease-fire" agreement that "saved" Srebrenica. The UN was putting the best face on what Bosnian government officials admitted was actually Srebrenica's surrender.[25]

That day in New York, April 16, the UN Security Council passed Resolution 819, a vaguely worded measure declaring Srebrenica the world's first UN "safe area." No one was quite sure what the term meant. The words "safe haven" were avoided because they suggested full protection under existing international law.

Three weeks later, after the Serbs again rejected the Vance-Owen peace plan, the Security Council declared the besieged Muslim towns of Sarajevo, Tuzla, Goražde, Žepa and Bihać safe areas on May 6, 1993. The crucial resolution came a month later. Resolution 836, enacted on June 4, stated that UN peacekeepers were to "deter" attacks on the safe areas and was vague on the use of airpower to defend them. The Clinton administration—whose proposal to arm the Bosnian government and launch air strikes against the Serbs had just been rejected by the Europeans—feared being drawn into the conflict and insisted that NATO airpower be used only to defend UN personnel. The final compromise language could be interpreted either way.[26]

The nonaligned nations—led by Venezuelan ambassador Diego Arilla—had proposed the safe haven concept but Venezuela and Pakistan abstained instead of voting for the final, vague resolution. Arilla felt the use of the word "deter" instead of "protect" and the loose wording on airpower constituted a false promise. The UN had stumbled into the worst of both worlds. It was grossly violating its ideal—neutrality—for "safe areas" it could not protect.[27] But the bottom line was that the safe areas served the short-term domestic political needs of the United States, Britain and France. The West looked active in Bosnia and was not using large numbers of troops.

To Bosnian Muslims, Morillon was the "Hero of Srebrenica" and the UN had promised to protect the safe areas. To policy-makers, he had helped the West ease into the creation of the safe areas. Largely because of his actions in Srebrenica, Morillon was relieved of his command that summer. Approximately 700

French soldiers were sent to Bihać and 300 British to Goražde—two new safe areas. French and British officials were also still trying to avoid being sucked further into the unpopular conflict. The Clinton administration, whose proposal to lift the arms embargo had been rejected by the Europeans, refused to send U.S. troops to the safe areas.

The United States and Europe had stumbled into creating the boldest experiment in peacekeeping in the history of the UN.

Two years later, Marc Klaver and other Dutch peacekeepers were cursing Morillon, the Security Council and the United States. At a brief ceremony held for Raviv van Renssen in the Dutch headquarters compound in Potočari, some Dutch soldiers wept. In the Srebrenica compound, Captain Groen decided his men didn't have time for a ceremony. Groen's Bravo Company, the unit van Renssen had been a member of, had fifty men trapped in five other isolated observation posts. Groen worked furiously with his staff that night trying to map out safe withdrawal and reinforcement routes.

Van Renssen's death cast a pall over the compound. His murder, as some Dutch called it, confirmed their long-running suspicions. While some burst into tears after hearing the news, other Dutch, like Klaver, silently resolved not to risk their own lives for Srebrenica.

The hostility was so great that Vahid Hodžić, a twenty-five-year-old Bosnian Muslim who had worked as a translator for the Dutch for the last year and a half, found himself shunned. Dutch soldiers he'd played soccer with three days earlier refused to speak to him. The usually relaxed cantina on the Dutch base, where a Dutch soldier had hand-painted a life-size tropical island scene complete with a beckoning blonde in a grass skirt, suddenly felt cold and alien. Almost none of the Dutch soldiers would speak to him.

At 10 p.m., the translator retreated to the small cubicle that he slept in inside the Dutch base. He pulled the curtain so none of the peacekeepers could see him. Crushed by the hostility of the Dutch, and fearful of the Serb guns he knew would resume pounding the enclave in the morning, Hodžić began to weep.

SUNDAY, JULY 9, 1995

BOSNIAN SERB ADVANCE, JULY 9, 1995

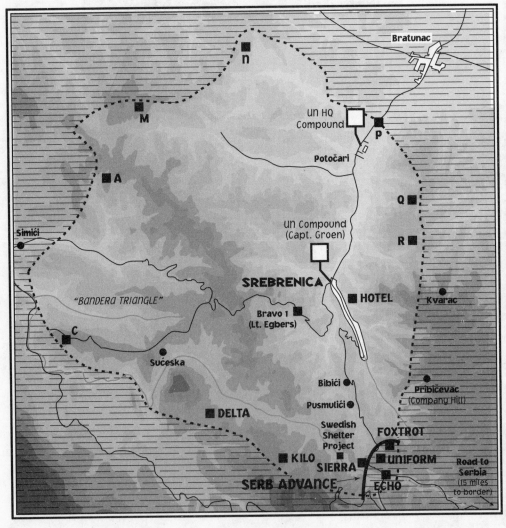

Bratunac

n

M

un HQ
Compound

P

Potočari

A

Q

Simići

R

un Compound
(Capt. Groen)

SREBRENICA

HOTEL

Kvarac

"Bandera Triangle"

Bravo 1
(Lt. Egbers)

C

Sućeska

Bibići

Pribićevac
(Company Hill)

Pusmulići

DELTA

Swedish
Shelter
Project

FOXTROT

KILO

UNIFORM

SIERRA

Road to
Serbia
(15 miles
to border)

SERB ADVANCE

ECHO

Serb-controlled   ■ un observation posts   - - - - Safe Area boundary

(Serb advance is approximate)

Ćamila Omanović watched from her balcony. Some scrambled down the steep hillsides on narrow footpaths. Most trudged down the asphalt road leading to the southern end of town. Grandmothers clutched blankets, bags and grandchildren in their sagging arms. Stooped old men drenched with sweat pushed wheelbarrows full of clothes and food. Panicked young mothers led toddlers by the hand. Bony cows—prized possessions in the slowly starving enclave—walked lazily in the midst of their uneasy masters. Sweltering in the July heat, the throng smelled of sweat and desperation. It was 8 a.m.

She greeted the refugees from her balcony. Most of them said they were from the Swedish Shelter Project in the southeast corner of the enclave. Serb gunners could easily see the long vulnerable column from their positions on Mount Kvarac, a 3,000-foot peak that loomed over the town from the east. Srebrenica itself sat in a deep ravine, 360 feet below sea level, and was surrounded by high hills. There were no panoramic vistas in Srebrenica. There was no open space. There was only a sense of vulnerability in the surrounded town.

Every ten to fifteen minutes shells and rockets whistled overhead, and landed with a thunderous crack. At first, each impact sent the human herd scurrying. As time passed, people ignored the danger. For now, the Serbs weren't directly targeting civilians.

The gunners seemed to begin at the same time every morning. Over 200 shells had hit the town the day before.[1] The constant tension of not knowing where the next projectile was hurtling was wearing Ćamila down. She had sent her thirteen-year-old son to her seventeen-year-old daughter's concrete apartment building in the center of town; it would be safer there.

Ćamila had seen it all before. Srebrenica's chattel were running for their lives again, just as they had when the Serbs nearly took the town two years ago. Since the night before, approximately 3,000 civilians had streamed into Srebrenica from the south. They were encamped inside the local elementary school. If one shell hit there it could kill dozens, just as the volley of Serb artillery had killed fifty-six people on April 12, 1993—including fourteen children on the playground.

The refugees were parking carts piled high with wheat, corn and other crops on the outskirts of town. Few had forgotten the slow torture of starvation from the beginning of the war. When forced to flee their homes people took food first. The Serbs had blocked 70 percent of the UNHCR food convoys planned for Srebrenica that year. Food supplies were the lowest they had been since Srebrenica became a safe area. By early July, people had started begging for food on the streets. The town, already overcrowded, was taking on the savage air she hated.

Ćamila turned and went back into her house. The Srebrenica she had grown up in had disappeared long ago. With no electricity, natural gas or running water, the town existed in the Stone Age. Fire was the primary source of heat. All food was cooked on woodstoves. Enormous stacks of wood seemed to fill every yard. Vegetable gardens lined the bare hillsides ringing the town. Trees that once flourished there had been chopped down and burned. Makeshift lanterns and candles were the primary sources of light. Lanterns consisted of a thin strip of cloth with one end placed in a can or cup of oil while the other slowly burned. As the oil burned, the room was filled with an acrid smell. The black smoke and dim light gave the apartments and houses a cavelike feel.

In the winter, smoke from thousands of fires hovered over Srebrenica. Makeshift chimneys of tin tubes spewed sparks from the walls and windows of what had been modern apartment buildings. The town was blanketed in soot and cinder. With glass in short supply, plastic sheeting covered windows blown out by shells or bullets. Unless you stood right next to a fire, you were never warm.

In the summer, the stench from the overcrowded apartment buildings where refugees lived twelve to a room was unbearable. Every inch of floor space was used. At night, kitchen and bathroom floors became beds. Dozens of people shared a single toilet. The town's sewage system was constantly overflowing and filling the air with the smell of feces. Fetid heaps of garbage lay where they had been dumped six months earlier. With the Serbs blocking resupply convoys, there was no fuel for trash removal. Lice, fleas and rats thrived inside and outside buildings.

Ćamila's was one of the lucky families in town. The house had a private spring and was one of a handful with running water. A Swedish aid worker had smuggled some money from her brother working in Germany into the enclave. Because her brother was a cook for the aid group Médecins Sans Frontières (MSF, or Doctors Without Borders), her son occasionally got to eat meat and other extra or leftover food. Most of the children in the enclave wouldn't have meat for months at a time.

Ćamila had been chief bookkeeper at the car brake factory, and had been forced to learn how to grow food, care for chickens and cows and shovel manure for the first time in her life. She converted the house's flower beds into a vegetable garden. Decorative plum and apricot trees in the front yard suddenly became valuable sources of food. A precious cow and a few chickens were kept in one of the house's single-car garages. With little fuel in the enclave, cars were useless for most people.

Whatever Ćamila cooked, their meals always seemed to be monotonous variations on rice, the staple of UN aid convoys. Salt cost twenty-five dollars a pound on the enclave's black market. Sugar was only slightly less. Almost anything that wasn't homegrown was too expensive.

Her husband taught chemistry in the high school when it was open. School was held only during warm weather because the buildings couldn't be heated. There was so little paper in the municipality that lessons and records were kept on the backs of old receipts. One of the most valuable gifts a Dutch peacekeeper could give a child was pen, pencil or paper.

Ćamila was proud of her son. Using electricity from a waterwheel her brother had built in a nearby stream, the thirteen-year-old had set up a movie theater in the house's other single-car garage. Crowds of fifty people and more would cram into the room to watch blurry videotapes on a TV set of American action movies starring Arnold Schwarzenegger and Jean-Claude Van Damme. The price of admission was a cigarette.

Ćamila put on her shoes and got ready to go outside and speak to the refugees. A short, plump woman with shoulder-length brown hair, she unconsciously gave off the air of a doting mother or benevolent schoolteacher. Ćamila's most remarkable feature was her eyes. Incandescent blue, they seemed to glow when she smiled. She was worried, but not yet panicked. The Serbs had overrun the southeast corner of the enclave. True, it was by far the most intense attack the town had suffered since it became a safe area, and she had already packed a bag with clothes and food in case the worst happened. But she was confident that if the Serbs got close to the town the UN would stop them, as General Morillon had in 1993.

Before the war, no place on earth made her feel safer than Srebrenica. Ćamila's father had been a locksmith and her mother a housewife. After high school, she had journeyed to Tuzla—the largest city in northern Bosnia—and studied business at the local university. There she met her husband, Ahmet, a gentle, soft-spoken man with glasses that hid his bright blue eyes. He had caught her eye in the library of their dormitory. "A couple of looks over the books, a couple cups of coffee, then you start holding hands with each other and taking long walks down railroad tracks," she recalled. "It was like that." The two began going steady on April 10, 1974. Three years later they were married.

Jobs had brought them back to Srebrenica. He became the chief technical engineer in the zinc processing factory north of town, while she kept the books at the car brake factory next door. The couple moved into a comfortable one-bedroom apartment and bought a car, a VCR, a washing machine and other modern appliances. In 1977 they had a daughter and in 1981 a son was born.

Their life took on a comfortable routine. Weekends were spent in a small summer house on a hill overlooking the town, or camping in the lush forests ringing Srebrenica. During winter vacations, they skied near Sarajevo. The monthlong European-style August holiday was enjoyed on the coast of Croatia, or visiting her husband's family in southern Bosnia. Ćamila joked that her husband was the first man in Srebrenica to do dishes and vacuum the floor. Strong-willed, she dominated the relationship.

Ćamila and her Serb friends had watched with shock, but not alarm, as the former Yugoslavia disintegrated. Three nationalist parties representing Bosnia's Muslims, Serbs and Croats won 85 percent of the vote in November 1990 elections. But even as war raged in neighboring Croatia between July 1991 and January 1992, Ćamila and her best friend and co-worker, a Serb named Nada Krsmanović, remained confident that blood would not run in Bosnia.[2] It was the most ethnically integrated of the six Yugoslav republics. Its Muslims lacked the long traditions of nationalism that belonged to Yugoslavia's Serbs and Croats. Forty-four percent Muslim, 31 percent Serb and 17 percent Croat, Bosnia had no overwhelmingly dominant ethnic group.

But in December 1991 Serbs voted against Bosnia's seceding from Yugoslavia in a referendum largely boycotted by Muslims and Croats. Capitalizing on the results of the referendum, Serb nationalist politicians declared their own state in Bosnia, the Republika Srpska. Ćamila and the vast majority of Muslims and Croats then voted for independence in a March 1992 referendum that was boycotted by Serbs.

That spring, the Muslim Bošnjak Party (MBO)—a small Muslim party that supported Bosnia's remaining in what was left of Yugoslavia—tried to negotiate a compromise with local Serb moderates as tensions rose across Bosnia. The MBO had won more votes in Srebrenica than in most other towns in Bosnia. In a perverse strategy carried out throughout the country, the Muslim nationalist Party for Democratic Action (SDA) and the nationalist Serbian Democratic Party (SDS) formed a coalition to keep moderate parties out of power.

As the crisis deepened that spring, conversations in Ćamila's office turned to whether Serbs would be discriminated against in an independent Bosnia. Some of her Serb co-workers admitted their unease.

"You're not endangered," Ćamila had said to Ljubica Đurić, a Serb whom Ćamila supervised in the bookkeeping department. "We take the same bus to get to work. We eat in the same cafeteria. I have the same things as you."

Đurić broke into tears. "They keep calling us on the phone at night," she said, referring to Serb nationalists. "They keep telling us if we don't do something to move out, the Muslims will kill us. But I'm not afraid of Muslims, I'm afraid of these Serbs."[3]

Fighting erupted in Sarajevo on April 5, 1992. Ćamila and her Serb friend Nada were convinced it would all be over in a few days. Ultranationalist paramilitary groups from Serbia—including the Arkan Tigers—crossed into Bosnia and began expelling Muslims from the Muslim-majority towns of Bijeljina, Brčko and Zvornik, thirty miles north of Srebrenica. Talks between moderate Serbs and Muslims broke off in Srebrenica and Bratunac.

In Muslim and Serb villages around Srebrenica, men began arming themselves and setting up patrols. Naser Orić, then a twenty-six-year-old policeman in the village of Potočari, seized the department's assault rifles, grenades and other weapons. Unlike many others, Naser anticipated the worst.

The Serb nationalists issued an ultimatum. Muslims were ordered to give up all of their weapons by April 17, 1992. In shock, Ćamila, her family and some neighbors fled at dawn to their summer house overlooking the town. The paramilitaries had expelled tens of thousands of Muslims from Brčko, Bijeljina, Zvornik and the other Muslim-dominated towns they now held.

Thousands had been killed and hundreds raped, according to the news from Sarajevo.

Twenty stunned men, women and children watched from the summer house as men armed with semiautomatic rifles and clad in black uniforms and ski masks—the Arkan Tigers—entered what had been a quaint mining town. Muslim houses were set on fire and Muslim stores were looted. Ćamila thought she saw two elderly Muslims scurry into a house that was then ignited by paramilitaries. She watched as the Serbs set up weaponry on the hillside across from them.

Shells began impacting around the town and then near the summer house as Ćamila and her family cowered inside. In the midst of the panic, her son turned to her. The two of them had heard on a radio broadcast that a Muslim father in Zvornik had died of sorrow after seeing his son killed.

"Please don't die of grief if I die," he told her.

They soon realized that the Serbs were firing the shells near the house to scare them into leaving. At dusk, the town quieted. Ćamila and her family made their way back into town and slept fitfully in an abandoned Muslim house. The following day, Ćamila was still convinced that the dispute would be over as soon as the paramilitaries and local nationalists departed. She decided to try to return to her home. As she walked through town, she saw paramilitaries looting nearby stores and houses. She realized that if she acted naturally, she could pass as a Serb.

When Ćamila was a block away from her apartment she saw a group of paramilitaries standing at the gas station across the street. When she entered her building she saw their faces clearly and was stunned. Several of her Serb neighbors were in the group. One neighbor, a Serb named Novica, had dropped his cigarette on seeing her, amazed that she would dare return. Their daughters had gone to school together. She waited for him to shout that she was Muslim. There was only an awkward silence. Her neighbor spared her.[4]

Later that day, she was horrified to see her friend Miloje Simić enter the apartment building next to hers. The forty-eight-year-old literature teacher in the Srebrenica high school was dressed in a uniform and carried a rifle. He had been working with the paramilitaries. Furious, she taunted him. "Good luck, hero," she said, her voice dripping with sarcasm. "Don't get wounded!" Shocked to see her, Simić stammered, "I wasn't wounded." He ducked into his building.[5]

Ćamila spent the next five days hiding with her husband and children in the house of her Serb friend, Nada Krsmanović. Nada was horrified by the Serb paramilitaries and local extremists, but thought it would all be over in a matter of days. Ćamila's experience was not uncommon. Around Srebrenica, many Serb neighbors refused to turn in Muslims when they crept back to their houses for food. Other Serbs cared for Muslims' farm animals and pets or invited their terrified Muslim neighbors into their homes for food and coffee. One Muslim was even given painted eggs by her Serb neighbor on Orthodox Easter.[6]

But at the end of the first week, Muslim nationalists from Srebrenica, led by Naser Orić, began to fight back. Several Serbs were killed by Muslims firing from the woods. Ćamila decided it would be safer for both her family and Nada if they hid in the forest. She and Nada said a quick goodbye on April 22, 1992, convinced the standoff would soon come to an end. No more than thirty local extremists, Muslim and Serb, had started the war in Srebrenica, she felt.

For the next three weeks, she, her family and thousands of other embittered Muslims stayed with relatives in surrounding villages or camped in the woods. Tents people had used for camping and old Yugoslav Army tarps were erected. Women snuck into abandoned houses on the outskirts of Srebrenica to gather food and cook. For the first time in her life, Ćamila learned how to store food without a refrigerator and regularly cook over an open fire.

On May 18, Naser Orić's forces ambushed a convoy of Serb cars as they drove from Srebrenica to Bratunac. Twenty-eight Serbs were killed in the attack. Not a single Muslim was hurt. Naser's men later said they didn't know it when they sprang the ambush, but Goran Zekić, the newly appointed nationalist Serb mayor of Srebrenica, was one of the ill-fated passengers. The Serbs remaining in Srebrenica fled in a panic as word of the attack spread. Led by Naser, Muslims returned to Srebrenica in triumph. For one of the first times in the war, Muslims outside of Sarajevo had fought back against the better-armed Serbs and won.

One of the first things Ćamila did when she returned to town was to look for the Serb who had hidden her for five days. But Nada and her family were gone. Three years later, as the shells rained down on Srebrenica, Omanović still wondered where her best friend was. She had tried to take care of Nada's house, but twenty Muslim refugees expelled from their homes in other towns had moved into it. She only managed to get some of Nada's valuables out and place them in storage.

She and her husband gave their apartment to relatives who had lost their home and moved in with her brother. Three families—approximately fifteen people—moved into Ćamila's 170-square-foot apartment, consisting of one bedroom, a living room, a kitchen and a bathroom. Ćamila no longer went there, because of the smell.

She had sat on hillsides holding torches with thousands of other Srebrenicans hoping it would lead the American C-130 cargo plane pilots to drop food near her when the enclave was on the verge of starvation and collapse in March 1993. People had been killed in the fights that erupted over the pallets of U.S. Army "Meals Ready to Eat," or MREs. Ćamila had learned to use a liquid in the packets called Tabasco as a way to spice up food. Chocolates called M&M's were precious sugar, and women burned the plastic wrappings as fuel and made shirts and pants out of the nylon parachutes.

Life improved with the creation of the safe area. When she and her husband heard that the son of his Serb colleagues from work, Ilija and Milena Miladihović, had died in 1993, they had sent their condolences in a Red Cross message. They never heard back.

Ćamila headed outside to talk to some of the refugees. Like everyone else, she tried to ignore the shells intermittently whizzing overhead. She chatted with several women. The three miles between the Swedish Shelter Project and the town were lined with steep hills and ravines. The exhausted women were shaken by what was happening, but confident the Serbs would be stopped.

"We won't be left at the mercy of the Chetniks," said one woman, using a pejorative term for Serb nationalists dating back to World War I. "Someone will come help us."

"This a protected area," Ćamila said. "We'll be protected."

Lieutenant Vincent Egbers focused his binoculars on the road below. If the Serbs were going to take the enclave, their tanks would have to roll up the winding strip of asphalt. From OP Foxtrot, the road gradually sloped downward for almost two miles. It then descended steeply through a series of switchbacks to the town itself. The narrow road was the only route tanks could take into Srebrenica town from the south.

Parked at the hairpin turn he and Captain Groen had chosen the night before, Egbers' two APCs were in a perfect position to observe—and that was all they intended to do. Groen's orders were to "fly the colors," or stay in a visible position where both sides could see that the UN was watching the fighting. A second APC, commanded by Sergeant Johan Bos, had arrived during the night to reinforce them.[7] Equipped with full combat gear and light blue UN helmets, the twenty peacekeepers spread out in the brush lining the dirt road. It was 8:30 a.m., and they waited nervously for the battle to unfold below them.

At first glance, the enclave's beautiful, but jagged terrain favored whoever was trying to defend the town. The road from the south ran along the top of a narrow ridge. There were sharp, 500-foot drop-offs on either side. Disabling one tank could be enough to block the crucial route. That morning, it looked deserted. No Serbs or Muslims could be seen moving in either direction.

But Bosnian Serbs held the peaks ringing the safe area, and the terrain was an artilleryman's dream. A moderately skilled gunner could see his potential target directly below. Even if a first shot missed, the second or third could easily be adjusted to hit home. Egbers felt exposed. He couldn't see the Serbs, but knew they could see him from their positions on much higher hills to the south and east. The abandoned OP Foxtrot was clearly visible—a bright white dot on a hill a mile and a half away. He was glad he hadn't been there yesterday.

About two dozen Muslim soldiers and their families had intermittently walked past their position during the night. The civilians begged the Dutch to stay. Most of them were heading north with their families, away from the Serb advance. None of them had threatened the Dutch, but Egbers was beginning to wonder how organized the Muslim defense of the town would be. They had never impressed him as soldiers. The only officer the Dutch thought had any authority in the enclave, Naser Orić, was gone. In a fuel-starved enclave where the Dutch had resorted to using mules, Naser drove a black VW Golf or a Mercedes. He was rumored to profit heavily in the town's black market and to be running a prostitution ring. The Dutch could not understand why the people were so fiercely loyal to him.

Egbers' position in the Quick Reaction Force was not his primary duty in the battalion. He was a member of Charlie Company, the unit responsible for observation posts in the northern part of the enclave. Egbers commanded a thirty-man platoon that rotated in and out of four observation posts on the northern edge of the enclave.

They had good relations with the local civilians; they traded coffee for bread and played impromptu soccer games with local teenagers. He and the Dutch had learned to communicate with the Muslims through a combination of English, German, Bosnian and hand gestures. English was mandatory in Dutch schools and half of the Dutch officers spoke fluent German. Before the war many Bosnians had worked in Germany for one or two years, saved money to build a home and then returned to Yugoslavia. They picked up English from the American movies they watched endlessly inside the enclave.

Egbers had never wanted to go to Bosnia. In fact, it was only later in life that he wanted to be a military officer. After receiving a business degree from a two-year college in Rotterdam, where he had grown up, he entered the army as a conscript officer and found that he liked it. He applied to the Royal Military Academy—the Netherlands' equivalent of West Point—and was admitted at the age of twenty-three. At first, he was out of place. Most cadets are only eighteen years old, and enter when they graduate from high school. But Egbers, a tall, dark-haired bear of a man, emerged as one of the leaders in his class. He used his personal skills to become president of the student senate. When he graduated in 1993 as a second lieutenant, he received the Academy Medal—the institution's highest honor. Soon he was promoted to first lieutenant.

When his battalion was chosen for a six-month deployment in Srebrenica, he knew it would be professional suicide to opt out. Egbers' father was a deputy principal in a vocational high school that trained waiters, butchers and bakers. His mother was a housewife. He had two brothers and two sisters. His family was proud of him for being in the military but they worried about him in Bosnia.

Just after his battalion, Dutchbat-III, arrived on January 18, 1995, Egbers was at the center of a confrontation between Dutch and Muslim soldiers that set the tone for the next six months. Srebrenica's commanders were furious that the Serbs had again sneaked forward while a new battalion of peacekeepers entered the safe area and took strategic positions along the enclave's front line. On January 21, Naser Orić and Zulfo Tursunović, the Bosnian Army commander for the southwest corner of the enclave, barred the Dutch from entering an area known as the Bandera Triangle. A Dutch observation post—OP Charlie— would have to be abandoned.

When negotiations failed, the UN headquarters in Sector Northeast ordered the Dutch to try to enter the triangle. On January 27, Egbers and a patrol of seven men entered Tursunović's territory from the north while other groups of Dutch entered from the south and east. The Dutch hoped to show the Bosnians that they were in control. Muslim soldiers shouted "Heil Hitler!" and "Mines! Mines!" at Egbers and his soldiers as they entered the triangle. Thirty of Tursunović's soldiers encircled Egbers' group. The Dutch entering from other directions were also surrounded. Tursunović, a six-foot-four giant who had been imprisoned before the war for killing two men, personally confronted a group of Dutch Special Forces soldiers led by the battalion's deputy commander, Major Robert Franken. Tursunović stuck a tree limb under one of the Special Forces' jeeps and tried to flip it off a hillside.[8]

More than 100 Dutch peacekeepers were held hostage by Muslim soldiers. Egbers and his seven men spent three days inside a small UN snowcat. Older Muslims gave the Dutch food and built them a fire. After three days, the Dutch were released after agreeing that they would take only a certain route to OP Charlie, and not patrol other parts of the triangle.

Egbers had learned a valuable lesson. The best way to get out of a confrontation was to remain calm and be as friendly as possible to Muslims or Serbs. He realized that treating people with respect was crucial in the former Yugoslavia—a country whose culture was far closer to that of Latin nations such as Italy and Spain than to that of the United States or Northern Europe. Bosnian men tended to be tough-talking, "macho," and expected to be treated with respect. The Dutch and British peacekeepers serving in the enclave, by contrast, tended to be seen as cold and unemotional by Bosnians who worked for the UN.

Dutch relations with Muslim soldiers remained troubled throughout the spring. Observation posts were sometimes robbed, and on every fifth or sixth foot patrol Egbers or his soldiers heard bullets whiz over their heads. The Dutch were never sure where the shots were coming from. The Serbs fired at them sometimes, but Egbers was convinced that the Muslims would also snipe at the Dutch from the direction of the Serbs to trick the peacekeepers. The Muslims emphatically denied it, but on a few occasions Egbers or his men believed Muslims had positioned themselves near Dutch observation posts and fired on the Serbs, apparently hoping to draw the Dutch and Serbs into a firefight.

...

Egbers listened to the constant radio checks between the observation posts and the operations room in Srebrenica and scanned the horizon. He saw no activity. At approximately 8:45 a.m., a tense voice came over the radio. OP Uniform, the only remaining Dutch observation post in the southeastern part of the enclave, had been taken by the Serbs. As Egbers and the other Dutch posts in the southern half of the enclave listened, Sergeant Jan Bresser, commander of OP Sierra, said the Serbs were giving the Dutch a choice of going to Srebrenica or Serb-occupied Bratunac.

After a tense night, Bresser had stepped out of the OP at the suggestion of Captain Groen to see whether the Muslim soldiers in the area had withdrawn. As soon as Bresser appeared, twenty Serb soldiers emerged from the woods and approached the OP from two different directions. The Dutch were immediately disarmed and the OP looted.

"Sierra, this is Romeo. Can you get back to Srebrenica?" Groen asked.

"Romeo, this is Sierra. There may be some Muslims behind me," Bresser answered. "I'm not sure what to do."

Groen told Bresser to do what he thought was best. The twenty-nine-year-old sergeant had been threatened by the local Muslim officer when the attack started. If the Dutch withdrew, the officer said, RPGs would be fired at the peacekeepers' APC. With thoughts of Raviv van Renssen's fate, Bresser opted to go with the Serbs. At 9:15 a.m., the Dutch departed for Bratunac. After having hand grenades thrown at him the night before, Egbers supported Bresser's decision.

Later that morning, Bresser was on the radio again. He nervously reported that Serb artillery could be seen as he passed through the Serb-held village of Pribičevac. For the second night in a row, fifty Serb soldiers were firing ten light 81 mm mortars, one howitzer and one World War II-era T-34 tank gun down at Srebrenica. Seated just behind Bresser on the APC, the Serbs were either allowing him to use the radio or somehow they didn't notice it. On the road between Pribičevac and Bratunac, Bresser saw no artillery. The Serbs told him that the peacekeepers would be allowed to return to the Netherlands. Bresser thought the attack was a large one, but was unsure whether the Serbs wanted to take the entire enclave.

The morning passed slowly. The Serbs were firing fewer shells into town than the day before. Egbers could hear the sound of gun battles in the south of the enclave. Every fifteen to thirty minutes, Egbers would see the flash from a distant muzzle and then wait for the report. His men were bored. Neither the Serbs nor the Muslims seemed to be advancing on the road below. The heat was stifling and mosquitoes were beginning to swarm.

A jeep arrived with a British commando and Sergeant Voskamp. Both were Forward Air Controllers (FAC) or Tactical Air Control Parties (TACP).[9] The two soldiers were specially trained to guide NATO airplanes to their exact target. Equipped with secure communications, the FACs were not required for an air attack, but they helped cautious UN commanders approve one. They minimized the chances of a bomb being dropped on civilians or peacekeepers by mistake. There were only two British and two Dutch FACs left in the enclave. The Dutch officer in charge of the group had not been allowed back after he went on leave.

After the jeep arrived,[10] Egbers thought he heard voices speaking Bosnian above him. His men had been speaking with Bosnian soldiers hanging around their position all morning.[11] He decided to investigate and walked up the hill. He was amazed. Thirty yards up the slope, a half dozen Muslim soldiers were standing around a Yugoslav Army M-48 field artillery gun. All Muslim tanks and artillery were to have been turned over to the UN when the safe area was created and the enclave demilitarized. For two years, the Muslims had successfully concealed the aging artillery piece. They must have captured it from the Serbs at the beginning of the war. With a range of three miles, it was effective against infantry, but had to score a direct hit to disable a tank.

Egbers had driven down the dirt road next to the bluff dozens of times while on patrol and never noticed the Muslim position. The gun must have been hidden in some brush. The Muslims had even dug a large bunker, which they probably built at night.

He began to wonder what other surprises the Muslims had in store.

"Good morning," he said to the soldiers in Bosnian. The Dutch had run out of cigarettes a month ago and he had nothing to offer to break the ice. The Bosnians eyed him suspiciously. He decided to just make his point.

"Don't shoot it, don't shoot it," Egbers said slowly in English as he pointed at the artillery piece to make himself clear. He looked at a middle-aged soldier and said, "No good, no good," in German.

The middle-aged man, clearly an officer, smiled. He seemed amused by Egbers.

"You shoot, no NATO," Egbers said, using his hands to indicate a plane on a bombing run. "NATO," he said, and he pointed to the south toward the Serb lines.

The officer laughed out loud. He seemed to be enjoying the spectacle. "Ramiz decides if the gun shoots," the officer said slowly in Bosnian. Egbers understood that Ramiz meant Ramiz Bećirović, the acting Muslim commander in Srebrenica.

The group walked back down to the APC. The officer pointed at Egbers' pocket and said "Paper, paper," in Bosnian. Egbers fished in his pocket for a piece of scrap paper and a pencil. He handed them to the Muslim officer. The officer scribbled the number 30,000 and pointed to himself and his men. "Thirty thousand Muslims," he said. Egbers was puzzled.

The man then scribbled the number 30 and pointed to Egbers. "Chetniks have thirty Dutch," he said slowly in Bosnian, referring to the Serbs. He pointed again at the number 30. "Chetniks, Chetniks have thirty Dutch," he said.

"Thirty thousand Muslims," he repeated in Bosnian, pointing at the number 30,000. "Nothing."

"Serbs thirty Dutch," he said, pointing at the number 30. "No NATO, no NATO."

Egbers realized what the man was saying. There would be no NATO air strikes because of the Dutch hostages. UN commanders or the Dutch government would hold back, fearing the Serbs would kill Dutch hostages in retaliation. The lives of thirty

Dutch soldiers were worth more than the lives of 30,000 Muslims.

Egbers stared at the ground and suddenly felt very uncomfortable. It won't come to that, he thought. They can save all of us.

As Egbers talked on the bluff dozens of Dutch peacekeepers filed out of the main building of the UN headquarters compound in Potočari. Each peacekeeper carried a rifle, wore a light blue beret and was dressed as neatly as possible. The peacekeepers formed two lines and created a column leading from the doorway on the side of the building to a white UN four-ton truck. There was a noticeable decrease in the amount of Serb shelling in the area after they appeared.

The six survivors from OP Foxtrot emerged from the main building carrying a wooden casket draped with the pale blue flag of the United Nations. The Dutch peacekeepers lining the route snapped to attention. Marc Klaver held the right rear corner of Raviv van Renssen's casket on his shoulder. In front of him were Jeroen Yak and the medic Jeffrey Schijndel. Sergeant Frans van Rossum, Jeroen Dekkers and Steven Mungra carried the left-hand side.

As they walked, Klaver told himself he was glad to have the chance to honor Raviv one last time. Schijndel wept, as did some of the peacekeepers lined up on either side of them. Because Serbs had blocked resupply convoys into the enclave, Dutch doctors were unable to find a coffin that van Renssen would fit into. In the end, they had to remove the coffin's zinc lining to accommodate him.

The peacekeepers from OP Foxtrot loaded the coffin onto the truck. They and a captain from the headquarters in Potočari were to take van Renssen to a small soccer stadium in the Serb-controlled city of Zvornik. A UN helicopter would then take the casket and three of the peacekeepers to Holland.

The Dutch left the compound but were immediately stopped at a Serb checkpoint when they tried to leave the enclave. Serb soldiers demanded that the coffin be opened so they could inspect the contents. Klaver and the others refused. For thirty humiliating minutes, the peacekeepers waited. A Serb officer finally arrived and gave them permission to drive on.

When the Dutch reached Zvornik, a Bosnian Serb TV crew was waiting for them. They filmed van Renssen's coffin and started asking the Dutch questions. "I can understand how you feel," one of the Serbs said. "My brother was killed by the Muslims." Klaver and the others refused to answer.

Two green helicopter gunships, apparently from neighboring Serbia, flew in and circled the stadium. Klaver thought they were there to intimidate anyone from disrupting the transfer. A white UN helicopter landed. Klaver, Steven Mungra and Jeroen Dekkers helped the others load the coffin onto the chopper. They said their goodbyes. Van Rossum, Jeroen Yak and Jeffrey Schijndel would escort van Renssen home. Klaver and the other two peacekeepers were needed in the manpower-short enclave. The Dutch piled into the truck and drove south to Srebrenica.

As the Dutch bid farewell to van Renssen, a small group of Muslim soldiers reached Kožlje, a hill half a mile north of OP Foxtrot, unbeknownst to the Serbs or Lieutenant Egbers.[12]

The Muslims hurriedly assembled their most potent weapon, a Chinese-made TF-8 Red Arrow antitank missile that had been smuggled into the enclave via a secret helicopter flight that spring. A half dozen such flights had been made to Žepa between January and May.[13] The contents were split between Žepa and Srebrenica. Soldiers then hauled the Red Arrow missiles, approximately 300,000 rounds of ammunition, 44 rocket-propelled grenades, 6 light mortars, 60 mortar grenades, 100 AK-47 semiautomatic rifles, a half dozen Motorola walkie-talkies and cartons of cigarettes and salt on their backs to Srebrenica. The trip, at times through waste-deep snow, was fifteen miles long and ran through hostile Serb territory.

No one was quite sure how to use the Red Arrow. No soldier in the enclave knew anything about Chinese missiles, and the forty pages of instructions that came with them were in English.

Naser Orić had ordered two Muslim translators who worked for the UN to render the instructions into Serbo-Croatian, but the instructions and translation were then lost. In May, the first attempt to assemble the missiles ended in disaster. Working inside the building next to the town hall, three soldiers had carefully pieced the weapon together. Everything but the warhead was installed, but then one of the soldiers accidentally hit the wrong button. The rocket fired and slammed into the wall at the opposite end of the room. All three men were seriously injured.

This time, the rocket was fully assembled, including the warhead. Aiming at the Serb tank firing on the town from the Serb-held village of Pribičevac, the Muslims fired. The rocket flew wildly off the launcher, soared through the air and careened into some trees, missing the tank completely. Worried that the Serbs would identify their position, the soldiers hurriedly loaded another rocket onto the launcher.

They fired again, but the missile flew even more wildly off course, crashing into the ground a few hundred yards away. The Red Arrows were totally unreliable.

When they tried to load another rocket, they noticed that something was wrong with the launcher. The trigger mechanism was broken.[14] The launcher, the only one they had, was now useless. Eleven missiles left, with no way to fire them.

That morning, UN Force Commander Janvier was returning to Zagreb from Paris. Janvier had just suffered the latest in a series of setbacks. The new 13,000-troop Rapid Reaction Force created by France, Britain and Holland in the wake of the hostage crisis would not change its name. He feared "Rapid" would raise expectations that the UN would go to war against the Serbs and had asked that the new force be called the less provocative Theater Reaction Force. After Janvier's proposal leaked to the press and was criticized as another example of UN timidity, the name was set as the Rapid Reaction Force.

What Janvier feared was that pressure would quickly mount to use the force to create corridors to funnel supplies to the enclaves. More than anything else the fifty-four-year-old Janvier, a Foreign Legionnaire and commander in the Gulf War, was cautious. He complained to his friends about the loneliness of his position, the crushing responsibility he had and the lack of clear political guidance. At meetings, he often appeared tortured, furrowing his brow and grimacing.

Janvier's top priority was the safety of his peacekeepers. Largely reflecting Akashi's view of the conflict, he was extremely hesitant to use force or to appear to be taking sides. And like Akashi, he believed that the role of the UN was to pacify the situation, not inflame it.

Janvier refused to speak with the media, but on May 22 he expressed his views on the safe areas in a closed-door session of the UN Security Council. Every six months the mandate of the peacekeeping mission expired. UN officials in New York and the former Yugoslavia had prepared an exhaustive report on the troubled mission UNPROFOR and were recommending that it be urgently reformed, or it would soon be forced to withdraw.

The safe areas, especially Sarajevo and Bihać, were routinely shelled or attacked by Serb troops; at times, Bihać was even bombed by Serb airplanes in violation of the NATO-enforced "no-fly zone." Peacekeepers were routinely sniped at. The three-year death toll for the mission, now at a UN record 173 peacekeepers, was steadily rising.[15]

The Serbs had allowed 30 percent of UN aid convoys to reach their destinations. Food supplies in all of the enclaves were dangerously low. Sensing the UN's weakness that spring, Serbs, Croats and Muslims commandeered over 500 UN vehicles. Humiliated, nearly all UN officials in the former Yugoslavia were desperate for a new, clearer mandate that lightly armed UN peacekeepers could actually carry out.

Secretary General Boutros Boutros-Ghali laid out several options for the Security Council to reform the dying mission's mandate. Increase the number of peacekeepers and use force to deliver aid and protect safe areas; keep the number of peacekeepers the same but decrease the UN's responsibilities; or stay the course. Boutros-Ghali recommended reducing the scope of the mission—diplomatic language for abandoning the safe area concept.

The safe areas became the Achilles' heel of the UN peace-keeping mission. After limited support in 1993, NATO countries were no longer willing to deploy troops in them. French forces had pulled out of Bihać and been replaced by Bangladeshis in 1994. Canadian troops pulled out of Srebrenica in January 1994 and were replaced by the Dutch. Now the British and Dutch governments said they were pulling their soldiers out of Srebrenica and Goražde by January 1996. After a long and difficult search, Ukraine had offered to send its peacekeepers to the two isolated enclaves. But the Ukrainians, who were already in Žepa and Sarajevo, were infamous for corruption, black marketeering and their failure to enforce UN mandates.

In his briefing to the UN Security Council, Janvier recommended that all but a handful of UN peacekeepers who were Forward Air Controllers withdraw from the eastern enclaves. A small group of the specially trained peacekeepers would be left in the enclave to guide NATO air strikes if needed. British general Rupert Smith backed the proposal because it would allow the UN to use force against the Serbs without being handicapped by the existence of hundreds of potential hostages.

"Let us be pragmatic . . . and above all let us be honest with ourselves and those we have pledged to protect," Janvier had told the Security Council. "One shouldn't play in the storm if one cannot throw lightning bolts."[16]

The military situation had changed since 1993, Janvier asserted. Bosnian government forces were now strong enough to defend the enclaves themselves. With the support of the Russian ambassador, he alleged that the Bosnian Army had repeatedly abused the safe area concept and used the enclaves to launch offensives. He also pointed out that it was the Bosnian government that had broken a four-month cease-fire negotiated by former U.S. President Jimmy Carter the previous December. The last three French soldiers killed by snipers in Sarajevo were shot by Bosnian Muslims, he asserted. In fact, only one of the shots was confirmed to have come from the Bosnian side.[17] The U.S.

ambassador to the UN, Madeleine Albright, chided Janvier for criticizing the Bosnian government for fighting back against the Bosnian Serbs; the Muslims had a right to defend themselves, she maintained. The United States would oppose any reduction in the commitment to the safe areas. But at the same time the Clinton administration refused to send any U.S. ground troops to bolster the flagging mission.

Janvier's proposal to effectively withdraw from the safe areas was flatly rejected. Unable to agree on how to change the mandate and unwilling to commit additional troops, the Security Council instructed UN officials and commanders to simply soldier on as they had for the last two years. As Janvier arrived in Zagreb, Srebrenica presented him with yet another watershed.

In Srebrenica, Ibran Malagić[18] and his nine men dug in at what they thought was the last point where they could stage Srebrenica's defense. They were all volunteers.

Malagić and the other men had grown impatient and left the town just after dawn. Ramiz Bećirović was convinced the Muslims should force the UN to defend Srebrenica. He didn't trust the Dutch and was worried that if the Muslims seized the weapons they had turned over to the UN in 1993 or showed that they had hidden weapons of their own, the enclave would lose its demilitarized safe area status and not be defended by NATO. Bećirović had issued strict orders concerning the artillery piece that Egbers had discovered: it was not to be fired.[19] No NATO air strikes would occur, he thought, if the Muslims fired the gun.

Malagić and his two younger brothers, Meho and Ferid, were convinced the opposite was true. The Muslims needed to do everything possible to stop the Serbs. They didn't trust the UN to defend the town and knew that if Srebrenica fell the Muslims had nowhere to retreat. In a practice common throughout the war, the three brothers split up, so that a single shell could not wipe out the entire family. Ibran headed down the road south of town with the nine other men; Meho went to man the M-48 artillery piece above Egbers; Ferid, the youngest brother, waited in Srebrenica.

At approximately 8 a.m., Ibran Malagić and the nine other

men had reached Bibići, a settlement of half a dozen houses a mile south of Srebrenica. They chose to make their stand there. A trench dug by Muslims defending the town in 1993 ran across a small hill overlooking the asphalt road. It was a strong position: a 150-yard-long stretch of pavement with no trees or houses the Serbs could use as cover lay in front of them. The Serbs would have to dislodge Malagić's men to take the town.

But Malagić, like many of the enclave's soldiers, was rusty. He fought fiercely in 1992 and 1993, but had barely fired a gun since. After Srebrenica became a safe area, he worked as a volunteer geography instructor in the local elementary school, and he looked the part. Tall with broad shoulders, he was half bald at twenty-six and looked like a teacher. He had married his girlfriend, Alma, the previous spring. With her, life in the enclave was almost bearable.

Before Srebrenica became a safe area, Malagić was a member of an elite maneuver unit made up of refugees from Bratunac commanded by Mido Salihović. Naser Orić's maneuver unit and Salihović's were the two best in the enclave. Salihović's unit had merged with what was left of Naser's. For the first time, the charismatic twenty-nine-year-old would not be leading Srebrenica's defense.

According to local stories, the brawny former bodyguard of Serbian President Milošević drank a mixture of honey and walnuts—an aphrodisiac—before battle. As Naser passed through villages on his way to the front line, farmers had jars of the potent concoction ready for him.

Naser was loved because he always led his men into battle. He was always first out of the trench. His soldiers told their wives they loved Naser more than them. Soldiers named their sons Naser.

Just after noon a Serb tank, a Serb APC with a 12.7 mm PAM antiaircraft machine gun and a half dozen Serb soldiers were moving slowly up the asphalt road. They were only 600 yards in front of them and Mido Salihović and reinforcements were nowhere to be seen. Malagić and his nine men faced a tank, an APC and an unknown number of Serb soldiers. Malagić motioned for the other men in the trench to hold their fire. They had one 64 mm RBR M-80 antitank grenade launcher, a 7.9 mm M-53 machine gun and a 7.62 mm M-80 machine gun. Each man was armed with a 7.62 mm Kalashnikov semiautomatic assault rifle. Malagić waited for the Serb infantry to get closer. They had to conserve their ammunition. One of the Serbs was wearing what looked like a stolen Dutch uniform. When they were 150 yards away, Malagić and the other men opened fire.

Three or four of the Serbs immediately fell to the asphalt. Others scrambled for cover in a nearby grove of pine trees. One dove behind a wood pile on the side of the road. When he tried to run back toward the tank, the Muslims killed him.

For the next fifteen minutes, both sides waited. The Serb tank and APC were still 750 yards away. Apparently unable to locate the Muslim position, neither fired. Malagić saw Serb soldiers pulling back and fired the M-80 machine gun at them. The road was strangely quiet for the next half hour. The Serbs were regrouping.

Unaware of the Serb push north toward the heart of the enclave, Colonel Thomas Karremans, the Dutch commander in Srebrenica, faxed a new assessment of the Serb attack to his superiors in Tuzla and Holland at 11:56 a.m. Karremans believed the Serbs would move west toward the strategic Mount Kak to secure their control of the southern half of the enclave. The conquest of the entire safe area was a possible consequence of the attack, Karremans said, but not in the short term.[20]

The Serbs would first overrun UN Observation Posts Delta and Kilo—the only two remaining Dutch OPs in the southern half of the enclave. He also believed the Dutch soldiers taken hostage by the Serbs would be "treated [with] courtesy." The Serbs, he maintained, were operating according to a "well-organized plan." They would achieve their goals "in due time."

Confident that the Serbs did not intend to take the entire safe area at this time, Karremans opposed calling in a NATO Close Air Support attack to defend UN positions. "Using Close Air Support in all possible ways is not feasible yet. It will provoke the Bosnian Serb Army in such a way that both Srebrenica itself and observation posts and compounds will be targeted by all means," he wrote. "Especially the multiple rocket launcher M-63 north of Observation Post Papa, the multiple rocket launcher M-77 within Bratunac and all their artillery and mortars with their missiles and rounds at fixed targets. Unless these weapons systems can be eliminated at one time, which is [possible]."

The six rockets fired over the main Dutch compound when the attack began at 3 a.m. Thursday appear to have made an impression on Karremans. The Soviet-made rockets make an ear-shattering noise before they pulverize whatever they hit. Between six and forty-two rockets can be fired in a volley, which means an acre of territory—the size of one of the Dutch compounds—can be incinerated in fifteen seconds. Since the attack began on July 6, whenever a Dutch vehicle left the UN compounds in Srebrenica and Potočari, shells would follow. Houses outside the main UN base in Potočari had also been pummeled by Serb gunners. The attempt to intimidate the Dutch was working.

Karremans had adopted the philosophy of the men in OP Foxtrot: a NATO Close Air Support to destroy a single tank firing on a UN position would be suicide—the equivalent of putting a red cloth in front of a bull. On the other hand, a massive NATO air strike could take out all fifteen Serb artillery positions and tanks the Dutch had identified. Karremans decided that unless you had the power to definitively stop the Serbs, it was better not to confront them.

In Sarajevo, a Dutch UN legal adviser was taking away what Karremans thought was the backbone of his defenses. Dutch general Cees Nicolai, the UN chief of staff, was trying to figure out what kind of NATO air attacks he could use to defend Srebrenica, large-scale NATO air strikes or only more limited NATO Close Air Support.

The difference was crucial. Air strikes allowed NATO planes to bomb Serb targets in a wide area around Srebrenica in retaliation for an attack. Close Air Support was more difficult to trigger and permitted NATO planes to bomb only individual tanks or artillery pieces if they fired on UN peacekeepers in Srebrenica.

The problem was with UN Security Council Resolution 836, which defined the UN's mandate in the safe areas. France demanded that air strikes be used to defend the safe area. The Clinton administration—heeding the advice of Chairman of the Joint Chiefs of Staff Colin Powell—insisted NATO airpower should only be used to defend UN peacekeepers.

As a result, exactly how UN commanders were supposed to "deter attacks on the safe areas" was unclear. In one line of the resolution the peacekeepers, "acting in self-defense, [were authorized] to take the necessary measures, including the use of force." Another section authorizes UN commanders to use "airpower" to carry out their mission in the safe areas.

Officials interpreted the mandate however they wanted to. Cautious UN legal advisers took the resolution to mean that only NATO Close Air Support could be called upon for the "defense" of UN peacekeepers in the safe areas. Much more effective large-scale NATO air strikes could not.

But other UN officials insisted that NATO air strikes *could* be used to defend the safe areas. In the end the decision was political.

With the disastrous results of the May air strikes and Janvier's new May 29 guidelines on using airpower in mind, General Nicolai in Sarajevo decided not to request air strikes.[21] UN Secretary General Boutros Boutros-Ghali still had to personally approve air strike requests. Getting air strike approval from New York could take days.

Nicolai decided that Close Air Support was the only type of air attack he had a chance of getting approved in the current political climate. It would take the direct targeting of a UN position to trigger NATO Close Air Support. What appeared to be a technicality would prove to be pivotal.

· · ·

Back in Srebrenica, Captain Groen anxiously waited. Without any satellite or aerial reconnaissance to aid him, he sent another of his APCs on a patrol to "find" the enclave's new front line.

Just after 1 p.m., Sergeant Johan Bos arrived at the Swedish Shelter Project. The vast complex of over 800 prefabricated houses that accommodated more than 3,000 refugees just half a mile from the southern border of the enclave was deserted. He could hear gun battles between Muslim and Serb soldiers around him, but he wasn't sure how far the Serbs had advanced.

That morning, Bos left Lieutenant Vincent Egbers' position and was instructed to take a long dirt road to get to the enclave's southeast corner, because Captain Groen feared Muslim soldiers would attack the APC if it went down the main asphalt road.

As he made his way south, Bos found hundreds of frightened refugees walking north. He and his men dreaded the assignment. Like Egbers' the day before, Bos's job was to do little more than drive south until he became a target.

Just before 1:30 p.m., fifteen to twenty Serb soldiers abruptly advanced from behind a cluster of Shelter Project houses and encircled the APC. The Dutch were disarmed and ordered to go to Bratunac. The Serbs said the Dutch would be allowed to leave for Holland the next morning. Bos was relieved in a way. He was convinced the Muslim soldiers would never have let the Dutch survive the trip back to Srebrenica. Bos radioed Captain Groen.

"Romeo, this is Bravo Two. Over," Bos said.

"Bravo Two, this is Romeo. Where are you?" Groen asked anxiously. Bos had been out of radio contact for ten minutes.

"We were surrounded by Serbs," Bos said. "We've been disarmed. They're ordering us to go to Bratunac."

Groen was furious. Why couldn't he get any aerial reconnaissance? Why did he have to keep sending his men on suicide missions? Planes could give him almost all the information he needed. Groen wished Bos good luck. The radio went dead. The Serbs now had twenty Dutch hostages.

...

In Bibići, at 2 p.m., the Serb antiaircraft gun started firing on the trench where Ibran Malagić and his men had taken cover. Bullets from the 12.7 mm antiaircraft gun burrowed into the ground in front of them. For the last hour, the outgunned Muslims had watched helplessly as the Serbs entered Pusmulići, a village to the west of their position, and pillaged and burned it.

One of Malagić's men started shouting for help. Blood poured from his hip. A bullet or fragment from the antiaircraft gun had somehow hit him. Malagić told two men to carry the wounded man back to Srebrenica and ask for help. He lifted the M-80 machine gun over his head and fired it over the edge of the trench without looking. The two Muslims carrying the wounded man slipped away without being hit, but Malagić's gun abruptly stopped firing. It was jammed. There were now only six men left in the trench. Afraid to lift their heads, they lay face down in the trench as the earth vibrated around them.

The tank opened up. Methodically shifting its fire, it tried to incinerate the trench. Each impact felt like an earthquake. Bits of dirt and rock showered onto the Muslims. Malagić thought they'd be buried alive. But the men who dug the fortification in 1993 had placed it well. A small rise in front of the trench absorbed most of the shells. The sound of the Serb tank's engine grew louder. The Muslims lay prone, afraid to look over the lip of the trench as the tank approached.

Malagić took out a knife and frantically tried to unjam the machine gun. He burned his fingers on the hot barrel, fighting off panic. He hadn't looked out from the trench in fifteen minutes. Serb soldiers could be crawling toward them. Malagić forced the jammed cartridge out of the gun, raised it over his head and fired it wildly without aiming. The gun jammed again after only a few rounds. Malagić threw it to the ground. He had fired between 500 and 600 bullets. The firing chamber was probably dirty.

A tank shell tore into the pine trees just behind the trench. Malagić grabbed a Kalashnikov assault rifle and fired it over his head without looking. A full cartridge—thirty bullets—was gone within seconds. He jammed a new cartridge into the gun, stood up and started firing again. A Serb tank was now a hundred yards away.

Malagić crouched. As one of his friends covered him, he crawled to an adjoining trench and grabbed the 64 mm RBR grenade launcher. Malagić then fired the Kalashnikov, as one of his men aimed the grenade launcher at the tank. The missile soared toward the Serb tank, but missed it by two yards. The vehicle quickly took cover behind nearby trees.

They heard a new rumble in the distance. A second Serb tank was approaching.

A half mile away, Ibran Malagić's brother Meho watched helplessly as the trench his brother was in was pounded by Serb tanks. He was manning the Muslim cannon thirty yards above Lieutenant Egbers. Meho begged the officer in charge to check with Ramiz Bećirović one more time. Using a walkie-talkie, the officer received the same order he had all day. The Muslims were not to fire the artillery piece. They were to leave it to the Dutch to defend the enclave.

Peacekeepers in Kilo and Delta, the only two Dutch observation posts remaining in the southern half of the enclave, reported that the sounds of battle were moving past them at 2 p.m. Captain Groen cursed again. The Serbs were advancing around the OPs.

An hour later, Serb artillery shells impacted within 100 yards of OP Kilo. Groen was furious. A single shell could kill all eight peacekeepers. At nearly the same time in the northern end of the enclave, several mortars impacted near OP Mike after the Dutch ignored shouts from Serbs in a nearby trench to leave. The UN observation posts were being directly targeted by the Serbs. The conditions for UN Close Air Support had been met. But Colonel Karremans and his deputy, Major Robert Franken, did not request it.

General Nicolai in Sarajevo had explained Janvier's new guidelines. Karremans and Franken followed them and gave the peacekeepers permission to abandon the OPs. But when Nicolai suggested NATO planes fly over the enclave to intimidate the

Serbs, Karremans and Franken said no, fearing it would antagonize the Serbs and "stir up the bees."[22]

The crew of OP Mike withdrew from the OP and parked
their APC 200 yards behind it, just to the north of the village
of Jaglići, at 4:30 p.m. The Serbs, apparently afraid of Muslim
soldiers in nearby trenches, made no attempt to occupy the strategic hilltop compound.

But once the Dutch halted their APC near Jaglići, a crowd of
furious Muslim soldiers and civilians quickly surrounded it. The
Dutch sealed the hatches and cowered inside. Muslim soldiers
shouted in a combination of English, German and Bosnian for
the Dutch to return to the OP, but the Dutch refused. The Muslims then demanded that the Dutch hand over their weapons.
The Dutch again refused. Finally, two Muslim soldiers with
rocket-propelled grenades took up positions behind the APC.
The Muslim who appeared to be the ranking officer made it
clear: if the Dutch withdrew, they would die.

At 4:30 p.m., Major Franken gave permission for OP Delta
and OP Kilo, in the south, to withdraw if it was safe. Obeying
Janvier's guidelines and Colonel Karremans' strategy, the outgunned Dutch were ceding the southern half of the safe area
without firing a shot.

At 4 p.m., with little ammunition left and no word of reinforcements, Malagić and his men decided to abandon the trench. But
they were trapped for the next thirty minutes as the second tank
blasted away. Malagić estimated that the two tanks had fired a
total of twenty shells from point-blank range that afternoon.
Dust and dirt from the impacts covered their faces and clothes.

By 4:30 p.m., there was a lull in the shelling and Malagić
gathered the ammunition they had left. He had partially repaired
one of the machine guns, so it could at least fire single shots.
They crept to the far end of the trench and saw that they were
no longer within sight of the Serb tanks. Malagić fired at the
Serbs, as the six men sprinted down the back of the hill. Then
he ran down himself. The area appeared deserted, but Malagić

thought there were Serbs still hiding in the grove of pine trees. He could still see Serbs looting and burning houses in Pusmulići on a hilltop 500 yards away. Malagić found Mido Salihović and twenty to thirty soldiers in an abandoned house.

"Why didn't anyone come help us?" Malagić asked. "Why?"

"We tried to get to you two or three times," replied Salihović, the soft-spoken commander of the group. "We couldn't because of the shelling."

Five or six men decided to try to secure the trench again. Tired and hungry, Malagić and his men spread out across the living room. Six men filled the two couches; he sat on the floor. One of Mido's men sniped at the Serbs from the kitchen window as Malagić devoured a meat pie he found in the kitchen. Mido stood in the doorway and, with his walkie-talkie, tried to listen in on Serb communications. "Give me an eighty-four to finish the job," he heard a Serb officer say.

A few seconds later, the wall behind them imploded. Men started screaming. (The Serb had been referring to an M-84 tank.) Two rounds had hit the side of the house. Because he was sitting on the floor, Malagić was the only man in the living room who wasn't wounded. He and Mido started dragging the six men into the backyard. Red dust from vaporized bricks covered their faces. Malagić couldn't recognize any of them.

Mido's other men quickly returned to the house. Hurriedly they carried the wounded down the steep hill leading to the town. No one was willing to stay in the trench or in the house to face the Serb tanks. The road leading into Srebrenica from the south was completely undefended.

From the dirt road to the west, Lieutenant Egbers watched with increasing alarm. The Serbs weren't stopping at Bibići. They were heading straight down the asphalt road toward Srebrenica town.

"Romeo, this is Bravo One. Over," Egbers said quickly. The response seemed to take forever.

"Bravo One, this is Romeo. Over," Captain Groen answered.

FURTHER BOSNIAN SERB ADVANCE, JULY 9, 1995

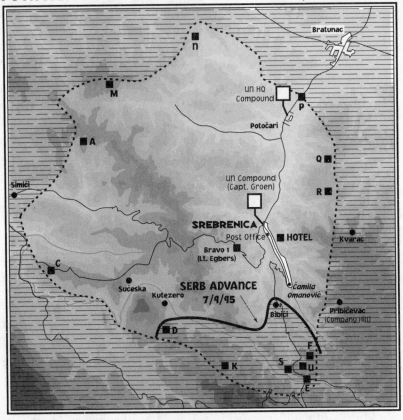

Serb-controlled ◼ UN observation posts ▪▪▪ Safe Area boundary
(Serb advance is approximate)

"One Serb tank backed by fifty Serb infantry are advancing north," Egbers said. "I repeat. One Serb tank is advancing north toward the town."

The Serbs were only a half mile away from Srebrenica.

The Serb push north set off alarms in Zagreb. By 6 p.m., the Serbs had penetrated three miles into the enclave and were only a half mile south of Srebrenica. Karremans reported that the

Bosnian soldiers in the town were putting up no resistance. He repeated that only massive NATO air strikes could halt the Serbs. For the first time, Karremans and Colonel Charles Brantz, the UN commander in Sector Northeast headquarters in Tuzla, thought the Serbs might want to take the safe area.

Colonel Harm De Jonge, the chief of operations in Zagreb, decided to propose what he hoped would maximize the meager military tools the UN had on hand. After talking it over with General Nicolai, De Jonge drew up a plan for the Dutch battalion to form a blocking position a half mile south of Srebrenica. Dutch soldiers and APCs would be deployed on the three main roads leading into town. The Serbs would be publicly warned that if they attacked the blocking position, the UN would call in NATO Close Air Support.

De Jonge's idea was for the blocking position to serve as a trip wire which would make Serb intentions unmistakable and force the UN to use Close Air Support to defend Srebrenica. The concept was simple and gave cautious UN commanders in Zagreb little room to hesitate.

De Jonge took the proposal to General Janvier, who was infamous for taking a long time to make a decision. Janvier quickly approved the request. The usually cautious Legionnaire even suggested that the warning to the Serbs include a demand that their forces withdraw to the former front lines of the enclave by 9 p.m. that evening. The proposal was discussed with Yasushi Akashi, the Japanese diplomat criticized for being too reluctant to use force. He quickly approved it too.

In Sarajevo, General Nicolai called the Bosnian Serbs at 5:50 p.m. and demanded that the Serbs immediately withdraw to the enclave's original borders. General Zdravko Tolimir, one of Ratko Mladić's top generals, denied that the Bosnian Serbs were attacking the enclave. He said he would check with his subordinate commanders and asked Nicolai to call him back in a half hour.

Nicolai called again at 7:30 p.m. Tolimir was evasive and

condescending. "I passed the message on to my subordinate commanders," he said. "The Bosnian Serb Army has no particular problem with UNPROFOR or the civilian population in Srebrenica. The UNPROFOR soldiers are being treated well."[23]

"They might not be having any particular difficulties now," Nicolai replied, "but if your troops do not withdraw from the demilitarized zone, they will undoubtedly have some."

Nicolai again insisted that the Serbs withdraw and added that both the UN Force Commander, General Janvier, and its civilian head, Yasushi Akashi, supported the warning.

"Only because of the good discipline of our soldiers have we not used our weapons yet," Nicolai bluffed. "I can't guarantee that we won't use our weapons if the present situation continues."

Tolimir countered that the Serbs' only problem was with the Bosnian Army soldiers in Srebrenica. "They have launched an offensive to link Srebrenica and Žepa," he said, lying, "but we have halted it."

"The attack was launched by the Bosnian Serb Army from the south," Nicolai responded. "Your troops are now approaching the town of Srebrenica." A direct attack on the safe area and the Serbs' failure to withdraw could cause a "very serious reaction," he warned. Anticipating Tolimir's response, Nicolai pointed out that the only party using heavy weapons was the Serbs; all of the Bosnian Muslim heavy weapons remained under UN control.

"The Muslims are using the heavy weapons that were never handed over to the UN," Tolimir rejoined. "They are also using six APCs they were either given by the UN or that they took away from them."

"That's absolutely untrue, especially the part about the six APCs," Nicolai responded. "I guarantee that is one hundred percent false. Your forces must withdraw within two hours. Otherwise, UNPROFOR will be forced to use all available means."

"The essence of the problem is that the Muslims are constantly attacking from the safe area," Tolimir continued. "It has never been demilitarized. They've burned Serb villages. We don't want an escalation of the situation either. I will contact my subordinates."

"You have been warned repeatedly not to attack the demilitarized zone," Nicolai said. "You are directly attacking the safe area. This is far beyond self-defense."

The conversation was at an end. Tolimir was obviously lying. Nicolai, who had been in Bosnia for four months, expected it from both sides. But on one crucial point, Nicolai wasn't sure if Tolimir was telling the truth.

Nicolai had asked repeatedly over the last few days to speak with General Ratko Mladić, the commander of the Bosnian Serb Army. Tolimir and other Serb officers had told him that Mladić wasn't available. If the charismatic Mladić was leading the attack on Srebrenica, the Serbs wanted the entire enclave. If local commanders were organizing it, the Serbs wanted only part of it.

Nicolai called Karremans later that night to relay and talk over the orders to create the blocking position at dawn the next day. The reaction was tepid. After waiting for two hours, the Dutch had withdrawn from OP Delta at 6:15 p.m. After a half mile, they were stopped by furious Muslim soldiers in the village of Kutezero. OP Kilo was surrounded by the Serbs at 6:30 p.m. The Dutch surrendered and were taken to a bauxite mine just south of the enclave. A busload of local Serb leaders "welcomed" them there and forced the Dutch to do interviews with Bosnian Serb TV.

The Dutch from OP Kilo were now on their way to Milići—a Serb-held town southwest of Srebrenica.

By sundown, the Serbs had thirty Dutch hostages, were a half mile south of Srebrenica and controlled the entire southern half of the enclave. Nicolai outlined the terms of the UN warning to the Serbs, and the conversation came to a close.

"Do what you can," Nicolai told Karremans. "Deploy some of your antitank weapons in the blocking position."

"But most of them are in the observation posts," Karremans responded.

"Try to use them," Nicolai said. "Just the sound of the weapons will frighten them."

Somehow, Nicolai misrepresented the warning or Karremans misinterpreted it. Each man would later blame the other for the confusion. After speaking to Nicolai, Karremans informed his officers in Srebrenica that massive air strikes would be launched against the Serbs the following day if they did not withdraw from the enclave.[24]

But the actual warning—which was also faxed to Karremans—stated only that the UN "demands" that the Bosnian Serbs withdraw from the enclave. There was no mention of massive air strikes if the Serbs failed to withdraw. The only reference to force was with respect to the Dutch blocking position. "If the blocking position is attacked by BSA forces," the carefully worded and very public warning stated, "NATO Close Air Support will be employed."

In Zagreb, UN commanders planned to approve NATO Close Air Support if the Dutch came under direct attack. In Srebrenica, Karremans expected any Serb forces still in the enclave to be incinerated in massive NATO air strikes.

Once again, the UN commanders themselves were confused by the UN's Byzantine system for approving NATO air attacks. The disarray in the nearly all-Dutch command chain was as tragic as it was inexcusable.

Meanwhile, in UN posts across Srebrenica, spirits soared when people were told an "air strike ultimatum" had been delivered to the Serbs. Captain Groen, the commander of the southern half of the enclave, heard yet another version of the warning at 8:30 p.m. If the Serbs didn't withdraw to a position a mile and a half south of the town, there would be massive air strikes at 9 p.m. For the first time in days, Groen thought Srebrenica might have a chance.

At 9 p.m., nothing happened.

...

That evening, Zoran Radić, the Bosnian Serb police officer, heard from a friend that the attack on Srebrenica had been launched. Sitting in a bar near Skelani, he had no idea what was happening in his former hometown, but he knew that defeating Srebrenica's men would be impossible.

He thought there were at least 5,000 well-armed Muslim soldiers in the enclave. Radić had heard rumors of secret helicopter flights and was sure the Muslims were well armed. But it wasn't the Bosnian soldiers that made Radić so confident his hometown would never be liberated; it was NATO. He was sure that no matter what the Serbs did, the Muslims would somehow trick NATO into bombing the Serbs.

The high school gymnasium was packed with soldiers. Ramiz Bećirović, Srebrenica's acting commander, Hakija Meholjić, the town's police chief, Fahrudin Salihović, Srebrenica's mayor, and Osman Suljić, Srebrenica's war president, stood before their people. Bećirović was having difficulty finding volunteers. Most of the soldiers in the room saw all three as little more than Naser Orić's puppets. Outside, a sense of panic began to envelop the town.

Naser had still not appeared; the politicians and military officers in the room knew he wasn't going to. Even if he tried to walk to the enclave, it would take him five days to reach the town. Srebrenica would have to make its stand without him.

Meholjić opened the meeting. The Serbs had halted their advance at dusk. They were now a half mile south of town. The UN was promising air strikes if they didn't withdraw, he said. He then made a desperate offer, which the town's leaders had agreed to before the meeting.

"Any man who destroys a tank will be paid five thousand marks [$3,000]," he said. "Anyone who goes to the line will get two hundred marks [$130] and their family will be given food."[25]

Thousands of deutsche marks had already been paid to men who had dared to get close enough to a tank with a *zolja*—a bazooka-like weapon—or a rocket-propelled grenade in the beginning of the war. A dozen Serb tanks had been destroyed and five captured in 1992 and 1993.

Bećirović spoke next. "We have to defend ourselves," he explained. "We have no choice." A counterattack would be mounted the next morning and every man in the enclave was needed to defend the town. Bećirović was literally a shadow of the man he was trying to replace. Arrogant and charming, Naser Orić was twenty-nine and built like a linebacker; he had been wounded three times but carried himself with a bravado and confidence that drew others to him. At forty-five, Bećirović was graying, thin and frail. The helicopter crash he survived had taken its toll on the deputy commander. He had fractured his pelvis, and been bedridden for a month. Bećirović could still barely walk.

The meeting concluded with grandiose statements by the mayor and the war president about how the Muslims would defeat the Serbs again. The mercenary offer seemed to work. Many of the men who had shown up vowed to defend the enclave.

Srebrenica's military and civilian leaders resumed the discussion at the post office, but they were divided over strategy.[26] Bećirović and others, like the UN, had thought the Serbs only wanted to take the southern half of the enclave until they advanced north from Bibići that afternoon. They believed the attack was in retaliation for the burning of Višnjica the month before.

Bećirović and the enclave's leaders were still unsure where the next Serb push would come from. The enclave's front line was thirty miles long and the Serbs were doing everything they could to stretch out its defenders. The main attack appeared to be coming from the south and consisted of four tanks and about 200 infantry. Several key hills on the eastern border of the enclave held by Ejup Golić's soldiers had already been heavily shelled by the Serbs that day. The Serbs were also pushing from the west. A PT-76 tank had been off-loaded from a truck in

Simići, on the enclave's western border, and attacked with a T-55 tank. Sućeska, a village to the southwest, was heavily shelled. Bosnian positions and UN Observation Post Mike in the north had also been shelled. Some officers feared an infantry attack from Bratunac.

They had received no clear orders from Tuzla or Sarajevo in conversations with Bosnian President Alija Izetbegović or Prime Minister Haris Silajdžić over the course of the day. Just don't harm the Dutch, the Srebrenica commanders were told, and hold on until NATO air strikes arrived.[27]

Karremans had told Bećirović on July 6, the day the attack began, that the Muslims could take back the weapons they had turned over to the UN when the safe area was demilitarized in 1993. Two tanks, two howitzer artillery pieces, an antiaircraft gun and 150 homemade rifles had been put in storage in the UN base in Srebrenica town when the safe area was created in 1993.

But the town's leaders still didn't trust the Dutch. If they took the weapons, the UN could just as easily take away the enclave's safe area status. Besides, they had almost no ammunition for the tanks, artillery and rifles. They'd be useless if the Muslims seized them.

Ejup Golić finally proposed a risky, but daring counterattack. While one column of men approached the Serbs from the northern side, a second would loop behind the Serb tanks in the southern half of the enclave before dawn. They would ambush the sleeping Serbs from behind and try to capture the tanks. In the end not enough volunteers could be found, and the proposal was dropped.[28] Bećirović thought it was too risky. He didn't want to lose his best men in one action. Bećirović decided instead on a frontal attack against the Serbs. The meeting broke up at midnight. The men would gather the following morning at 5:30.

Later that night, the town's war president spoke to Bosnian Prime Minister Haris Silajdžić by radio. But Silajdžić had no new instructions for the men in Srebrenica. In their talks with Sarajevo, Srebrenica's leaders—just like their Dutch counterparts— had the same unnerving realization. People outside Srebrenica didn't seem to grasp how close the town was to falling.

MONDAY, JULY 10, 1995

BOSNIAN MUSLIM COUNTERATTACK, JULY 10, 1995

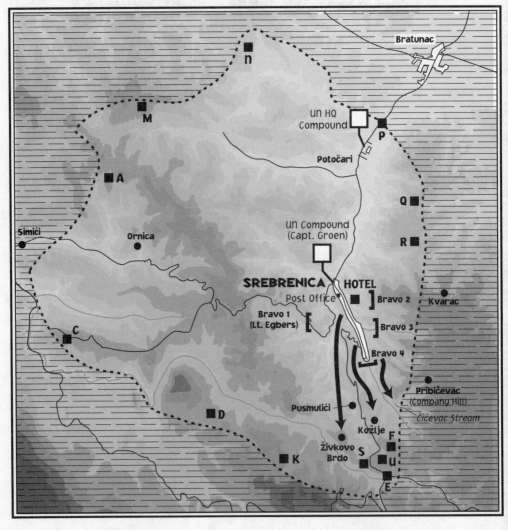

Serb-controlled ▪ UN observation posts - - - Safe Area boundary

◀— Bosnian Muslim counterattack ⊏ Bravo 1, 2, 3 – Dutch blocking positions

Captain Mido Salihović and his men had somehow reached the spot without being seen. A Serb T-54 tank sat in the center of the road 100 yards away. A car and some kind of truck were parked next to it. About thirty Serb soldiers slept peacefully in the open air. It was 6:50 a.m.

Salihović, twenty of his men and two unarmed volunteers had crept through the woods that morning from Srebrenica town to Kožlje, a hill half a mile north of OP Foxtrot. The Serb sentries were unaware of the Muslims lurking in the trees to the west. Salihović, a stocky twenty-six-year-old, moved quickly. Deputy commander of Naser Orić's elite maneuver unit, he had done this many times before.

Salihović was still angry that they had not been able to hold the Serbs at Bibići the day before. Using hand signals, he positioned his men. The soldier next to him aimed a rocket-propelled grenade at one of the tank's tracks. If they blew it off, the Muslims could capture a precious tank and use it to block the road and fire on the Serbs. Salihović nodded to the soldier.

As the grenade launched, the sentry spun his head toward the flash in the trees. Trailing smoke, the grenade plowed into the rear of the tank. Red sparks showered the ground. Salihović and his men opened fire with Kalashnikov assault rifles. Some Serbs went down immediately. Terrified and disoriented, the others sprinted for the woods in the opposite direction.

The tank's engine started abruptly. The driver slammed it
into reverse and began speeding down the road backward. The
Muslims fired, but the bullets pinged off the tank's armor. Salihović was surprised by how fast it was backing up. One of the
two unarmed volunteers reached for another RPG from his
knapsack. It was empty. The grenades had fallen out of the
knapsack somewhere in the woods.

The tank, whose track had been damaged, finally jerked to
a halt near a bend 300 yards away. Salihović and his men peppered the tank with bullets, hoping the Serbs would abandon it.
The tank's hatch stayed closed. Then they heard a second tank
engine. Another T-54 was approaching slowly from the south.
The undamaged tank moved up behind the damaged vehicle.
Figures were seen running between the tanks. Salihović and his
men fired but there was little they could do without another
RPG. The T-54 began backing up. The damaged tank moved
with it. The Serbs were towing it away. The roar of the tanks
slowly faded in the distance.

It was all over in fifteen minutes. The Serbs had retreated.
Salihović was astonished. While the Dutch did nothing, the Bosnians had pushed the Serbs back. To his right, a second group
of thirty Muslims commanded by Veiz Šabić was moving west-
erly through the woods to retake a hill known as Živkovo Brdo.
To his left, Ibro Dudić and another thirty men had moved into
position along a stream called Ćićevac. The Muslims' strategy
was simple. They too were ceding the southeast corner of the
enclave and control of the strategic road there to the Serbs.

The encampment they had attacked appeared to be the north-
ernmost position the Serbs had taken. Almost a mile and a half
of the territory the Serbs had gained the day before was left
unprotected. Either the Serbs had withdrawn because they feared
being surrounded in a Muslim counterattack or they decided to
comply with the UN ultimatum.

Salihović sent a messenger to town to ask for 200 reinforcements. He wanted to retake the high ground around OP Foxtrot.
As he and his men approached the Serb encampment, they noticed a car and some kind of truck that looked like a field
kitchen. Rifles, grenades and other equipment lay scattered

around the site. Four dead Serbs lay in contorted heaps. The Muslims searched them for valuables.[1]

Then they gathered the Serbs' weapons and ammunition. One volunteer beamed as he was given a Serb assault rifle. Salihović smiled. It had been a spectacular morning.

While Salihović collected his spoils, Lieutenant Egbers and his men were greeted by the roar of an armored personnel carrier. After a second night on the bluff, they were being reinforced. While the Muslims did nothing, Egbers thought, the Dutch were trying to stop the Serbs. Bravo One was now the western tip of the Dutch blocking position, which consisted of sixty Dutch peacekeepers and six APCs stationed on the three main roads leading into town. Captain Peter Hageman was commander of the entire blocking position.

Because of the steep hills and his lack of manpower and equipment, Captain Groen placed APCs and peacekeepers at the four possible entrances to Srebrenica. Egbers' position on a bluff to the west of town, known as Bravo One, and one group near OP Hotel, which sat on a hillside to the east, referred to as Bravo Two, also had a clear view of the southern approach. Two other APCs, known as Bravo Three, were to stake out the road that led to the Serb lines to the east, while the two APCs in Bravo Four were to take a position near the castle ruins on the hill to the southeast.

Four Forward Air Controllers were placed at Bravo One and Bravo Two. Equipped with secure satellite telephones to contact Sarajevo, radios to communicate with NATO attack jets and lasers to "illuminate" targets for laser-guided bombs, the FACs were the most important weapons in the blocking position. The success of any air attack would depend largely on them.

To support the blocking position, an 81 mm mortar was set up in the center of the Dutch compound in Srebrenica.[2] Weaponry continued to be a problem. Each APC had highly accurate Dragon antitank missiles, but they had a range of only 500 yards. By contrast, a Serb T-54 tank had a range of at least 1,500 yards.

In his briefing to peacekeepers the night before, Captain Groen had made one thing clear. Firing on the Serbs was to be used only as a last resort. He believed that the most valuable weapon the Dutch had—and their best tool for protecting the town's civilians—was their role as impartial observers. Fighting the Serbs was hopeless; it would only make the situation worse for the Dutch and the civilians. Protecting civilians and his own soldiers remained Groen's top priority.

By 7 a.m., three of the four blocking positions were in place. But Captain Hageman found the road leading to the hilltop castle where Bravo Four was to be established too narrow for his two APCs. After consulting with Groen, Hageman sent his APCs up the winding road leading to the ridge south of Srebrenica. At 7:15 a.m., an explosion rocked Hageman's APC. The driver swerved, went off the road and barely stopped in time. The APC dangled over the side of the hill. Hageman thought it was a hand grenade thrown by a Muslim soldier that caused the explosion. The Dutch squeezed into their one remaining APC and headed back to the UN base.

Ćamila Omanović watched the Dutch from her balcony. She knew where the shell had come from. It was fired by the Serb tank in Pribičevac that had been shelling the town for days. She couldn't understand why NATO planes had not destroyed the tank yet.

She and her husband had walked up the stream running through the center of town and sneaked into their house that morning. They hoped to gather diapers for their grandson and feed their precious cow and chickens. They had fled to her daughter's apartment in town the night before in a panic. A neighbor mistakenly told them that the Serbs were advancing toward the southern end of the town.

She peered anxiously at the forest and hillsides for signs of Serbs, and tried to figure out how to get her grandson's diapers off the clothesline without exposing herself to sniper fire. Her husband cut each end of the clothesline and the diapers fell into the garden below. Ćamila then ran downstairs and reeled the clothesline into the house. Still convinced the UN would stop the Serbs, Omanović expected to be back home in a day or two.

But all morning Serb artillery and mortars pounded the town in the most intense bombardment since the attack began. The roar of artillery fire and thunderous detonations echoed off the hills. Dozens of high explosives careened into houses, streets and apartment buildings. The town itself was deserted. Civilians huddled in basements and the stairwells of apartment buildings, desperate for cover.

At 8:30 a.m., a guard in the Dutch compound reported that a fire had broken out in one of Srebrenica's buildings. Captain Groen radioed the report to his commanders in Potočari. The Serbs were shelling the town. The Dutch weren't sure if the Serbs had withdrawn and abided by the ultimatum.

The night before, Sarajevo had requested a list of the exact positions of all known Bosnian Serb artillery and tanks around the enclave. The Dutch had faxed back fifteen locations. Colonel Brantz, the UN commander in Sector Northeast, had been told that forty planes would be in the air circling over the Adriatic. Brantz says he was also told by Sarajevo that all forty were fighter-bombers to be used in massive air strikes. General Nicolai and his military aide in Sarajevo, Colonel Andrew de Ruiter, deny ever saying such a thing.

At 8:55 a.m., Karremans filed his third request for Close Air Support. Sarajevo rejected the request, telling Major Franken that because the Dutch were not one hundred percent sure that the firing on the blocking position was coming from the Serbs, Close Air Support could not be approved.

By 10:30 a.m., forty planes began to circle over the Adriatic, but they were there only for Close Air Support if the Serbs attacked the blocking position. At most, six of them could actually carry out attacks around Srebrenica. The rest were electronic warfare escorts and support planes that were part of the strict new safety standards NATO commanders had put in place since U.S. pilot Scott O'Grady had been shot down on June 2.

What the Dutch didn't realize was that their blocking posi-

tion *had* been attacked by the Serbs. Still convinced that it was
a Muslim hand grenade that had blown the Dutch APC off the
road near Ćamila Omanović's house at 7:15 a.m., Karremans
had not included the incident in the 8:55 a.m. Close Air Support
request.

When Mido Salihović's messenger reached Srebrenica with news
of how far south the maneuver unit had pushed the Serbs, he
was nearly in tears. "The Serbs are running!" he shouted. "They
didn't even have time to take their cars!" Officers leapt to their
feet and shouted in glee. Even the cautious Bećirović smiled
broadly.

The group had listened to the gunfire from the south nervously. "They're fucking them," one officer had said, half praying. "I know they're fucking them." While they waited, Osman
Suljić, Srebrenica's war president, and Zulfo Tursunović, the brigade commander who had barred the Dutch from the Bandera
Triangle, had broken into the locker of the abandoned UN Military Observers' office in the building. For the first time in years,
they ate fruit salad and chocolates. The enclave's British, Dutch
and Kenyan UN Military Observers had retreated to the main
base in Potočari on Sunday. Their two Bosnian translators
stayed in the town and relayed reports on where and how often
shells were landing.

Near Kožlje, Salihović and his men still waited. Some of them
tried to move up to the trenches near OP Foxtrot, but shells fired
from behind abruptly careened into the hillside. Puzzled, Salihović and his men hid in the woods. A Serb tank in Pribičevac
had shot at them. A devastating volley of shells and mortars
rained down on the Bosnian soldiers who had occupied the hill
to Mido's right, Živkovo Brdo.

This dynamic occurred throughout the war in Bosnia. Once
Bosnian Muslim infantry gained new territory, long-range Serb
artillery would pulverize them. After several hours of shelling,
either there were no Bosnians left in the new positions or they
had fallen back, unable to fire back at the Serb artillery in the
distance. The one hundred soldiers who had volunteered for the

counteroffensive hid in houses or behind trees as Serb shells shook the ground beneath them or tore through the branches above them. The number of wounded slowly began to rise.[3]

The daily briefing convened in UN headquarters in Zagreb at 11 a.m. Force Commander Janvier opened the meeting. "A Kenyan soldier died in a car accident," he said through a translator. "In BH [Bosnia], the situation is quiet except in Srebrenica. The BSA [Bosnian Serb Army] attacked south to north—in retaliation perhaps for last week's attack by the BH [Bosnian Army] out of Srebrenica."[4]

"I spoke yesterday with General Tolimir," he continued. "He explained that the Dutch are free and have their weapons. They are in Bratunac and not POWs."

In truth, all of the Dutch hostages had been disarmed. Twenty were under armed guard in the Hotel Fontana in Bratunac and ten were under armed guard in a house in Milići. None were allowed to leave.

"The Dutch asked to be taken in by the BSA for their own safety," Janvier went on. "I demanded the BSA stop their action and hope to talk with the BSA this morning."

Colonel De Jonge, the chief of operations, then gave a more detailed report on the attack and the situation in Bosnia and Croatia.[5]

Janvier spoke up after he concluded. "The BH blocked Canadian resupplies to two observation posts, fired rounds against [UN] troops in Sarajevo and killed a [UN] soldier in a deliberate attack in Srebrenica. I will report this to New York," Janvier pledged. "In Sarajevo, [UN and UNHCR] convoys reached Sarajevo without firing by the BSA."

Since arriving as Force Commander in February, Janvier had repeatedly criticized the Bosnian Army for launching offensives and sniping at UN troops while blaming it on the Serbs. Janvier's suspicions about the Muslims were not unusual. Many Western military officers serving in the UN mission felt that the Bosnian Muslims were not the helpless, outgunned victims of Serb "genocide" that the media portrayed. The Muslims were better armed than the press realized and highly effective at getting fabricated or exaggerated accounts of Serb war crimes publicized.

Some officers went further and believed that the Muslims fired shells at their own people to demonize the Serbs and generate international sympathy, including the one that killed seventy-two people in the infamous February 1993 Sarajevo marketplace massacre which led to the creation of the heavy weapons exclusion zone around the besieged capital. No proof of the allegations was ever produced, but suspicion ran deep among some senior French officers and UN officials that the Bosnian Muslims were trying to draw the UN and NATO into waging war against the Serbs.

As the July 10 daily briefing drew to a close, Janvier accused the Bosnians of trying to draw the UN into fighting in Srebrenica.

"I remind everyone that the BH troops are strong enough to defend themselves. Also, access to Srebrenica is not being defended by the Bosnians. The situation is not the same as 1993," Janvier said. "I've just received information that [Bosnian soldiers] are shooting on Dutch troops blocking the route into Srebrenica and shooting at NATO planes over Srebrenica."

The claim that the Bosnians fired on a plane over Srebrenica was false.[6] Serbs may have been firing on the planes, but no Dutch reported seeing Bosnian soldiers shooting at them. The report of the Bosnians firing on the Dutch was apparently a reference to the "Muslim hand grenade" that the Dutch thought had knocked their APC off the road near Ćamila Omanović's house that morning.

"The Bosnian Army is trying to push us into a path that we don't want," Janvier warned.

Yasushi Akashi agreed. "The BH initiates actions," he said, "and then calls on the UN and international community to respond and take care of their faulty judgment."

In a village outside Srebrenica that morning, Hurem Suljić, a fifty-five-year-old Bosnian Muslim, hobbled around his house. The day before, he had watched groups of ten to fifteen women, children and old men walk through the field near his village, Ornica, with growing confidence. All of them said they were fleeing from the southern half of the enclave and were going to the Dutch headquarters in Potočari. Suljić was sure that once all the refugees got to the Dutch base and the UN commander saw them, he would call for help. The Serbs would be ordered to withdraw, and it would all be over in one or two days. Two days at the most.

Short and frail, with only wisps of thin brown hair, Suljić had large ears and a big nose. His face was deeply wrinkled and his eyes were brown, soft and round. His right leg was nearly useless.

Suljić's life had ended more or less twenty years before, on July 3, 1974, when he was working as a carpenter and slipped and fell. His right leg shattered when he hit the concrete three floors below. The doctors in Sarajevo considered amputating it, but instead saved the lifeless limb. He was hospitalized for four months. The neural damage was so severe that he could feel nothing in the leg. It was as if he had been paralyzed. To walk, he locked his knee in place and then slowly put weight on it. After the accident, Suljić was forced to become a night watchman at one of the factories in Potočari. He hated the hours, sitting in the dark, and he was never outside, as he had been as a carpenter.

He and his family were lucky; they lived in the countryside. A mile from the western edge of the enclave and three miles from Srebrenica town, Ornica was relatively safe. There were only eleven households in this tiny Muslim village. Suljić lived with his wife, two daughters, son, son-in-law and two grandchildren. They grew all the food they needed—peppers, onions, garlic, carrots, cabbage. Cornmeal and bread they bartered for salt and sugar with the traders who came once a week from Žepa.

Suljić and three neighbors had worked together to jury-rig a century-old water mill normally used to grind corn. Steel bars and a truck tire held the waterwheel to a cement mixer motor that generated electricity. They built a small dam in the river to make the water run faster, creating more revolutions, and therefore more electricity. Still, their generator produced only enough electricity to power one or two lights or a radio in each of their houses.

The trick was modulating the amount of electricity. Too much voltage could blow precious fuses and lightbulbs. To watch TV, lights and radios in all four houses were turned off. Suljić or a neighbor would then measure how much current the waterwheel was generating with a voltmeter. The men shouted to their wives to turn on lights in the four houses one by one. Once the meter gave an acceptable reading, it was possible to turn on a television set in a communal living room. There were only two options—state-controlled Bosnian Serb TV from Pale or state-controlled Bosnian government TV from Sarajevo. Suljić usually watched the evening news from Sarajevo, and then turned the TV and VCR over to the younger people.

If the outbreak of the war surprised Suljić, its viciousness astonished him. Like so many others, he had talked with Serb friends as tensions rose in Bosnia. A few days before Arkan's soldiers arrived in Srebrenica in April 1992, he was chatting with Rajko Pajić, a Serb friend from a neighboring village. "It's not going to be good," Pajić had told him. The next day, the Serb cattleman and his family gathered their belongings, abandoned their house and moved to Serbia. Suljić had always thought his friend had been trying to warn him.

As the crippled ex-carpenter hobbled around his house that morning, his idyll was barely disturbed by the distant thunder of artillery. Suljić knew Naser Orić was not in the enclave, but he had no doubts that the UN would defend Srebrenica. There was no one else to stop the Serbs. The town's soldiers had turned over all their weapons. The Dutch commander just needed to call UN headquarters and ask for help.

Lieutenant Vincent Egbers scanned the hills south of the enclave. He had heard the firefights erupt early that morning but was unable to determine exactly what was happening. The Muslims sitting on the hill a few feet above him had still not fired the enclave's lone artillery piece. Ramiz Bećirović's orders had not changed. The soldiers were to wait for the UN to defend them.

Just after 11 a.m., Meho Malagić, the brother of the man who had held off the Serb tanks in Bibići the previous day, watched the Serb tank in Pribičevac fire on the town. A puff of smoke left the barrel. Something—the sound of the shell or his instinct—told him it was coming. "Grenade!" he shouted in Bosnian. Egbers and his men never saw it coming.

A twenty-foot plume of smoke and dust rose from the ground in front of them. Bits of rock and shrapnel whizzed through the air. The Dutch dove to the ground. The shell had landed twenty yards away.

A second round landed just behind them. Rocks, dirt and shrapnel showered down. The Dutch leapt into the APCs and the jeep parked on the bluff. A third explosion followed. The earth shook. Bits of shrapnel could be heard pinging off the sides of the APCs. In the back of the jeep, blood poured from the British Forward Air Controller's elbow, neck and knee. In total disarray, the Dutch turned the vehicles around. A fourth shell impacted and the Dutch sped down the dirt road until they were hidden by trees, out of sight of the Serb gunners.

At almost the same time, a UN salvage APC arrived on the road overlooking the town to tow the APC driven off the road that morning. As it prepared to pull the vehicle up the embankment, a loud explosion ripped through the trees thirty yards away. The Dutch scrambled into the salvage APC and sped back to the UN base. The driver was so panicked that he drove the vehicle into a wood pile in Srebrenica town, injuring some of the Dutch soldiers inside. Several hours later, the Dutch realized that the tank in Pribičevac had been attacking them; it was not a Muslim with a hand grenade.

Up ahead, Lieutenant Egbers checked if everyone was in the APC. He radioed Captain Groen. Egbers' mind was following patterns that had been drilled into it in training. He felt as if he'd just been in a car accident. His body was trembling. His men were in shock. They couldn't hear each other because their ears were ringing so loudly. The medic started bandaging the wounded peacekeeper. He had been hit by shrapnel, but the wounds weren't serious. Shrapnel had torn through the spare tire on the back of the jeep. Egbers was astounded that no one had died.

His soldiers started cursing the UN. They were stationed in hell compared with the other peacekeepers. They had heard about how the peacekeepers in the UN headquarters in Zagreb lived. All the food and beer they wanted, tennis courts and swimming pools on the main base at Camp Pleso. The Dutch received no extra pay for risking their lives in Srebrenica. The UN didn't even supply them properly. Food, fuel and ammunition could all have been air-dropped into the enclave, but the Dutch had been left there to rot. None of them had come to Bosnia to die.

Egbers couldn't make radio contact with Groen, but he was able to radio the men in OP Charlie on the far western edge of the enclave, who relayed to Groen what had happened. When Groen asked Egbers if he was sure the Serb tank was targeting him, Egbers balked. The Serb tank could have been firing at the Muslim artillery piece thirty yards above them. The Muslims could have been firing the gun when the Serbs fired and masking the noise. Egbers wasn't sure.

When the Dutch deputy commander, Major Robert Franken, contacted his superiors in Tuzla about the shelling attack, he was told it did not qualify as an attack on the blocking position. Baffled, he assumed it was because of the nearby Muslim artillery piece. He still thought it was the Muslims who had fired on the two UN APCs on the road above Ćamila Omanović's house, not the Serbs.[7]

Another opportunity to pressure Janvier, Akashi and other reluctant UN commanders in Zagreb to launch Close Air Support had been missed.

In Srebrenica town, Ramiz Bećirović was having difficulty finding reinforcements to send south. As the shelling intensified, each brigade commander worried that his own line would collapse, exposing his own village, house and family to the Serbs.

Few men had shown up for the counteroffensive that morning. In an enclave which had 3,000 soldiers in 1993, there were only 100 volunteers. Many men were insulted by Bećirović's offer of 200 deutsche marks and food for their families. When they'd needed food a week ago, the town's corrupt leaders had hoarded it for profit, the men complained. Now that the town's leaders needed their help, they were doling out food and money. In the end, the men leading the counterattack with Mido Salihović, Veiz Šabić and Ibro Dudić went out of personal loyalty to their commanders. The enclave's long-running divisions were widening.

Approximately 70 percent of the population consisted of refugees from villages already held by the Serbs. Many of the refugees were not motivated to fight. No matter what the politicians in Sarajevo said, most men fought to defend their village, house and family, and *not* for the ideal of an independent Bosnia. With their houses already destroyed, many refugees felt they had nothing to fight for in Srebrenica; they were eager to go to Tuzla in Bosnian government-controlled central Bosnia.

Then there was an entirely separate class of people who dominated the local government, lived in larger homes and generally had more food than most. They controlled the few jobs in town. They were those with close ties to Naser Orić.

Not surprisingly, few people trusted the town's leaders. Stories of corruption were rife, and whether true or not, they were believed.

After being adored by nearly all of the town for his heroics in 1992 and 1993, Naser Orić was seen in a different light by some in the town in the following years. Many still believed that Naser was clean but those around him were corrupt. But others said he was the head of a vast, highly profitable black-marketeering enterprise.[8] Naser's soldiers now spent most of their time hauling goods and food back and forth from Žepa. It was a lucrative trade.

With Naser Orić and a few families dominating it, the enclave's political structure was basically feudal. Orić's associates were named the town's war president and mayor in 1992. The offices rotated among several men, but all of them were seen as loyal to, or controlled by, Orić.[9] It was rumored that the mayor, the war president and other officials in the municipal government had sold much of the UN humanitarian aid. The salt, sugar, coffee and gasoline sold at a tremendous profit on the black market. They hoarded rice and other foodstuffs, it was said, in municipal warehouses to drive up prices. Municipal officials of course denied the rumors; few believed them.

Since his helicopter had been shot down on May 7, Ramiz Bećirović had been at the center of a storm of rumors. Bećirović carried 150,000 deutsche marks ($100,000) in cash into the enclave from a charity in Sarajevo. The money was to be distributed to the orphans of the roughly 1,500 soldiers from Srebrenica killed during the war. Naser Orić was supposed to later carry in a large amount of deutsche marks that was back pay for soldiers.[10]

Bećirović said he distributed 100,000 deutsche marks ($70,000) of the charity money to four of the five unofficial "brigades" in the town. When the attack started in early July he said he had 50,000 deutsche marks ($35,000) left that he said he still intended to distribute.[11] The rumor was that Bećirović had distributed none of the money and that he and his wife had pocketed it all. Zulfo Tursunović, the brigade commander in the southwest, denied it, but he was rumored to run his own black-market operation, as were several of the enclave's other officers.

The news disseminated to the outside world was frequently false. In impassioned shortwave radio interviews, for example, Srebrenica's leaders reported that people were starving. Suljić, the war president, told Sarajevo radio on July 6 that thirteen people had died of starvation due to food shortages. But according to Médecins Sans Frontières officials within the enclave, food was in very short supply at the time, but the story was blatantly untrue.

Médecins Sans Frontières also feuded with Avdo Hasanović, the director of the local hospital. Dr. Hasanović wanted the aid group to allow him to distribute its free medicines. But Hasanović, a member of Orić's inner circle, allegedly sold the medicine on the town's black market. He was even reputed to have charged people for performing operations, such as abortions,[12] which was unheard of in siege conditions and against the Hippocratic oath. He denied all of the charges; few believed him.

The sale of UN aid and rampant black-market activities were

not unusual for Bosnia. The United Nations High Commissioner for Refugees (UNHCR) aid operation in the former Yugoslavia was the first ever to allow local authorities to distribute the aid they received. UNHCR predictions that Srebrenica, Sarajevo and other enclaves were on the verge of starving were always based on loose estimates. UNHCR officials were never sure exactly how much food government officials had actually distributed versus stockpiled, given to the army or sold on the black market.

In each of the five surrounded enclaves and along key supply routes in Bosnia, the war, for some, was enormously profitable. Hundreds of thousands of dollars were made by leaders, smugglers and racketeers.

Opposition was not tolerated in the enclave and few people dared to challenge Naser. He and his men were primarily from small villages around Srebrenica and were viewed as dangerous primitives by some of the original inhabitants of the town. When the Bosnian government replaced the entire senior command in the enclave of Goražde in the winter of 1994–95, hope had risen in some quarters that the same would soon happen in Srebrenica.

In June, three leading opponents of Orić were ambushed in Srebrenica. Ibran Mustafić, a member of the Muslim nationalist Party of Democratic Action and the town's representative to the national assembly, was wounded in the nighttime attack. Orić had accused him of being a coward and the leader of a pro-Serb "fifth column" trying to destabilize the enclave.[13]

A bullet grazed Mustafić's face, leaving a scar running from the corner of one of his eyes to his hairline. Hamed Salihović, Srebrenica's police chief before the war, wasn't so lucky. He died in the attack. A third person, Mohamed Efendić, survived unscathed.[14]

As the shelling intensified in the south, Bećirović was finally able to find some reinforcements. Accounts of how many men were sent and exactly what time they left vary widely,[15] but the effort was too little too late. Lacking the authority and charisma of Naser Orić, Bećirović was losing control of the enclave's soldiers.

...

By noon, Egbers had found a new position where the view to the south was nearly as good as it had been on the exposed curve. But he still did not have direct radio contact with Captain Groen in Srebrenica. The Serbs had probably targeted the bluff in case a Forward Air Controller was there.

Their strategy had worked in more ways than one. The wounded British Forward Air Controller had been evacuated, and the remaining Forward Air Controller—Sergeant Voskamp of the Dutch contingent—was on the verge of a nervous breakdown. He sat silently in the APC, not speaking to the soldiers who tried to get him to talk. He refused to eat or drink. When he finally spoke, he vowed not to go back to the exposed curve. "You guys are crazy," he said. "You guys are playing with your lives."

Egbers couldn't believe it. The other Dutch Forward Air Controller, Sergeant Roelof Groenendal, had fallen to the ground and started screaming, "I don't want to die, I don't want to die," on Saturday as he walked toward the APC that would carry him from Potočari to Srebrenica. Now Egbers and his men were risking their lives so this Forward Air Controller could be in position. They desperately tried to calm him. Without a Forward Air Controller, air strikes could not be carried out.

Egbers was frightened, but he was willing to go back up to his former position. After the shelling that morning, he had trembled for several minutes. He calculated in his head how he wanted his $60,000 life insurance policy divided if he died. He wrote down the names of his beneficiaries and the amounts and tucked the information into his uniform where it could be easily found.

Gun battles were erupting again along the road. The Serbs seemed to withdraw their forces from the enclave every night so their soldiers could go celebrate in Bratunac. This was nothing like World War II, Egbers thought; fighting was like a nine-to-five job for these people. Unaware of the Muslim counteroffensive, he remained unimpressed with the resistance the Muslims were putting up. The Serbs were attacking toward Srebrenica and shelling the enclave with everything they had, but there were still no NATO planes overhead. Sometimes fear gave way to simple exasperation.

Egbers and a few of his men walked back up the hill to the Muslim artillery position. He wanted to know if the gun had fired, and if that was why the Serbs targeted the position. The Muslim who had scribbled "30 equals 30,000" lay on the ground surrounded by his men. Blood poured from a shrapnel wound in his stomach. His soldiers carried him away on a make-shift stretcher.

The mood of the Bosnians had darkened. They pointed at Egbers' two APCs nestled in the trees below. Another conversation began in Serbo-Croatian, German and broken English.

"Why don't you shoot at the Serbs?" they asked Egbers.

"Why don't you shoot?" Egbers answered. He pointed at the gun and wrote on the paper that his antitank missile had a range of only 800 yards. He pointed at the Bosnians' artillery piece and wrote 3,000 yards.

The Muslims shook their heads. Their orders had still not changed. Their forty shells were unused. Srebrenica's only artillery piece had still not fired.[16]

In the enclave's northwest corner, Mevludin Orić was waiting eagerly in his home village of Lehovići for the NATO planes to go into action. Since the first day of the attack when he had watched the Serb shelling from Mount Zvijezda, he had been waiting for NATO's high-tech arsenal to be unleashed. Distant cousins who lived in the Swedish Shelter Project arrived that morning telling exaggerated stories of dozens of tanks and thousands of soldiers from neighboring Serbia swarming the southern edge of the enclave. Mevludin believed them, but he knew the Dutch and NATO had the firepower to crush the Serbs.

Mevludin himself had been caught by a Dutch patrol the previous summer. His unit regularly carried out secret patrols along the enclave's northwestern front line to check for Serb raiding parties entering the safe area. They patrolled with semiautomatic rifles—something Muslim soldiers were not allowed to have in the demilitarized enclave. The precious rifles were hidden at night and shared by the unit's soldiers. His thirty-man platoon had only ten rifles.

Just before the Dutch caught him, Mevludin was leaning against a tree and dozing in the hot afternoon sun. When one of his friends shouted, "Look out, it's UNPROFOR!" he thought it was a joke they often played on each other. But Dutch peace-keepers abruptly encircled Mevludin and pointed their rifles at him. In his hands was one of the most valuable items in the en-clave—a Kalashnikov assault rifle that had been captured from the Serbs during the attack on Kravica. Mevludin at first tried to play dumb, quickly smiling and trying to shake hands with the Dutch soldier. "Rifle!" the peacekeeper said in Bosnian. "Rifle!"

There were at least eight Dutch. Mevludin knew he wouldn't survive if he fought. Grudgingly, he handed the Kalashnikov over. Mevludin knew he would be ridiculed by his unit for losing it. He despised the greedy Dutch and had heard that they re-ceived ten days' vacation for every rifle they seized.[17] Mevludin couldn't believe they were taking away his right to defend him-self. One year after losing the rifle, he still loathed the Dutch. But he expected the UN to be as hard on the Serbs as they had been on him.

By the early afternoon, Captain Groen and another officer had counted thirty-two consecutive explosions. A multiple rocket launcher was clearly firing on the town. Groen wondered what had happened to the NATO air strikes.

The only good news had come at noon. The Dutch from OP Delta who were surrounded by the Muslims in Kutezero the day before finally arrived in Srebrenica. Groen had worried more about the fate of the ten Dutch held by the Muslims than about the thirty Dutch held by the Serbs. The shelling continued as the afternoon crawled by; no NATO planes appeared.

...

By 3 p.m., the new positions the Muslims had taken in the south of the enclave were nearly empty. In the dynamic of the war, the Bosnian Serb advantage in tanks and artillery was so overwhelming that the Muslims did not have enough time to dig adequate bunkers or simply failed to do so.

Ten of the approximately thirty Muslim soldiers on Živkovo Brdo had been wounded by shrapnel from distant Serb tanks and artillery. Demoralized by their inability to return fire and fearing more casualties, the group pulled back.[18] Mido Salihović and most of his men had left their position on Kožlje at some point that morning. Salihović, confident the Serbs would not counterattack, had waited for several hours for reinforcements to arrive. When none did, he left ten men to hold the position and returned to the town to rest and meet with Ramiz Bećirović.[19]

When a Serb tank backed by 100 infantry began to advance up the asphalt road, it met only token resistance.

Egbers watched the tank inch north. There was still no sign of NATO planes. At 4:30 p.m., he radioed that the Serbs had passed Bibići and were only a half mile south of the town center. Still afraid the Muslims would attack the Dutch, Groen had not sent APCs down the main asphalt road to block the Serb advance. Thirty minutes later, Groen ordered Egbers to return to base. He was worried that the Serbs would soon pass Bravo One and the Dutch would be captured.

As Egbers sped down the hill toward Srebrenica, he heard bullets ping off the armor of his APC. The gunner grabbed his arm and disappeared inside the vehicle. Convinced the Dutch were retreating yet again, the Muslim soldiers manning the artillery piece were firing at them.

Once they reached town, Egbers was shocked by the anarchy. Thousands of people packed the streets. Hundreds of panicked Muslims surrounded them, shouting "Fuck you!" in English. Heavily armed Muslim men pointed rocket-propelled grenades and shouted at Egbers to drive south toward the Serbs. Others tried to leap onto the vehicle and use its .50 caliber machine gun. He and his men fought them off.

Egbers slowly drove south. Muslim men armed with rocket-propelled grenades followed him. His orders were to reinforce the two other APCs in the market near the southern edge of the town. Nervously eyeing the Muslim soldiers, he readily complied.

Four thousand people from neighboring villages and the Swedish Shelter Project filled the town. In the market, Muslim women and children clustered around Dutch APCs, hoping the Serbs would be less likely to shell peacekeepers. They circled the UN compound and begged sentries to let them in. Thousands of others huddled in the stairwells of apartment buildings trying to avoid the random shells.

Chaos reigned. Men broke into stores and looted. Muslim soldiers sat with their families, taunted the Dutch or wandered aimlessly. Naser Orić's absence was glaring.

In the post office, the town's leaders were divided. Ramiz Bećirović, the acting commander, still believed NATO air strikes would come. Fahrudin Salihović, the mayor, thought the Muslims should invite the Dutch commander, Colonel Karremans, to a meeting, take him hostage and threaten to kill him if NATO didn't attack.

In the southern end of Srebrenica, Ćamila Omanović was trying to have dinner in her house with her husband and brother. After seeing the Dutch APCs shelled, there had been no other indications that Serb soldiers were so close. She had spent the day doing busywork in the house, desperate to keep her mind off the situation around her.

They ate in silence.

"They're behind you!" a man suddenly shouted from outside the house. "Get out of the house!"

Ćamila, her brother and her husband froze.

"They're close!" he cried. "Get away!"

Ćamila and Ahmet tore out of the room. Her brother, Ab-

BOSNIAN SERB ADVANCE, JULY 10, 1995

Serb-controlled ■ UN observation posts - - - - Safe Area boundary
(Bosnian Serb advance is approximate)

dulah, ran to the balcony and jumped to the yard ten feet below. She and her husband sprinted down the stairs and burst out the front door. As the three crossed the street and headed toward the tree-covered stream, bullets hit the side of their house. Only later did they realize what had happened. The Serbs were on the ridge overlooking the southern end of town. From the top of it they had a clear shot at Ćamila's house.

...

At 6 p.m., a panicked voice filled the Dutch operations room in Srebrenica.

"Romeo, this is Hotel!" Dutch peacekeeper Sergeant Frank Struik shouted over the radio. "A company of BSA infantry are on the hill overlooking Srebrenica! I repeat, eighty BSA infantry are on the hill overlooking Srebrenica town!"

It was happening, Groen thought. Srebrenica was falling.

"Hotel, this is Romeo," Groen shouted. "Are they advancing toward the town?"

"Negative," answered Sergeant Struik, who was on a hill just east of town. "They're lined up on the hill facing the town but not moving."

The Serbs were halfway down the hill overlooking the town center. They were 400 yards above his APCs in the market. How had they gotten so close? Groen wondered. Where were the Muslims?

Groen radioed the APCs in the market and ordered them to watch for any signs of a Serb advance. He ordered two other Dutch APCs to pull back from their positions south of the market and join the others already there. He checked to see if the mortar in the compound was ready, and then waited for the Serbs to make the next move.

Ibran Malagić stared at the Serbs through the scope of his sniper rifle. His fingers were burnt from trying to fixed the jammed machine gun on Saturday, but he could still shoot. Crouched behind the base of a power pole at the southern end of Srebrenica, he saw three Serbs moving in a clearing about 1,000 yards up the hill. Malagić fired three shots and ran across the road. His wife, along with eight soldiers, followed him. They reached a house they could hide in, and momentarily relaxed.

Mido Salihović had banged on Malagić's front door at 5 p.m. to tell him the Serbs were on the edge of town. A hodgepodge of two dozen men from Mido's and Ibro Dudić's units were taking up positions on the southern tip of the town. Malagić's twenty-one-year-old bride had insisted on coming with them.

Five hundred yards up the hill, a house was burning. Malagić hoped this was the Serbs' most advanced position. Mido was leading a second group of soldiers who were taking positions along the stream that flowed into town from the south. He peered through his sniper sight and saw a Serb standing in the clearing 1,000 yards away. Malagić traded his sniper rifle for a Kalashnikov assault rifle. He didn't know how many other Serbs were nearby.

His group decided to split up and try to move closer to the burning house, as Malagić, his wife and two soldiers walked down a small street hidden from the Serbs' view. Mido's group began shooting near the stream and ran out from behind the house. A Serb soldier scrambled for cover in the woods. Malagić fired all thirty of his bullets, knowing he wouldn't hit anything. His goal was to scare the Serbs into thinking that taking the town wouldn't be easy.

The firing died down. The Serbs had disappeared. Malagić and his wife silently smoked a cigarette. He trusted Mido completely, confident that the Serbs would never enter Srebrenica. But what he didn't know was that a second, larger group of Serb soldiers was advancing toward the town a half mile to the north. The only thing standing in their way was the Dutch.[20]

At 6:30 p.m., Sergeant Struik started shouting over the radio again.

"Romeo, this is Hotel!" Struik implored. "BSA is advancing! BSA is advancing!"

Groen had prepared for this moment dozens of times. He ordered his second-in-command in the market to fire over the heads of the Serbs with the APC's .50 caliber machine gun. He ordered the mortar in the compound to begin firing as well, but only to send up flares.

Bedlam erupted in the market. Instead of cheering, confused Muslim soldiers hurled themselves at the Dutch vehicles, screaming, "Stop! Stop! Those are our soldiers!" The Dutch kept firing.

OP Hotel instructed the mortar to adjust its fire. The flares were now falling directly over the heads of the advancing Serb infantry. Still, they came.

Groen wanted his men to shoot directly at the Serbs only as a last resort. He thought that if it came to a battle, the Dutch could not stop the Serbs. The best the Dutch could do was to try not to antagonize the Serbs or lose their status as neutral UN observers. As long as the Serbs still thought the Dutch were neutral, they could escort convoys of fleeing civilians and, he hoped, the Serbs would not fire on them.

The Dutch continued to fire, and the Serbs continued to march downhill. The frightened women and children gathered around Groen's compound finally broke through the fences. Hundreds of women and children swarmed in. Groen screamed for soldiers to clear them out.

The command center of the Dutch headquarters in Potočari came on the radio. "Be ready for an air strike." The blocking position was clearly being attacked. The trip wire created in Zagreb two days earlier had finally been triggered. Colonel Karremans was requesting Close Air Support.

The request for Close Air Support reached Sarajevo at 7:15 p.m. Knowing how hesitant Janvier was to use airpower, General Nicolai had denied any request he thought Janvier would not approve. He had waited for a clear-cut signal that Zagreb could not question. This was it. The Dutch general took the request to the acting UN commander in Bosnia, General Hervé Gobilliard, and recommended that it be approved. Gobilliard signed the form immediately.

In Zagreb, Colonel De Jonge received the request at 7:30 p.m. He had been waiting for this moment since he came up with the blocking position idea. De Jonge rushed into the office of Force Commander Janvier and announced that a company of Serb infantry was on a hill overlooking Srebrenica. The Serbs were advancing toward the town. The Dutch blocking position was firing over their heads.

Janvier, who was notoriously indecisive, hesitated. The French general called a meeting of his Crisis Action Team. The forms for the Close Air Support, code-named Blue Sword, were ready. They needed only Janvier's signature. Yasushi Akashi was in the Croatian city of Dubrovnik for the day and had delegated the authority to approve Close Air Support to Janvier.

By 7:50 p.m., Janvier's ornate, wood-paneled office, located on the third floor of Building A in the UN headquarters complex in tranquil Zagreb, was filled with the senior military and civilian leadership of the UN mission. Akashi was represented by his special assistant, John Almstrom.

General Ton Kolsteren, the chief of staff, opened the meeting. "Fifteen minutes ago, sixty to eighty BSA infantry attacked the southern end of Srebrenica town. Two tanks are one and a half kilometers behind them with three trucks and they are moving toward the confrontation line."[21]

"How soon can the planes be ready?" asked Janvier, speaking through his interpreter.

"In less than an hour," answered Colonel Cranny Butler, of the U.S. Air Force, the acting NATO liaison officer.

"We can ask them to change to cockpit standby," said Colonel Robert, the UN's chief of air operations.

"Have them stand next to the cockpits," Janvier said.

The NATO liaison officer left the room.

"Last night we issued an ultimatum," Janvier said. "They've fired on it, but the problem is we have no targets."

"We have two tanks, we don't need a smoking gun," De Jonge retorted. He was referring to a nuance in UN rules that allowed NATO Close Air Support to destroy a tank that was approaching a UN position in a hostile manner even if it had not fired yet.

"If the TACPs [Forward Air Controllers] can't see them we can change to an airborne Forward Air Controller," said air operations chief Robert.

"We have two TACPs in the area," De Jonge said.

"We can also spot artillery from the air," added Robert.

"Are we in a SAM ring?" Janvier asked, referring to surface-to-air missiles only a few miles away from Srebrenica in Serbia and in the Bosnian Serb Army headquarters in Han Pijesak.

"We're not sure, but we'd go in with a formation that included SEAD [Suppression of Enemy Air Defenses] planes," Robert replied.

"Would there be any preemptive strikes against SAMs?" inquired Colonel Thierry Moné, one of Janvier's military aides.

"Not unless they locked on to us," Robert answered.

"What is the Dutch government's position?" Janvier asked General Kolsteren. Many of them expected the Serbs to threaten to kill the thirty Dutch hostages if Close Air Support was carried out.

"It is focused on avoiding casualties among its own soldiers," Kolsteren responded. Janvier asked Kolsteren to telephone the Dutch government to confirm their position on the use of Close Air Support.

"What do you recommend?" Janvier asked De Jonge.

"Because you made a strong statement to Mladić yesterday and he is countering it, I believe you must launch CAS [Close Air Support]," De Jonge said.

"I agree that the troops are at risk," added Robert. "Although there is a risk to those detained, we must act."

"There's no choice if troops are under attack," said Almstrom, Akashi's deputy. "If they're not under attack, it's different. Then the question is how much shelling can civilians stand? There's also a problem being near FRY [Serbian] airspace. We don't need to wait for the SRSG [Akashi]. We only need him to authorize air strikes not CAS."

"It is absolutely necessary to speak with Mr. Akashi," Janvier said.

Colonel Butler, the NATO liaison officer, entered the room. Butler said he had spoken to the Coordinated Air Operations Center in Naples, Italy. After having planes circle over the Adriatic from 10:30 a.m. to 2 p.m. that day without being called on, the head of NATO's southern command, U.S. admiral Leighton Smith, said he needed a signed Close Air Support request before he would launch more planes.

"Are their planes on alert?" Janvier asked.

"If the Force Commander calls, the planes will be ready," responded Butler.

"Despite the risks, it's a situation where CAS is necessary," said Colonel François Dureau, Janvier's military assistant. "But the targets must be confirmed. The FAC [Forward Air Controller] has the last word on launching the attack."

Janvier asked to have a call placed to Sarajevo so he could speak with General Gobilliard, the acting UN commander in Bosnia, who had already approved the request. Gobilliard was not in and Janvier did not want to speak to General Nicolai, the Dutch chief of staff.

Janvier's assistant military assistant, Colonel Moné, was the first to oppose the request. "I'm in favor of CAS, but not tonight. Once the BSA infantry advances there will be confusion. There's also a problem with targets. It's better to do it tomorrow morning."

The meeting was interrupted. Janvier had a phone call. He went into an adjacent room with Moné.[22]

Colonel De Jonge began to fidget. The light outside was fading. The debate continued without Janvier.

"We can also attack infantry with aircraft," said air operations chief Robert. "We need F-18s swooping down right now!"

"I agree. We need action," said General Kolsteren. "I don't agree with Moné."

"The aircraft will choose their targets based on attackability and economy of effort," said Robert. "It's always better to choose a single target like a tank; infantry requires several passes. It's about a twenty-minute flight. NATO would love the ability to do its job."

As Colonel Moné came out of the adjacent room, Janvier was heard raising his voice to whomever he was speaking to. It was a heated discussion. At 8:30 p.m., General Gobilliard returned Janvier's call from Sarajevo. Janvier ended his conversation and began speaking with Gobilliard.

The 7 p.m. request for Close Air Support was now an hour and a half old. Colonel Karremans in Srebrenica was calling General Nicolai in Sarajevo every fifteen minutes to see if it had finally been approved. Nicolai had no answer for him. De Jonge, whose idea it was to create the blocking position, could not believe how long it was taking.

At 8:45 p.m., Janvier was still on the phone. One of De Jonge's aides announced that the Dutch were now firing directly at the Serbs. A few minutes later, a report arrived that the Dutch and the Muslims, fighting side by side, were engaged in a heavy firefight with the Serbs.

Kolsteren went to his office. Like his British, French and American counterparts, Kolsteren had a secure telephone line to the Ministry of Defense in his home country. In previous UN missions it had been clear that a military officer's primary loyalty lay with his home country. But the mission in the former Yugoslavia had set new standards for intervention by individual countries in UN decision making.

Janvier's request that Kolsteren call his government was an overt admission of what was well known in UN headquarters—the country with the most at stake on the ground in Bosnia had tacit control over UN decision making. During the May hostage crisis—when most of the hostages were French—it had been clear that the French government determined how the crisis would be handled.

Srebrenica was a Dutch dilemma. Carrying out Close Air Support might result in the Serbs killing thirty Dutch hostages. The flag-draped coffins would be returning to Holland, not UN headquarters in New York. In the end, Dutch politicians would suffer the consequences of the decision.

Kolsteren found Defense Minister Joris Voorhoeve in the basement bunker of the Dutch Defense Ministry at approximately 8:50 p.m. During every stage of the crisis all of the Dutch commanders—Karremans in Srebrenica, Brantz in Tuzla, Nicolai in Sarajevo and Kolsteren and De Jonge in Zagreb—had been conferring with their superiors in Holland on all major decisions.

The conversation was brief. Voorhoeve had known for days he might have to face this decision. After consulting with Dutch Prime Minister Wim Kok and Dutch Foreign Minister Hans Van Mierlo, Voorhoeve made one of the few courageous decisions surrounding the attack on Srebrenica. He decided that the lives of thirty Dutch peacekeepers were not worth more than the lives of 30,000 Muslims. The UN safe area and its people should be defended, Voorhoeve had concluded, no matter what the consequences were for the Dutch hostages. He told Kolsteren that the Dutch government had no objections to Close Air Support.

After the phone call ended, the mood in the Defense Ministry bunker was bleak. Dutch military officials expected the worst from the Serbs. Voorhoeve's press aides sketched out the rough draft of a press release announcing the deaths of Dutch peacekeepers.

Over 450 Dutch lives hung in the balance. The Defense Minister appeared on the national news at 10 p.m. Over the last three days the Netherlands had become increasingly focused on Srebrenica.

Air strikes appear to be "inevitable," a somber Voorhoeve warned. There is a "strong possibility" of Dutch casualties.

But in Zagreb, Janvier had not yet made up his mind. After speaking to Gobilliard in Sarajevo, the Force Commander continued to be on the phone. The unsigned forms waited on his desk.

At 9:05 p.m., Janvier spoke with Yasushi Akashi. He then spoke with Bosnian Serb general Zdravko Tolimir, the man who the day before denied to Nicolai that the Serbs were even attacking Srebrenica.

At 9:40 p.m., Janvier finally came back to the meeting. "We will be able to attack in half an hour," he said. "The night option is OK if we have tanks or artillery attacking."

Then one of Janvier's aides entered the room and announced that fighting had stopped in Srebrenica. The Serbs had withdrawn from the hill overlooking the town. But the Serbs had issued an ultimatum of their own at 9 p.m. If the UN and all aid organizations surrendered all their weapons and equipment, they would be free to leave the enclave the next morning. All Muslims would be free to leave within forty-eight hours. But if the enclave did not surrender, the Serbs would resume their attack. Karremans himself, the aide said, had held a meeting with the Serb officer in command in the southern part of the enclave.

"If there is no move by the NGOs [aid groups] in the morning, the commanding officer said the Serbs will attack," the aide warned. "The Dutch commanding officer does not consider it useful to have Close Air Support tonight. He wants it tomorrow morning."

Karremans also wanted to know if he should abandon his remaining observation posts, which he felt should be "a command decision," Janvier's aide said, "not a tactical decision, because of the military and political impact."

"No, I refuse to accept that," Janvier said. "It's a decision to be made on the ground."

"It's out of the question to leave the OPs at night anyway," Janvier's aide said.

As the discussion dragged on, a waiter in a red blazer began serving canapés and pouring red wine for each participant. The UN officers and officials had missed dinner and Janvier or one of his staff had ordered refreshments. As Srebrenica's fate hung in the balance, Janvier's Crisis Action Team sipped wine and nibbled on gourmet sandwiches.

Air operations chief Robert continued to lobby Janvier to approve Close Air Support. "The aircraft are already airborne over the Adriatic," he said.

The planes were from the USS *Theodore Roosevelt* and were circling over the sea, awaiting orders. U.S. F-15s and other aircraft were equipped to carry out attacks at night. The flight to Srebrenica would take only twenty minutes.

"Can they keep them up all night?" Janvier asked.

"No. They wouldn't have anything left for tomorrow," he replied.

"If firing has stopped, it's an indication that maybe the attack has stopped," Janvier said. "Maybe Mladić has given an order."

"If the fighting has stopped it is not due to Mladić's order," a frustrated De Jonge retorted. "It's due to the fact that they can't advance because of the Dutch blocking position."

Janvier had finally made his decision. "If someone asks why there was no CAS," he said, "we say it was an infantry attack and CAS was too dangerous." Janvier ignored the UN air operations chief's and NATO liaison's opinions that it was not dangerous.

De Jonge refused to give up. "The question is why is the BSA acting this way," he said. "Is it to conquer Srebrenica? If so, the attack will continue."

Robert warned that an air attack in the morning wouldn't work. "There will be fog in Srebrenica tomorrow morning."

Janvier ignored him. "I do not think Mladić wants to punish the enclave. He wants to punish Bosnia," Janvier said, referring to the offensive to break the siege of Sarajevo and two others launched by the Muslim-led Bosnian Army that spring. "The Serbs are now involved in a process of negotiation, so it's very strange they act this way."

"The attack started on Thursday," said one of De Jonge's aides. "Maybe it was because of Lanxade's comments on the RRF." He was referring to French Army chief of staff Admiral Jacques Lanxade's statement that the Rapid Reaction Force would be used to open up corridors to Sarajevo and then the other surrounded safe areas.

Janvier disagreed. "It's very, very clear that the BSA and Mladić have no fear of the RRF," he said. "I've spoken to Mladić at length on this."

John Almstrom, Akashi's special assistant, indicated that he too was opposed to Close Air Support. "I think we're in a good pause now," he said, referring to the halt in the fighting in Srebrenica.

Janvier agreed and later disclosed what General Tolimir had told him.

"I spoke to Tolimir and he says they do not intend to take the enclave," Janvier said. "I believe him. If they do take the enclave, I'll draw my conclusions."[23]

In Srebrenica, events had progressed far faster than Janvier and his Crisis Action Team. For the last three and a half hours, in fact, the situation had been calm. After the Dutch fired over the soldiers on the hill at 6:30 p.m., the group had stopped walking toward the town. A few minutes later, they slowly retreated up over the crest of the hill. By 7 p.m. they had disappeared.

The report that the Dutch were firing directly at the Serbs

and fighting alongside the Muslims was false. The report that Colonel Karremans had met with the Serbs also was false. It was one of the Dutch hostages in Bratunac who was forced to read the Serb ultimatum over his APC's radio. Where the false information came from in the labyrinthine UN command chain was unknown, but such mistakes were not unusual.

As the debate raged in Zagreb, Srebrenica was still jittery, but comparatively tranquil. Bosnian soldiers even helped the Dutch clear Muslim civilians from the UN compound. But Muslim soldiers in the market insisted that the Dutch were firing at a group of Bosnian soldiers on the hill. Egbers and the crew of his APC weren't sure what to believe. Sergeant Struik, the peacekeeper in OP Hotel who saw the Serbs advancing down the hill, made a tape recording for his girlfriend. He hoped it would get to her if he didn't.

"It's the tenth of July. It's ten past nine in the evening. The situation is as follows. The Serbs have taken by surprise and overrun almost every observation post. All are overrun. I'm at OP Hotel, the last OP, and we are completely surrounded."

Bosnians who worked for the UN were convinced the town would fall and began shuttling their relatives to the relative safety of the Dutch base in Potočari. At 5:05 p.m., the Bosnian who worked for the UN High Commissioner for refugees sent a frantic cable to his superiors.

"Urgent, urgent, urgent," the cable read. "BSA is entering town of Srebrenica. Will someone sto[p] this immediately and save these people, thousands are gathering around the hospital. There is nothing to be confirmed anymore. Please help. At least half of the enclave has been taken. Please help withany [sic] means."

A half mile away from the Dutch base a cluster of several hundred Bosnian soldiers were meeting on a dirt road behind the post office. They were demanding to speak with Ramiz Bećirović, but the town's acting commander had sent only a representative. The soldiers deemed the situation hopeless, and were debating whether to abandon the enclave that night.

After three years of siege many men despised life in the rancid, claustrophobic enclave. The chief topic of conversation in town that spring was what route men would take through the woods to Tuzla. It happened every spring. Over 400 men had walked from Srebrenica to Tuzla in the summer of 1994, prompting the Bosnian government to order a crackdown by Naser Orić and his men. The exodus was especially large in 1995 after flash floods in May destroyed many of the town's waterwheels.

The lack of NATO air strikes, the departure of Naser Orić and fifteen officers and the paltry Dutch resistance were confirming long-running suspicions in the isolated enclave that Srebrenica was being sacrificed. From the first days of the war, Srebrenicans had been suspicious of Sarajevo. The enclave had always felt expendable. In three years, no senior Bosnian government officials had visited it. They had gone to Goražde and Bihać, two strategically more important enclaves, but not to Srebrenica. Rumors that the enclave was going to be traded to the Serbs, or abandoned, circulated constantly.

The split with Sarajevo first emerged in 1993 after the Srebrenicans took Kravica and were only five miles from Muslim-held central Bosnia and the Bosnian Army made no attempt to liberate Srebrenica. Sarajevo had instead ordered the Tuzla-based 2nd Corps to try to break the strategic Posavina corridor—a two-mile-wide strip in northern Bosnia that connected Serb holdings in western and eastern Bosnia. The Serbs held in Posavina and the men from Srebrenica never forgave their leaders in Sarajevo for failing to liberate them.

Tensions had also risen when the town was declared a safe area in April 1993. Sarajevo insisted that few people be evacuated to central Bosnia. Critics accused the Bosnian government, which also blocked civilians from leaving Sarajevo, of using its people as cattle. Naser Orić moved aggressively to halt the evacuations. Any men caught trying to leave the enclave for Tuzla were jailed.

The final straw came in June. The Dutch and UN officials—including Janvier—didn't know it, but Sarajevo had secretly ordered Srebrenica's men to carry out the largest raid since the creation of the safe area. Two hundred men had linked with soldiers from Žepa and carried out the raid as a way to aid the ongoing offensive to liberate Sarajevo. The Serb village of Viš-njica had been burned on June 26 and one Serb soldier killed and three civilians wounded. Many men were convinced Sara-jevo had set up Srebrenica by ordering a raid that would obvi-ously provoke the Serbs.

Faced with the choice of using up their meager ammunition to defend Srebrenica or saving it for the dangerous walk to Tuzla, many men opted for the latter. A dangerous delusion was also spreading. The men were convinced that the Serbs would open up a corridor for them to retreat to Tuzla. The trip through forty miles of Serb territory would be difficult, but not impos-sible.

Like the Dutch, few Muslim soldiers were willing to die in what they viewed as a futile battle. Small groups of men had already left the front line and headed for Tuzla on Sunday. By Monday evening, entire units were departing.

On the Serb side of the front line, Sergeant Dražen Erdemović settled in for the night with his unit. He and eight other soldiers had occupied a hill that afternoon and encountered no resis-tance.

Erdemović was worried about what the next day might bring. They were to move into the town. Erdemović was an anomaly in the Bosnian Serb Army, one of a handful of Croats on the wrong side of the front line. Most Croats were technically allied with Bosnia's Muslims against the Serbs. Erdemović was one of the hundreds of hustlers trying to profit from the war as much as possible. He had fought in all three of Bosnia's armies—Mus-lim, Croat and Serb.

He had grown up in a small village outside Tuzla, making money through one scheme or another as a teenager. When the war began, he joined the Muslim-led Bosnian government army and quit because he didn't like the food. He then joined the Croat Defense Forces unit, but was caught smuggling people across the front line.[24]

"Human trafficking" was a common practice in multiethnic

Bosnia. When war erupted, tens of thousands of Serbs, Croats and Muslims found themselves on the wrong side of the front line or separated from their families. It was a lucrative business. Erdemović and his friends got $500 to $1,000 for each person smuggled.

In 1993, he was caught smuggling Serbs out of Muslim-held Tuzla to Serb-occupied territory. He faced a two-year jail sentence, but jumped bail before trial and quickly crossed the front line with his pregnant wife.[25] She was half Serb and was theoretically safer on the Serb side. Before the war their mixed marriage had been nothing unusual. Now they didn't know where they belonged.

Life in Serb territory quickly became a never-ending series of loyalty tests. To receive housing, he was told, he'd have to join the Bosnian Serb Army. To be promoted, he had to kill Muslims. To be trusted, he had to kill fellow Croats. Always hunting for more money, he joined a special Bosnian Serb Army "maneuver unit" made up of Muslims and Croats to earn extra money. He quickly realized that the dirtiest jobs were left for them. He was demoted the previous year for disagreeing with his commanders. His commanding officer now constantly harassed Erdemović and questioned his loyalty.

The twenty-three-year-old didn't realize it yet, but Erdemović had outhustled himself.

Since the offensive had begun, UN military spokesman British colonel Gary Coward had told journalists that it was possible that the Serbs wanted the entire enclave, but the UN's position was that their goal was to take only the southern half of it. Journalists were skeptical of the assessment, but Bihać and Goražde had withstood Serb offensives and no town in Bosnia had changed hands in the war in Bosnia in two years. Many believed Srebrenica would fall if there were no NATO air attacks, but it might take several days for the Serbs—who had shown no affinity for house-to-house fighting—to see to it.

Reports from Bosnian government-controlled and Bosnian Serb-controlled media that night were little more than propa-

ganda. The Bosnian government's 6:30 p.m. news claimed that
hand-to-hand combat had broken out on the outskirts of Srebrenica and the Bosnian Serbs were firing shells with poison gas
at the town. Osman Suljić, Srebrenica's war president, made an
appeal for help in an interview by shortwave radio.

Suljić requested "the intervention of NATO or of the RRF
[Rapid Reaction Force]. If they don't prevent the massacre, I will
not guarantee the safety of the UN soldiers in the pocket. If
anything happens to us, they will suffer," Suljić warned. "We
have delivered our weapons to the UN, and UNPROFOR is responsible for our lives. In spite of that, there has been no water,
food, clothes and electricity since, and the UN has not done
anything to improve the situation. Now we are left alone to be
slaughtered." He ended the interview by stating that it was impossible to assess the number of casualties because they were
increasing by the minute.[26]

The 7 p.m. Bosnian Serb radio news was Orwellian. The Bosnian Serbs were not attacking Srebrenica, the Muslims were attacking the Serbs. General Milan Gvero, a member of the
Bosnian Serb Army general staff, was quoted as saying: "The
problem of Srebrenica is mainly the result of media manipulation. Muslims are trying to bring the attention of the media to
that little town they have already used as a joker in the war
game. Srebrenica is a perfect example of the flagrant breaking
of international regulations. In that so-called demilitarized zone
weapons were in fact never collected; otherwise there wouldn't
be any problems now. UNPROFOR has never implemented the
resolutions and agreements, and the Muslims considered the
presence of the UN a cover for their terroristic actions."[27]

The general went on: "Since the proclamation of the demilitarized zone they have killed more than 100 and wounded more
than 200 Serbs. They have recently burned down the village of
Višnjica and massacred its inhabitants. They had tried, engaging
all their units in Srebrenica, to make the connection to Žepa. So,
the current activities of our army are merely a response, an effort
to neutralize Muslim attacks and not in any case an attack on
UNPROFOR. There is no reason the UN and foreign media
should be involved in the problem, since it would only serve the

Muslim cause. Some UN members in the Srebrenica area felt they would be safer with us and they crossed to our territory. They are our guests now."[28]

After reporting again the failure of the Muslim offensive to lift the siege of Sarajevo, and that self-inflicted wounds and desertions among demoralized Muslim soldiers were increasingly frequent, Bosnian Serb radio quoted an interview with Bosnian Serb Army commander Mladić that had run in the British newspaper *The Independent*.

"War and weapons are too dangerous to play games with, as it is now in the Balkans," Mladić reportedly said. "The word 'war' would not even be in the vocabulary and only toy weapons would exist, if the world listened to me."[29]

On that crucial night, no Tony Birtley was poised to save Srebrenica. Birtley—the freelance British reporter and cameraman whose reports and videotapes for ABC News had played such a crucial role in saving Srebrenica in 1993—had been banned from Serb territory. After allowing a handful of foreign journalists into the enclave in 1994, the Bosnian Serbs had barred visits that spring. Most journalists, including the author, made no efforts to get into the enclave via a Bosnian Army helicopter flight as Birtley had.[30] In early July 1995, coverage of the war was almost completely focused on Sarajevo.

Colonel Karremans arrived late. Ramiz Bećirović shook his hand curtly. Mayor Fahrudin Salihović glared at the tall, skinny Dutchman. He still wanted to take Karremans hostage, but none of Srebrenica's other leaders would back him. It was 12:05 a.m.

Karremans walked up to the second floor of the post office. The Bosnians had turned the former UN Military Observers' office into their war room. Colorful posters declaring "UNPRO-FOR—Working for Peace" filled the walls. They were forty feet from the window where Philippe Morillon made his famous declaration in 1993.

Karremans sat down. The eyes staring at him were bloodshot, worn and hostile. Along with the mayor, the town's war president and several of its brigade commanders sat around the

table. There were about fifteen of them in all. A sense of exhaustion and desperation hung in the room. Karremans started
to speak.[31]

"I have heard from my superiors that between forty and sixty
planes will be arriving over Srebrenica by 6 a.m. tomorrow," he
said slowly. "There will be a massive air strike."

There was barely any reaction from the Muslims. The Dutch
colonel stood and pointed at locations on the map. Karremans
explained how forty different Serb tanks, artillery pieces and
multiple rocket launchers identified by the Dutch were going to
be destroyed. He was referring to the latest target list the Dutch
had faxed to Sarajevo, which now contained thirty-eight potential targets.

"An ultimatum was sent to the Serbs," Karremans said.
"Withdraw to their old positions of 1993 or be bombed." He
recommended that the Muslims pull all of their troops to within
a half mile of the town.

"This area," Karremans said, pointing at the wide swath of
territory now held by the Serbs south of Srebrenica, "will be a
zone of death in the morning. NATO planes will destroy everything that moves."

He explained that General Smith or someone on his staff
would come to verify whether the Serbs had actually withdrawn.
Karremans sat down.

"What will happen if the Chetniks withdraw and do what
they're told?" Bećirović asked.

"We will retake our old positions," Karremans said.

Mayor Salihović tore into the Dutch commander. "I don't
have much confidence there will be an air strike," he growled.
"I don't believe the air strike will happen. We've learned from
experience we can't believe anything you say."

Karremans assured him he was telling the truth. Osman Suljić, the war president, looked straight at Karremans. "Tell me,
man to man," Suljić said. "Do you believe there will be air
strikes?"

"Yes," Karremans answered.

"What should people do if the air strike takes place?" Bići-
rović asked.

"People should stay as far away as possible from the confrontation line," Karremans said, "and try to take cover in houses."

Just before Karremans left for the meeting, Dutch deputy commander Major Franken had been told by General Nicolai in Sarajevo the UN's response to the Serb ultimatum that the enclave surrender the following morning at 6 a.m. If the Serbs did not withdraw from the enclave by 6 a.m., Nicolai said, they would face air strikes.

But Nicolai was wrong, confused or exaggerating. Janvier had been precise with his final instructions in Zagreb that night. Before leaving the headquarters Janvier said that if a tank or artillery piece attacked the town or moved toward it during the night, Close Air Support would be approved. If tanks or artillery attacked the Dutch blocking position or moved toward the town tomorrow morning, Close Air Support would be approved. No ultimatum about the Serbs withdrawing was issued. The term "air strikes" had not even been mentioned in Zagreb.

After giving more assurances that there would be air strikes, Karremans stood up to leave. He sensed that most of the men around the table didn't believe him.

"Don't shoot the piano player," the Dutch colonel quipped. The Muslims had no idea what he was talking about.

SREBRENICA SAFE AREA, JULY 11, 1995

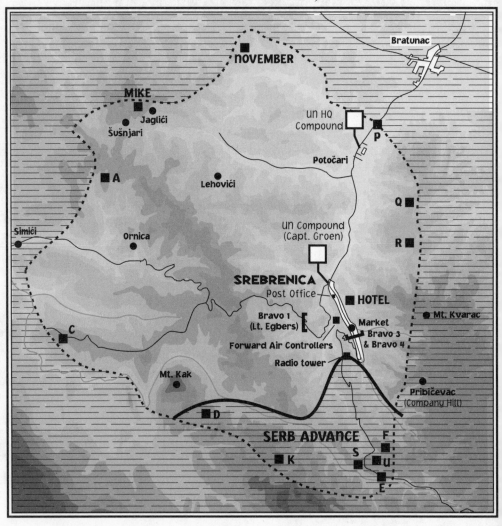

Bratunac

NOVEMBER

MIKE

Jaglići

Šušnjari

UN HQ
Compound

P

Potočari

A

Lehovići

Q

Simići

UN Compound
(Capt. Groen)

R

Ornica

SREBRENICA
Post Office

HOTEL

Mt. Kvarac

Bravo 1
(Lt. Egbers)

Market
Bravo 3
& Bravo 4

C

Forward Air Controllers

Radio tower

Mt. Kak

Pribičevac
(Company Hill)

D

SERB ADVANCE

F

K

S

U

E

Serb-controlled   ■ UN observation posts   ▪ ▪ ▪ ▪ Safe Area boundary

(Serb advance is approximate)

At 5 a.m., the sky began to glow to the east of Srebrenica. In the Dutch compound, Captain Groen anxiously looked at his watch. Colonel Karremans had told him that NATO planes would be circling over the Adriatic at 6 a.m. All night, Groen had worried, constantly checking the time. The Serbs could have moved into the town at any moment. The shelling seemed endless. UN Military Observers counted 182 detonations over the course of the night. The Serbs would have at least one full hour of light to move into town before NATO planes were in the air. Just one more hour, he thought, and the enclave would be saved.

In the market square, Lieutenant Egbers ordered his driver to start the APC. He and his men were edgy, but optimistic. They had been informed of the air strikes over the radio and relayed the news to the Bosnian soldiers. NATO strikes would finally be coming at 6 a.m.

The eight men crammed inside each of the APCs parked around the market had slept fitfully. Afraid of both Muslim hand grenades and Serb shells, they had sealed their hatches while they tried to rest. Trapped in the hot, claustrophobic vehicles, they listened as shells randomly careened into the town. A mortar had landed ten feet from one of the APCs at 2:15 a.m., sending shrapnel pinging off the vehicle's armor. Muslim soldiers had shouted "Fuck you!" in English at them during the night. At dawn, they were happy to be alive, and eager to leave.

Egbers waved goodbye to the officers commanding the other three APCs and rolled out of the marketplace. His orders were simple: return to the bluff and guide the massive air strikes against the Serb positions to the south.

In the Bosnian headquarters, Ramiz Bećirović's mood was hopeful for the first time in days. The Serbs were finally going to get the pummeling they deserved. He remembered General Morillon's visit to the town and the eagerly anticipated arrival of General Smith or one of his deputies.

With the support of the town's mayor and war president, Bećirović had pulled the few men still under his control out of the "zone of death" after the meeting with Karremans.[1]

The town's leaders had spoken by radio with Bosnian Prime Minister Haris Silajdžić in Sarajevo early that morning, and Silajdžić urged them not to harm or take any peacekeepers hostage. The Prime Minister said the UN had assured him there would be NATO air strikes.[2] Bećirović's standing order, to the dismay of his enraged troops, was unchanged. Bosnian soldiers were not to harm, disarm or take hostage Dutch peacekeepers. The artillery piece on the hill behind Lieutenant Egbers was not to fire. Bećirović was betting the future of the enclave on the UN.

Egbers reached the area near the bluff at 5:45 a.m. He parked his APC in the trees where it couldn't be seen by the Serbs. A thick fog hung over the enclave. Srebrenica was eerily quiet. No artillery fire, no tank engines, no machine guns. The Muslim soldiers on the hill above them—the ones who probably shot at them yesterday—smiled and waved, clearly happy to see the Dutch return.

At 6 a.m., Srebrenica's mayor, Fahrudin Salihović, war president Osman Suljić and commander Ramiz Bećirović listened for the sound of jets streaking overhead. Soldiers in the street scanned the fog-shrouded horizon. People strained their ears, desperate to hear at least the low hum of a distant jet engine. Nothing. Only a horribly empty silence.

On the dirt road, Lieutenant Egbers and his men were in position to guide air strikes; but they received no orders. In the Dutch compound in Potočari, peacekeepers huddled in the base's bunker in case of retaliatory Serb shelling after the air strikes.

In preparation for the morning NATO attack, a formal request for Close Air Support with an updated target list had been sent from Srebrenica at 10 p.m. the night before. At 5 a.m., contact had been made with the UN Sector Northeast headquarters in Tuzla. The target list was adjusted and planes were expected over Srebrenica at 7 a.m.

In anticipation of the air strike, Tuzla went from green alert status to orange alert at 6 a.m.

By 6:15 a.m., Captain Groen in the UN compound in Srebrenica was sure the planes were now in position over the Adriatic. They could be over Srebrenica in twenty minutes. All his men had to do was verify that the Serbs had not withdrawn from the enclave. Nothing could go wrong.

At 7:15 a.m., two white UN jeeps skidded to a halt in front of the post office. Two British commandos stormed into the building. They found Ramiz Bećirović and tried to tell him they needed a soldier who could point out the Serb positions. He couldn't understand them.

Alma Hadžić,[3] a twenty-seven-year-old Bosnian woman who worked in the cantina in the Dutch base, was called downstairs. She spoke broken English and recognized the commandos. They had always offered her precious cigarettes and been friendlier and more professional than the other soldiers.

"We need someone who can show us exactly where the Serb positions are around the town," the commando barked as Alma translated. "We have to hurry."

Ramiz Bećirović quickly chose Sanel Begić,[4] the Bosnian officer who had unsuccessfully tried to fire the Chinese-made Red Arrow missiles two days before, and one other soldier. "Let's go! Let's go!" the commando shouted. Three Dutch soldiers were waiting for them in the jeeps.[5] They jumped in and tore through the town, their tires screeching around curves.

Alma at first had felt sorry for the peacekeepers when she started working in the cantina. They were totally unprepared for Srebrenica. In the winter, they would slip and fall on the slick ice that covered the town. There seemed to be countless broken ankles and wrists. The Dutch had been sent to Srebrenica to protect the Muslims, but they couldn't even take care of themselves.

Then she began to resent some of them. The soldiers spent their time in the cantina talking about how much money they made, about the new clothes or new cars they were going to buy when they got back to Holland. A handful even threw candy in the mud and took pictures of Muslim children rolling in the mire to get it.[6] She knew most of the Dutch didn't do that, but she still found it infuriating. Now the fate of her town and the lives of her family lay in their hands.

The commandos pointed to a hill just above the post office, and Alma directed them to the nearest road. When it dead-ended, they jumped from the vehicle and walked up the steep slope. Alma didn't notice at the time, but none of the commandos were wearing telltale bright blue UN helmets. Twenty minutes after the commandos arrived at the post office, the group was on the hill surveying the southern approach to the town.

They scanned the area with binoculars. In each direction red-roofed farmhouses, golden hay and lush trees dotted the hillsides. It was too picturesque for a battle. They could see the abandoned Dutch OP Foxtrot two miles to the south. The asphalt road the Muslims and Serbs had battled over for the last three days wound its way to Srebrenica in front of them.

Two Serb trucks—presumably carrying infantry—were moving north from Pusmulići. Behind them, approximately 100 Serb infantrymen were walking north along the road. A truck with an antiaircraft gun mounted on the back was parked near Bibići. To the Bosnians, it was obvious that the Serbs were massing for a final assault. But the town was eerily silent that morning. The bombardment had more or less ceased.

Begić pointed out the other Serb positions. The southeast corner of the enclave had been turned into a shooting gallery. Serb artillery or tanks were positioned on the three most strategic hills along the southern and eastern border of the enclave. Anyone or anything moving in the area could be caught in a withering cross fire.

Due south of town, some kind of artillery emplacement had been set up on OP Foxtrot. To the southeast, the tank that had been shooting at Egbers' bluff sat on a hill near Pribičevac or Company Hill. Due east, a Serb artillery piece was atop Mount Kvarac, the 3,000-foot peak that loomed over Srebrenica.

The commandos unfolded a large, highly detailed military map of the enclave, better than anything the town's defenders had. One of them began speaking on the radio. Alma's hopes rose, and for some reason, she felt safe for the first time in days.

After the fog burned off and no NATO planes appeared by 8 a.m., the Dutch in Potočari filed a request for air strikes to the UN's Sector Northeast headquarters in Tuzla. It was their fourth since the attack began. The Serbs were pressing the attack again. Fighting had broken out near Mount Kak in the southeast corner of the enclave. With forty NATO planes circling over the Adriatic, the Dutch expected jets over Srebrenica within thirty minutes.

From the southern tip of Srebrenica to the central market, Ibran Malagić, his twenty-one-year-old brother Ferid and forty other men took their positions in houses. Mido Salihović was again in command. All volunteers, the men were a hodgepodge from four different units, but confident they could still hold the town if NATO bombed the Serbs, as promised. Salihović didn't think the Serbs were willing to engage in house-to-house fighting with the Muslims.

They had not advanced up the hill, because it was in the "zone of death" that NATO planes would create. To their left,

Ejup Golić, one of the enclave's brigade commanders, was blocking the route into Srebrenica from the east with 100 men. To their right, members of a unit commanded by Smail Mandžić, one of the commanders who was pulled out with Naser Orić, were positioned near Egbers, blocking the approach from the west.

The Bosnian artillery piece located just behind Egbers still had not been fired. The tanks and antiaircraft guns turned over to the UN in 1993 had still not been seized. Seizing them would give the Dutch an excuse to cancel air strikes.

At some point that morning, civilians broke into the municipal warehouse. To the horror of local residents, it was filled with food. Between twenty and thirty tons of rice, flour and other aid had never been distributed.[7] Men began hauling the food away. In a bizarre sight, men remembering the starvation of 1993 ignored Serb shells and scurried past Muslim soldiers and Dutch APCs that morning with fifty-pound sacks of rice on their backs.

The cache appeared to be larger than it really was. UN High Commissioner for Refugees officials estimate that, based on ration sizes in Sarajevo, twenty to thirty tons would be used up by the enclave's 40,000 residents in three to six days. The town's leaders had amassed a large war reserve of food, but like so many other rumors in the isolated enclave, it was grossly exaggerated.

By 9 a.m., no jets had appeared. On top of the hill near the post office, Alma Hadžić, the translator, and Sanel Begić, the Bosnian officer, were confused. It was clear the Serbs hadn't withdrawn from the enclave as the UN had demanded. "Why isn't that enough for an air strike?" she asked in broken English. "We don't make the decision," the oldest of the Dutch peacekeepers said. "Zagreb does."

Begić was furious. His walkie-talkie was buzzing. Ramiz Bećirović and the town's leaders wanted to know where the NATO planes were. It was clear the Serbs were preparing to attack the town. The Muslims had done exactly what the UN told them. They were staying out of the "zone of death."

At 9:30 a.m., Captain Groen ordered two of the APCs parked in the market to drive south and confirm how far the Serbs had advanced. The Bosnians reported two tanks south of Srebrenica; one of the commandos on the hill spotted two "hard targets" on the road. Groen wanted irrefutable proof that the Serbs had not withdrawn before he requested Close Air Support.

In the market, Corporal Hans Berkers, the driver of one of the four APCs, silently groaned when he heard the order. For Berkers, the instructions were simple: it was his turn to drive south until you get killed. As the two vehicles roared out of the market, an APC driven by Captain Hageman followed and took a position in the south to support them. After climbing out of Srebrenica town, the Dutch APCs crept down the road with their hatches sealed. In the driver's seat, Berkers was ready to slam his vehicle into reverse.

Slowly, they edged around a hairpin turn a quarter mile south of town. A Serb tank and several trucks were parked near the radio tower. Berkers slammed the vehicle into reverse and punched the gas. He waited for the walls of the APC to implode on him as a tank round hit. Nothing happened. The APC roared backward around the curve. The firing stopped. Berkers sighed.

The APC commander radioed to Captain Groen that Bosnian Serb infantry were a quarter mile south of Srebrenica. The Serbs had not withdrawn.

Groen relayed the information to his superiors in Potočari. Major Franken, the Dutch deputy commander, had already called Tuzla at approximately 9 a.m. to find out what had happened to the air attacks they had requested at 8 a.m.

The chief of air operations in Tuzla, a Dutch officer, was on vacation. The chief of operations, a Pakistani colonel, told Franken the 8 a.m. request for air attacks had been rejected because it was not on the proper form. The Dutch had filed a request for air strikes, not a Close Air Support form. They needed to resubmit the request on the proper form with an updated target list. Franken was furious. More than an hour had been lost.

Finally, at approximately 9:45 a.m., Dutch colonel Brantz in Tuzla forwarded a Close Air Support request to Sarajevo. He then had to resubmit it twice because Sarajevo said it did not include a proper targeting list that identified Serb positions to the north and south of the enclave. The secure fax in Tuzla was broken for a short time also. At 10:45 a.m., a proper Close Air Support request was finally received in Sarajevo. It was already too late.

At about 9 a.m., General Nicolai in Sarajevo had been contacted by NATO. The Dutch chief of staff was told that the planes circling over the Adriatic since 6 a.m. were running out of fuel. Unless the UN expected an immediate request for Close Air Support, NATO planes would fly to their bases to refuel and be unavailable for two hours.

Nicolai, unaware that the CAS request had been made from Srebrenica, allowed the planes to depart for Italy.[8] The Dutch general heard no reports of problems in Srebrenica that morning and assumed the situation had stabilized. Colonel Brantz, the acting commander in Tuzla, said he had warned Sarajevo that a request was on its way, but Nicolai denied it. Whoever was at fault, yet another opportunity for Close Air Support was missed.

By 11 a.m., Sanel Begić stood on the hill above town cursing the British commandos in Serbo-Croatian. Alma Hadžić had no idea what to do. For four hours they had watched the Serbs slowly mass for the attack. The sky overhead was empty.

Twice, the oldest of the Dutch soldiers had announced that an air strike was going to happen in fifteen minutes. Twice, he had announced it had been delayed. To Hadžić the British and Dutch went about their business showing little emotion, but she could see frustration in the oldest Dutch peacekeeper's face and sadness in his eyes.

The post office radioed and ordered Hadžić and Begić to leave. There would be no air strike. Enraged, Begić was convinced the town was being sacrificed. He radioed Ramiz Bećirović with a question about the Dutch and British in front of him.

"Can I kill them?" he asked.

A half mile west of the commandos, a second APC—the one driven by Corporal Berkers—arrived to reinforce Egbers' position. Major Franken ordered Captain Groen to get Egbers' men back up on the exposed curve where they had been shelled yesterday. The Dutch needed to show the Serbs they were being watched; the position also gave Egbers better radio communications.

When Egbers told his men, a mutiny erupted.

"I won't go back up there," said Sergeant Voskamp, the Forward Air Controller.

"Yes, you will," Egbers said slowly. "We're going back up."

"No way," the Forward Air Controller said. "I won't do it."

"We're not going," added an engineer. "It's too dangerous."

"I know it's dangerous," Egbers said. "But it's our job to go back up on the hill."

The Forward Air Controller said nothing. He was freezing up as he had the day before. The engineer stared at the floor. Egbers understood the danger. He knew one well-placed shell could incinerate an APC. Fifteen of them could be dead in a split second. The day before, they had just been lucky.

Without a Forward Air Controller, it was pointless. Egbers gambled.

"We're going up without you," he said.

Egbers climbed into the commander's seat of the APC. The Forward Air Controller was left sitting by the side of the road with Sergeant Frank Struik. Other Dutch soldiers got into position. The APC's engine started. Egbers was relieved. The soldiers were obeying him.

In the other APC, Berkers grudgingly agreed to go up on the bluff—but only if he could back the APC up the hill so they could flee quickly if needed. "As soon as a shell hits," he warned, "I'm leaving."

The two armored vehicles crept up the road toward the exposed curve. This is crazy, Berkers thought. We're all crazy. He could feel the adrenaline pulsing through his body. He wasn't as frightened as he had been that morning. He just felt incredibly alert. They reached the bluff. He turned the engines off. Nothing happened.

"Romeo, this is Bravo One," Egbers radioed at approximately 11:15 a.m. "We are in position." Egbers got out of the APC. His stomach began churning. He told himself that this was his job. That nothing was going to happen. The soldiers in the other APC also got out. "If you get out, it's your problem," Berkers warned. "If something happens, I'm leaving."

Egbers walked to the edge of the road. He looked through his binoculars. He saw some kind of armored personnel carrier and two trucks. Fifty Serb soldiers were walking up the road. The attack was continuing. He reported to Captain Groen what he saw below. Five minutes later, a Serb T-54 tank lumbered up the asphalt road from the south. Inside the APC, Berkers urinated into a paper cup. He was afraid he'd be caught outside the vehicle when the Serbs started shelling.

Egbers thought the tanks and trucks were all perfect targets for an air strike. Captain Groen said he had no information on where the planes were. Egbers felt like a fool.

The ground shook abruptly beneath his feet. Stones and shrapnel ricocheted off the APCs. Egbers dashed toward the APCs. The Serbs were shelling them again.

Berkers started his vehicle and slammed it into gear in one fluid motion. As he accelerated, the Dutch outside the APC grabbed on to its sides. He drove through the smoke; dust enveloped the road. Berkers glanced in his mirror. Three peacekeepers were dangling from the handgrips on the APC. He stopped and let them inside. One of them was a trembling Lieutenant Vincent Egbers.

A detonation directly in front of the APC stunned Berkers for a moment. He pressed down on the accelerator again. They quickly arrived at their old position, hidden by the trees. Berkers was shaking. It slowly dawned on him and the other Dutch. If he hadn't stopped to let the men inside, the shell would have made a direct hit.

After the quiet morning, Serb guns had opened up all across the enclave. Three mortars landed directly on top of OP Hotel. The Serbs were on a hill just east of town, and appeared to be shelling the positions where they thought Forward Air Controllers would be. OP Mike and OP November, located on the northern edge of the enclave, were attacked with mortars and heavy machine guns at 11:10 a.m. OP Mike's peacekeepers had already withdrawn and OP November's hid inside their bunker. The attacks in the north seemed designed to stretch out and confuse the town's defenders. The final assault was beginning.

In the post office, Ramiz Bećirović ordered Sanel Begić not to kill the Dutch and British commandos on the hill and to come back to town. Begić grudgingly complied.

The Serb shelling and the lack of NATO air strikes all morning confirmed the Bosnians' worst suspicions. Men who hadn't done so already went home to find their families and pack bags of food for the long march to Tuzla. Bećirović still held out the hope of air strikes. The mayor, Fahrudin Salihović, and others decided the town was being intentionally sacrificed by the Bosnian government and the UN.

Under pressure from the United States, Britain and France, the Bosnian government had finally agreed to the much-rumored secret deal with the Serbs, the mayor thought. He was convinced Srebrenica was being traded for one of the suburbs surrounding Sarajevo that was controlled by the Serbs. The capital would finally have a land link to the rest of government-held Bosnia. The siege of Sarajevo would finally end, Salihović thought, but Srebrenica was the price.

When the Close Air Support request finally arrived in Zagreb just after 11 a.m., Colonel Harm De Jonge rushed into Janvier's office with it. The French general again hesitated. Even though

Zagreb had been informed of the fighting around Mount Kak in the southern end of the enclave at 8 a.m. and the Dutch patrol had found Serbs a half mile south of town at 10:15 a.m., UN officials were still unsure whether the Serbs wanted to take the entire enclave, because the shelling had slowed that morning. At the daily briefing at 11 a.m., the UN intelligence assessment was that "the pressure is mounting, but as long as there was not significant shelling they do not intend to take the enclave."[9]

Reports of OP Mike and OP November being shelled arrived in Zagreb at approximately 11:30 a.m. As Colonel De Jonge and General Kolsteren waited anxiously, Janvier consulted with Akashi in the Japanese diplomat's office.

Finally, at 12:05 p.m., Janvier signed the request four hours after it had been originally sent from Srebrenica to Tuzla. NATO planes began taking off from their bases in Italy at 12:06 p.m. Akashi signed the request at 12:15 p.m. He later called Serbian President Slobodan Milošević to explain that the UN had been forced to use airpower and to ask for his help in halting the Bosnian Serb attack. Milošević said he would contact Mladić immediately but said he doubted that Mladić would understand the difference between Close Air Support and air strikes and that he might react strongly.[10]

The earliest the NATO planes would be over Srebrenica was 1:45 p.m. Five days after the Dutch filed their first request for air attacks, one had finally been approved. It was the sixth request they had made since the attack began.

Alma Hadžić had finally descended from the hill at 11:30 a.m. She felt like a fool, as if all the commandos were laughing at her. Only the oldest one seemed to understand. The town's leaders cross-examined her when she got back to the post office. A half dozen men in their thirties and forties pleaded with the twenty-seven-year-old to make sense of it all.

"Do you think there will still be air strikes?" one of them asked.

"No," she said.

"Why?"

"They don't care," she replied.

Ramiz Bećirović made contact with the 2nd Corps in Tuzla between noon and 1 p.m. Using the modem communications system, he typed the message that the Serbs were at the entrance of the town. Tuzla replied that they were doing everything they could and that the UN had promised air strikes. To Bećirović, the reply was essentially a noninstruction. It was useless. Osman Suljić, the war president, radioed Sarajevo. "This will be my last contact with you from Srebrenica," he said. "We must move to a safer location."

All men of fighting age were instructed to gather in Šušnjari, a village in the northwest corner of the enclave. All women, children, invalids and elderly men were to go to the Dutch base in Potočari. Across the enclave, wives embraced husbands, mothers said farewell to sons and sisters bid goodbye to brothers. Few had any sense of what was about to descend upon them.

In Šušnjari, Bosnian Muslim soldier Mevludin Orić reported for duty. A messenger had arrived in his home village of Lehovići saying he had to report for duty. In Šušnjari, Orić was told by Mirky Mandžić, a local brigade commander, that the Serbs were retreating and Srebrenica would not fall. Mevludin was ordered to report to his platoon for duty.

Orić walked to the village of Jaglići, where his platoon was based. He saw the Dutch APC that had withdrawn from OP Mike and approached with several other Muslim soldiers. He was disgusted. He wanted to take their weapons, but he was told Ramiz Bećirović had issued the order not to touch the Dutch.

"Where are the airplanes?" one soldier asked the Dutch. "Why don't they come?"

The Dutch answered with a combination of hand gestures and Bosnian and English words. They told the Muslims to be patient. They were calling all the time for air strikes but didn't know why they were not coming.

Sickened by the Dutch, Mevludin found his commanding officer and was told there were no rifles left but he was needed in the trench. Mevludin was given two hand grenades. He made his way to the front lines. Two years before, ammunition had been so low that there were only seven bullets for the rifle he shared with several other men. The secret helicopter flights that spring had brought the Red Arrow missiles and more rifles to the enclave but many of Srebrenica's 3,000 to 5,000 potential fighters still had only hunting rifles.

In 1993, each soldier in the enclave was supposed to have dug twenty yards of trench. After the UN arrived the Muslims were barred from digging in, and at times Canadian and Dutch peacekeepers filled in the trenches. The result was that in July 1995 the Bosnians had an unfinished trench near OP Mike. The only way to get into it was to sprint through fifty to sixty yards of open field.

The Serbs were firing at the Muslim trench with mortars and heavy machine guns. Mevludin was told that one man had two of his fingers blown off that morning when he tried to make it to the trench. An antiaircraft grenade had exploded near him. Once five or six men had gathered, Orić readied himself. There was little mystery to the technique. They just ran as fast as they could, one at a time. It was much worse for the men in back because by then the Serbs had time to aim their weapons better. When Orić's turn came, he sprinted and dove into the trench unscathed.

Mevludin was now ready for war Bosnia style. As the Serbs shelled the enclave into submission as they had in so many other towns in Bosnia, Mevludin waited. His role was simple. If the Serb infantry charged the trench, he was to throw the hand grenades.

Inside her daughter's apartment in Srebrenica, Ćamila Omanović had finished making lunch for her husband, children and grandson when her husband, Ahmet, abruptly announced they had to leave. The Serbs were rumored to be entering the town. Pandemonium was erupting outside. Thousands of people were emerging from houses, apartment buildings, and basements with sacks on their back. The exodus north had begun.

Ćamila turned back to the stove, put the food on separate plates and placed it all in a plastic bucket. She poured the broth from the pan into a container. She planned to eat lunch later and make noodles with the broth when they returned in a few days.

Her seventeen-year-old daughter, Đermina, picked up her baby. He was only four months old. Đermina had fallen in love with and married one of Naser Orić's bodyguards during the war. The baby was named Naser.

Ćamila filled a bag with diapers and baby clothes, clothing for her son and herself, a radio, photographs, some jewelry. The family's entire savings amounted to $600. She gave $150 to each of her children and kept $300 for herself. She gave the bag to her thirteen-year-old son and grabbed the baby carriage.

She locked the door to the apartment, grasped her son's hand firmly and headed downstairs. The stairway, which had been packed with refugees fleeing the shelling, was empty.

Outside, grandparents, soldiers, mothers and children moved in clots in a vast river of people. Fifteen thousand people moved toward the Dutch base in the northern end of town in search of protection. Gunfire echoed off the hills to the south and east of the town. Shells whizzed overhead. She threw the bag in the baby carriage and followed the horde.

They headed for her old apartment building across the street from the post office and a few hundred yards from the UN base. The stairs were crowded with people when they got there. But Ćamila fought her way to their first-floor apartment. The one-bedroom apartment was packed with their relatives. There was no place for them to eat.

She heard her husband outside. He was screaming her name. There was a panicked tone in his voice that unnerved her.

"Come out! Come out!" he shouted. "Hurry up!"

They gathered their things again and went back into the stairwell. Ćamila pushed through the crowd. Children screamed. Women angrily shoved each other. Someone shouted, "The Chetniks are in town." She ignored them.

Ćamila met her husband outside and they headed toward the UN base. The crowd swept them past the gas station where she'd seen her Serb neighbors who had turned nationalists, but she didn't notice it. Every store had been looted. The streets were filled with clothes, pieces of bread, trash and bags dropped by people who had packed more than they could carry. Bewildered elderly souls sat on the side of the road but no one paid any attention to them.

Ćamila Omanović's mind was focused on her children and grandson. The shelling and gunfire were getting to her. They had to move north. They had to get away from the Serbs. There was no time to wonder where the NATO planes were or where the town's defenders were. The bookkeeper only wanted to move as fast as she could. All she wanted was for these people to get out of her way. All she wanted was to get her children and grandson to the safety of the UN base.

What happened next in the chaos that ensued is unclear. The Dutch insist they were the last to leave Srebrenica; the Muslims insist they were.

Between 1:30 p.m. and 2 p.m., the few Muslim soldiers who had been threatening to fire on the Dutch APCs in the market if they retreated, departed themselves.

Worried that the Dutch would be overrun by the advancing Serbs, Captain Groen ordered his APCs to begin retreating north. He had given up on air strikes hours ago. He instructed Captain Hageman to keep the APCs between the advancing Serbs and the retreating Muslim civilians. Standing and fighting the Serbs was hopeless, Groen thought. The Serbs could not be stopped; peacekeepers would die needlessly, and the Dutch would lose the neutrality they needed to protect civilians. If the Muslims were making no effort to save the town, it made little sense that the Dutch should.

After Mido Salihović's men saw the Dutch pulling back, they too began to withdraw, according to Ferid Malagić, Ibran's brother. The Bosnian soldiers stayed 100 yards in front of the retreating Dutch, Ferid said. The poorly armed Muslims saw little point in defending Srebrenica if the UN was not going to launch air strikes and the Dutch were going to pull out. Their main goal was to keep the Dutch in town until all Muslim civilians had a chance to leave.

Whoever started the process, the Dutch and Muslim withdrawals played off of one another. Both groups were completely demoralized by the failure of NATO planes to appear and thought the situation was hopeless. At 200-yard increments, the Dutch slowly retreated north out of Srebrenica. No determined effort was made to stop the Serbs. A handful of retreating Muslims fired wildly at the advancing Serbs. The Dutch, following Captain Groen's strategy of staying neutral, didn't fire a shot.

On the Serb side of the front line, Dražen Erdemović and his unit began to move forward. Their commander, Lieutenant Milorad Pelemiš, had arrived early that morning with their latest orders. Their objective was simple, take the town itself.

Erdemović had never been to Srebrenica. He was worried about possible house-to-house fighting. Dislodging a single sniper could take hours and cost many lives. The Muslims had nowhere to retreat to. Taking the town could be bloody.

But as Erdemović slowly moved down the hill with the seven other men in his squad, they encountered no resistance.

Between 12:30 p.m. and 1 p.m., the town's civilian leaders abandoned the post office. Osman Suljić, the war president, wept. The tall, arrogant figure whom people thought had ruled the enclave like a feudal lord sobbed. Mayor Fahrudin Salihović's face was ashen. The man seen as a war profiteer who allegedly sold some of the humanitarian aid sent to the enclave said little.

As in a funeral procession, Srebrenica's leaders filed out of the post office onto the street. Leaving the building, they passed beneath the window where General Philippe Morillon had made his once daring and now infamous declaration.

...

Fifteen thousand feet over the Adriatic Sea, eighteen NATO jets slowly fell into formation. Following the new rules established by NATO after the June 2 downing of U.S. pilot Scott O'Grady, the attack package included FA-18s, F-18s, EA-6Bs, six F-16s (both Dutch and American), two F-111s armed with Suppression of Enemy Air Defenses (SEAD) systems, two tanker planes for refueling, a C-130 acting as an Airborne Command, Control and Communication Center (ABCCC), an AWACs airborne radar plane and several other escorts.

NATO was running nearly an hour behind schedule. Instead of being over Srebrenica at 1:45 p.m. as planned, the planes would be over Srebrenica at 2:30 p.m., six and a half hours after that morning's initial request and six days after the first Dutch request for Close Air Support from OP Foxtrot.

At 1 p.m., Captain Groen ordered every available soldier in the Dutch base outside. Marc Klaver, lookout at OP Foxtrot, was on watch; he was shocked by the chaos before him.

The entire enclave, it seemed, was descending on the Dutch base. Over 5,000 civilians clamored inside and outside the UN camp. The compound that Captain Groen and his men had struggled so hard to keep in spit-and-polish condition was seething with desperate people. Panic spread with chilling speed. Klaver and the other Dutch urged the people to walk north to the Dutch headquarters in Potočari, but the mob swarmed onto the base. Screaming and shouting, they begged the Dutch to protect them.

Ignoring the constant shelling, Dr. Daniel Golden and Kristina Schmidt from Médecins Sans Frontières and local staff workers from the UN High Commissioner for Refugees had gradually transferred the hospital's patients to the UN base in pickup trucks and cars. Klaver helped set up a medical aid station in the cantina and cordoned off parts of the compound for the elderly and wounded. Fifty-nine wounded lay on stretchers in the bar, television room and dining hall.

Captain Groen ordered his men to drive the company's five one-ton trucks to the center of the compound. They intended to load the wounded and evacuate them to Potočari. But as soon as the trucks were in the open, civilians swarmed onto them. Young people pushed old people off the trucks. Women fought each other viciously. The first in were crushed as dozens more clawed their way onto the overcrowded vehicles. People sat on the roofs, clung to the sides and even hung in front of windshields. Vahid Hodžić, the translator who had been shunned by the Dutch after Raviv van Renssen's death, urged the civilians to allow the wounded onto the trucks. None would listen.

The Dutch gave up and sent the desperate caravan to Potočari. After the first trucks departed, the peacekeepers finally succeeded in getting some of the 5,000 people in and around the base to begin walking north to Potočari. But old men and women who had been brought to the Dutch base in wheelbarrows were abandoned by their relatives or friends who could walk.[11] As the Serbs closed in, an instinct to survive enveloped the safe area.

Ibran Malagić arrived at the post office at 12:30 p.m. The man who had briefly held the Serbs at Bibići was disgusted to find men filling backpacks for the trek to Tuzla.

"What are you doing?" he asked.

"Preparing for the breakout," a soldier answered.[12]

"Do you know what you're going to find?" Malagić asked. He was convinced the forty-mile journey to Tuzla would be impossible.

"There's a chance the Serbs could cut us off," the soldier warned, "and we won't be able to leave."

"But who's going to take care of the wounded?" Malagić asked, worried about the men who had fought with him in the trench in Bibići. The soldier said they would organize something with the UN. In shock, Malagić left to find his wife.

Mido Salihović arrived at the post office at 1 p.m. Soldiers were trying to pack up the shortwave radio, the modem connection and car batteries to operate them. He found Ramiz Bećirović.

"They're not going to bomb the Serbs," Bećirović told him. "The Serbs are going to take Srebrenica."

Bećirović's face was white. He looked gaunt. His eyes stared blankly ahead.

"Maybe we can resist for one more day," he said plaintively, "but then we will run out of ammunition." Salihović left to look for his family.

Ćamila Omanović abruptly found herself in front of the Dutch base. Her deaf-and-mute forty-nine-year-old aunt Hadzira had spotted them in the crowd near the apartment building and joined the family. Ćamila saw hundreds of men walking up the dirt path that led to the northwest corner of the enclave.

She grabbed the bag of clothes for the children that her husband was carrying. She handed him $150. Ahmet was forty-seven but had always been frail. His mind was always far more powerful than his body. He had been operated on only three weeks earlier for goiter and he still had not fully recovered. It was all happening at the worst possible time. In a split second, he was gone. Ahmet and his blue eyes and gentle disposition disappeared into the column of men. Neither had said a word.

At 1:30 p.m. a ghostlike figure stood in the middle of the Dutch operations room. Captain Groen didn't recognize him at first. Amid the tumult, Ramiz Bećirović had simply walked into the nerve center of the Dutch compound.

"Will there still be an air strike?" Bećirović asked.

"I don't believe it's going to happen," Groen replied. "We have to get as many civilians as possible out of here."

Bećirović didn't say anything. His eyes were empty. His face was blank.

"Is there anything I can help you with?" Groen asked.

Srebrenica's commander walked off in a daze.

...

Just as Bećirović and Groen finished speaking, a Serb artillery shell careened into the compound without warning. A new wave of pandemonium struck. As the crowd scurried away from the detonation, a half dozen civilians lay writhing in bloody puddles on the ground. One woman stared in shock at her leg. Her foot had been blown off. Somehow, none of the Dutch had been hit.

Klaver and other peacekeepers tried to calm the crowd. The wounded were taken into the cantina for treatment by Dutch and Médecins Sans Frontières doctors. Groen, worried that the situation was spinning out of control, radioed Lieutenant Egbers and ordered him to return to Srebrenica. At 12:30 p.m., Serb mortars had hit OP Hotel, which the Dutch had abandoned and was apparently being used by Bosnian soldiers. Egbers radioed back that a second tank was now parked on the asphalt road near the radio tower. Its barrel was pointed at the dirt track that he and his men had to take to get back to town. Groen left it up to Egbers to decide when he wanted to challenge the tank and try to get past it.

At 2:15 p.m., an English-speaking voice came over the radio on the battalion's command channel. It was a Serb interpreter. The Bosnian Serbs issued a new ultimatum: no civilians were to go to Potočari.

In Washington, President Clinton was making a brief statement to reporters before meeting with the congressional leadership in the cabinet room of the White House to discuss the ongoing budget dispute, a rescission bill and terrorism and welfare legislation. At 8:30 a.m. Washington time, 2:30 p.m. Srebrenica time, Clinton was first asked about the health of Russian President Boris Yeltsin, who had been hospitalized that morning. The second question was about the besieged safe area.[13]

"Sir," the reporter asked, "the Bosnian Serbs are moving into Srebrenica fast, according to reports. Is it time for NATO air strikes?"

"We may have something to say on that later today," the President said. "But let me say I'm concerned about the people

who are there, and I'm also concerned about the UNPROFOR
troops—the Dutch—who are there. And we may have something
to say later today about that."

Back in Srebrenica, a Forward Air Controller came over the radio in the Dutch operations room just after 2:30 p.m. NATO
planes were overhead. Groen wanted to laugh. The planes had
finally arrived—only two of them. The British and Dutch Forward Air Controllers were furious. The planes had been in the
area for twenty minutes, but they were unable to make radio
contact with them.

There wasn't much time. The British had seen a group of
Serb troops walk along the stream called Čićevac and enter Srebrenica. The Serbs were moving slowly through the houses in
the southern end of the town. The commandos had been guided
by Bosnian soldiers to a trench only 200 yards from the Serb
tanks. If they were captured with the equipment they used to
guide the airplanes, the Serbs could kill them. The Serbs knew
exactly what they were there for.

The jets roared high overhead. On the path leading to the
northwest corner of the enclave, the column of fleeing men
halted. Ramiz Bećirović, who had just left Srebrenica, scanned
the sky. The mayor and the war president, well on their way to
Šušnjari, stopped and listened. On the road to Potočari, Ćamila
Omanović's spirits rose. In the northern end of the enclave, the
Serbs abruptly stopped shooting at a trench Mevludin Orić was
cowering in. In the western end of the enclave, Hurem Suljić,
the crippled carpenter, watched the planes from his field. All
over the enclave, Serb, Muslim and Dutch eyes turned to the
sky.

The two planes were F-16s from the Royal Dutch Air Force.
The Forward Air Controller with Egbers, Sergeant Voskamp,
was hidden in the trees nearby and had calmed down. He guided
the planes toward the road south of the town. As they homed
in, the Dutch closer to the tank took over. The nervous Forward
Air Controller broke NATO procedure and began speaking
Dutch instead of English. Officers monitoring the operation in

the Airborne Command, Control and Communication Center over the Adriatic could not understand what was happening.

At 2:40 p.m., the planes streaked over the Dutch base in Potočari and bore down on the Serb tanks on the asphalt road. Within seconds they were over Srebrenica town. A woman piloted one of the Dutch planes. The first bomb dropped by the Royal Dutch Air Force since World War II would be released by a female.

"If you see an antenna there," the Forward Air Controller said to the planes in Dutch, "very close to it is also a tank."

"The straight part after the small curve," the pilot replied. "I see between a house with a red roof and a curve . . . I see a few tanks driving."

"Roger," the Forward Air Controller answered. "Get that son of a bitch."

"Roger," the pilot said. "Coming in."

The F-16s dove toward the winding asphalt road. Serbs panicked. Muslims and Dutch prayed. One plane released a bomb and climbed sharply upward. A detonation reverberated throughout the enclave. Slightly louder than a howitzer or tank firing, it could be heard five miles away. Dust and smoke engulfed the hill where the Serb tanks had been.

As the smoke cleared from the area around the radio tower, Egbers and his men thought they saw a tank ablaze. Cheers erupted from the Dutch APCs. On the roof of the Dutch headquarters in Potočari, peacekeepers shouted with glee at the crack of the bomb.

The two planes circled high overhead. They dove intermittently toward the tanks, but dropped no bombs. Small specks in the sky, they were difficult to follow. The planes could be seen clearly only when the sun momentarily reflected off their wings. One of them circled and came in low over the Dutch base in Potočari with its engines roaring. It swooped over Srebrenica town, released a bomb over the hill and climbed straight up. Another explosion reverberated across the hills.

Cheers again erupted from the men gathered on the bluff with Egbers. It was difficult to see through all the dust and smoke, but one of the Serb tanks seemed to be retreating to the south. "Good luck," the Dutch pilot told the Forward Air Controller. It was over. The planes disappeared as quickly as they arrived.

The town's police chief, Hakija Meholjić, and a Muslim officer near Egbers' position reported seeing only smoke. "We can see the bombs," the police chief radioed over a walkie-talkie to the mayor and the war president. "They're smoke bombs. They didn't hurt the Serbs at all." The Muslim men continued retreating toward the northwest corner of the enclave.

In the town, Mido Salihović and Ibran Malagić were unimpressed. The Serb shelling continued unabated. Salihović thought the attack was some kind of NATO training exercise. On the road to Potočari, Ćamila Omanović was crushed. Only two NATO planes arrived. The bombs were so unimpressive that she finally faced the obvious. No new Morillon would emerge to save them. Even Dutch peacekeeper Marc Klaver was disappointed. He had expected all the Serb tanks and artillery around the enclave to be targeted, not merely two tanks.

The planes were not carrying NATO's most accurate bombs. They had free-fall bombs, not laser-guided ones that locked on to a laser beam the Forward Air Controller directed on a target. The Serbs had prevented the Dutch from bringing the equipment into the enclave.

As they departed, the pilots reported to their commanders that Serb forces were seen retreating after the air attack. In the village of Ornica that afternoon, all twenty-one residents, including Hurem Suljić, clustered around the radio when the news from Sarajevo came on at 3 p.m. Government radio announced that NATO had bombed Serb armored vehicles and the Serbs were withdrawing. Ecstatic, Suljić decided the Serbs had been stopped and went to buy some hay.

What the bombs actually hit is unclear. According to Egbers, a Serb tank was destroyed. But Bosnian Serb television that night showed only a jeep with a smashed windshield and a small crater in front of it. Ratko Mladić complained to Colonel Karremans that the bomb nearly hit him and killed eight of his soldiers. But General Milenko Živanović, the commander of the Bosnian Serb Drina Corps, said the bombs were more than just symbolically late. Bosnian Serb soldiers had parked vehicles on the hill above the town and descended on foot into Srebrenica. No soldiers were killed by the bombs because when they finally fell, the Serbs were already in Srebrenica town itself.

Lieutenant Egbers decided his chance to get to the town had arrived. The Serb tank targeting the road either had been destroyed or pulled back. His men piled into the two APCs and roared down the dirt track. Bullets ricocheted off the APCs. Corporal Hans Berkers, who was driving, felt something hit the back of his helmet. The Muslims with the artillery piece were shooting at them again.

The artillery piece had still not been fired. At some point Tuesday afternoon, frustrated Bosnian soldiers turned it on its head and stole the firing pin. They had obeyed Ramiz Bećirović's orders. The forty shells they had for the gun were never used.

As Egbers and his men raced away, Berkers whipped around a corner. A Bosnian soldier was sitting in the road. With no time to stop, Berkers' massive vehicle ran over the man's legs. The Dutch kept going.[14]

Nearby, the Dutch Forward Air Controller and the British commandos emerged from the woods and tumbled down the hill, bullets whizzing over their heads. Captain Hageman, who had withdrawn from the market and parked his APC 200 yards from the Dutch base, nearly began firing at them. Without their bright blue helmets on, the commandos were at first mistaken for Serb soldiers.

Mido Salihović, Ibran Malagić, his younger brother Ferid and twenty other men clustered in front of Srebrenica's post office. The building and the city were deserted.

Ibran had said goodbye to his young wife in front of the post office. Alma agreed to separate temporarily only after he said he would join her later and together they would walk to Tuzla. They had been inseparable since they married in May.[15]

Some in the group cursed; others wept. It was over. Three years of cold, hunger and deprivation for nothing. More than 1,500 soldiers' lives for nothing. They had failed Naser. They had failed their dead friends. They had failed themselves. Srebrenica had fallen.[16]

In the Dutch headquarters in Potočari, a Dutch Forward Air Controller made contact with two U.S. F-16s circling near the enclave at 3 p.m. Two other U.S. F-16s had departed after being unable to find Serb targets on the smoke- and dust-covered ridge south of town.

It took fifteen minutes for the Forward Air Controller to guide the new NATO planes in. The Americans were to bomb the Serb artillery positions on the western edge of the enclave that had shelled OP Mike and OP November. But the pilots also had difficulty finding the targets. As the U.S. planes prowled the area, a shoulder-fired antiaircraft missile streaked toward one of them. The missile missed by a wide margin, but the planes disappeared anyway.

In the operations room in Potočari a Serb translator abruptly came over the radio. "If the NATO attacks do not stop immediately, all Dutch peacekeepers in Serb custody will be killed," he said in a trembling voice. "The Dutch compound in Potočari, where civilians are gathering, will also be shelled."

At 3:30 p.m., Lieutenant Egbers and the Dutch Forward Air Controller arrived at what was left of the UN compound in Srebrenica. It was chaos beyond description, Egbers later said.[17] People were crammed onto "anything that had wheels." Clutching their children, mothers begged the Dutch to save them. The fifty-nine wounded and mental patients from the hospital still lay on stretchers scattered throughout the compound. Shrapnel from mortar and artillery had ripped holes in what were once pristine UN buildings and Mercedes jeeps.

With the Serbs closing in, all of his men back in the compound and most of the able-bodied civilians already headed for

Potočari, Captain Groen decided to abandon the town. He went into the operations room to dismantle radios and collect code books and other sensitive documents. The trucks that had been swarmed by Muslims were now returning and picking up the wounded. Dr. Daniel Golden and Kristina Schmidt from Médecins Sans Frontières assembled a final caravan of misery with the help of the Dutch soldiers.

Almost everyone who was physically able to had already fled north. Only the elderly, infirm and insane were left. The wounded and mentally ill were stacked on top of one another inside the APCs and jeeps. Mothers with children and the elderly were piled onto whatever space was left. A handful of elderly refused to come, saying they would put themselves at the mercy of the Serbs. Vahid Hodžić, the translator, and Marc Klaver, from OP Foxtrot, tried to coax elderly people into believing they had the strength for the journey.

Hodžić heard someone calling for help and stepped inside a small prefabricated container. An old man and woman were lying on stretchers. With one of his wrists broken, Hodžić picked up the man's stretcher and with one hand dragged it outside to the APCs. When he returned, he was so tired that he could only pull the woman for thirty-yard intervals, resting between each one until he got her to a vehicle.

Under the hot July sun, Srebrenica's residents and the peacekeepers slowly streamed north. As the cavalcade departed, children shrieked. The Dutch stared blankly ahead of them. Egbers and Berkers were eager to get to Potočari. Neither had slept for nearly four days. On the way to Potočari, Berkers thought he saw an old man fall in front of his vehicle. The vehicle rose up on one side as if it had run over something. When Berkers looked in his rearview mirror, he saw that the body of an old man, severed in two by the APC, lay in the road.[18] He cursed. The wounded stacked on the APC in front limited his vision. He had to get them to Potočari. He kept driving.

As the column moved north, Klaver saw a small boy walking back toward Srebrenica. Klaver scooped him up and gave him to a Dutch sergeant in one of the Mercedes jeeps. Klaver had no sense of defeat as they trundled toward Potočari. The Dutch had come to Srebrenica to act as the eyes of the UN. They had done that. It had been up to people on higher levels to decide how to respond to the Serb attack.

Captain Groen focused on getting as many civilians and peacekeepers to Potočari as possible. As a military leader, he was conceding defeat. Instead of turning and fighting the enemy, the Dutch were running from him. But Groen didn't see himself as a warrior; he saw himself as a neutral monitor. Except for a few random shells, the Serbs were not shelling the two-mile-long column of 13,000 refugees. Groen had made sure that there were peacekeepers and UN vehicles scattered throughout the horde. Their ridiculous white vehicles and blue helmets were finally useful. The Dutch appeared to have kept their neutrality.

Srebrenica was lost, but the lives of Groen's soldiers and 13,000 innocent civilians could still be saved.

As Srebrenica emptied out, the executive committee of the ruling Muslim nationalist Party of Democratic Action began meeting at 3:30 p.m. in the government-held city of Zenica in central Bosnia. President Alija Izetbegović and army commander Rasim Delić were present. Prime Minister Haris Silajdžić, who was not a member of the SDA, was in Sarajevo monitoring events in Srebrenica.[19]

The first order of business was naming a temporary replacement for Vice President Ejup Ganić, who had been badly injured in a car accident. General Rasim Delić, commander in chief of the Bosnian Army, then announced the NATO air strikes and turned to the situation in Srebrenica. Delić, whom Western military analysts viewed as far less competent than Bosnian Serb Army commander Ratko Mladić, said he had expected the UN's passivity. He warned of the "Goražde syndrome," referring to the attack on Goražde in 1994. Delić apparently felt that Bosnians had believed the UN would save them and had not done enough to organize the defense of the town.

Without explaining why the army had pulled out Naser Orić and the enclave's fifteen best officers, he warned that there was no one strong enough in Srebrenica to create "cohesion in the resistance." "Srebrenica has enough arms," he said. "The only problem is how to create resistance." The general pointed out that the army had "made sure over the last few months" that more arms and ammunition were in Srebrenica than there had been in three years. He mentioned the Chinese-made Red Arrow antitank missiles. "Four tanks mean nothing," Delić said, referring to the attack from the south. "If a launcher with enough missiles is present."[20]

The Serbs, according to Delić, had entered the first few houses on the edges of Srebrenica. He criticized Srebrenica's war president, Osman Suljić, for making exaggerated comments about the Serb attack on Bosnian radio that would further lower morale in the town and for not organizing the town's resistance.[21]

He then began a long analysis of the offensive to break the siege around Sarajevo and the current situation inside the army. Western analysts had concluded weeks ago that the stalled Sarajevo offensive had been a military disaster that resulted in approximately 1,000 casualties, but Delić discussed it as if it were still continuing. The army's withdrawal of Srebrenica's commander and much of its senior military leadership was never mentioned.

Only five minutes of Delić's twenty-five-minute speech were devoted to Srebrenica. The commander of the Bosnian Army either failed to grasp the gravity of the situation or was intentionally downplaying it.[22]

After the Dutch abandoned their compound at 3:30 p.m., Ejup Golić, one of Srebrenica's brigade commanders, led the last group of Bosnian soldiers through town.[23] Golić and about twenty men descended from the hills east of Srebrenica. They entered the Dutch compound and grabbed some abandoned flak jackets and rifles for the trek to Tuzla.

At approximately 4:15 p.m., soldiers from the Bosnian Serb Army entered the Dutch United Nations compound in Srebrenica town. They had encountered no resistance from the Dutch and almost none from the Bosnians.

The world's first United Nations safe area had fallen.[24] Approximately one Dutch peacekeeper and 50 to 75 Muslim soldiers died defending the safe area. In the most stunning victory of the war, approximately 50 to 75 Bosnian Serb soldiers died conquering it.

In the basement bunker of the Dutch Defense Ministry, the country's Prime Minister, Foreign Minister and Defense Minister made their decision quickly. At 4:50 p.m., Defense Minister Joris Voorhoeve called Yasushi Akashi, the civilian head of the UN mission in the former Yugoslavia, and asked that no further Close Air Support attacks be carried out in Srebrenica. With the Bosnian Serbs in control of the town, there was no point in risking the lives of the thirty Dutch hostages. Ten minutes before Voorhoeve called, UN Force Commander Bernard Janvier had already canceled the attacks.

As word of Srebrenica's fall spread, governments around the world reacted with shock and outrage at the conquest of the safe area. The Clinton administration, which at first limited what kind of airpower could be used, always refused to send any U.S. troops to protect the safe areas and blocked Janvier's proposal in May, harshly criticized the attack. White House spokesman Michael McCurry saw it as the latest example of the "repugnant" behavior of the Bosnian Serbs and called on them to withdraw. But there was no change in the long-running U.S. policy of refusing to deploy ground troops in Bosnia.

French President Jacques Chirac, who halted air strikes in May, signaling to the Serbs that taking hostages could curb NATO attacks,[25] said France would be willing to supply troops from the Rapid Reaction Force to invade Bosnian Serb territory and to reestablish the safe area. Few Western or UN officials took the pledge seriously.

And British Prime Minister John Major, whose government championed the policy of avoiding confrontations with the Serbs, condemned the fall of the safe area. Fearing that British troops deployed in the surrounded safe area of Goražde might soon face the same dangerous and humiliating fate as the Dutch in Srebrenica, he called on NATO to aggressively defend the remaining safe areas.

Getting the Serbs to release the 450 Dutch peacekeepers surrounded in Potočari immediately became the UN's top priority. Officials in UN headquarters in Zagreb feared that the Bosnian Serbs would carry out random atrocities against Muslims. It was crucial that UN and International Committee of the Red Cross personnel get access to Srebrenica to supervise any evacuation.

Only one person seemed to immediately grasp what lay ahead for Srebrenica—General Philippe Morillon, the man whose impromptu trip and off-the-cuff promise had led to the creation of the safe area. Seated in his plush office in the Ministry of Defense in Paris, Morillon was told by the French Defense Minister that the safe area had fallen. One of the first thoughts to enter Morillon's mind was chilling: the Serbs are going to kill all the Muslim men.

General Ratko Mladić, the commander of the Bosnian Serb Army, triumphantly entered Srebrenica. With a camera crew in tow, the burly general swaggered past Srebrenica's abandoned post office. "On to Potočari!" he shouted, jabbing his finger to the north as the television camera captured his every move. "On to Potočari!"

The general paused and gave a brief interview to a Bosnian Serb TV journalist.

"Here we are in Srebrenica on July 11, 1995. On the eve of yet another great Serbian holiday," Mladić said. "We present this city to the Serbian people as a gift. Finally, after the rebellion of the Dahijas, the time has come to take revenge on the Turks in this region."

The Serb general was referring to Srebrenica's Muslims as Turks. The "rebellion of the Dahijas" was a Serb uprising that the Turks brutally crushed in 1804. Over one hundred and ninety years later, General Mladić was looking for revenge.

...

At 4 p.m. in Potočari, a Dutch officer standing outside head-quarters radioed Lieutenant Eelco Koster, "You better come see for yourself what's coming."[26]

The fifteen-foot-wide asphalt road from Srebrenica was filled with a solid wall of refugees. As far as the eye could see, thousands of bedraggled women, children and old men marched toward the Dutch. The sight was both tragic and spectacular.

Thousands of women dressed in bright blue, red and green *dimijes*—baggy Muslim pantaloons with intricate patterns—carried children or led them by the hand. Hundreds of stooped old men in soiled white shirts and navy blue berets hauled red, brown, green and yellow bags and blankets. Lush green grass and trees bordered the column on both sides. The mob produced a cacophony of children crying, women shouting and weeping and old men cursing the Dutch. The light blue helmets of ex-hausted peacekeepers and white UN APCs dotted the crowd.

At first, the Dutch allowed approximately 5,000 civilians to enter the base itself. When the main hall of the factory building was filled, the Dutch blocked a hole they had cut in the base's barbed-wire fence. The refugees were enraged. Although they would have to sit in the open air, all of the refugees could easily fit inside the three-acre complex. Translators with megaphones pleaded with the people to remain calm and promised that the Dutch would also protect refugees outside the base. Grudgingly, the hordes moved into the abandoned factories and bus station outside.

In English, German and Serbo-Croatian, women and the el-derly asked the Dutch what was going to happen to them. Vahid Hodžić, positioned outside the base next to a Dutch APC, was interrogated by other Muslims. Men and women fainted in the heat and chaos. A handful of pregnant women, overcome by the tension, went into premature labor.

Adults moved through the crowd shouting the names of the relatives, friends and children they had been separated from. As the wounded arrived with Captain Groen and his men, a Dutch doctor and orderlies worked feverishly to move the most serious cases to the Dutch hospital inside the compound. Corporal Klaver again found the young boy wandering along the side of the road, walking back to Srebrenica. The woman who promised the Dutch sergeant she would care for him had lost control of him. The boy was convinced that his parents—or their bodies—were in Srebrenica.

On the Bosnian Serb side of the front line, Dražen Erdemović was disgusted. The town was rancid. Thirty-foot-tall mounds of garbage rose above the streets. The smell of feces wafted from manholes. The Muslims had lived like animals. Huge stacks of chopped wood sat in front of apartment buildings. Soot covered every structure. Cars sat on the side of the road where they had run out of gas years ago.

The Serbs encountered no resistance. Srebrenica was deserted. Moving slowly from house to house, they kept waiting for a Muslim sniper to open up on them. Nothing happened.

The first person they found was an elderly man who said he had stayed because he was too old to leave and wanted to protect his home. Lieutenant Milorad Pelemiš, the unit's commander, sent him to the local soccer field. The Serb soldiers' orders were not to harm anyone they found.

But near the center of town, a Muslim man who looked to be about thirty years old surrendered to the group. He was of military age and could have been a soldier. Pelemiš didn't tell him to go to the soccer field. Erdemović tensed. Pelemiš was unpredictable. He loved to hold huge parties in neighboring Serbia after the unit carried out difficult operations. The missions sometimes involved some kind of payment, but Pelemiš rarely shared the money with the unit.

Pelemiš eyed the Muslim. "Slaughter him," he said to Zoran, a new man in the unit.

In one swift motion, Zoran stepped behind the terrified man, drew his knife, pulled his head backward and slashed his throat.

Blood spurted across the pavement. The Serb soldiers let the man fall forward. His body quivered as if he were having a seizure. Loud wheezing and gurgling sounds came from his throat. Gallons of blood seemed to gush from him. His entire body shook violently. His legs kicked the pavement, and finally slowed. The pool of blood was twice as large as the man's body, which was limp.

At 4:30 p.m., after walking for an hour from Srebrenica, Ćamila Omanović arrived in the midst of the mob outside the Dutch base in Potočari. She, her son, her daughter, her grandson, her deaf-and-mute aunt, a friend and her friend's mother had managed to stay together.

Pushing the baby carriage filled with their bags, she walked between two Dutch APCs. Shells had exploded intermittently on the side of the road, but her daughter Dermina refused to put Naser in the carriage or let anyone carry him. Dermina weighed only 105 pounds and clearly struggled during the two-mile walk. She enveloped the child with her arms, desperately trying to shield him from shrapnel.

The peacekeepers urged them on, saying, "Hurry, hurry!" She heard that the Dutch were allowing small children onto the base. But when she reached the fence around the former car battery factory, Ćamila was crushed. "There is no more room," a translator for the Dutch said over a megaphone. "Go to the factories."

Omanović had worked as a bookkeeper in the car brake factory across the street for fourteen years. She had been in the complex that was now the Dutch base dozens of times. The family doctor and dentist offices were there, and she often had lunch with friends in the cafeteria. She had spent lunch hours and breaks lounging on the grass that she longed to sleep on. But now that her life depended on it, foreigners who were half her age and spoke a strange language told her she couldn't go in.

Humiliated, she and her family moved through the throng of whimpering children and exhausted mothers. Naser was shrieking. Every inch of abandoned building, grass or parking lot close to the Dutch complex was occupied. Petrified of the Serbs, Ćamila didn't dare move too far away from the base. Eventually she found a small patch of pavement in the parking lot of the zinc processing factory where her husband used to work. She laid out on the ground a two-foot-wide plastic container top and a piece of cardboard they had found. She and her children sat down. She could see her husband's old office window from where she sat in the parking lot.

They tried to quiet Naser. Đermina breast-fed him. They placed him in the carriage and somehow the child slept as dozens of other babies screamed. Ćamila unpacked the radio to hear what the United Nations was going to do to help them. At 7:30 p.m., Srebrenica was finally mentioned, but the newscaster talked about ongoing fights there. He said nothing about the fact that the town had fallen, that its people were desperate for help.

Around her refugees sat on hay or pieces of wood they had collected from nearby houses. Families were encamped three feet away from her in every direction. An old man retched onto the asphalt. People stood up and relieved themselves wherever they could find an empty spot. The humid air began to stink of vomit, urine and excrement.

They took turns trying to calm the baby. The Serbs fired three salvos of shells and bullets over the compound before sunset. Each time, they landed on the other side of the street but set off a panic among the refugees streaming in from across the enclave.

Ćamila's aunt looked at the tired, haunted faces and saw fear. She kept waving her hand across her chin. None of them knew sign language, but the family had developed a primitive language of its own. Her aunt was asking about the Chetniks— who were known to grow long beards. She wanted to know how close they were.

When word arrived at 6 p.m. Mevludin Orić refused to believe it. Srebrenica could not have fallen. Furious at the Dutch, he ran from the trench determined to see his parents, wife and two daughters off to Potočari. But in Jaglići, he came across a neighbor who told him his mother, wife and daughters had already left. His father had headed toward Šušnjari.

As Mevludin walked to Šušnjari, a sense of dread swept over him. He had made the journey before. He had walked with a surgeon and forty-six other men from Tuzla to Srebrenica in June 1992. When the war broke out, Mevludin was in Croatia at his uncle's house in Kutina. To get back to Bosnia, he took a job in security and carried a rifle and rode shotgun on an aid convoy from the Croatian capital of Zagreb to Tuzla. He then joined the group and began the risky journey to Snagovo— which at that point was the western tip of the nearly 100-square-mile Srebrenica pocket. The men walked the nerve-racking ten miles at night, stopping repeatedly to scout the area and check for Serb patrols. The trip had nearly killed him, but this would be far, far worse. In 1992, roughly ten miles separated Srebrenica from Muslim-held central Bosnia. After 1993's disastrous battlefield losses, forty miles now separated Srebrenica and Tuzla.

When he reached Šušnjari he was overwhelmed. Thousands of men had arrived since he had been there at noon; hundreds more streamed in. It seemed to take forever, but he finally found his father and some neighbors from Lehovići. His father, sixty-one, was a soft-spoken farmer and easily frightened by shelling. He always urged Mevludin not to get involved in military action and to be careful. His father came up only to Mevludin's shoulder, but he was the central figure in Mevludin's life. The two had built the family's house together. Mevludin had learned everything he knew about building and farming from his father.

A few minutes after they met in Šušnjari, Mevludin broke down and started sobbing in front of his father. "Don't worry," his father said. "Forget about the house, it's not important. The only thing that's important is to stay alive."

But Mevludin wasn't crying because of the house; he was weeping because he knew what lay ahead.

Back at UN headquarters in Zagreb, the mission's senior leadership convened for a 6:30 p.m. meeting.[27] Akashi pointed out that Dutch Minister of Defense Voorhoeve had requested that the air attacks be stopped.

Then Janvier, who in press accounts was already being criticized for failing to call in NATO planes, spoke. "I think we've reached the end of the safe areas. Following the successful attack on Srebrenica, I fear that Žepa and Goražde will follow. The Serbs will have achieved their objectives regarding the map," he said. "Given the pretext that the BH attacked [from Srebrenica ten days ago], we still acted. We opposed the Serbs with firm intentions. We did battle with the Serbs on the ground and used airpower to protect our units. But the force ratios on the ground did not allow us to continue fighting."[28]

"I ordered, at the moment when the air attacks were initiated, that the OPs in Srebrenica should regroup, but they couldn't because the BH [soldiers] stopped them," Janvier said.[29]

"How do I see the future?" Janvier asked rhetorically. "A military solution is not possible." Janvier opposed retaking the enclave by force as French President Chirac had suggested. There would be potential reprisals against UN soldiers elsewhere, and to cross forty miles of Serb-held territory would take an armored division. They needed to review NATO's plans for extracting the Dutch from Srebrenica, he said. "I would only allow the extraction of the battalion—not their equipment," he said, "and of course not the refugees."[30]

"If Srebrenica disappears, Žepa disappears. There's the whole problem of the enclaves. There are 450 soldiers in Goražde without a mission. The BH have taken all other OPs," Janvier said, without mentioning that the UN had already left the OPs. He said the safe areas should be abandoned. "In Žepa, the Ukrainians are only involved in the black market. The only way to proceed is to negotiate an exit with the Serbs.[31]

"The problem is the reaction from the international community. They will demand an invasion of the safe area and demand something be done—air strikes, etc. . . . which is practically impossible," he predicted. "The only way out is to sit down with the Serbs in Pale and discuss a way out."

"What happened to the ABiH [Bosnian Army]?" Akashi asked.

"I've been asking that question. They disappeared," Janvier said. "In our communications we must say the BH was not effective in defending the safe areas."

"[Special Adviser to the Secretary General Chinmaya] Ghar-

ekhan remembers your statement to the Security Council," Akashi said, "that we should withdraw because the ABiH was
capable of defending. Obviously they are not."

"Or they chose not to," interrupted Major General Barry
Ashton, of Canada, the Deputy Force Commander.

"Did Mladić have a plan from the beginning?" Akashi asked.

Janvier, who was unsure of Serb intentions the night before,
had changed his mind. "Yes. Sector West was a good example,"
Janvier replied, referring to the Croatian Army's lightning conquest of the Serb-controlled pocket in Croatia in May. "He
wants to make the map ethnically pure in eastern Bosnia."

When Hurem Suljić and his wife returned to their house at 7
p.m., he was startled. His neighbors were gathered around. As
he rode his horse Dorat into the village, two of his neighbors
rushed out to meet him.

"Why haven't you been at home?" one of them asked. "Srebrenica has fallen."

Suljić couldn't believe it. "I was getting hay," he stammered,
noticing bags near the houses. "Why are you packed? Where are
you going?"

"The civil defense came and said all the men should go to
Šušnjari," his neighbor said. "Invalids, old men who could not
carry guns, women and children should go to Potočari."

"Don't wait for me," he said. "I've got to pack."

Suljić was in shock. He had no idea what to take and what
to leave from a lifetime's possessions. Suljić and his wife slowly
packed some valuables, a little food, some clothes, one or two
blankets. He had been sure that once all the refugees got to
Potočari the Dutch commander would do something. After an
hour, he, his wife, his daughter, his daughter-in-law and granddaughter were ready.

One thing made them hesitate—his fifty-eight-year-old
cousin Ismet, who was partially paralyzed by a stroke. He was
able to walk but not for long distances. Suljić urged his cousin
to come with them to Potočari, but he refused. "I cannot even
go far on the horse," Ismet said. "There's no other way to go."

Hurem's son Kadrija was the last person to see Ismet. At 8 p.m., Suljić's cousin was found alone in the tiny deserted village, weeping.

"Where are the others?" Kadrija asked.

"They all went," Ismet answered, sobbing.

They left him a month's worth of flour and other food. If he was lucky, two old Serb friends who lived in nearby villages would return to the area and care for him. If he wasn't, he would slowly starve to death, unable to gather additional food or prepare the food in front of him.

Colonel Karremans was summoned by the Bosnian Serbs for a meeting in Bratunac at 8:30 p.m.[32] He had received new orders from Sarajevo at 6:30 p.m. He was instructed to begin negotiating a cease-fire with the Serbs and not give up any of his weapons, which "was not a point of discussion." The Dutch were to withdraw from all the OPs and concentrate in Potočari, to provide medical assistance to refugees and prepare to coordinate the distribution of humanitarian aid. He underlined the order to "take all reasonable measures to protect civilians in your care," and wrote "not possible" in Dutch next to it. He wrote "not possible" next to one other order—the instruction to "defend your forces including the use of Close Air Support."

As soon as Karremans and two of his liaison officers arrived in the Hotel Fontana and entered the restaurant, a deep voice boomed across the room. TV cameras and klieg lights were shoved in his face. "Are you the one that ordered the NATO strike?" a burly figure bellowed from across the room. "You killed eight of my soldiers!"

As he approached, Karremans was dumbstruck. Ratko Mladić, the bull-necked commander of the Bosnian Serb Army, was berating him. "Your soldiers tried to kill me!" Mladić bellowed. "Your soldiers shot at me!"

Mladić's face was bright red and as wide as a shovel. His graying hair was combed straight back. His piercing blue eyes glared or sparkled at whomever he was speaking to. Just over six feet tall, barrel-chested and overweight, Mladić used his loud voice and large frame to intimidate. "You failed in your mission!" Mladić barked. "You never disarmed the Muslims in the enclave!"

Drinks were given to the peacekeepers. The infamous scene was captured on film and video. Karremans and Mladić stood face to face holding wineglasses. The Dutch colonel sipped what appeared to be champagne or wine, but later he said it was water. The Bosnian Serb commanders toasted their victory as the tall, skinny Dutch colonel stood by.

Earlier in the evening Mladić had walked up to twenty Dutch hostages eating dinner. "Stand up like soldiers," he said, "and salute me." The Dutch hesitated, but with armed guards nearby, awkwardly saluted the Serb general. Mladić later told the Dutch his dream was "coming true" and an aide said he was referring to taking all the enclaves.

Karremans tried to explain the dire situation around the Dutch base. He said he needed food, water and medicines immediately to prevent a catastrophe. "You'll have to return for a second meeting at 11:30 p.m." Mladić replied. "Bring with you one representative of the refugees and one representative of the opština [municipal government]."

Karremans returned to the compound. After a frantic search, the peacekeepers found the director of Srebrenica's high school—thirty-two-year-old Nesib Mandžić—at 9:30 p.m. Mandžić was hesitant. If the Serbs decided he was a local leader he was doomed. Karremans and his officers said negotiations were the only way the Dutch and the Muslims would be safe. They said there was no alternative. Mandžić decided to risk it.

In New York, the fall of Srebrenica set off a flurry of activity. The UN Security Council convened, and France was the primary proponent of a draft resolution that condemned the attack, demanded that the Serbs withdraw and authorized the Secretary General to use "all means at his disposal"—including force—to restore the safe area.

During a briefing the Security Council was told that a Serb force "of approximately 1,000 to 1,500 troops with more than

20 armored vehicles" attacked the Dutch blocking position at 10:30 a.m. local time. Two Serbs tanks were destroyed by the NATO air attack, but a "flanking operation" allowed the Serbs to enter the town. Reports from UN headquarters in Zagreb had exaggerated the size of the attack and the Dutch effort to defend the safe area.[33]

In Washington, President Clinton's foreign policy advisers, who were already meeting to prepare the announcement on rees-tablishing diplomatic relations with Vietnam, briefly discussed Bosnia. The meeting was chaired by National Security Adviser Anthony Lake, and included Secretary of State Warren Christopher, Secretary of Defense William Perry, Chairman of the Joint Chiefs of Staff John Shalikashvili and CIA director John Deutch. The prospect of U.S. ground troops being sent to Bosnia had suddenly moved one giant step closer.

The immediate focus in Washington was on whether or not the Dutch would request that a NATO mission—led by American troops and attack helicopters—be sent to Srebrenica to pull out the peacekeepers. At a July 11 background briefing on the Vietnam announcement, National Security Adviser Lake refused to address the issue, saying it was a "fluid situation."[34] White House spokesman Mike McCurry also refused to answer whether a Dutch request for help in pulling out from Srebrenica would come under the terms of President Clinton's promise that U.S. troops would aid a UN withdrawal.

Senior State Department officials contacted the U.S. ambassador in Holland, K. Terry Dornbush, with a simple message. The American ambassador should encourage the Dutch to "hang tough" in Potočari and try not to leave the enclave before the refugees did. Clinton administration officials hoped the Dutch would not call for American marines on the USS *Kearsarge* cruising in the Adriatic to come rescue them. As always, the administration's top priority was keeping U.S. troops out of Bosnia.

In Bratunac, Colonel Karremans and Nesib Mandžić returned to the Hotel Fontana at 11:30 p.m. The Muslim high school director and the Dutch met with Mladić and seven or eight Serb military and civilian officials in the hotel's restaurant. This time, Mladić was more cordial. As Mandžić expected, he was quizzed to see whether he was a leader or soldier in the enclave during the war.

"What is your profession?" Mladić asked.

"I was director of the high school," Mandžić answered nervously.

"Where did you graduate?" Mladić asked.

"Sarajevo," Mandžić answered.

"Where were you born?" Mladić asked.

"Skelani," Mandžić answered, a town twenty miles southeast of Srebrenica that the Serbs held throughout the war.

Then Karremans spoke. He again explained the situation in Potočari. He asked for an immediate cease-fire and requested that humanitarian aid convoys be allowed to travel to the enclave.

"I need medicines, water supplies, food and fuel," Karremans said as Mladić took notes. "I have a hundred wounded."

At that point Mladić began a long monologue. He told Karremans and the representative of the refugees that all Muslim soldiers should surrender and turn their weapons over to the Bosnian Serb Army. "I have a clear message for the Muslim soldiers," Mladić said. "Survive or disappear."

Mladić agreed that a cease-fire would be in place until 10 a.m. the following day, when another meeting would be held, but he issued a warning. "I will shell the UN compound and the refugees if they do not stop air strikes," he said. "That will be our retaliation against the Dutch and the refugees."

The Serb general criticized Bosnian President Alija Izetbegović. "Izetbegović's troops killed many Serb civilians," Mladić said. "But I am not willing to use military power against women and children."

Mladić asked Karremans if he could bring Naser Orić to the next meeting. The Dutch colonel explained that Orić had not been seen in the enclave since April. Mladić then offered to provide medical treatment for the wounded and promised they would not be harmed and would be treated according to the Geneva Conventions.[35] He told Karremans again that he should return the next morning with a delegation from the refugees and, if possible, the town's civilian and military leaders.

The Serb commander repeated his threat to the Muslim soldiers. "If they keep their weapons, that will be their death," he said.

"In the end," Mladić said, "the fate of Srebrenica's Muslims lies in my hands."

As the Bosnian Serb general spoke, a macabre lottery was being held in Šušnjari. The enclave's leaders held a closed meeting to decide what route to take to Tuzla and which groups would march at the front of the column.

At midnight, Ramiz Bećirović briefly made contact via modem with the Bosnian Army's 2nd Corps in Tuzla before his batteries went dead. "We are leaving Srebrenica. The Chetniks took the city," Bećirović said. "The civilian population which is not able to fight is in the UNPROFOR base in Potočari and the other part of the population is headed for Tuzla."

"Is that the best decision?" a 2nd Corps officer asked.[36]

"We don't have any other choice," Bećirović typed. "We will go to Srebrenica—Udrč—Balkovica." The communication ended. Bećirović had hoped the 2nd Corps would have instructions about where to meet in Serb territory. He hoped an offensive would be launched from Tuzla. The sense of abandonment among Srebrenica's men deepened.

The 10,000 to 15,000 men gathered in Šušnjari's moonlit fields knew the stakes couldn't be any higher. Only one-third of them were armed. The first groups to leave would have the best chance of survival. The last ones would face Serb troops who could pick and choose when to ambush the Muslims they'd seen coming for days.

The enclave's leaders decided that they and their families would be near the front of the column. Men originally from Konjević Polje and Čerska, where the column was headed first, would be in the first scout group because they knew the terrain. The best unit in the enclave—Mido Salihović's—would march near the town's leaders and their families in the front and middle of the column. Arguably the most poorly equipped unit in the enclave—Ibro Dudić's, which failed to hold the lines in the south—was given the assignment of guarding the mostly civilian rear.

Bećirović later claimed that he initially proposed a counterattack against the Serbs, but no one was interested. He also says he proposed that half the men go to Žepa, whose mountainous terrain was almost impossible for the Serbs to conquer, but no one was willing to go. Everyone wanted to head for Tuzla. Many hoped the Serbs would open up a corridor and let them pass.

As the order of the column was announced, bitter arguments broke out. Earlier in the evening, the Dutch at OP Mike had watched as a Muslim officer killed two of his soldiers who had refused to let the Dutch leave and take the officer's wife and children to Potočari. It was clear that the least armed and least influential people in Srebrenica were being forced to walk at the rear of the column. But the men had no choice. A Serb minefield ringed Šušnjari. Dozens, possibly hundreds of soldiers were able to cross the minefield before the town fell, but hundreds of civilians were forced to wait in Šušnjari for the minefield to be cleared after Srebrenica fell.

Clearing a path through the minefield proved far more difficult and time-consuming than expected. In the end, the path was only wide enough for one man to walk on. It would take hours for all 10,000 to 15,000 men to file out of the enclave. At midnight, the lead scouts in the column slipped out of the enclave. What would become known as the "Marathon of Death" had begun.

WEDNESDAY, JULY 12, 1995

COLUMN AND CONVOY ROUTES, JULY 12, 1995

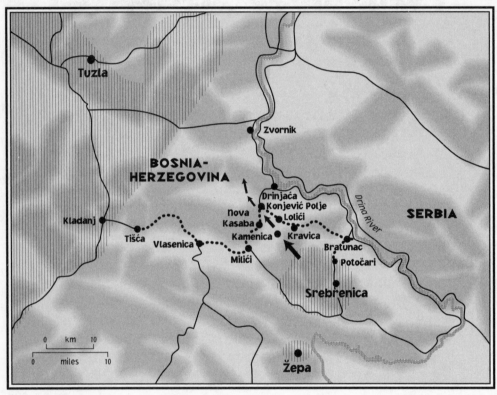

Tuzla

Zvornik

BOSNIA-
HERZEGOVINA

Kladanj

Tišća

Vlasenica

Milići

Nova
Kasaba

Kamenica

Drinjača
Konjević Polje
Lolići

Kravica

Drina River

SERBIA

Bratunac

Potočari

Srebrenica

Žepa

km

miles

Muslim- and Croat-controlled   Column of men   Convoy route, women and children

When Ćamila Omanović woke up, she was still lying in the parking lot. A few hours of fitful sleep had given her the luxury of thinking it was all a twisted dream, but the ground still smelled of vomit and excrement. Her bleary eyes surveyed the 20,000 wretched people clustered around her, and it hit her once again. Srebrenica had fallen.

At 8 a.m., three familiar faces appeared. They walked through the parking lot straight toward her. Zina Ćivić, a woman she knew from Srebrenica, Nesib Mandžić, the director of the local high school, and Ibro Nuhanović, a factory manager from the town of Vlasenica, greeted her. They asked her to join them as a representative of the refugees.

As members of her family held up a blanket around her, she changed out of her dirty sweat suit into the set of clean clothes she had packed yesterday—a blouse and skirt. She and the two male negotiators entered the battery factory and met with the Dutch. They asked for food, water, toilets and medical supplies for the civilians. No one was sure how many people were encamped around the base. The Dutch said there were 5,000 inside the base and 20,000 outside of it. Ćamila thought there were more. The response from the Dutch commanding officers was simple. We have nothing. Ask Mladić.

At 10 a.m., Ćamila and the two male representatives climbed into a Dutch jeep. For the last three years her world had been two miles long and half a mile wide. Afraid of shells and snipers, she had rarely ventured outside the town itself. As the jeep passed OP Papa and entered Serb territory, her stomach turned. There were several dozen of them—young and old, muscular and fat—clustered around four tanks and standing in trenches near the road. Bosnian Serb soldiers dressed in all kinds of camouflage uniforms glared at them. The jeep jerked to a halt at a Serb checkpoint.

Ćamila relaxed somewhat. The soldier walking toward the car was Milisav Gavrić. She and his wife had gone to high school together. But as he approached the car a dark look spread across his face. "Who are they?" Gavrić growled at the Dutch. When Gavrić looked at her there was nothing. No flicker of recognition swept across his face. One thing resonated from his squinting eyes and curled mouth: hatred.

They were allowed to pass. As they drove slowly north, she tried to concentrate on her speech to Mladić. The outside world she had not seen for three years flew by her window, but she barely noticed. She had to say the right things to Mladić.

They arrived at the entrance to the Hotel Fontana in the center of Bratunac. Ćamila and the two other negotiators got out of the jeep. Everyone seemed to be staring at them. They entered the front door and stepped into the lobby. Jelena Mušić, a Serb who was a friend of Ćamila and married before the war to a man who was half Muslim and half Gypsy, stood behind the reception desk. She stared at Ćamila as if she had never seen her before.

Ćamila's stomach tightened. She started to sweat. They entered the main dining room. She felt a wave of relief spread across her. Miroslav Deronjić, a Serb she went to high school with, was in a military uniform. He must have been a local commander. Just before the war, Deronjić had become active in the nationalist Serbian Democratic Party. She rushed toward him.

"Miroslav, my brother, if you have something human inside your body help us," she blurted out. "Can't you see there are thousands of people down there waiting and your people are still firing shells at them?"

Deronjić's face turned red. "Who are you?" a deep voice

interrupted her. Ćamila turned and nearly fainted. General Ratko Mladić, commander of the Bosnian Serb Army, stared down at her. According to Sarajevo TV, Mladić had overseen the expulsion of 300,000 Muslims and Croats from western Bosnia. His soldiers had killed thousands of civilians and raped hundreds of women. He had established the first concentration camps in Europe since World War II. Mladić could have her killed or raped, she thought, with a wave of his hand.

"Were you involved in politics?" he asked. He spoke slowly and deliberately.

"No. I've never been involved in politics," she stammered. "I'm the representative of the women and children."

Mladić's face was enormous. It was sunburned, covered with sweat and broader and flatter than any she had ever seen.

"Ma'am, where is your husband?" Mladić asked.

"He went through the woods," she answered. His speech and gestures were exaggerated. He reminded Ćamila of an actor.

"Tell your husband if he gives up his weapon he is free to go," Mladić said.

"My husband has never been a soldier and didn't have any weapons during the entire war," she said.

"Tell them to give up their weapons," Mladić said, "and they will be free to go."

"I have no contact with them," she answered.[1]

Mladić turned and swaggered into the dining room. A half dozen Serbs dressed in military and civilian clothes were gathered around a long table. Mandžić noticed that there were more Serb officials and officers present than the night before.

"Don't be afraid, just sit down. Everything will be OK. We're here to reach an agreement," Mladić said as they crossed the room. "No one will be missing a single hair from their head. You can choose where you want to be transported."

The three Muslim negotiators, Colonel Karremans and two Dutch officers sat down awkwardly across from the Serbs.[2] At the head of the table was Mladić. With a TV camera capturing his every move, he clearly relished the moment.

He introduced the men around him, local Serb military commanders and civilian officials. Finally, Ćamila, Ibro Nuhanović and Nesib Mandžić introduced themselves. It was clear this was their time to speak. Ćamila hesitated for a moment and then plunged forward in a faltering voice.

"I'm here for a thousand women and a thousand children to beg for help," she said with her voice trembling. "Because all of these people are helpless. They are afraid. They need help.

"Women and children are not responsible for what happened in the enclave over the last three years," she said. "We are all civilians. There are no soldiers or politicians among us."

Ibro Nuhanović then introduced himself. "Please don't blame the refugees," he said. "We need many things. We need medicine, food, water and other supplies.

"We and the Dutch were unable to contact anyone in the Bosnian government last night to ask for specific points for this meeting," he said. "We do not have any instructions."

Nesib Mandžić, who had met with the Serbs the night before, said nothing. Karremans and the two other Dutch officers were silent. Mladić began to speak.

"In 1992, Naser Orić's soldiers attacked many villages around Srebrenica. They killed many Serb soldiers, families and civilians. They devastated those villages," he said. "As soon as the safe havens were established in 1993, the fate of the people of Srebrenica was in Serb hands. It is again in Serb hands. It is too late for Sarajevo or the UN to help.

"There has been much misery over the last three years. The Muslim soldiers in the enclave have murdered many outside the enclave in raids in search of food, revenge and terror," Mladić continued. "This a great success, we've had great losses here. We had big losses in the villages along the Drina."

Miroslav Deronjić, Ćamila's schoolmate from before the war, suddenly spoke. "Do you know that seventeen people in my family were killed?" he said. "I'm going to get revenge for it. Whoever was responsible will pay."

With one glance, Mladić silenced him. The general continued with his monologue.

"I am willing to assist the refugees, but I need the help of local civilian and military leaders," he said. "Anyone who wants to stay in Srebrenica can stay or they can be evacuated to Serbia, to Muslim territory around Tuzla or even to foreign countries.

"The Muslim soldiers have a choice: survive or disappear. The ones who are guilty of crimes will answer for it. Whoever gives up their arms will be untouched," he said. "The fighting should stop. I cannot assist the refugees as long as the attacks continue. The Muslim soldiers can even hand over their weapons in the presence of UNPROFOR. I am willing to assist in the evacuation."

The tone of his voice softened. "Life used to be good around Srebrenica. I'd like to have that same situation—the good life before 1992—back again. I do not like what happened in 1992 and 1993. I am a professional soldier. I take no joy in killing either civilians or soldiers. I will help you," he said, turning to Ćamila and the two other representatives. "You should think over how best we can assist you in the evacuation. What are your basic needs? What do the refugees need in terms of food, water and medicines. How many refugees are there?"

"About twenty-five thousand," Mandžić answered. "Most of the refugees would like to go to Tuzla and be with their families."

He turned to Karremans. "I will need diesel oil for the evacuation."

Mladić, whose soldiers had not allowed a UN convoy carrying diesel oil to enter the enclave in five months, knew exactly how much fuel the Dutch had. "I have no diesel oil to give you," Karremans said meekly.[3]

"Then my soldiers will provide an escort during the evacuation," Mladić said.

"If there is going to be an evacuation, then my battalion should escort it," Karremans protested. "I can put one Dutch soldier on every vehicle."[4]

"No one will be forced to be evacuated," Mladić said, again looking at the Muslim representatives. "But on the other hand, if NATO attacks anywhere else in Bosnia I will be forced to use my weaponry."

It was the third time in three meetings that Mladić had

threatened to shell the Dutch compound and the refugees. As Mladić spoke, many of the Serb units involved in the attack on Srebrenica were pushing south. The safe area of Žepa appeared to be Mladić's next target. The long-term analysis produced by the UN intelligence unit in Sarajevo in March was proving prophetic.

The Bosnian Serb leadership had apparently[5] decided to bring the war to a spectacular conclusion that summer. The Muslims were only growing stronger with time, so Serb tanks would have to sweep through eastern Bosnia and eliminate Srebrenica, Žepa and Goražde. The Bosnian Serbs would finally complete their central goal from the outset of the war. After expelling hundreds of thousands of Muslims and Croats and creating an "ethnically pure" strip of Serb-only territory in western Bosnia in 1992, they would finally complete the process in eastern Bosnia in 1995. Once they took the three Muslim enclaves, the Serbs would have a de facto Serb-only state that stretched from eastern to western Bosnia. They could negotiate from a position of strength in the fall, and Bosnia could finally be partitioned into a Serb half and a Muslim-Croat half.

Only massive NATO air strikes, could stop them, but with the fall of Srebrenica, the number of cards Mladić held had mushroomed spectacularly. He now had 430 Dutch peacekeepers and 25,000 Muslims he could threaten to kill if NATO planes bombed his troops.

"Have you contacted any of the soldiers I mentioned to you last night?" Mladić asked, apparently referring to Orić or Srebrenica's commanders.[6]

"There are no BiH soldiers available at the moment," Karremans said, referring to the Muslims. "We are unable to look for them because we are surrounded in the same very, very small area as the refugees. We have lost our eyes and our ears in the rest of the enclave. We cannot find the military leaders."

Mladić turned to the representatives. "They have twenty-four hours to hand over their weapons. If they continue to fight, they will never be able to break through. There are eight rings of my soldiers around the enclave,"[7] Mladić said. "Even young soldiers can turn in their weapons and they will be free to go where they want. I will provide the transportation for them."

Then he turned back to the subject of evacuation. "If I am able to assist, I would prefer to help the wounded first, then the elderly, then the women with small children, then the rest of the refugees," he said. "You should make a list of the neediest. Transportation will start as soon as possible. I'll provide it. No one will be hurt. Coordination with UNPROFOR is one of my priorities."

"Can you make it humane transportation?" Ćamila asked. "Five babies were killed when people climbed on the trucks from Srebrenica to Potočari."[8]

"You will be given food, water and decent transportation," Mladić replied. "It won't be luxury buses, but it will be decent transportation."

The Serb general paused. He seemed to relish the moment. "Allah can't help you now," he said slowly. "But Mladić can."

The men walking in front of and behind Mevludin Orić stood out on the green hillside. Slowly climbing a treeless slope, the civilians in their white, blue and brown clothes could be seen a mile away.

As the meeting slowly progressed in Bratunac, Mevludin and the men of Lehovići were finally beginning the trek to Tuzla. For twelve hours, they had waited for their chance to cross the front line. They were one of the last groups in the single-file column, which by now was more than five miles long.

They walked in silence. Mevludin had watched as the enclave's best-armed soldiers departed first with the town's leaders. No speeches were given; they just disappeared. From what he could see, only every third man was armed. Mevludin himself had a single hand grenade. Forty miles of hostile territory lay between them and Muslim-held central Bosnia.

The Serbs had taunted them when they crossed the front line that morning. "Hurry up!" a Serb shouted with glee. "Hurry up!" Mevludin was convinced they were waiting for the right moment to ambush them. Tracking the Muslims was easy. The hills of eastern Bosnia were relatively open. Centuries of farming and sheep herding had created hundreds of open pastures and fields. There were few continuous stretches of dense forest in which to hide. Even at the height of summer, when the trees were thick with leaves, as much as 20 percent of the territory between Srebrenica and Tuzla was dangerously open.

Mevludin, dressed in fatigues that gave him some cover, knew the civilians made him more vulnerable, but he didn't care. The entire male population of his village marched together. There were forty-five of them in all. Farmers, carpenters and factory workers. Forty-one of them were fathers. Four were teenagers.

Mevludin, his father and his half brother Dašan, forty-three, walked together. Dašan had been born from his father's first marriage and he and Mevludin were close. Each family faced a dilemma. If they walked together, one shell could wipe out every male member of a bloodline. After a few miles, Mevludin let his father and Dašan drift away. He thought it was better if they walked in separate groups.

Haris Hasanović, Mevludin's twenty-four-year-old first cousin and best friend, was the only man in the group with an assault rifle. He walked with his father and brother.[9] Nearly everyone in the isolated village of twenty-five houses was related to each other. Hasanović was by far the most common last name.

The different branches of the Hasanović clan walked in clusters. Osman Hasanović, fifty-four, was a former Yugoslav National Army officer. His brother Ismet, fifty-two, was a construction worker. Their younger brother, Nusret, was forty-three and worked in the car battery factory in Potočari. Ismet's son Jusuf, eighteen, also trudged along.[10]

Several pairs of fathers and sons dotted the column. Fifty-nine-year-old Edhem Hasanović walked with his sixteen-year-old son, Haso. Fifty-six-year-old Sevko Hasanović walked with his twenty-five-year-old son, Sefik. Redzep Hasanović, the tallest man in the village by a foot, loped along in long strides. His three teenage children were all already over six feet tall. A basketball hoop with a grass court sat next to his house in Leho-vići.[11]

The terrain was cruel. Endless hills and valleys ate away at a man's strength. They had enough food for one day, but it was a six-day journey. The plan was to walk during the night and sleep during the day, but they were already behind schedule. The rhythmic sound of mortars firing and detonating echoed across the hills. Occasionally, bursts of gunfire whistled over their heads.

Mevludin thought of his wife, Hadzira, his mother and two daughters. They were all in Potočari by now. "Not a single woman or child will survive Potočari!" a Serb had shouted from a bunker that morning. He didn't trust the Dutch cowards to protect them. During the war, Mevludin had been intensely proud of being Naser Orić's distant cousin. Now he prayed that his family and friends would not utter their name. One word had gone from a rallying cry to a death sentence in Srebrenica: Orić.

After comparing himself to Allah, Mladić assured the Muslims and the Dutch in the Hotel Fontana that his men would harm no one.

"I give you my word," Mladić said. "Do not panic, do not be afraid. Please give that message to all of the refugees."

Mladić proposed that they be bused to Kladanj, a Muslim-held town on the border between Bosnian Muslim and Bosnian Serb territory. The "evacuations" would begin in a few hours. He again issued his warning that Muslim soldiers had to surrender their weapons within twenty-four hours.

"It is better to live than die," Mladić said. The Serb general then lapsed into another speech.

"I knew everything that went on in the enclave. I knew everything that happened day by day," he said, repeating a claim he had made in the meetings the night before. "I had people in the enclave who were informing me of everything that happened. I was well aware what was going on."

Mladić glanced at one of the Serb soldiers. He disappeared
into a side room and quickly returned. The soldier carried a
book and a sign that read "Municipality of Srebrenica." The
sign had been on the front of the town hall. It had a blue coat
of arms with six white fleurs-de-lis on it—the symbol of the
Muslim-led government in Sarajevo. Mladić was showing off his
trophies.

"Yesterday I entered Srebrenica," Mladić said. He opened the
book. It was some kind of municipal log. "The last wedding in
Srebrenica was on June 29," he noted. He read the names of the
last two people married in the enclave and smiled. "You see, I
know everything about you."

He went on. "I'm pleased we conquered Srebrenica. Many
Serb soldiers have been killed here and it was a great honor for
me to do it."[12]

A Bosnian Serb soldier entered the room to report that Muslim refugees from Potočari had walked to the soccer stadium in
Serb-held Bratunac. The Muslim representatives knew it was impossible for Muslim civilians to have crossed the front line. The
soldier was simply creating an excuse to pull Mladić out of the
meeting.

It was 1 p.m. Mladić turned to Ćamila. "You are a fine
woman," he said. "You have been frank in your statements to
me."

He said nothing to the two male representatives and stated
his warning to the Muslim soldiers one more time. He was fixated on them. "I urge you to contact the Muslim soldiers," he
said, "and convince them to hand over their weapons within
twenty-four hours."

As they left the hotel, Mladić spoke to Ćamila again. "If
you're afraid, you should bring your family here. You'll be the
last ones to be transported," he said. "You can stay here with
me. I will guarantee your security."

Ćamila declined. "Whatever happens to the twenty-five thousand people," she said, "can happen to me."

• • •

While Mladić met with the Dutch officers and Muslim representatives in Bratunac, the daily briefing was held in Zagreb.[13]

Akashi was concerned that the UN was being blamed for the
lack of NATO Close Air Support. "There's criticism of our CAS
as too late and too little, but the Dutch put up a strong defense.
It was very admirable," he added. "When the Dutch Minister of
Defense asked that air actions be suspended because of threats
against his soldiers who were held captive, we had no choice."

The Dutch Ministry of Defense had launched what would
become an extremely effective public relations effort. Colonel
Karremans had repeatedly requested Close Air Support, the
Dutch stated, but it was denied by his superiors. The Dutch Ministry of Defense made no mention of the fact that a Dutch general—General Nicolai in Sarajevo—had turned down three of
the four CAS requests. The mistakes made by the Dutch chain
of command—ranging from using the wrong forms to errone-
ously promising massive air strikes that were never discussed in
Zagreb—were never aired.

"There is a very good military argument for stopping CAS,"
Janvier said. It was inappropriate to use force "when units were
so close to each other. It made it impossible to continue CAS."

"I don't know that we saw any lucrative targets that we
could have attacked, except for two tanks," Akashi's special assistant, John Almstrom, continued in the same vein. "Airpower
is not at all effective against infantry."

Air Commodore Mike Rudd, the British NATO liaison, interrupted. "I spoke to Admiral Smith. He doesn't want to debate. He's been repeatedly asked why CAS was so late. He said
he only sends airplanes when asked," Rudd said. "But if we do
get into a debate, he said CAS was too late, there were targets
and it could have worked."

"I would totally contest this approach," Janvier retorted.[14]

Later that day, Akashi would send a cable and sample letter
to the UN in New York criticizing the French Security Council
resolution calling for the UN to use force to retake the safe area.
Akashi said the resolution raised "unrealistic expectations" and
it "blurs the lines" between neutral "peacekeeping" and taking

sides or "peace enforcement." The Rapid Reaction Force's Anglo-French multinational brigade would be operational in three days but was not "strong enough to reach Srebrenica and resolve the situation" and was "more likely to compound than solve the problem."[15]

In the Zagreb meeting, Akashi partially blamed the Bosnian government for the situation. "We must remember that the BH arms, trains and equips troops in safe areas and launches attacks out of them," Akashi said, "which is a provocation to the Serbs."

Tomiko Ichikawa, an aide who almost never spoke at meetings, challenged her superior, Akashi. She pointed out that the Bosnian government had promised to demilitarize the safe areas if the UN would defend them. The six-month report on the mission Zagreb submitted to the Security Council in May had said the demilitarization of Srebrenica was a model even if everyone knew it wasn't complete.[16] "Srebrenica has very strong symbolic value," she warned. "We're likely to have a very strong reaction from the international community."

"It would help," Akashi said, "if we had some TV pictures showing the Dutch feeding refugees."

At approximately 1 p.m. in Potočari, Dutch lieutenant Eelco Koster heard what sounded like a tank or APC engine roaring from the direction of Bratunac. He received a message over the radio that a Serb tank and APC were driving south toward the Dutch base. Klaver tensed. Most of the Muslim refugees around him panicked, moved away from the road and hid inside the abandoned factories.

A few minutes later, twenty to thirty Serbs appeared on the road coming from the direction of Potočari. The Serbs swaggered and radiated confidence, casually approaching the Dutch in groups of three or four. Kalashnikov assault rifles were in their hands, strips of bullets crisscrossed their chests and hand grenades hung from their shirt pockets. But their uniforms were mismatched. Some of them were wearing stolen Dutch Army pants, green Dutch Army T-shirts, blue UN T-shirts.

Koster's orders were contradictory. The Dutch were not to cooperate with the Serbs but not do anything that might lead to a confrontation. Koster, who was armed with an Uzi machine gun, was not to threaten the Serbs with his gun or handle it in a hostile way.

Karremans had filed a report to his superiors early that morning describing Tuesday night's meetings. Karremans said the Serbs had deployed "two guns, two tanks, three MLRs and one AA gun" within direct sight of the compound. "I am not able (a) to defend these people; (b) to defend my own battalion." Negotiations "at the highest level" is the only "way out."

Thousands of eyes inside and outside the Dutch base peered at the Serbs as they took the last few strides toward the UN base. Aside from the wails of children and the buzzing of flies, silence hung over Potočari. The Dutch had strung a flimsy red-and-white plastic tape across the road. The Serbs reached the tape and abruptly stopped. One of them stepped forward.

"Where is your commanding officer?" he asked.

"I am," said Koster as he stepped forward. The twenty-six-year-old officer was short by Dutch standards, just under six feet, but the Uzi machine gun was slung over his shoulder.

A Serb officer stepped forward and the two men introduced themselves.[17] Koster asked what the Serbs were going to do. The officer gave him a vague answer and walked back to his men.

The Serbs moved to the edges of the road and shouted questions at the Muslims. "Where is Naser now?" they taunted. "Look what he has done to you." Some Serbs sat down in the middle of the road and started singing Serb nationalist songs. Koster saw a group of Serb soldiers enter a gutted house whose walls had been blown out by shells. When they reached the second floor, the Serbs set up a .50 caliber machine gun. It was aimed directly at the Dutch.

From every direction, Serb soldiers closed in on the UN compound. Koster ordered his men to follow any Serbs that entered the crowd of refugees. Groups of Serbs dressed in matching uniforms moved slowly through the houses and fields around the UN base. Each group seemed to have a commanding officer. The better-organized Serbs, whom the Dutch thought must be combat troops or soldiers from neighboring Serbia, shouted signals and covered each other as they methodically searched houses room by room.[18]

In the factories, the Serbs started stealing CDs, personal possessions and other equipment from the Dutch. At the southern end of the crowd of refugees, Bosnian translator Vahid Hodžić and Private Marc Klaver waited anxiously. Small groups of Bosnian Serb soldiers were approaching their position from the south. Hodžić, Klaver, Captain Groen and twenty other Dutch had spent a sleepless night in and around four APCs parked a half mile south of the Dutch base. All night and morning, women and elderly men had begged Hodžić to tell them what was going to happen. He and the Dutch had no answers.

Eager not to provoke the Serbs, Groen and the officers had decided to disarm all of the Dutch and put all of the peacekeepers' weapons in one APC. The .50 caliber machine guns on their APCs were turned away from the Serbs.

As they closed in, Hodžić was petrified; Klaver was calm. His experience at OP Foxtrot had hardened him. Hodžić was struck by the fact the Serbs looked too clean, as if they weren't coming from battle. Klaver thought they looked less professional than the Serbs he had seen at OP Foxtrot. Neither thought they looked like combat troops—more like reservists on their way to being filmed in a movie.

"Good day," one of the Serbs said casually. Hodžić began frantically translating.

"Good day," said one of the Dutch officers.[19] Groen had gone inside the Dutch base just before the Serbs appeared.

"Would you like some brandy?" the Serb said, taking a flask from his pocket. The offer was customary in Bosnia. Some of the Dutch took a sip. The Serbs opened their backpacks and pulled out packs of cigarettes which they offered to the Dutch.

Other Serbs were mingling with the crowd. Klaver saw one Muslim woman hug a Serb she apparently knew from before the war. Hodžić heard some of the women ask if they could go get water. The July heat was stifling.

"Of course you can, of course you can," one of the Serbs said. "Don't suffer."

"Do you need anything?" a second Serb asked. "Do you need any food? Do you need any water?"

Hodžić thought they acted as if they'd controlled the area for centuries. He was sure the Serbs had orders to treat the people well at first.

Major Nicolić, the Serb commander in Bratunac, arrived at the northern tip of the crowd. He told Koster he wanted to inspect the crowd and walk through it to the other Dutch position. He refused to tell Koster what the Serbs' intentions were. "Just wait and see," he said. Escorted by a Dutch liaison officer and a UN Military Observer, Nicolić made his way through the refugees. Koster complained to Nicolić about the Serbs stealing things from the Dutch. Nicolić acted as if he was angry, said he would do something about it and departed for Bratunac.

Just after Nicolić left, the Dutch positioned in the factories radioed Koster. The Serbs were rounding up the men in the crowd. The Serbs were interested in one man especially—a gray-haired man in his forties who said he worked as a cook for Médecins Sans Frontières. The Serbs said he was an old Muslim fighter.

Koster and the liaison officer complained to the Serb officer standing near their position. "We want to take them away for further questioning," the Serb said. Koster and the liaison officer said no. The group of Muslim men were allowed to sit down and were guarded by the Dutch. The man who said he was a cook for Médecins Sans Frontières was allowed to enter the Dutch base. His name was Abdulah. He was Ćamila Omanović's brother.

At the southern end of the crowd, Vahid Hodžić was startled when one of the Serbs started shouting at him.

"You," a tall, burly Serb said, and pointed at Hodžić. "Come here."

"Just me?" the translator replied.

"Yes."

Vahid walked over to the man slowly. He was standing with three other Serb soldiers. Worried that Hodžić might be taken prisoner by the Serbs because he was a male in his twenties,

Captain Groen had offered him a full Dutch uniform the night before. Hodžić had put the uniform on and then panicked. If he was ever discovered he would be shot on the spot. He took it off quickly, saying, "I'll be what I am. Maybe it's better." That afternoon, he looked like any American or European teenager. His dirty-blond hair was longer than the Dutch crew cuts and he was dressed in Levi's jeans, a green U.S. Army surplus T-shirt and stylish purple-and-white Adidas running shoes the Dutch peacekeepers had given him.

As Hodžić walked toward the Serbs, the tall, burly one who had shouted at him stared.

"Do you know me?" the Serb officer asked.

The man looked vaguely familiar. He was a local teacher who worked in Hodžić's vocational high school in Bratunac before the war. Hodžić remembered that his name was Josipović. He thought his first name was Želko. Hodžić had studied traffic engineering and never had him as a teacher, but he remembered Josipović constantly telling the kids to be quiet. Hodžić had graduated from high school in 1988. He could not believe that the man remembered him seven years later.

A Serb soldier walked up to his old teacher and called him "Vojvoda," a term from the World War I era that meant "Duke." The Kingdom of Yugoslavia was dominated then by Serbs, and nationalists talked longingly of re-creating it.

Hodžić's old teacher asked the soldier if he had anything to report. "Nothing," the soldier replied. "Everything is under control." His teacher seemed to have become some kind of high-ranking military official. He barked some orders into a walkie-talkie and turned again to Hodžić.

"Where are your soldiers?" he snapped.

"You know! You know! Tell us!" one of the Serb soldiers insisted.

"I don't know," Hodžić replied.

"You know everything," his former teacher said. "Where did you learn English?"

Hodžić said he had studied it in college before the war. His teacher seemed to lose interest and wandered off, but one of the young Serb soldiers started berating Hodžić.

"You see, your Alija, look what he's done for you," the soldier said, referring to Bosnian President Alija Izetbegović. "You're living in the eighteenth century, not the twentieth." He was wearing running shoes with his military uniform and said he had just come from fighting in Ilidza, a Serb-held neighborhood in Sarajevo.

"If I was told of the misery here I wouldn't believe it. He made you very happy," the soldier quipped. "Do you know what massacres your people are involved in with the Croats? Do you know what happened in western Slavonia? Do you know what crimes they have committed?"

Serb nationalists seized control of western Slavonia, a region of neighboring Croatia, after Croatia declared independence in 1991. Like Serbs in Bosnia, Serbs in Croatia had captured chunks of the country, declared their own state and hoped to eventually link it with Serbia to create a "Greater Serbia." But the Croatian Army had retaken western Slavonia in a lightning strike on May 1. It had been the first major defeat for Serbs in Bosnia or Croatia since Yugoslavia disintegrated. Western Slavonia was one of four Serb-held regions of Croatia the UN dubbed "protected areas" as part of a 1992 cease-fire agreement. Though this was as misleading a concept as the "safe areas" in Bosnia, the Serbs were furious when the UN failed to defend the western Slavonia "protected area."

"I don't know," Hodžić answered. "I have been here for four years. I just want to leave."

"I know," the soldier said. "But I just came from there and saw what you've done."

The soldier looked at the horde of women and children spread out in front of them. He turned to Hodžić. "Who should I let live?" he said. The soldier shrugged his shoulders and walked away. Hodžić was speechless.

Only one Serb soldier remained. He had dark hair and was the same size as Hodžić—five feet ten with a medium build.

"How long have you been working with the Dutch?" the soldier asked.

"From the beginning," Hodžić answered. He was lying. He had fought in the army in 1992 and 1993.

"Stick to them. Try to get out with them," the Serb soldier said. "Fuck Bosnia. Fuck these hills." Hodžić was surprised.

"There was nothing you could do. The world has allowed us to do this," the soldier said. "Tomorrow they will allow us to do the same in Žepa."

"They allowed the Muslims to do the same around Sarajevo," he said, referring to the failed Muslim offensive to break the siege of Sarajevo. "Who is to blame when they are not able to scratch our lines even though UNPROFOR is helping them with artillery?

"If I could, I would go anywhere," the Serb soldier said. "I wouldn't stay here. There's no future here."

Hodžić noticed that they were both in their mid-twenties. They could've been classmates before the war. "If I can leave, I will. It depends on whether they want to take me," he said. "I've been waiting for four years to get out of this hell."

"Don't be afraid," the soldier said. "If you did something wrong, perhaps you wouldn't be here."

"Of course I didn't," Hodžić said. "But how can I prove it?"

"Don't be afraid," the soldier repeated. He walked away and joined the other Serb soldiers. Hodžić returned to the Dutch. They saw that the young translator was shaken. Captain Groen, who had gone into the base just before the Serbs arrived, had returned. He offered him a cracker from their combat rations.

"What did they say?" Groen asked.

Hodžić repeated what the Serb had told him. He told Groen the Serb soldier had motioned toward the refugees and asked whom he should let live.

A strange look spread across Groen's face. He was known among the Dutch peacekeepers and Bosnian workers as an extremely strict, almost machinelike officer. Hodžić had worked with him for six months and never seen him show emotion or weakness.

All at once, it was hitting the thirty-two-year-old Dutch officer. Captain Jelte Groen realized he was powerless. The Serbs had overrun the safe areas. On a whim, the Serbs could kill his soldiers and the women and children they were supposed to protect. All of the work, all of the by-the-book procedures, all of the effort to stay neutral, Raviv van Renssen's death—all of it was for nothing.[20] A look of frustration and fear Hodžić had never seen before spread across Groen's chiseled face. The usually domineering captain realized he was at the mercy of the Serbs.

While other Serb soldiers encircled the Dutch base, Bosnian Serb police officer Zoran Radić triumphantly returned to his hometown. He was satisfied. The war was over for at least this part of the country.

Radić was still astounded by the fact that Srebrenica had fallen. A joke was spreading among the Serb soldiers. The key to their easy victory was a statement allegedly made by Bosnian President Alija Izetbegović on Bosnian radio before the town fell. Izetbegović had said 40,000 Serbs were attacking Srebrenica and demanded NATO bombing. Radić and his friends joked that Alija's statement had frightened Srebrenica's Muslims so much that they had turned and run.[21]

The sight of the town saddened him. His high school had no windows. The hospital he visited as a boy had been hit by an artillery shell. Sixty percent of the Hotel Domavija, the resort he'd always dreamed of running, was gutted. Srebrenica was in ruins.

He and his squad had left Serb-occupied Skelani early that morning. The road they had taken into Srebrenica ran through Obadi—Radić's home village. As a teenager, he had used the road hundreds of times to go to school, the movies and sporting events in Srebrenica. That morning, he crept along it, convinced that Muslim fundamentalists were waiting to ambush him.

The town itself was a grim caricature of the community he had grown up in. Buildings and houses were pockmarked from shells and bullets. Enormous piles of wood filled every yard, garbage rotted in the streets and fumes from the backed-up sewage system hung in the air. Serb soldiers told him they found rats, cockroaches and lice in the houses. I'd rather surrender, Radić thought, than live like this.

...

When Ćamila Omanović returned to Potočari with the other two representatives and saw Serb soldiers already around the UN base, she panicked. She wondered if the Serbs had gotten to her son, daughter, grandson and aunt. Ibro Nuhanović and Nesib Mandžić stayed inside the base to try to contact Sarajevo. Ćamila went outside to compile a list of who should be evacuated first. She made a beeline for her children and found them in the parking lot. They had worried about her, but were fine.

At approximately 3 p.m., a Serb officer approached Lieutenant Koster. "There's a truck coming with bread for the people," he said. "You should make room." Marc Klaver and several other peacekeepers from the back of the crowd were brought forward to help control the refugees.

A small truck driven by civilians as well as several jeeps and cars materialized. As the truck backed into position, a television camera crew emerged from one of the cars. The Serb soldiers threw bread to the people, and the TV crew then captured the scene on video. The truck drove off.

The soldiers smiled for the cameras, but muttered "dirty pigs" as the Muslims lunged and fought each other to catch a loaf of bread.[22] Bread was also handed to the Dutch, their first in two months. The peacekeepers tore into it like savages. Klaver was disappointed to see Muslims taking four or five loaves for themselves and sharing them with no one.

A few minutes later, the truck reappeared, bringing another load of bread, which was given to the refugees. When a fire truck arrived, women were allowed to come forward and fill their jugs one by one. The Serb TV crew recorded it all, and departed.

Serb jeeps continued to shuttle back and forth between Bratunac and Potočari. Koster recognized one of them—a Mercedes the Serbs had stolen from the Dutch. At around 4 p.m., more jeeps and cars arrived in front of the Dutch base. "I think I see Mladić," Koster's translator said. The Dutch lieutenant radioed Major Franken. Koster's orders were not to cooperate with the Serbs and also not to do anything that might incite violence. One of the battalion's liaison officers was sent outside to deal with the Serb general.

The barrel-chested Serb general walked straight toward the Dutch and the crowd of refugees behind them. A Serb interpreter and several massive, heavily armed bodyguards hovered around him.

"Who is the commanding officer?" Mladić asked the UN interpreter.

"I am," Koster answered. The liaison officer hadn't arrived yet. Koster and Mladić introduced themselves to each other.

"What's going on?" Koster asked. "What do you want to do?"

"I want to speak to the people," Mladić said.

"You have to speak with Colonel Karremans first," Koster replied.

"I'm not doing that. I'm going to talk to the people," Mladić said. He walked past Koster and headed toward the crowd. His bodyguards, his translator and the Serb TV camera crew followed him.

"You have to talk to Colonel Karremans," Koster protested, following the general.

"I'm in charge here," Mladić scoffed. "I don't have to do anything."

Mladić broke through the line of red-and-white ribbon and reached the wall of Dutch peacekeepers holding the crowd of Muslims back. The shoving immediately stopped. The refugees were dumbstruck—half terrified, half in shock—to see the infamous commander before them.

"There is no need to be frightened," Mladić shouted, and smiled. "You'll be taken to a safe place. Don't be afraid of any hostile actions by the Serbs."

As the cameras rolled, his men gave chocolate candies to children. Mladić played the doting grandfather.

"No one will be harmed. No one will be harmed," he repeated as he patted a young Muslim boy on the head. "You have nothing to fear. You will all be evacuated."

"Thank you," the bewildered refugees answered. "Thank you."

Mladić turned away from the crowd. Buses and trucks began to pull up. Koster had radioed Major Franken and was told to confront Mladić again.

"You must go speak with Colonel Karremans," Koster repeated.

"What is your rank?" Mladić asked.

"Lieutenant," Koster said.

Mladić smiled. He seemed amused. "You've done your best," he said in a patronizing tone. "I am in charge here. I'll decide what happens. I have my plans and I'm going to carry them out. It will be best for you if you cooperate."

"We will not cooperate in any way," Koster said. "You are not allowed to take the people away without our permission. What are you going to do?"

"We are going to take the refugees to a better location," Mladić said, clearly irritated. "Nothing is going to stop us." The general and his entourage walked away.

Koster tried to follow but one of Mladić's bodyguards pushed him aside. Koster pushed back, but the general was gone.[23] The Uzi machine gun still hung from Koster's shoulder. He thought firing it would only lead to a massacre of Dutch and civilians. He radioed the operations room inside the base, but Franken only reiterated his orders.

The buses and trucks turned around and parked in a long line.

"Why are the buses here?" one of the Dutch asked a Serb.

"We're going to take the people whether you're here or not," the Serb replied.

A group of Serb soldiers walked forward and pulled two or three Dutch out of the human wall that was holding back the crowd.

"Run! Run!" the Serbs shouted at the Muslims. "Run to the buses!"

About fifty Muslim women, children and elderly men tore through the opening in the Dutch wall. Marc Klaver, who was in the wall, didn't know what to do. Civilians rushed by. The Serbs grabbed two or three of the men. Koster was dumbfounded. There were fifty heavily armed Serbs and thirty mostly unarmed peacekeepers.

He radioed Major Franken again and was told to continue to refuse to cooperate, but to try to put men on each of the buses and trucks. Koster sent several soldiers to get on the buses. They quickly returned and said Serbs blocked them from entering. He radioed Franken, who said the Dutch would try to escort the buses in Mercedes jeeps.

The Serbs continued to allow groups of women, children and men through the wall. Klaver kept his arms linked with the peacekeepers next to him. The Muslims rushed toward the buses and trucks as the Serbs shouted insults at them. Koster saw the Serb soldiers wrest a teenage boy from his mother. He walked up to them.

"You can't take him away," Koster said.

"No?" one of the Serbs answered.

"I'm a lieutenant," Koster said.

The Serb let the boy go and shook his head, apparently puzzled by the fact that the Dutch officer cared. The situation was out of control. Other peacekeepers were being robbed of their helmets and flak jackets at gunpoint. The buses were gradually filling. The Serbs were leading the Muslim men away with little or no resistance. A deep wave of depression washed over Koster. The Serbs were arresting, taunting and expelling the people the Dutch were supposed to be safeguarding. Koster's deputy sat on the ground with his head in his hands. Their humiliation was complete.

Clutching their blankets and bags of food, Hurem Suljić, his wife, daughter, daughter-in-law and granddaughter fought their way to the front of the crowd. The crippled fifty-five-year-old and his family were eager to leave.

The family had finally arrived in Potočari at 11:30 p.m. the night before after being trapped in the long column of civilians fleeing the western half of the enclave. Even with Hurem riding Dorat, his horse, the journey had taken them three and a half hours. When they arrived, they asked people encamped outside the Dutch base why they weren't inside the UN compound. Refugees told them the Dutch weren't allowing people in. Exhausted and confused, they spent the night in an abandoned house.

Hurem lay on the floor of an overcrowded room. There were no candles and he knew few of the people lying around him in the darkness. The night had been cold and he had barely slept. He still believed the UN would order the Serbs to leave the enclave. He would be headed home the following day.

In the morning, a Muslim civilian had come to the house and said there were going to be rides to central Bosnia. "There will be no going home?" someone asked. No one was sure what to say. Hurem went to his horse and set it free. He and his family made their way to the asphalt road. They asked UN soldiers what was going to happen. The Dutch said they didn't know.

When word passed through the crowd that trucks and buses would be coming soon, Hurem and his family began fighting their way forward. They were too far back to hear Mladić's speech or see any of the bread being thrown. After two hours, they finally breached the front section of the crowd, but their view of the road was blocked. As the first convoy arrived, groups of Muslims flowed through the opening the Dutch created. The Suljić family inched forward.

Their opportunity came with the second convoy. The family squeezed through the narrow gap in the wall of peacekeepers and quickly headed for a bus. Suljić's limp was as glaring as ever. For each step, he had to stop and lock his right knee in place. As he passed the row of Serb soldiers, someone grabbed his arm. Suljić froze.

"Don't go that way," a Serb soldier said.

"I must follow my family," Suljić protested.

"No, go to the left," the soldier growled.

Trapped in the crowd, he hadn't seen the other men being taken away. If Suljić had known, he wouldn't have tried to get on a bus.

"Let's go!" the Serb shouted. "Let's go!"

Suljić hesitated.

"Back!" the soldier barked. "Back!"

Suljić gave in. His family would be leaving without him. He shouted "Good luck" to his wife, daughter, daughter-in-law and granddaughter. The women hesitated and then scurried onto a bus as the Serb soldier led him away.

"Just let me get a piece of bread," Suljić asked the Serb, referring to the food his family was carrying. The soldier was amused. He glanced at the other Serbs and quipped, "Look at him, he has the nerve to speak!" The soldier grabbed Suljić's arm again and warned him, "Don't say a word." Suljić silently hobbled toward the house with the other old men.

When he reached the house, the bags and blankets of other old men were already strewn across the grass. A soldier pointed his Kalashnikov assault rifle toward a doorway. "Get in the house!" he shouted. "Get in the house!" The entire ground floor of the house was one room. Roughly twenty-five by fifteen feet, it was packed with men. It reeked of body odor. Wrinkled faces peered at him in the darkness. Almost every man in the cramped, stifling room was over fifty or handicapped.

Hurem Suljić couldn't believe this was happening. He hadn't been in the army in thirty years. He could barely walk, let alone fight.

Inside one of the buses, Suljić's family was in a state of disbelief. Suljić's wife, like many other women on the bus, began to weep. She was sure she would never see her husband again. His six-year-old granddaughter, Merima, kept asking the women around her what had happened. "Grandpa stayed," she kept repeating, "Grandpa stayed."

Inside the Dutch base, Muslim negotiators Nesib Mandžić and Ibro Nuhanović confronted Major Franken. Colonel Karremans was incapacitated with diarrhea; Franken was the acting commander. The two negotiators complained about the men being separated. Franken said he was doing his best but the Serbs were in control.

The two negotiators then frantically tried to contact someone in the Bosnian government on one of the UN satellite telephones. After half an hour, they finally got through to the office of Bosnian Prime Minister Haris Silajdžić.

Silajdžić's assistant at first didn't believe Mandžić was actually calling from the fallen safe area. The Prime Minister got on the phone. Mandžić explained that the Serbs had arrived with buses and trucks and were taking the civilians away. The men were being separated from the women and the Dutch had no control over what was happening.

Silajdžić was supportive, but told Mandžić to speak with Hasan Muratović, the Bosnian government's minister for relations with the UN, who was in Silajdžić's office.[24]

"Stay there. Don't get on the buses," Muratović said. "If you get on the buses something horrible is going to happen. Stop the people."

"It's impossible," Mandžić said. "There's complete panic. Mladić and his soldiers have entered the UN base. They're among the refugees."

"England and France have agreed they will deliver an ultimatum to Mladić's units to get out of Srebrenica," Muratović said. "Or their joint air forces will attack."

Mandžić put the phone down and Ibro Nuhanović began speaking. Mandžić feared the worst. He also knew no planes were coming to Srebrenica.

Bored with standing at the back of the crowd of refugees, Lieutenant Leen van Duijn was given permission by Captain Groen to go to the front of the mob.[25] Van Duijn had been in the blocking position, and was a giant who stood at six feet seven inches tall. He had been directing refugees and patrolling the area around the UN base since they arrived the day before. He was eager to do something, to make order out of the chaos.

When he arrived at the front of the crowd, he found the Serbs barking orders at the Dutch and hurling insults at the Muslims. He asked the Dutch peacekeeper sitting by the side of the road whether he was going to do anything. He said he would, but after a few minutes van Duijn took matters into his own hands and asked a Serb officer what was going on. "We have two options," the Serb said. "The Muslims are going away. Two hundred buses will be here in twenty minutes. The Dutch can take care of the deportations, or we will take care of the deportations and do it our own way."

"We'll take care of it," van Duijn said. "We'll do it on our own terms. I have to talk to my commander." Van Duijn radioed Franken and told him he had "run his mouth" and agreed to coordinate the expulsions with the Serbs. Van Duijn felt it would be safer if the Dutch tried to deal with the crowd instead of the Serbs. Franken said he had heard that the Serbs had plans for transporting the refugees, but seemed surprised that the expulsions were beginning so quickly. He wished van Duijn good luck and promised to send some food and water to the peacekeepers.

It was over 90 degrees, and the heat was taking its toll on the crowd. The wounded and exhausted streamed into three tents that Médecins Sans Frontières was allowed to set up to perform triage and rehydrate those with heatstroke.[26] People suffering from nervous breakdowns and festering, untreated wounds continued to pour into the base hospital. The Dutch estimated that after providing the refugees with two meals that day and two meals the following day, their food reserves would be exhausted.[27]

Van Duijn spoke with a Serb captain who called himself "Mane"—a common nickname in Bosnia—who said he was the head of the military police unit overseeing the "evacuation." Captain Mane's translator called himself "Mickey"—slang in Serbo-Croatian for "pal." Both were obviously using false names. Van Duijn and Mane agreed that the Serb captain would call out the number of Muslims needed and the Dutch would then release them. The Serbs agreed to stay twenty yards behind the Dutch and the crowd.

But as the crowds passed through the row of Serb soldiers, Muslim men were separated from their families and led to a small house twenty yards from the road. "What are you going to do with those guys?" Van Duijn asked one of the Serbs.

"We're going to interrogate them and see if they are war criminals," one of the Serbs said. "We have a list with the names of war criminals."

Van Duijn reported this to the operations room in the base. "Can you see the men in the house?" the officer in the operations room asked.

"I can see them constantly," van Duijn answered.

"I'll report it to Major Franken," the officer said.

As the afternoon passed, van Duijn protested when he thought the men being taken away were too old or too young. Mane acted surprised, saying, "Why are you making such a big fuss?" But he would release each of the men van Duijn complained about. The Dutch peacekeeper was able to get seven or eight old men and young boys onto the buses, but the house steadily filled.[28]

In the wall of peacekeepers holding the refugees back, Klaver was shocked by how badly the Muslims smelled and how merciless they were to each other. Desperate women and old men viciously pushed and elbowed their way to the front of the crowd. He thought it was better for the Dutch to keep the Muslims under control so the Serbs wouldn't do anything rash.

The women wept as they watched the old men being led away, knowing what fate awaited their loved ones. Klaver didn't understand the words, but he saw their tears and knew they were begging him to save their husbands, fathers and sons. Some women kissed him, handed him deutsche marks or prayer cards, and thanked him as they departed. Others cursed him, spitting words in his face that he barely understood. "Chetnik!" was one name the idealistic peacekeeper understood well. But another name burned each time he was called it.

"Nazi."

In the Serbian capital of Belgrade, U.S. chargé d'affaires Rudolf Perina visited Serbian President Slobodan Milošević. The United States hoped that Milošević, who was paying the salaries of the Bosnian Serb officer corps and was widely believed to be supplying their weapons, could rein in Mladić and his troops.

Perina expressed the American concern for the plight of the Muslims in Srebrenica and urged Milošević to halt all military supplies to the Bosnian Serbs. He warned that the fall of Srebrenica was a serious blow to ongoing peace talks. Mladić had been seen repeatedly in Belgrade during the weeks leading up to the attack. But, as he had claimed so many times earlier in the war, the Serbian leader said he had no control over the situation. "Why blame me?" Milošević said. "I have been unable to contact Mladić."[29]

Forty miles west of Srebrenica, Lieutenant Vincent Egbers was relieved. The Serbs really were taking the Muslim civilians to central Bosnia. Egbers had driven one of the two UN jeeps that escorted the first convoy of refugees to Tišća—a Serb-held village four miles east of Muslim-occupied Kladanj.

Escorting the convoy had been chaotic. Egbers and a sergeant had packed their jeep with several days' worth of food and water. Their orders from Major Franken were to follow the buses wherever they went. As the convoy sped across Serb territory, the Dutch described over the radio the direction they were heading and the rivers and mountains they saw. Back in the operations room in Potočari, Dutch officers tried to track the convoy's route across their maps of eastern Bosnia.

Crowds of Serbs in Bratunac jeered the Muslims and threw stones at the bus, though no one was seriously hurt. One bus engine caught fire and Egbers and the sergeant stayed until it was repaired. A Serb cameraman who was filming the evacuation posed for a picture wearing Egbers' light blue UN beret. A second bus arrived; the passengers were transferred and the journey continued. An elderly woman died during the trip, but her death appeared to be due to exhaustion.

Egbers' orders were to make sure nothing happened to the women and children. But what the Dutch were supposed to do if the Serbs started harming people was unclear. Egbers was unarmed and the standing order to the peacekeepers was to "do what they thought was best" if the situation became dangerous.

In Tišća, a Serb major oversaw the evacuation. "OK," he told

the women as they got off the buses. "You can walk to freedom." The exhausted Muslim women were forced to walk four
miles to Muslim-held Kladanj.[30] Captain Voerman, who had rid-
den in the lead jeep, crossed with the first groups of refugees to
Muslim-held central Bosnia. Once Voerman was safely in central
Bosnia, he stayed there.

On the Muslim side, Bosnian government soldiers and UN
peacekeepers from Pakistan doled out food and water to the
traumatized women and children. The refugees were then bused
by the Muslim-led government to the gate of UN Sector Northeast headquarters in Tuzla—a sprawling former Yugoslav Air
Force base—and dumped there.

Thousands of refugees clustered in front of the gates of the
UN headquarters. Gradually they were registered by the UN
High Commissioner for Refugees staffers and other aid groups.
A massive tent city was frantically being erected on the air base's
main runway, a site that was within range of Serb artillery in
the nearby Majevica Hills.

The government, blaming the UN for the fall of the enclave,
said it was the UN's responsibility to care for the thousands of
refugees. But the air base lacked adequate shelter, water and
toilet facilities, and parts of it were still littered with mines left
by the retreating Yugoslav Army troops. Critics accused the Bosnian government of yet again using the people of Srebrenica as
cattle to make a political statement.

As the afternoon passed in Serb-held Tišća, Egbers was impressed by the efficiency and organization of the Bosnian Serbs.
In just a few hours, they produced dozens of trucks and buses.
The expulsion of the town's Muslims had obviously been well
planned. One Serb soldier later told a Dutch peacekeeper that
the Serbs had been ready to launch the offensive a week earlier,
but they had been waiting to gather enough vehicles. It appeared
that Serbia was providing its Serb brethren in Bosnia, who were
usually short on fuel, with significant amounts of diesel—if not
troops—to help conquer the safe area.

But as the day progressed, Egbers saw more convoys and
fewer peacekeepers. The Dutch arriving in Tišća reported that
convoys were being formed so quickly in Potočari that escorts

couldn't be organized fast enough. Any semblance of control the Dutch appeared to have was disappearing. After being delayed for several hours, a seven-vehicle medical convoy carrying 54 wounded was finally allowed to leave Potočari for Tišća at 6 p.m. Its only escort was a Dutch doctor and some nurses.

What happened to Egbers on his way back to Potočari at 6 p.m. disturbed him. The Serbs were deploying troops along the road from Bratunac to Konjević Polje. Serb soldiers had stopped Egbers along the route and demanded that the peacekeepers hand over the jeep. "I'm a first lieutenant," he said, pointing at the insignia on his shoulder. "No!" The Serbs backed off.

Around Konjević Polje itself, there were Serb soldiers with assault rifles and sleeping bags positioned every few yards along the road. Egbers wondered what was going on in the woods.

As the afternoon passed, the Serbs in Potočari gradually became more emboldened. At first, they would ask the Dutch if they were willing to trade their flak jackets, rifles or pistols for some Serb weapons or souvenirs. When the Dutch refused, the Serbs gave up.

By late afternoon, Serbs would simply walk up to the Dutch and point at the pistol or flak jacket they wanted. "This is a nice one. I need one," a soldier might say. Most Dutch who refused found an assault rifle pointed at their heads or chests.

The Dutch were still under orders to do nothing that might lead to an armed confrontation. Confronting or antagonizing the Serbs would only lead to Dutch peacekeepers or Muslim civilians getting killed. Major Franken eventually ordered peacekeepers who left the Dutch compound to keep their weapons and flak jackets on the base.

As the Muslim men were rounded up, they were taunted shamelessly. "Fuck your Turk mothers!" the Serbs shouted at the refugees. "Where is your Naser now? Naser fucks your mother up the ass!" The Muslims were blamed for their own suffering. A young Muslim boy who had a bullet wound in his mouth was told, "Do you see where they have brought you? And now they are even shooting you," a Serb soldier said, suggesting the Muslims had shot the boy for propaganda reasons. "What would they do if these children were ours?"[31]

Women were ridiculed. One Serb soldier saw a Muslim woman walking with two children. "Where are your children?" he asked her.

"With me," she answered.

"Only two? You don't have five of them?" the soldier said sarcastically. "I cannot believe my eyes."

The slurs and the obsession with birth rates were nothing new. The notion that there were too many Muslims in Bosnia was at the core of the Serb nationalist thinking. Srebrenica and all of eastern Bosnia was Serb land even though the majority of the prewar population was Muslim. According to Serb nationalist propaganda, the Muslims followed secret instructions from the Koran and their imams—or priests—to have as many children as possible as a way to spread Islam. The Muslim majorities in Srebrenica and eastern Bosnia were temporary abnormalities created by a high Muslim birth rate. If all Muslims weren't expelled, over time the Muslims would outbreed the Serbs and become the majority again. Most of Bosnia's large landowners were Muslims, another source of resentment for the Serbs.

By castigating Srebrenica's Muslims as "Turks," the Serbs were referring to the brutal 500-year rule of the Ottoman Turks over Bosnia and Serbia which ended only in 1918. Bosnia's Muslims were descendants of Slavs who converted to Islam under Turkish rule—people whom the Serbs viewed as traitors. The Turks rewarded those who converted.

Some Serb nationalists saw themselves as the latest generation of Serbs defending themselves and Europe from the Islamic horde—a recurring image in Serb mythology. Before the defeat that ushered in the 500 years of Turkish rule—the Battle of Kosovo in 1389—the Serbian epic hero Miloš Obilić told his vastly outnumbered knights, "If all of us were turned into salt there wouldn't be enough to season a Turkish dinner."[32]

During World War II, eastern Bosnia and the area around Srebrenica and Žepa suffered some of the most brutal fighting of the conflict.[33] The book Bosnian Serb police officer Zoran Radić had read, *Bloody Hands of Islam,* inaccurately stated that all Muslims fought with the Nazis and portrayed the Serb nationalist Chetniks as the war's victims. The activities of the "Handjar Division," an all-Muslim unit that fought with the Nazis and was alleged to have killed hundreds of Serb civilians, were detailed.[34]

For fifty years, Tito's slogan of "Brotherhood and Unity" and state-controlled media buried the old stereotypes and resentments. But as soon as fighting flared in 1993, the stereotypes became truth and old rumors were concrete atrocities that cried out for revenge. For two years, the Serbs had listened to exaggerated stories of atrocities committed by Naser Orić and his men, who adopted an eye-for-an-eye strategy with the Serbs. If a Muslim village was burned, a Serb village was burned. If a Muslim civilian was killed, a Serb civilian was killed. Serbs estimated that 2,000 Serbs—mostly soldiers but also several hundred civilians[35]—had died around Srebrenica since the outbreak of the war. Over 50 Serb villages were burned, according to Serbs, and dozens of Serb graves desecrated.[36]

The bitterness was deeply personal. Senior Bosnian Serb commanders were obsessed with Srebrenica and Naser Orić. General Milenko Živanović, the commander of the Bosnian Serb Army's Drina Corps, came from a tiny hamlet near Ratkovići, a village south of Srebrenica. According to Živanović, Naser Orić's soldiers burned his village and his house to the ground on June 21, 1995. Twenty-seven Serbs died in eleven towns around Ratkovići. Naser's men desecrated the graves of his mother and other Serbs by knocking over their headstones.[37]

The two most potent examples of Muslim atrocities cited by Serbs were attacks on the villages of Zalazje and Kravica. Forty-six Serb men were allegedly missing after the attack on Zalazje on the Serb holiday of St. George's Day in May 1992. A St. Peter's Day attack on July 12, 1992, left 120 dead in Zalazje. In Kravica, more than 100 Serbs, including ten to fifteen women, were allegedly killed; civilians were burned alive in their houses when the Muslims took the town in the surprise Orthodox Christmas attack in January 1993.[38]

Some of the more spectacular accounts involved Muslims beheading Serbs, cutting bodies in half with chain saws, nailing men to trees and skinning them alive. One story Serb propagandists seized on was that Muslims kept sheep in the Serbian Orthodox church in Srebrenica. The story was partially true. One group of men returning from a successful trip to Žepa or a raid on an outlying Serb village[39] had corralled several dozen sheep in the local church. The sheep were held there for several days before they were sold for as much as 100 deutsche marks apiece.[40]

Orić's men did commit atrocities, but how many is unclear. He was cavalier enough to show a videotape of a burned-down Serb village and headless Serb corpses to foreign journalists visiting the enclave in February 1994.[41] Several Muslims and Dutch peacekeepers reported seeing a photo of Orić standing over a Serb corpse in the ruins of a village.[42]

In July 1995, Serb nationalists viewed Srebrenica as the "epicenter of genocide" that the Muslims had been carrying out against the Serbs for centuries.[43] It was a pretext for invasion, and as the afternoon wore on, it became clear the nationalists didn't care if Naser Orić and the Muslim soldiers who may have deserved retribution were in Tuzla or not. They were simply eager to get their hands on any men from Srebrenica.

While the Dutch watched, five Muslim prisoners getting out of a Serb minibus tried to escape. Two were shot dead on the spot. The other three immediately surrendered.[44] In a separate incident, five Muslim men were marched into the factory across from the UN base by a Serb soldier armed with a pistol. Minutes later, five or six shots were heard, and the Serb soldier emerged alone.[45]

Shots also resonated from the hills behind the house where the old men were taken. When Lieutenant van Duijn, Dutch peacekeepers or a UN Military Observer briefly inspected the building that afternoon, they found only terrified Muslims.[46] Later, the haunting sound of single, methodical shots from Kalashnikov assault rifles still echoed for two to four hours from the woods.[47]

...

At 6 p.m., Vahid Hodžić tried not to make eye contact with the Serb soldiers. The Bosnian translator was petrified he would be noticed. A Dutch soldier had brought Hodžić to the front of the crowd. Lieutenant Leen van Duijn handed Hodžić a megaphone and asked him to calm the people.

"Don't you have anyone else who can do this?" Hodžić asked the Dutch officer.

"There is no one else," van Duijn said. "They are all in the camp."

Hodžić froze. He was the only Muslim translator outside the base. He was probably the only Muslim male in his twenties left in the safe area. If the Serbs decided to take him away, there was nothing the Dutch could do to stop them.

"Tell them to calm down. Tell them to sit down," van Duijn said. "It's very hot, they'll suffocate each other."

Hodžić looked at the sea of faces in front of him. Desperation was written across them. One thought consumed the crowd: survival.

Hodžić lifted the megaphone to his dry lips. He felt the stares of the Serb soldiers behind him.

"You will be taken to Kladanj as has been agreed," he said, trying to counter rumors apparently running wild in the crowd. He repeated exactly what the Dutch lieutenant told him. "You will go to Tuzla and be sheltered there."

His voice quavered. "You will go group by group depending on which kind of vehicle we have. If fifty can fit in a truck, fifty will go. If one hundred can fit in a truck, one hundred will go," Hodžić translated. "We will let all of you go. Don't push each other. We will let this part go, then the other. You will all have your turn.

"The first convoy has already arrived at the destination point. We have a continuous radio connection with them. They are already coming back."

"Who are you?" a gruff voice roared to Hodžić's left.

He turned and flinched. The enormous, sweat-covered face of General Ratko Mladić was six inches away.

"Who are you? What are you doing here?" roared the sunburnt commander of the Bosnian Serb Army. "What lectures are you giving these people?"

Hodžić was petrified.

"I'm working as an interpreter for the Dutch battalion of UNPROFOR," he stammered.

"Do you have an ID?" Mladić barked.

"Yes."

"Show it to me."

Mladić glanced at the plastic UN ID. "Take it," he said to one of his bodyguards. The soldier grabbed the ID and tucked it in his pocket. Hodžić panicked. The ID was the only thing that differentiated him from the Muslim men being led to the house.

"Do you know that you are not allowed to say anything without my permission?" Mladić lectured. "Do you know that you are not allowed to leave the base without my permission? Which base do you come from?"

"From Srebrenica," Hodžić said. "The small one."

Mladić stood only just over six feet tall, but he seemed to fill the space around Hodžić. He seemed enormous.

"Whose is this?" Mladić said, grabbing the flak jacket Hodžić was wearing.

"It's theirs," Hodžić answered, referring to the Dutch.

"Whose is that?" Mladić said, pointing at the megaphone.

"It's theirs also."

Mladić glanced at one of his soldiers. The Serb grabbed the megaphone from Hodžić's hand.

"Did you know that I sent you all back to the base?" Mladić asked.

"No, I didn't," Hodžić said quickly. "If I knew, I would not be here. They brought me here."

"How can they bring you here?" Mladić said, referring to the Dutch. "They are prisoners of war just as you are."

Mladić turned to the crowd. The shoving ceased. The women and old men were dumbstruck like the others before them.

Ibro Nuhanović and Nesib Mandžić, the two Muslim negotiators, stepped forward. They had been told by Major Franken to go to the front gate. As soon as they stepped off the Dutch base, a Serb soldier had punched Nuhanović in the face and the Dutch officer escorting them was disarmed. Mladić had arrived and not said a word to the two negotiators; he had only indicated with his hand that the two should walk in front of him.

"Do you know these two?" Mladić asked the crowd.

"Yes, yes," answered voices.

"What did he do?" Mladić asked, referring to Nuhanović.

"Taught German," a voice answered.

"Do you know this man?" Mladić asked, referring to Mandžić.

"He was the high school director," a voice answered.

"How were they?" Mladić asked, referring to how they treated people in Srebrenica.

"Good, good," answered voices in the crowd.

Nuhanović stepped forward. "General Mladić and I have agreed that everyone will be evacuated," he said in a shaky, rehearsed voice.

Mandžić stepped forward. "General Mladić says that everyone will be evacuated," he repeated weakly. Ćamila Omanović, who was with her family in the parking lot, was spared the humiliation.

Mladić turned to the crowd again. "Nowhere was there a country like Yugoslavia and you have destroyed it," he thundered. "It was not bad to live together, but you have followed Izetbegovič, Orić and the Silajdžićes.

"He has accumulated a pile of money and left you," Mladić said, referring to Naser Orić. "And now he is sending the message: 'I am not able to help myself, so how can I help you?' " Hodžić thought Mladić must have been quoting an intercepted radio message.

"He orders you to go and burn Serb villages. You could live well in your protected area, work your land, plow your fields and bring in your harvest and no one would harm you. No one would do anything to you," Mladić bellowed. "Now you will be scattered from America to Australia and you will never see each other again.

"You will all be transported. All of you. No one will stay here. Tell those who are hiding in the forests they have no chance. This is the only way to get out of this iron ring. Tihić's unit has been captured. Zulfo's unit has been split up," he roared, referring to two of Srebrenica's officers. "One part has surrendered. No one will get out. This is the only way to get out of the iron ring. Everyone will pass this way."

Light applause rippled through the crowd. "Why are they applauding?" the Dutch lieutenant whispered to Hodžić. "To survive," he answered.[48]

Ratko Mladić was omnipotent. With a wave of the hand he could feed the hungry, cure the sick, spare the condemned. For the next five days he would hold the lives of 25,000 people in the palm of his hand. The timidity of the United States and Europe and the at best incompetence of the Bosnian government had turned a small man with a small army into a deity. Every Dutch and Muslim in Potočari was forced to accept the bitter truth on July 12, 1995.

General Ratko Mladić was God.

After his speech, Mladić disappeared. But to Hodžić's alarm, a Serb soldier in a black uniform decided Hodžić was a Muslim officer he had met. He kept walking up to Hodžić and saying, "Don't you remember me? We negotiated together." Hodžić was sure the soldier would talk to Mladić and he'd be hauled away with the other men.

Mladić abruptly returned after a few minutes and swaggered over to Hodžić with his bodyguards in tow. The twenty-five-year-old translator tensed. "How was it in there? Did they mistreat you?" Mladić asked amiably, referring to the safe area. "When did you start working for them?" He meant the Dutch.

Hodžić thought it was a trick question. Mladić was trying to find out if he was a soldier.

"From the beginning," he said. "I don't know what to say. Now it's over."

"Don't be afraid," Mladić said softly. "You can talk freely. There are none of them here." He was referring to Naser Orić and his men. The general sounded genuinely concerned.

"I don't know what more I can tell you," Hodžić replied. "You know as much as I do."

"Where are your parents?" Mladić asked nonchalantly.

"I don't know. They're somewhere in the crowd," Hodžić stammered. "I saw them last night at around three a.m. Since then I've been working all the time. I don't know where they are now." Hodžić was lying. His father and fifteen-year-old brother were trying to make it through the woods and he knew where his mother was in the crowd.

"Try to pull them out of there," Mladić said, motioning toward the crowd.

Hodžić's mind raced. What does he want? Does he think I'm really stupid enough to bring them here? I don't even know what he's going to do with me. If I don't bring them here, then I'm signaling that I think he's going to kill everyone in the crowd.

"I don't know what I can do," Hodžić said. "They'll go when it's their turn."

Apparently bored, Mladić turned and walked toward one of the Dutch officers.

"Hey, kid," he said. "Come over here. I want to talk to this Dutch gentleman." Relief swept over the translator.

Mladić introduced himself to three peacekeepers saying, "Where are you from? Holland?" To the third one, who was black, he said, "Where are you from? Ethiopia?"

"So what's the best soccer team in Holland?" Mladić asked Lieutenant van Duijn.[49]

"Ajax from Amsterdam," the puzzled officer answered.

"Who is the best player?" Mladić asked. Only a few feet away from them elderly Muslim men were being led away.

"Ruud Gillit," replied the officer. "Who is the best player in Yugoslavia?"

"Red Star is the best in Yugoslavia. The best player is Dragan Džajić, or he used to be," Mladić said. "Dragan Stojković is now the best."

Mladić gestured at the 5,000 women and children crammed onto the road. "Look at these. They've been doing nothing but making children for four years," he said, using a Serbo-Croatian tense that referred to the Muslims as objects, not people. "If they continue like this, in a couple of years they'll occupy even Holland."

"I don't think so," van Duijn replied. "In Holland we have all cultures, from blacks to many European nationalities. Some of them have been living in Holland for more than thirty years and we have never had any problems. I hope we won't."[50]

"It doesn't matter," Mladić replied. "These have been living here for more than three hundred years and this is the third war they have started in this century."

Mladić wandered off, but the Serb soldier in black started harassing Hodžić again. "Hey, kid, I'll be right back," he said. "Wait for me right here." Hodžić panicked. He went to a Dutch military policeman, Sergeant Major Bert Rave, who had somehow gotten Hodžić's ID back from Mladić's bodyguard with Lieutenant van Duijn's help.[51] The sergeant major was one of the four Dutch who had actually stood up to the Serbs. When a Serb soldier pointed at his flak jacket earlier, Rave said, "You have enough." The Serb was amazed at such an insolent answer, and he backed off.

"A soldier is threatening me," Hodžić said anxiously, referring to the soldier in black. "Please get me out of here."

"I don't know how," Rave said. "The lieutenant said a new shift is coming to replace our soldiers in five minutes. We can go with them."

"I don't have five minutes," Hodžić said. "I need to go now."

"Since Mladić didn't want you here, let's go ask if you can leave," Rave said. One by one they approached the Serb soldiers, asking where Mladić was. They moved through the Serbs, inching toward the Dutch compound. "Don't turn around," the sergeant major whispered. "Let's keep going until they stop us."

Out of the corner of his eye, Hodžić could see two Serb soldiers. He and Rave were fifty feet from the gate. He heard the two Serbs speaking. "Those two . . ." The sentence trailed off. Hodžić asked Rave to walk between him and the Serbs. They were twenty feet from the gate. The Serbs didn't shoot. Ten feet. Hodžić entered the base.

Inside, other translators told Hodžić he was overreacting. But

Hodžić knew how powerless the Dutch were. Most of the workers inside the base still thought they were well protected by the UN. Only one other translator seemed to understand what was happening outside. Hasan Nuhanović had brought his father, mother and twenty-year-old brother to the Dutch base because he was sure the Dutch would protect Srebrenica's civilians.

Nuhanović's father—Ibro—was one of the civilian negotiators. The three negotiators and local Muslims who worked for the UN would be allowed to leave Srebrenica with the UN. The Dutch were telling Nuhanović that his brother and mother would have to leave the base. Nuhanović was sure the Serbs would kill his brother—a Muslim male of fighting age—if he left. Vahid Hodžić didn't know what to say.

At approximately 7 p.m., the Serbs guarding Hurem Suljić and the other retired farmers, factory workers and grandfathers snapped to attention. "Do any of you know Ratko Mladić?" one of them asked. Some of the men answered, "Yes." "If you don't," the guard said, "you're about to meet him."

Thirty seconds later, a heavyset officer with bodyguards approached the house. There was a young UN officer with him. Hurem recognized Mladić from television. The general stood in the doorway.

"Hello, neighbors," he said. "Do you know who I am?"

A half dozen voices responded, "Yes."

"I am Ratko Mladić. Those of you who don't know me have the opportunity to meet me," he said. "You see what has happened to your Srebrenica? It has fallen.

"Why did you follow Alija? You should have followed Fikret Abdić," he said, referring to a Muslim politician allied with the Serbs.

"Why are you separating us from our families?" Suljić asked. "We are old men and invalids."

"I have one hundred eighty Serbs who were captured last year and are in Tuzla," he said. "I need one hundred eighty of you for an exchange." Suljić began to relax. He knew Mladić was a powerful man. Some kind of deal would be cut.

"You will not be harmed," Mladić assured them. "The exchange will be done in a peaceful way. You will be rejoining your families." Mladić turned to the UN officer and said the Muslims would be given juice and food. The Serb commander and the UN officer departed.

No juice and food arrived. It had all been a show for the young UN officer.

Forty-five minutes later, two buses and a red car arrived on the asphalt road in front of the house. The Serb soldiers hustled the old men out of the house, shouting, "Quickly! Quickly!" The ground-floor room was so full that some men had been forced to sit out in the yard. Instead of going directly to the asphalt road, they were led across a field—apparently out of sight of the Dutch[52]—and loaded onto the buses. After the buses were full, Mladić stepped in the doorway of Suljić's bus and ordered the driver to shut the door and follow the red sports car. The vehicles rolled north toward Bratunac. We're too old to go to work camps, Suljić thought, what else can they do but exchange us?

But soon after the men were bused away, the Serbs began burning the hundreds of bags the old men had left in the front yard. When Serbs were no longer nearby, Marc Klaver and a Dutch officer crept over to the house to check for bodies. None were found. The Serbs, Klaver thought, aren't stupid enough to leave any evidence.

That evening, Bosnian Serb radio news reported that the Bosnian Serb Army, "in a powerful counterattack, liberated Srebrenica. The army is treating the civilians, UN members and Muslim soldiers who surrender according to [the] Geneva Convention. We expect the Muslim units in Žepa [to] also surrender."[53]

Earlier that day in Sarajevo, Bosnian President Alija Izetbegović had called for the UN to reestablish the safe area by force, blamed Akashi's "indecisiveness" for the fall of Srebrenica and called for Akashi to resign. Bosnian Prime Minister Haris Silajdžić sent a letter to U.S. Senate Majority Leader Bob Dole denouncing the UN and the international community as "accomplices to genocide" and urging the U.S. Congress to lift the UN arms embargo.[54] Žepa was under Serb attack from both the north and the south and Bosnian officials demanded that the UN defend it.[55]

French President Chirac stated that France was ready to reestablish the safe area and called on the UN Security Council to order the Rapid Reaction Force to do it. Akashi said that would be "impossible." British Prime Minister John Major's aides privately dismissed the French proposal as posturing. The Clinton administration danced around the issue. The UN, the United States and Europe were unable to agree on an appropriate course of action.

The evening news concluded with statements from Bosnian Serb President Radovan Karadžić and General Ratko Mladić. Karadžić, as he did throughout the war, portrayed the Serbs as the war's victims. "NATO became a Muslim ally, and so did the UN. The air strikes served no purpose, since we had to take Srebrenica," he said. "We couldn't tolerate Muslim terrorism anymore; they have killed more than thirty Serbs in the last twenty days."

Karadžić scoffed at the expected UN resolution calling for the reestablishment of the safe area. "There will be no withdrawal. Srebrenica belongs to us. Why didn't anyone ask [the] Croats to withdraw from western Slavonia?" he said, referring to the Croatian Army's May seizure of the Serb-controlled pocket. "There will be no massacre in Srebrenica, as happened in Slavonia. Srebrenica civilians are free to go or stay. The same applies for UN soldiers."

Mladić said that he had met with a delegation of local leaders who asked for permission to leave Srebrenica. The Muslims would be transported by "their [own] free will." "Civilians are not to be blamed for the wrong policies of their leaders," Mladić added. "There are several groups still trying to fight, but we will deal with them soon."[56]

Mevludin Orić and his neighbors were exhausted. It had taken them nine hours to reach Kamenica, a deserted, formerly Muslim village halfway between the edge of the enclave and Konjević Polje. It was just after 8 p.m.

They had picked up several men who were wounded by Serb shells along the way. Mevludin was one of the stretcher bearers. The stretcher consisted of a blanket wrapped around two tree limbs. The column was moving at a miserable pace. They had covered only three and a half miles. The trail was far too congested. Hundreds of men lay sprawled out across the steep hillside overlooking the deserted village.

The terrain was brutal. Already malnourished, bodies were flagging in the heat. The route ran over a series of ridges and deep valleys. In the course of the day they had climbed and descended from 2,000 feet to sea level three times. Potable streams coursed mercifully through the bottom of each ravine. It felt like it was over 90 degrees. They rested in a meadow, before beginning an extremely steep 1,500-foot descent to a stream below.

Mevludin wanted to go look for his father. After deciding they should walk apart, he had lost track of him when the men from Lehovići had begun to mix with other groups. During the trek, it quickly became clear that the threat to the column was as much psychological as it was physical. Shells abruptly whizzed overhead. Gunfire erupted with no warning. Corpses littered their route. A Serb mortar had landed ahead of them at 1 p.m. and killed five men. A human stomach and intestines lay across the green grass just below the intact head and torso of a man in his twenties. Mevludin had seen such things before; the others hadn't. The image would slowly eat at their minds. Some men were already saying it was hopeless. It was better to kill yourself, they said, than be captured by the Serbs. That was what Mevludin's hand grenade was for, but he hadn't reached that point yet.

Rumors were flying up and down the column about Serbs masquerading as Muslims. People from all over eastern Bosnia were in the march. They had randomly survived being expelled from their hometowns and been crammed into Srebrenica. A Serb could stand directly in front of Mevludin, use a fake Muslim name and say he was from Vlasenica, and Mevludin would have no idea if he was lying. No passwords had been agreed upon before the group left Šušnjari. Mevludin had seen a Serb standing near a tree silently watching them, but he didn't say anything. Identifying the man would only have led to unarmed people being hurt.

A few miles into the trek, Mevludin realized the trip would be far more difficult than his walk to Srebrenica three years earlier. They would have been much better off had they somehow fought off the Serbs. Life in Srebrenica no longer looked as miserable, boring and intolerable as it had. Making it to Tuzla would be nearly impossible, Mevludin thought, we should have fought to the last drop of blood.

At 8:30 p.m., Mevludin stood up to find his father. The hillside exploded. Screams filled his ears. He dove toward a cluster of trees. Other men piled on top of him. He hugged the ground. Mortars whistled overhead. Bursts of shrapnel from an antiaircraft gun careered across the hillside. Automatic rifles erupted from every direction. The gunfire was deafening.

All around Mevludin men sprinted down the hill, then up and across in a panic. Weapons and bags with food were dropped in the pandemonium. Men gasped or groaned where they had fallen. Those carrying stretchers threw the wounded to the ground and ran for the nearest cluster of trees or bushes for cover. Men running downhill tripped, fell and tumbled head over heels for fifty yards, the ground was so steep. The few with guns didn't know where to shoot because the firing came from so many different directions.

The Serb antiaircraft gun and mortar seemed to be positioned on the hillside directly across from the meadow where 3,000 to 5,000 Muslims had rested. It was a devastating position. The gunners had a half-mile-wide clearing filled with people for targets. For the first twenty seconds, it was a question of how many rounds the Serbs could fire, not whether they would hit anyone.

The next five minutes were the cruelest. The men who found cover in the foliage were trapped. In a macabre technique that would be fine-tuned over the next few days, the Serbs would estimate which clusters of trees were filled with the most men and then methodically saturate them with flak from the antiaircraft gun and mortar rounds. Bodies were found stacked on top of each other in the trees. The living pulled the dead on top of them and used corpses as sandbags.

In the end, at least 125 dead[57] and hundreds of wounded lay across the hillside. The injured were left alone, doomed to die slowly of their wounds. The living cowered under cover or sprinted headlong through the forest. Thousands of men had been separated from their relatives, friends and guides. The six-mile-long column was cut in two. Any vestige of organization was gone.

Marching at the well-armed front of the column, Srebrenica's leaders escaped the carnage. As the ambush was unleashed, the lead elements were three miles ahead, on the verge of crossing a crucial stretch of road just north of the village of Nova Kasaba. But they could hear the ambush behind them. Major Mido Salihović, the commander of the enclave's combined maneuver unit, halted the march. No one was willing to go back, but Salihović and his men stayed in the area for two hours, directing disoriented men across the road. Even after Salihović and the rest of the unit left, Ibran Malagić and another soldier stayed and directed hundreds more across the dangerous stretch of road and fields.

Whether by design or not, General Ratko Mladić had flushed 10,000 to 15,000 mostly unarmed Muslim men into a ten-square-mile killing zone. Behind them lay the fallen enclave. In every other direction were asphalt roads Mladić was trying to fill with Bosnian Serb soldiers. If Mladić could seal two crucial stretches of road—one running from Bratunac to Konjević Polje and the other from Konjević Polje to Milići—Srebrenica's men would be trapped in the Serb general's "iron ring."

Darkness enveloped the parking lot. Ćamila Omanović stared at her daughter Đermina's hair, long, silky and light brown. Even though she hadn't been able to wash it for days, it cascaded off her shoulders. As her daughter grew into a woman, Ćamila had braided and brushed it hundreds of times. Her long mane was beautiful, too beautiful, in the moonlight.

"We have to cut your hair off," she whispered to her daughter.

"No, Mom," she replied. "No."

"We've got to change your clothes too," Camila whispered anxiously. "We need to find a scarf and some *dimijes* [pantaloons]."

At dusk, Serbs had begun moving through the crowd of women, children and elderly men encamped outside the Dutch base. Elderly men sitting in factories were rounded up by the Serbs and taken to abandoned buildings for questioning. Some never returned. Those who did said they had been tortured. Men began talking of suicide. One old man was taken to the Dutch hospital for treatment after he picked up a large rock and started pounding it against his head.[58]

In the darkness, Serbs could start taking away pretty girls. Đermina was dressed in jeans and a T-shirt. Camila was desperate to get her to change her clothes. Throughout the day mothers dirtied their daughters' faces and dressed them in peasant clothes to make them unattractive. They gave their daughters babies to hold so they didn't appear to be virgins.

Abject fear enveloped Potočari. It consumed the 15,000 Muslims in Potočari's parking lots and factory buildings, hysterical, hungry, beyond exhaustion. It paralyzed the Dutch, who tentatively patrolled the area close to their base or hid inside the compound. And it intoxicated the predators among the Serb soldiers and police.

As two women sitting nearby silently prayed, four Serb soldiers raised the legs of a twenty-eight-year-old woman in the air and took turns raping her in the center of a crowded factory hall. The woman screamed for them to stop, but they stuffed a rag in her mouth.[59]

Dogs were heard barking in the nearby hills. The Dutch and the Muslims slowly grasped that the Serbs were using the animals to hunt down any men who tried to escape. Marc Klaver, the lookout from Observation Post Foxtrot, and Lieutenant Eelco Koster, who had tried to stand up to Mladić, volunteered to stay outside for the night. Groups of two or three soldiers moved through the crowded factories, fields and parking lots, at times armed with flashlights. But the refugees were unsure if they were Dutch soldiers patrolling the crowd or Serbs wearing stolen Dutch uniforms hunting Muslims.[60]

Men and boys hid under blankets or dressed as women. Young girls covered their faces. A pattern emerged. A beam of light would probe the sea of faces. Each person froze when it hit them, felt waves of relief when it moved. "You, come with us," a voice would sometimes say from behind the blinding rays of light. A wife or a mother would beg that a man be spared. "Now," the voice would command. A man would rise silently and disappear.

Ćamila and her family had moved closer to the base and now sat next to a gas pump in the parking lot of the bus maintenance depot outside the UN base. She made Đermin, her thirteen-year-old son, go sit with a sickly elderly man who had suffered a stroke and was sitting a few feet away from her. She thought if he sat with the old man the Serbs might spare him. He had nearly fled for the woods that morning while she was at the meeting. A friend had approached him with news the Serbs were rounding up all the men. He had waited for his mother, but one small group of men had avoided the Serb sentries by walking through an unguarded swath of urine and feces made by people using the woods as a latrine.

Earlier that day, a man sitting a few feet from Ćamila had been taken away by the Serbs for two hours and returned. She knew him, but had no idea what had happened to his wife and children. A construction worker, he lived just south of Srebrenica. After he returned he sat silently all night with an absent look on his face. He would occasionally blurt out things. "I was tortured. I was asked various questions," he said to no one in particular. "Maybe someday I'll be able to talk about it."

The crowd was a living, breathing creature to her. The moon was nearly full. She could see what was happening around her, but it was the sounds that haunted her. Screams suddenly filled the night. At one point, she heard bloodcurdling cries coming from the hills near the base. She later decided the Serbs must be playing recordings to terrorize them. Women gave birth or cried out as their husbands were taken away. Men wailed and called out women's names. Ćamila thought they were being tortured. "Hediba!" was one man's drawn-out howl. "Hediba!" Another man begged for "Nesiba!" He stopped abruptly after Ćamila thought she heard the sound of chains. Panic would grip the crowd. People would suddenly rise up and rush off in one direction. Then there would be silence, until the cycle of screams and panic started all over again. Nearly hallucinating, Ćamila could not sleep.

Several times during the night she saw a group of soldiers dressed in Dutch uniforms walk down a narrow gravel road. She put a blanket over her son's head and prayed they would not see him.[61] Dozens of men were taken away that night. Soldiers in Dutch uniforms carried men away on stretchers whom they said were "crazy," but Ćamila and her son didn't believe them. They were being taken away to be tortured by Serbs who were masquerading as Dutch.[62]

Exhausted, Ćamila was convinced she had doomed her children by meeting with General Mladić. Unaware that as a negotiator she could leave with the Dutch, she thought that she and her family were marked for execution and that it was best to try to blend in. She heard coughing. She thought she smelled something and she quickly had her children and grandson breathe through moist diapers. The Serbs were using some kind of poison gas, she thought. It was the gas, not the hours of sobbing, that made her and other women's eyes dry up to the point where they could shed tears no more.[63]

But it was the fear that didn't let her sleep. A fear more intense than anything she had ever felt. A fear that changed her forever.

In Bratunac that night, flashlights also stalked Hurem Suljić. Ratko Mladić led the men who had been separated from their families to an empty agricultural warehouse in the Serb-held town. The prisoners were hustled inside. After about an hour, a few Serb soldiers came to the door. They called out the names of Muslims unknown to Suljić. Finally one Muslim stood up after his name was called. He walked to the door and one of the Serb soldiers shook his hand warmly. The Serb offered him a cigarette. Other Muslims whom Suljić assumed were from Bratunac walked to the door. "How is your brother?" "How is your family?" echoed across the warehouse.

It lasted only an hour. At 10 p.m. a sharp, loud voice called the Serbs. Two Serb guards stood at either side of the door. "You twelve, tonight you must do as you've been ordered," the same voice was heard saying outside. "Do you understand?" Other voices answered yes.

A soldier appeared in the doorway. A flashlight cut through the darkness. Suljić and the other men stared at the floor, hoping to avoid being noticed.

"You," one of them said. "Get up."

The man walked outside. Gasps and moans from just outside the warehouse echoed in the darkness. After fifteen minutes the Serb returned with the flashlight. The beam of light again probed the darkness. Suljić stared at the floor in desperation.

In Srebrenica, the order made Bosnian Serb police officer Zoran Radić curious. A group of soldiers had been told to go to a house near the police station where fifty elderly Muslims were gathered. The soldiers were to round up all the men and leave the women. Radić followed them, wondering if he'd see someone he knew from Srebrenica.

They drove to the house at 11 p.m. A Serb who was a cobbler and drank too much had lived there before the war. The soldiers went in first, holding a single candle to illuminate the pitch-black rooms.

"Let's go," one of the soldiers barked, as he searched for men. "Let's go." Most of the people in the room were women. Radić scanned the men's faces and froze when he looked closely at the sickly man over sixty-five lying on the couch. Hašim Mustafić lay before him. Mustafić had been the maître d' and a vocational teacher at the Hotel Domavija in Srebrenica when Radić was a teenage student. He was a kind man who treated everyone well.

"I know this man," Radić said. "Let him stay."

No one objected. Radić didn't think about what he was doing. As the Serb soldiers led the other old men outside shouting "Quickly! Quickly!" he followed the Serb with the candle into the next room. Two dozen eyes filled with fear stared back at them.

"Get up, let's go," the soldier bellowed. "All the men."

A man who had been lying on the couch got up and challenged the Serb.

"Where are we going?" he asked.

Radić didn't recognize the first few, but a tall man he spotted brought a broad grin to his face. It was Edhem Lućanin, the former manager of the Hotel Domavija and Radić's favorite teacher in high school. He adored Lućanin. The man had treated all of his students with respect.

"Leave this man here," Radić said. "He was my teacher. He's a good man."

Lućanin couldn't see Radić's face or recognize his voice.[64]

An awkward silence. Radić was preventing the soldiers from carrying out their orders. He could easily be demoted and sent to the front line for what he was doing. None of the soldiers said anything. Lućanin continued to stare at Radić in the darkness but didn't seem to recognize him.

The sergeant walked toward Radić and his teacher. "That's OK, old man," he said as he passed by. "Next time, it'll be your turn."

The sergeant disappeared outside. Bewildered, Radić's former teacher walked back to the couch. Five stooped elderly men were led out the door, the last Radić saw of them as they were marched toward Potočari.

He thought Edhem and Hašim would be around for the night and headed back to an abandoned house he and the other police officers were sleeping in. The men were roasting a goat they had caught in the town.

None of the soldiers had complained. Radić didn't care anyway. He had prided himself throughout the war for being tough but fair. Edhem and Hašim had nothing bad in them and deserved to be protected. He knew there were many men in the town who had lost relatives in the fighting and might do something rash. His father was the same age as the two old Muslims. He didn't care what the soldiers thought. Radić thought that what he had done was not a mistake before man—or God.

Once the Serb ambush slowed, Mevludin Orić crawled out from the cluster of trees. The only man he recognized was Haso Hasanović, the youngest of the group from Lehovići. He couldn't find his cousin, the one he had been carrying before the ambush. The hill was strewn with bodies.

Mevludin and Haso loaded a wounded man into a blanket and walked downhill with a small group of men. After a few dozen yards, the Serbs opened fire on them again. He and Haso dropped the wounded Muslim and sprinted wildly downhill. The scene was nightmarish. No matter how far he went down the 1,000-foot slope the ground was strewn with corpses and wounded. He finally made it to the bottom, and tripped while crossing a stream. Soaked, he ran across a meadow and into a thick grove of trees. He didn't know where Haso was, but he was safe.

Mevludin heard voices close by and froze. The woods were teeming with Muslims and Serbs. The men were talking about the ambush. They sounded horrified. Mevludin decided to risk it. He emerged from the trees and ten civilians spun toward him, terrified he was a Serb. After speaking with them for a few minutes, Mevludin joined them and soon found himself in the middle of a half-mile-long, 300-man column walking west toward Tuzla. They quickly found their path blocked by a densely wooded hill. The group was divided over whether they should go left or right.

One man came forward and said he knew the way. He took the group to the right—toward the asphalt road connecting Konjević Polje and Bratunac. After thirty minutes he abruptly disappeared. The Muslims were puzzled until they heard the roar of an APC engine. They had been led into another ambush. Mevludin sprinted back up the path they came down. He squatted in the brush.

"You are surrounded," a Serb megaphone blared. "There is no way out."

Mevludin figured he was about 100 yards from the road, but knew he was well hidden if he stayed in the trees. Exhausted, he lay down on the ground to rest. After a few minutes, he heard voices around him. It was another group of men from Srebrenica. The Serb megaphone started again. He ignored it. Unarmed, exhausted and lost, Mevludin fell asleep fitfully.

As Mevludin passed out, hundreds of men from Srebrenica followed the lead section of the column and streamed across the asphalt road just north of Nova Kasaba. But between 7,000 and 12,000 other men, most of whom were unarmed civilians, wandered aimlessly like Mevludin. Too far from the crossing point or lost without their guides, they failed to cross either crucial road.

Just after midnight, Gerry Schouden, a Dutch doctor, felt a wave of relief. Six hours after leaving Potočari, his medical convoy of wounded had finally arrived in Tišća and was only one checkpoint away from crossing into Muslim-held central Bosnia.

He watched with growing alarm as two Serb soldiers wove their way toward his UN ambulance. They were heavily armed and extremely drunk. Schouden was only four miles from Muslim-held Kladanj. All he needed was a little luck.

The convoy included three unarmed male nurses, fifty-four wounded Muslims and ten Muslim nurses who worked for Médecins Sans Frontières. They were spread out in seven cars, ambulances and trucks. At first, Dr. Schouden couldn't understand what the drunk Serb soldier was saying. Then it was clear. Like the Muslim women earlier in the day, the wounded were to walk the last four miles to Muslim-held territory.

"No, no way," Schouden said. "We have to carry them on stretchers."

The two drunken Serb soldiers searched the vehicles. They were furious when they found twenty wounded Muslim men of fighting age. One soldier departed and returned with five more Serb soldiers. As Schouden protested, two fresh amputees were pulled from the trucks and made to stand on crutches. Eighteen other wounded were laid out on the side of the road in their stretchers. All twenty pulled from the truck would have to walk the four miles to their freedom. Some of the patients were so badly wounded they would only be able to make the journey by crawling.

Schouden tried to radio the Dutch base, but the Serbs ordered the convoy to leave immediately. They insisted that the twenty patients and four of the ten Muslim nurses stay with them.

As the convoy drove back to Potočari, Schouden noticed that the fighting they had heard near the village of Kamenica had died down. By 2 a.m., hundreds of Serb soldiers were sleeping on the road. Near Kamenica—the site of the ambush Mevludin Orić narrowly escaped—Serb soldiers forced the convoy to drive without lights for two miles. There was a danger, the Serbs said, of Muslims targeting them from the woods.

Near the halfway mark to Bratunac, they were stopped a second time. A Serb soldier pointed his Kalashnikov assault rifle at Dr. Schouden's throat and said "*Panzer.*" Schouden was confused at first and then realized the man was saying "armor" in German. The doctor quickly took his flak jacket off and handed it to him.

At 3 a.m., the convoy finally reached the front line of the safe area. They were a half mile from the Dutch headquarters in Potočari. But the Serbs manning the checkpoint refused to allow them to pass. Schouden was told he would have to wait until the soldier's commanding officer reported for duty at 8 a.m. The wounded had been on the trucks and ambulances for nine hours. Schouden distributed the few sedatives he had left. A half mile from the Dutch base's modern hospital facilities and stockpile of drugs, a wounded elderly man died.

Back at the Serb crossing point to Muslim-held central Bosnia, the drunken Serb soldiers began beating and kicking the twenty wounded Muslims after Schouden's convoy departed for Potočari. One wounded Muslim was severely beaten with an automatic rifle. A man with a broken leg was forced to walk without crutches.

The four Muslim nurses were taken away by drunken Serb

soldiers. The Serbs were convinced one of them was Naser Orić's sister. She was interrogated for an hour and allowed to begin walking to freedom. Thirty minutes later, two other nurses were allowed to leave, but a nineteen-year-old nurse was forced to stay. For the next several hours, she was raped.[65]

COLUMN AND CONVOY ROUTES, JULY 13, 1995

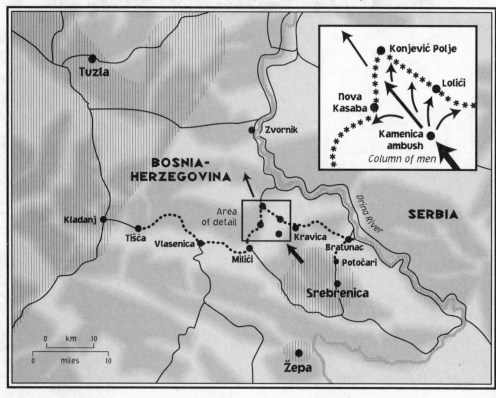

Muslim-and Croat-controlled

Column of men

••••••• Convoy route, women and children

✳✳✳✳ Serb soldiers

They found his body at dawn. A woman screamed when she saw him hanging from a truck with a belt around his neck. The construction worker whom the Serbs interrogated the day before decided not to let it happen again. After intermittently telling Ćamila Omanović that he had been tortured, he abruptly stood up in the middle of the night and walked away without saying a word. Now Ćamila watched as two UN soldiers with red crosses on their arms bore him away on a stretcher. She felt a wave of sadness wash over her. His family should be here, she thought.

Ćamila had seen the Serbs take dozens of men away during the night. She knew four of them: Suljo Bektić a forty-five-year-old technician and father of two; Nezir Osmanović, a forty-eight-year-old bookkeeper and teacher with two sons; Nutfet Purković, forty-five, a miner with three daughters and a son; and Mustafa Hašić a sixty-three-year-old retired salesman with two daughters, a son and seven grandchildren.[1] None had returned.

The Dutch found another suicide across the street.[2] Lieutenant Eelco Koster, the peacekeeper who had tried to stand up to Mladić the day before, inspected the scene. His deputy, Lieutenant Frank Schotman, was led to the spot by Muslims. A middle-aged man had hanged himself in a small building next to the Energo-Invest zinc factory. People had been using the room as a toilet. Feces and urine filled the floor a few feet beneath his dangling feet. Koster was overwhelmed.

The Dutch officer felt pity as he stared at the bloated body. The man had done it for a reason. Koster began to grasp the element of fear that seized the Muslims. Two of his men cut the body down and lay him outside. Koster wanted to give him a proper funeral. When the Dutch returned to collect the body, his shoes had been stolen. The man was identified by his brother. The Dutch buried him in a vegetable garden at his family's request.[3]

Serb buses arrived at 7 a.m., but there were no Serb soldiers around the base. Apparently the Serbs returned to Bratunac each night to celebrate. Koster and van Duijn began to organize their departure. For one precious hour, men were able to slip onto the buses and escape.

At 8 a.m., the medical convoy that had spent the night at the Serb checkpoint just a half mile away from the Dutch base was now ordered to proceed to Bratunac. Only the six Muslim nurses were allowed to walk to the UN base. Dr. Gerry Schouden stayed with the patients who were taken to Bratunac and placed on the grounds of a small, walled clinic. Serb gunmen initially demanded entry, but Schouden, the sole Westerner left in the group, blocked them. From Serb doctors and nurses he received the medical supplies he needed, but Serb police refused to let him and the wounded return to the Dutch base. The Serbs suspected that several of the wounded men were Bosnian soldiers. Four of them were, in fact, the very men who had held the Serbs in the trench in Bibići with Ibran Malagić four days before. The men who had actually resisted the Serb attack were delivered to their enemies by the UN.

As the morning progressed, more bodies were found in the factories around the UN base in Potočari. A fourteen-year-old girl who had been taken away by the Serb soldiers the night before was found hanging from a rafter. After spending an hour with the Serbs, she had returned with blood running down her legs. She slipped away from her family during the night and somehow found a belt.[4]

A baby, an elderly woman and two elderly men were also

discovered. They appeared to have died of natural causes. The Dutch buried nine bodies behind the UN compound. Families buried their loved ones in gardens and makeshift graves.[5]

After spending thirty-six hours outside the Dutch base without food, the refugees began raiding the gardens and kitchens of nearby houses. The smell of smoke and frying potatoes filled the air. Some of Ćamila's neighbors brought her potatoes they had cooked, which she fed to her grandson.

By 10 a.m., Ćamila could wait no more.

"We should go," she said to her daughter.

"Let's stay," Đermina answered. She had refused to change out of her jeans and T-shirt the night before. She had inherited her mother's strong will. The tension between Ćamila and her daughter was increasing.

"We're going now," Ćamila said firmly. "If you stay here they can do whatever they want to you. We've got to do our best to leave."

Đermina grudgingly agreed. Ćamila grabbed a baby bottle with a little juice in it. She gave her jewelry to her deaf-and-mute aunt. Ćamila had lost her patience, and asked two of her friends to take care of her aunt. All of their clothes and belongings were left behind.

"I don't have the strength for another night," Ćamila told her friends. "If I stay, I'll lose my mind. Whatever happens, happens. I can't stand it anymore."

She and her family waded into the crowd and headed toward the buses. Ćamila held her grandson in the air over her head to keep him from suffocating. Her daughter grabbed on to Ćamila's waist, and finally her son grabbed on to his sister. For half an hour she pushed and shoved her way through the crowd. As they approached the Dutch base, Ćamila could see a friend of hers. Mina Hasanković was standing next to a Dutch APC with red crosses on it. She worked as a translator for the Dutch. Ćamila yelled, but Mina couldn't hear her. They pressed on.

Finally they made their way to the wall of Dutch peacekeepers holding back the crowd. A half dozen buses and trucks arrived. Ćamila was swept onto the road by the pressure of the crowd. They walked hurriedly toward one of the buses.

"You're not going to get on a bus," a Serb soldier said. "You're going on a truck."

Ćamila and her daughter froze. Her boyish-looking son continued toward the buses. The soldier walked over to a large rock blocking vehicles from entering the Dutch base and picked up something. He returned and gave Ćamila a golden medallion and her a daughter a ring.

"Take this," the soldier said. "Someone is going to ask you for this in Bratunac."

Her son waited for them and the family climbed onto the truck together. Other women and children piled on. "Fill it up," one of the Serbs quipped. "Let them suffocate."

Two men she recognized were being led away. Their wives pleaded with the Serbs to spare them, but to no avail. Ćamila stared at the medallion. We're finished, she thought; we're marked. Even if we throw them away, we'll be found. Ćamila was convinced she had doomed herself and her children by meeting with Mladić. She started shrieking.[6]

"Help! Help!" she shouted in English as loudly as she could. "Help us!"

The Serbs and Dutch stared at her.

"Please stop, Mom!" her daughter shouted as a neighbor took the grandson. "Please! Please!"

"Please stop!" her son shrieked. "Please!"

One of the Serb soldiers spoke to the driver. "Start the engine. It doesn't matter that it's not full," he said. "Just take them to Bratunac and they'll get their fair share there. Fuck their Turk mothers."

The truck's engine turned over.

Ćamila panicked. The only way to save her children was to kill herself, she decided. Hysterical, she pushed her son and daughter away from her and jumped off the truck. She landed between a Dutch peacekeeper and a Serb.

"Stop!" the Serb shouted. "I'll shoot."

"All three of them are innocent children! Kill me!" she shrieked. "The whole world will find out about it!"

"You're not innocent. Fuck your Turkish mother!" the Serb

soldier bellowed. "Wait and see what happens to you when you get to Bratunac."[7]

Ćamila frantically sprinted toward the Dutch base. She waited for the crack of the rifle and the burning sensation in her back. She waited eagerly for the Serbs to kill her.

In Srebrenica, Zoran Radić was eager to check on his former teachers. His unit was supposed to be policing the town, but some soldiers were already taking valuables from stores, shops and houses. He worried that someone who had lost a relative might take revenge on his teachers. At some point in the morning, accompanied by another officer, he went to the house where they were held.

He opened the door and relief washed over him. Edhem Lućanin, the teacher he had held so dear in high school, was still there.

"Do you remember me?" Radić said to the confused old man.

"Dragan?" the teacher asked, recognizing the warm face but straining to remember his name.

"I'm not Dragan, I'm Zoran," Radić said with a smile.

The two men shook hands and embraced.

"That was you last night, wasn't it?" Lućanin said.

"Yes," Radić said. "I am helping you because I'm human. Please don't tell anyone my name." No one had said anything to him about the two old men that morning, but Radić was still worried that those who had lost close relatives wouldn't understand.

Radić offered his old teacher a cigarette. Lućanin thanked him profusely for the night before, took a few long drags and visibly relaxed.

"Don't worry, everything is safe. You'll be transported to Tuzla," Radić said. "Why didn't you leave Srebrenica before it fell?"

"I couldn't. My mother is bedridden," Lućanin said. He explained that she was ninety-two, was deaf and couldn't walk.

He had had a chance to be evacuated by the UN in 1993, but turned down that offer also because of his mother. Lućanin was sixty-eight and hoped the Serbs would spare an old man.

"You should've gone earlier," Radić said. "It's a war. Anything can happen. I can help you, but when I leave there's nothing I can do."

Some of the women said they were unable to leave because Muslims with cars or trucks had been charging for rides to Potočari during the town's fall. They didn't have the money, and didn't think they were strong enough to walk.[8]

Hašim Mustafić, Radić's other teacher, entered the room and warmly shook hands. "Thank you very much for last night," he said.

"I did what I could," Radić replied.

The men made small talk about old students and teachers.

"Has anyone brought you food?" Radić asked. The Muslims had received nothing for the last twenty-four hours. He turned to the other officer. "What's in that knapsack?"

"Two cans of meat and a loaf and a half of bread," the officer answered.

"Give them one can and half the bread," Radić said.

"What are we going to eat?" the officer protested.

"You can eat the rest," Radić snapped at his fellow Serb. "I'll starve."

As soon as Mevludin Orić saw the two Muslims lying across the path in the woods that morning, he knew they were doomed. A shell had blown off one man's foot. His best friend was cradling the injured man, promising never to abandon him. Their proposal was simple.

"Take us to the Chetniks," the wounded man said. "They'll either help us or kill us."

"We can't," Mevludin replied. "If we take you, we'll all be killed."

Mevludin had awoken at dawn and joined a dozen other men who were walking west toward Nova Kasaba. Their goal that day was to cross the asphalt road. He and the other men offered to carry the wounded Muslim. He readily accepted.

The effort ended after only fifty yards. The wounded man was heavy. Mevludin and the other men were exhausted. They left the two huddled together on the path. Throughout the hills, wounded were being left to die by friends and relatives. Other men were lost and wandering in circles. Mevludin was still optimistic that the Serbs would never catch him.

Two miles ahead of him hundreds of Muslim men stared at the cruel illusion Mevludin would soon be confronting. Perched on the hills overlooking the asphalt road between Nova Kasaba and Konjević Polje, Srebrenica's men gazed at the steep slopes on the other side which were covered by a striking patchwork of dark green forests and light green meadows bursting with yellow wildflowers. Wisps of white clouds floated in the royal-blue sky. It was Bosnia at its most beautiful.

Only a thirty-foot-wide strip of asphalt, a nearly dry riverbed and a 200-yard-wide field beyond it separated thousands of Muslims from freedom. Most of Srebrenica's men had driven through the area hundreds of times before the war. But the familiar valley and stretch of road between Konjević Polje and Nova Kasaba was now a killing zone guarded by old friends turned enemies. Crossing the road was far more difficult than it appeared.

The last few groups scurried across just before dawn. After that came the roar of heavy machinery. Serb armored personnel carriers began to take positions along the road. Serb foot patrols intensified. Psychological warfare began. "You are surrounded," Serb soldiers using megaphones said. "You will not escape. Surrender or die." Serbs dressed in stolen Dutch uniforms patrolled the area in stolen UN APCs. "You will not be harmed," the Serbs said over the megaphones. "UNPROFOR is overseeing the evacuation."

Just north of Konjević Polje in the village of Kušlat, a group of seventeen prisoners is led to the banks of the Jadar River. With no warning the guards begin firing. In the village of Zabrde, nestled in the woods off the main road, the guards walking in front of a group of twenty-five to thirty prisoners abruptly disappear. The guards behind the prisoners open fire.

Near Kravica, an antiaircraft gun fired at a column of Muslim men scampering across a nearby ridge. Serb soldiers patrolled the asphalt road. One of them wore weight-lifting gloves, toted a Kalashnikov assault rifle, but had difficulty quantifying how many Muslims had already surrendered. "A lot, a lot," he told a Serbian journalist with a video camera. "Thousands, several thousand."[9]

Dozens of exhausted, dazed and unarmed Muslims filed out of the woods in the 90-degree heat. Wounded were carried on makeshift stretchers made of tree limbs and blankets. Resignation and fear were etched across sweat-covered faces. They had been broken.

Prisoners were forced to remove their shirts, revealing malnourished torsos. Muslims who had already been captured were forced to shout their names over megaphones and swear that they were being treated well. "It's safe here. Come to the Serbs!" one prisoner shouted at gunpoint. Another Muslim prisoner told the Serb journalist he was unarmed and had spent the last two days in the woods. Asked if he was frightened, he answered, "Naturally," his face ashen. "How would you feel?"[10]

With Serb soldiers and APCs blocking the asphalt roads, as many as 7,000 Muslim men, including Mevludin Orić, were trapped inside Mladić's "iron ring." Haggard, hungry and demoralized, they began surrendering in droves.

In shock and horror, Ćamila Omanović's children watched her run toward the Dutch base, waiting for the Serb soldiers to shoot her. She ran wildly, shrieking, "Help! Help!" But the Serbs and Dutch did nothing. They dismissed her as crazy and went on with their work. The trucks and buses rolled forward. Afraid to jump from the vehicle, Ćamila's son, daughter and grandson departed without her.[11]

She sprinted toward the Dutch base, tripping and landing face first in a drainage ditch. Soaked from head to toe, she crawled out and spotted a hole in the chain-link fence. She was worried it might be mined, but didn't care. She wanted to die. She moved through the opening and ran straight toward the main building.

"I need a translator!" she shouted in Bosnian at a stunned Dutch soldier. Her sweat suit was drenched and covered with mud. Her faced was contorted and her voice cracked.

"My children are in danger!" she shrieked. "I am in danger!" Ćamila told the story of the medallion. The Dutch officer had her taken to the base's field hospital. A doctor injected a sedative into her arm.

"Calm down," he told her. "Nothing is going to happen to your kids."

Ćamila saw her brother Abdulah enter the room and ran to him. Médecins Sans Frontières had guaranteed that he could leave with them, but he was still deeply shaken by the Serb attempt to arrest him the day before. He told Ćamila how he had seen one of his former students when the Serbs briefly inspected the Dutch base. "You taught us a very good lesson," the young Serb said. "Now we will teach you a lesson when you get to Bratunac."

She was convinced the Muslims inside the Dutch base would eventually be seized by the Serbs. Ćamila knew the Dutch could do nothing to protect her. "Please give me something," she whispered to her brother. "I want to kill myself." Ćamila was sure Serbs were going to enter the Dutch base at any moment and demand that she be turned over to them.

"They know you're in here," her brother said, at first trying to comfort her. "They can't come in and get you."

"I don't want to wait," Ćamila said. "I just want to finish it and kill myself."

They fed each other's paranoia for the next thirty minutes. Abdulah finally gave her a piece of rope he had been saving in case he was captured. He had already tied a loop in it. Ćamila ran up a flight of stairs and found herself on a long, thin platform that overlooked the main hall of the factory. Five thousand refugees spread out across the floor below her. The refugees had huddled inside the hall for two days. The air reeked of urine and feces.

Ćamila surveyed the platform for a proper place. The corner she stood in was nearly deserted. A few children stared out a nearby window, watching the buses depart. "Go away," she told them. Ćamila had heard that people looked terrible when they hanged themselves.

There was a large machine, some kind of dryer, she thought, behind her. She climbed up a built-in ladder for workmen that ran up the side of it and sat down on top of the machine. An iron pipe was just a few feet above her head; it was roughly eight feet to the floor.

Ćamila looked down at the factory hall. A Serb soldier and two Dutch soldiers moved through the crowd. They made two wide circles and appeared to be searching for someone. She was convinced the Serbs were looking for her. She told the children not to tell anyone she was there. When they left, she tied one end of the rope around the pipe.

Earlier in the war, she had heard that the Serbs forced sons to rape their mothers and fathers to rape their daughters. She had heard that people were slowly skinned alive. As each section of skin was removed, salt was placed on the naked flesh. Ćamila then did something she hadn't done in years—she prayed.

"God, please don't take this as a sin," she whispered. "What I'm doing now I'm doing because I don't want to end up in their hands. I'm taking my life."

She said a short prayer in Arabic that she'd learned as a little girl, placed the rope around her neck and jumped.

Outside the UN base, Lieutenant Vincent Egbers was convinced the Muslims were overreacting. Egbers, who had escorted the first convoy the day before, decided he would see what was happening inside the house where the elderly Muslim men were being taken for questioning. He and a Dutch sergeant were supposed to escort a convoy leaving at 11 a.m. Two Dutch corporals had attempted to go into the house, but they were rebuked by the Serbs. Seeing that he outranked the Serb standing guard, Egbers tried to bluff his way in.[12]

"I'm an officer," Egbers said in English, pointing to the

stripes on his shoulder. "Of course I can go in the house. Do you have anything to hide?"

Egbers entered the house with Serb guards following him. Several dozen elderly Muslims cowered on the floor. They were clearly terrified of their Serb guards.

"We have to see if they are armed," one of the Serb guards said to Egbers in broken English. He motioned for Egbers to follow him and showed the Dutch officer several dozen knives the Serbs had found on the men.

Egbers had seen at least three buses full of old men depart that morning.

"What will happen to the men?" Egbers asked.

"We're taking them to Kladanj," the Serb guard answered, referring to Muslim-held central Bosnia.

In Bratunac, Hurem Suljić had somehow avoided being beaten. Over the course of the night, approximately forty prisoners were dragged outside the warehouse where the men who had been separated from their families the day before were being held. The beatings had finally stopped at 4 a.m.

Only five of the men returned. The Serbs dragged them back into the warehouse and dumped them on the floor. All were semiconscious and bleeding from the face and mouth. By morning, all five were dead.

"Please let us take them outside," one of the Muslims who hadn't been chosen for a beating asked the guard.

"Shut up!" the guards barked. "You're not allowed to say one word. Keep them."

The prisoners dragged the bodies to the back of the warehouse. At 9 a.m. two vehicles arrived outside. A Serb appeared at the door. "I need ten hardworking men to do something for me," he said. No one volunteered. Ten of the younger, healthier men remaining were chosen and the vehicles departed.

At 10 a.m., a Serb soldier entered and demanded that the Muslims turn over all their money. When the elderly men said they had nothing, he fired a burst from his assault rifle over their heads. "I'll kill ten men for every man who doesn't give up his money!" he said. "I'll bring dogs here to find it!" The captives turned over the money they had hidden in their clothes. Suljić fished the 400 deutsche marks—roughly $260—he had out of his pocket. He put the money and his watch in his nylon tobacco bag and buried it in the warehouse's dirt floor.

After the Serb left with the money, the beatings resumed. Muslims who were well known in Bratunac before the war and the younger and healthier prisoners were the target. As men were pummeled outside, the guards allowed the older prisoners to drink their first water and make their first trip to the toilet in twenty-four hours.

Taking his place in a long line of prisoners, Suljić hobbled toward the front of the warehouse. To the right was a corridor leading to the bathroom. To the left was a corridor leading outside. "When you go to the bathroom you have to look to the right. If anyone looks to the left, he won't be coming back," the guard warned. "When you come out, you have to look to the left."

As Suljić exited the bathroom, he peeked to his right. Seven or eight Serb soldiers had formed two lines. A Muslim prisoner was walking between them. On the left, one of the Serbs had what looked like an iron crowbar in his hand. He pummeled the prisoner with it. The man crumpled to the ground. On the right, one of the Serbs had an ax, which he embedded in the Muslim's back. The prisoner's body twitched. Blood splattered across the pavement.

Suljić immediately snapped his head to the left and looked at the wall, petrified he would be next. "Look to the left!" the guard commanded. "Look left!"

Suljić made his way back to his seat on the dirt floor. He realized it was all a game. Prisoners seated near the front of the warehouse heard the cries, gasps and groans of Muslims dying outside. The Serbs cursed as they tortured their prisoners: "Turk bastard." After a few minutes a Serb would mutter, "He's finished." The loud hiss of air and gurgle of blood rushing out of a man's throat was followed by the sound of feet kicking the ground. As prisoners' throats were slashed, their bodies went into seizures.

Then it started all over again. The guards slowly scanned the warehouse for their next victim. The 400 prisoners cowered. The victims cried out for help as they were dragged outside. The guards grunted and cursed. And finally, the sound of an ax hitting its mark.

A girl fetching water for her family in Potočari was the first to find them. A young boy then approached Dutch warrant officer Be Oosterveen, drew a finger across his throat and pointed toward a stream across the street from the UN base. He led Oosterveen and another Dutch soldier to nine bodies. Each man had gunshot wounds in the back, near the heart. Unarmed and worried the Serbs would soon find them, the Dutch quickly snapped photos of the bodies and hurried back to the base.[13]

At around noon, Lieutenant Koster, the ranking officer outside the base, returned to the site with Lieutenant Ron Rutten, the commander of the battalion's antitank platoon, A Serb with a radio saw them as they headed toward the bodies. The Dutch knew they had to work quickly. Rutten took close-up photos of the dead men and the wounds. Koster posed for photos next to the bodies to verify he was a witness. But as he and Rutten tried to cut through a field and enter the Dutch base behind the Serbs' backs, shots whizzed over their heads. The peacekeepers sprinted into the crowd of Muslim refugees. Convinced the Serbs would stop them, they nervously crossed through the wall of peacekeepers, surprised to make it to the base

Rutten was furious. He went back outside at approximately 2 p.m. and confronted Lieutenant van Duijn, who had made the deal with the Serbs about the Dutch releasing a certain number of civilians. "Why are you leading the deportation?" Rutten shouted at the tall, muscular Dutch officer. "Why are you collaborating with the Serbs?"

"You can either help or go back to the base," van Duijn shot back.

Rutten, a short thirty-seven-year-old, then approached Captain Mane, the ranking Serb, and started berating him. "This reminds me of fifty years ago!" Rutten yelled. "You remind me of the Nazis!"

The tall, burly Serb officer started screaming back at the Dutch officer. "Don't you call me a Nazi!" he howled. "My grandfather fought with the Partisans against the Nazis!" Van Duijn arrived and separated the two. "Ron, get the hell out of here! Get back in the camp!" The peacekeeper left.

The Serb officer was furious. He immediately halted all the buses and trucks and said they would not start again until van Duijn explained why Rutten had called him a Nazi. Van Duijn agreed to talk with the Serb officer, his translator and two other soldiers behind a house. The Dutch were supposed to be always within sight of one another, but van Duijn went anyway.

"He's so emotional because his family is Jewish," van Duijn said after sitting down on a log. He thought Rutten was Jewish but wasn't sure. "That's why he gets so upset." The Serb captain listened as van Duijn gave a long history lesson about the Nazi occupation of Holland during World War II and the deportation of hundreds of thousands of Dutch Jews. He said he thought some of Rutten's relatives had been killed in the Holocaust.

The captain said that most Serbs had fought with the Partisans against the Nazis, which was more or less correct. Croatia had sided with Nazi Germany, and many Serbs had fought with Tito's Partisans.[14] The Serbs suffered terribly. More than 300,000 were killed in a Croatian-run concentration camp in the town of Jasenova. But the officer couldn't comprehend why Rutten was so upset now.

"I understand his story, but I don't understand why you're making such a big fuss," the Serb captain said, referring to the deportations. "I understand why the guy gets so emotional, but they're not Jews, they're Muslims."

In Paris that day, French President Chirac called President Clinton regarding Srebrenica. Chirac was indignant. He said the Serb separation of the men from the women and detaining them in camps reminded him of World War II.

"We must do something," Chirac insisted.

"Yes," Clinton agreed. "We must act."

Chirac boldly suggested that American helicopters and French troops recapture the city. Stunned, Clinton asked Chirac what they would do with the town. Would they throw out the Serbs and then try to drive the Serbs out of all of Bosnia? Clinton made it clear that he thought the proposal was impractical and didn't support it.

Afterward, Clinton told his aides that the only time the West had ever accomplished anything was when NATO bombed the Serbs. Clinton turned to the young naval aide who had set up the phone call.

"What do you think we should do on Bosnia?" the President asked.

"I don't know, Mr. President," the aide stammered.[15]

Ćamila Omanović remembered jumping from the machine and feeling as though she was sinking. When she regained consciousness, someone was lying on top of her and weeping. It was her brother. She was on a stretcher.

Two Dutch soldiers had run to Ćamila and cut the rope. A Dutch nurse now hovered over her, giving her some kind of injection. "Please, Doctor, don't give me away to the Chetniks," Ćamila pleaded, still hysterical. "Please, Doctor, put me to sleep. Don't let them take me."

"I won't let you go," the male nurse said. He tried to let go of Ćamila, but she clung desperately to his hand. The sedative gradually took hold. Ćamila's mind slowed. Her grip loosened. For the first time in four days, she slept.

Lieutenant Egbers' reputation for staying calm in crisis situations was being tested again. The Dutch attempt to escort convoys of civilians was turning into a humiliating farce. His convoy had left Potočari at 11 a.m., as scheduled. Serbs lined the streets of Bratunac. Serb women and children had pelted the buses full of

Muslims with rocks and bottles. Egbers sped on. There was nothing he could do to control the people in Bratunac, he decided, it was best to keep the buses moving.

When they reached the five-mile stretch of road between Kravica and Konjević Polje, Egbers grew nervous. There were now hundreds of Serb soldiers on the road, which was now lined with military telephone wires. Serbs flagged down his convoy. As Egbers watched Serb soldiers board the buses and demand money from the Muslims, other Serbs surrounded his jeep and demanded that he hand over all his weapons. Egbers explained that he was unarmed, but the Serbs searched his jeep anyway. In order to avoid provoking a confrontation, and to prevent more theft, the Dutch escorting the convoys had been ordered to leave their weapons in the UN base. They were helpless.

A half mile down the road, Egbers and his jeep were stopped again. "I want your jacket and your helmet," a Serb soldier said as he pointed an assault rifle at his chest. Egbers quickly obliged. Twice more his jeep was stopped before he reached Konjević Polje. The buses were now far ahead of him.

He drove south toward Nova Kasaba, amazed by the concentration of Serb soldiers and armored personnel carriers. A stolen Dutch APC was being driven by Serbs. But what he saw just north of Nova Kasaba sent a chill through him.

Thousands of Muslim men were on their knees in the Nova Kasaba soccer field with their hands on their heads. Their eyes were downcast. Serb soldiers barked what sounded like orders or insults. A table was set up near the front of the field to register the prisoners. Hundreds of small bags and sacks the Muslims had been carrying lay on the grass.

There was something in the air. Egbers and other Dutch soldiers noticed a clear difference between the Serb soldiers who had taken over the enclave and these Serbs, who seemed obsessed with stealing as much as possible from the Dutch and the Muslims. Many of them appeared to be Drina Wolves, the local Serb military unit. But to Egbers, they looked and acted like convicts who had just gotten out of prison.

What bothered him more than the Serbs were the terror-stricken prisoners on the soccer field. Almost none of the Muslims were wearing military uniforms. Many of the men imprisoned on the soccer field weren't the trash-talking Muslim soldiers Egbers and the Dutch had resented so much; they were the proud, stubborn farmers the Dutch respected.

Mevludin Orić squatted on top of the hill overlooking Konjević Polje. By 2 p.m. he and the dozen men who had been walking since morning finally made it to the asphalt road. The whereabouts of his father, or any of the men from Srebrenica, still eluded him.

Serb armored personnel carriers, stolen UN APCs and the roar of megaphones greeted them. "Surrender," the megaphones droned. "No one will touch you." Sometimes the Serbs pretended to be Muslims, or they forced Muslims to speak: "UN-PROFOR is providing security for us to leave freely."

Mevludin and his group, led by a soldier armed with a machine gun, moved slowly down the hill. Mevludin was near the back. "Stop," a voice demanded from somewhere in the trees. The group froze. The lead man with the machine gun took a few steps forward. Bullets tore into his chest. Mevludin and the other men ran frantically back up the hill. "Stop!" the voice shouted. "Surrender." Another Serb ambush.

After running twenty yards, Mevludin tripped and fell. The back of his shirt was caught in barbed wire. He pulled frantically at his shirt, tore part of it off, and continued sprinting up the hill. An explosion erupted behind him and he dove behind a tree. Silence hung over the hillside, followed by the sound of men shouting and then quiet conversation. Three of the Muslims in his group approached him.

"Let's go see what happened," one of them said. Another handed Mevludin his rifle. "OK," he said nervously, "I'll go first." They crept back down the hill. Several others from his group were walking around and talking freely to two men he didn't recognize. A figure lay on the ground, an old man dressed in civilian clothes. Mevludin realized he was the one who had

ordered them to surrender. He looked like he was from Srebrenica, but Mevludin wasn't sure. The man's entire chest cavity was
missing. He had committed suicide with a hand grenade.

After two days of no food, little sleep and seemingly endless
ambushes, hysteria was setting in among the thousands of men
from Srebrenica trapped in the hills. Rumors of Serbs infiltrating
the column were multiplying. Real or imagined Serb patrols were
everywhere. Only people from one's own home village could be
trusted. For Mevludin and the thousands of other exhausted
men, the mind was becoming the enemy.

They tried to give the dead man some kind of burial by covering him with leaves. The entire group turned and headed back
up the hill. Despondent, they sat on the peak and watched Serb
and stolen UN APCs patrolling below. The Serbs intermittently
fired antiaircraft grenades blindly at the trees. Muslim men scurried for cover. The Serb line seemed impregnable. Hundreds of
other Muslims sat in small groups across the hillsides. Paralysis
gripped some; others decided to wait until dark to dash across
the road.

Then Mevludin was sure he was hallucinating. He saw Haris,
his cousin and best friend, from whom he had been separated
during the ambush, walking nearby.

"Haris?" Mevludin ventured. The figure turned toward him.

"Mevlo?" the man asked, using Mevludin's nickname.

Mevludin beamed. It was Haris. He stepped forward to em-
brace his cousin and was thrilled when he touched him. The
stocky frame of Haris, the weight lifter, was warm and real.

Ten miles to the northwest, the front of the Muslim column of
men forged through the wilderness. Scouts moved five hundred
yards ahead, probing for Serb ambushes or encampments before
the main column caught up.

Then came Mido Salihović and Ejup Golić and approximately 200 heavily armed Muslim soldiers. Ibran Malagić and
his two brothers were among them. The men were exhausted,
but well armed. The town's commanders had brought several
zoljas or bazookas to destroy tanks if necessary. They also had

rocket-propelled grenades and .50 caliber machine guns. Fearing a Serb ambush, the column headed northwest, not due west toward Muslim-held central Bosnia. They stopped to rest during the day and covered roughly fifteen miles at night.

The enclave's commander, Ramiz Bećirović, walked behind Salihović, Golić and their men. The town's mayor and the war president were even farther behind. The soldiers largely ignored the corrupt officials. Salihović and Golić were in command.

After the soldiers came the wives and children of the town's military and political leaders. Then a long column of 3,000 soldiers, mostly unarmed, wound its way through the woods and hills. The relatives of the town's leaders had chosen to walk with their fathers, uncles or brothers. They were afraid their identities would be discovered if they went to Potočari.

The leaders and their families were surrounded by the enclave's few armed men. Two elderly people were also among the group's most protected civilians. They were Naser Orić's parents.[16]

That afternoon in Srebrenica, a group of Serb officers approached the house that held Zoran Radić's two former teachers. A burly officer with a large, flat sunburned face stopped in the street in front of it. General Ratko Mladić peered at the elderly Muslims standing on the terrace.

"Who are you?" Mladić said gruffly. "Who are those people?"

"We are refugees," Edhem Lućanin, Radić's old teacher, answered.

"Why aren't you in the refugee center?" Mladić asked, referring to Potočari.

"Because we are too old and we are invalids," Lućanin answered.

Mladić briefly conferred with his officers. "Don't go anywhere," Mladić said. "A vehicle will come pick you up at four o'clock."

The general and his entourage abruptly left.

The Muslims were puzzled. Earlier in the afternoon, Serb soldiers had come and asked for "volunteers" to clean up the police station. Many women went. They asked about the nine old men who had been taken away the night before, but the Serb soldiers said they didn't know where they were.

That afternoon, Serb civilians the refugees had known before the war also arrived in Srebrenica. There were bittersweet reunions. The Serbs suggested the Muslims take a loyalty oath and stay; most were anxious to leave.

Zoran Radić checked on his former teachers one last time later that day. The teachers and the fifty elderly women were still there. The conversation was brief. Lućanin told his former student about Mladić's promise. Radić was relieved; he believed Mladić's word was golden.

"Please, please don't mention my name," Radić implored his former teacher. "Whether you want to say I helped you or did bad things to you, please don't mention my name."

He turned to leave. "All the best to you," Radić said. "Good luck."

"Good luck," Lućanin said.

The young policeman disappeared.

As the afternoon passed in Potočari, the factories outside the UN base slowly emptied. Inside the base, grim resignation set in among the 5,000 Muslims sheltered there. They would not be spared.

Around noon, Major Robert Franken had called the two remaining Muslim representatives to meet him in the conference room inside the Dutch compound. Nesib Mandžić and Ibro Nuhanović were told that once the deportation of the refugees outside the base was completed, the 5,000 refugees inside the base would be next.

"But what will happen to the men inside the compound?" Mandžić asked.

Franken said it was obvious that they couldn't resist the Serbs; the people had to leave the base. He asked the two representatives to make a list of all of the men between seventeen and sixty-five. Franken said he would show it to the Serb commanding officer and tell him that the list had already been faxed to Geneva and Holland.

Mandžić was worried about the list falling into Serb hands, but Franken promised to carry a copy of the list out of the enclave in his underwear. He said he thought the Serbs would think twice about doing anything if the UN had evidence of their identity.[17]

Outside the base, the deportations continued. The Serbs hurled insults at women scurrying by with screaming children in their arms. In the last twenty-four hours six babies had been delivered in Potočari. One was stillborn and all were delivered on stretchers in dark, muddy corridors where anyone could watch.

Kristina Schmidt, the Médecins Sans Frontières coordinator, was allowed to reenter the town to collect medical supplies from the hospital. She and a Dutch military observer found six elderly Muslims around the hospital and brought them back to the UN base. Serb soldiers were already looting the town. The Dutch discovered the bodies of three dead Muslim soldiers in the marketplace and snapped photos of them.[18]

In the afternoon, a Muslim father approached Schmidt. Accompanied by his one-year-old child and a Serb soldier, he was weeping. The man had been chosen for "questioning." Schmidt wrote down the man's name and took the baby—convinced the child would never see its father again.[19]

The brutality only worsened. A Serb soldier began to fire over the heads of the unruly Muslims moving toward the buses. But as the crowd pushed forward, he began shooting civilians in the arms and legs at point-blank range.[20]

Even though the Dutch knew the men would be separated from the women, had found nine bodies and witnessed at least one execution,[21] they still forced them to leave the UN base.

As the list of Muslim men inside the base was compiled, Dutch soldiers strung yellow tape from the cavernous hall where the refugees were encamped to the front gate. The path the Muslim men were to follow as they walked into the hands of their potential executioners was clear.

Hasan Nuhanović, the translator who had urged his family

to come to the base, began begging his superiors—UN Military Observers David Kingori, a Kenyan; André van de Haan, who was Dutch; and Joseph Tete, a Ghanaian—to add his brother's name to the list of Muslims who were UN staff workers.

If his brother's name was on the list he could stay. His father, Ibro, was one of the three civilian negotiators and was allowed to remain on the base. His mother would probably survive if she left by bus. His twenty-year-old brother was the only problem.

"Please," Nuhanović begged. "Please. The Serbs will kill him."

The Military Observers said they couldn't do anything without the permission of the Dutch. Major Franken had already said no. Colonel Karremans was still incapacitated with the chronic diarrhea that had plagued him and several other peacekeepers for the last month. Nuhanović began systematically working his way around the base, begging for help from every humanitarian aid organization.

The list of Muslim men was finished: 239 in all. Twelve men refused to put their names on it. Groups of five to ten refugees began making the long walk to the front gate of the base at 4:30 p.m. Serb soldiers stood on the other side, waiting.

Hakija Husejnović and what he estimated were 1,000 to 2,000 other Muslim prisoners[22] sitting in the meadow recognized him immediately. A "short, fat" figure with "lapels on his shoulders," General Ratko Mladić strode across the grass to inspect them. For four hours, the men had sweltered under the hot sun as their Serb guards robbed them. Finally, Husejnović thought, something would be done.

He had been caught in the ambush in Kamenica the night before. A fifty-one-year-old farmer from a village outside Srebrenica, Husejnović was disoriented after the attack and had no idea how to get to Tuzla. The men who had been guiding his group either were killed in the ambush or had disappeared. Wandering around the hills above Kamenica all morning, Husejnović and the other men were again shelled by the Serbs around noon.

Loudspeakers told them they were surrounded. The men decided to surrender. They were led down the hill to a meadow just off the asphalt road running between Bratunac and Konjević Polje.

Husejnović realized that they were in Lolići, a village just west of Kravica. He knew nothing of the atrocities that Serbs maintained Orić and his troops had committed there in the 1993 Orthodox Christmas raid.

At least three of the other prisoners were men from Lehovići who had set off with Mevludin Orić. Sefik Hasanović, twenty-five, and Haso Hasanović, sixteen, sat in the clearing.[23] Immediately after the ambush, Haso and Mevludin had sprinted down the hill, but had been separated when the Serbs resumed fire. Haso was captured that day, but when the Serbs sent him to get water, he found a teenage girl with her throat slit and other bodies near the stream and was able to slip into the woods.[24]

At first, the prisoners were treated relatively well. They were forced to hand over all their money and dump their rucksacks on the other side of the road. Serb guards recognized a handful of Muslim friends from before the war. They greeted them warmly and took them away. Younger prisoners were sent to get water in the sweltering heat. The Serb soldier sitting in an APC just to their right had pointed his gun at the prisoners and joked with another soldier. "Should I shoot them?" he asked. "Don't be silly," the other Serb said. The barrels of the guns were pointed down. Husejnović thought that Mladić's arrival would only improve their treatment.

Mladić was blunt with his prisoners. "Is it better this way or to get killed?" he asked without waiting for an answer. "Naser abandoned you. He escaped." Mladić paused. "It's not good to be at war with the Serbs. The sheep cannot leave the stable until the doors are open.

"We have evacuated your families. You will be evacuated yourself in a day or two," Mladić said. "Nobody is going to beat you or provoke you. If it's necessary we will give you some food. We'll move you to a cooler place than this."

The Muslims applauded Mladić. Husejnović dared to raise his hand.

"General, I'm barefoot and my shoes are in my rucksack," Husejnović said. "Can I get them?"

"You'll get new shoes," Mladić said. The general conferred with some of his officers, got in his car with his entourage and left. Twenty minutes later, a new Serb arrived who acted as if he was in charge, but he wore no insignia to show he was an officer.

"Line up in rows of four!" he shouted. Husejnović and the other Muslims dutifully obeyed. They formed a column roughly 600 yards long and began marching east toward Kravica. Serb soldiers carrying Kalashnikov assault rifles walked on either side of the prisoners. Husejnović was impressed by the amount of ammunition they had strung across their chests.

After twenty minutes, the column reached the outskirts of Kravica. A UN jeep with what looked like two Dutch peacekeepers passed, barely slowing down. The prisoners were led into a complex of three tan concrete warehouses with dark brown trim used by local farmers to stockpile goods. Husejnović and the other men were slowly herded inside the largest warehouse.

The building was divided into two rooms.[25] There were three or four narrow windows on the back walls of both. There was a narrow doorway in the room next to Husejnović; the one he was in had a twenty-five-foot-wide opening for farm vehicles. It was a relief for the prisoners to get out of the sun, but having so many men crammed into such a small space was claustrophobic. He and several friends from his home village of Sućeska sat down together in a corner.

The men closest to the door and the windows were probably puzzled when they saw the Serbs raise their rifles. Positioned in front of windows and doorways, the Serbs suddenly opened fire and then threw hand grenades into the warehouse. Chaos erupted inside. Men shrieked when they realized they were trapped. Others screamed as shrapnel and bullets tore into them. The few that leapt over the piles of bodies and made it outside were mowed down. The sound of the hand and rocket-propelled grenades exploding inside the warehouse was deafening. Bodies were pulverized. Blood and crimson bits of flesh were spattered across the gray cinder-block walls. Chunks of skull and brain matter flew sixteen feet in the air and stuck to the ceiling.

Husejnović dove to the floor. "Hakija, brother," his friend Salko Redjić shouted from behind him, "I've just died." More grenades. More machine-gun bursts. After five minutes, there was a lull in the firing. Piles of corpses, or what was left of them, lay strewn across the concrete floor. Wounded men moaned. The living hid under the dead.

Husejnović was delusional. He remembered standing and walking toward what he thought was some kind of reception desk. As he stepped over mutilated bodies, he thought he saw Zulfo Salihović—a man he knew from Srebrenica—staring up at him.

"Don't let me die," Husejnović stammered. "Is there any water here?"

"What water?" Salihović whispered back. "Lie down."

Just as Husejnović lowered himself to the floor, the Serbs sprayed his corner of the warehouse with bullets. He pulled a dead body on top of himself. Husejnović felt something warm spread across the right side of his body. It was someone else's blood.

Ratko Mladić apparently relished making speeches. He arrived at the Nova Kasaba soccer field roughly thirty minutes after addressing Hakija Husejnović and the other prisoners. In Nova Kasaba, another group of Muslims awaited his judgment.

One of them was sixty-five-year-old Smail Hodžić, a farmer who had volunteered to walk through the woods with the men because he had a horse that could carry wounded. His wife, daughter and grandson went to Potočari without him. The trip had gone wrong as soon as Hodžić and his group left the enclave. They had been randomly fired upon and shelled.

After the initial ambush in Kamenica, small groups of Serb soldiers had started "Muslim hunting" inside the killing zone Mladić created by blocking the asphalt roads. Heavily armed Serbs roamed the woods placing mines, setting booby traps and

sniping at Muslim soldiers and civilians. With only every third
Muslim armed, the hunt was bounteous.

But what had unnerved Hodžić the most was the way Muslims were acting. He was convinced that the Serbs were using
some form of chemical gas or lacing the streams in the area with
hallucinogens. At the site of an ambush Hodžić had stumbled
upon that morning, ten men who had survived sat amid a dozen
corpses and spoke incoherently. When they saw Hodžić and his
group they threatened to strangle them.[26]

As Hodžić and a group of 150 Muslims approached Nova
Kasaba, they came upon more and more dead soldiers. He
thought he'd seen as many as thirty-five with no chests or heads,
having killed themselves with hand grenades or pistols. Hodžić
found one old friend who was wounded. He asked simply for a
hand grenade and to be left alone.

At noon, Hodžić and 150 other men descended toward the
asphalt road and found themselves suddenly surrounded. "Give
up. We will not harm you. We will not touch you," the Serbs
said. "The elderly will be sent to Tuzla to join their families.
The young will be exchanged for Serb soldiers." Hodžić and the
150 men raised their hands or waved white bandages and surrendered.

They were ordered to keep their hands on their heads, and
started marching toward the Nova Kasaba soccer field. Along
the way, the Serb soldier guarding Hodžić begged him for for-
giveness. "I'm from Krajina," the soldier whispered, referring to
western Bosnia. "My future is no better than yours."

What the soldier said next filled Hodžić with a strange combination of trepidation and pity. "If there's any luck and any of
you survive and my child comes to your door, please give him
a piece of bread," he whispered. "If I don't do this, it will be
against orders."

"Make them go faster!" another Serb soldier shouted.

"Please go faster," whispered the Serb walking next to Hodžić.

When they finally arrived at the soccer field, Hodžić couldn't
believe his eyes. Over 2,000 Muslim prisoners were on their
knees with their hands behind their backs. New Serb guards or-

dered Hodžić and the other prisoners to dump their rucksacks in a pile and turn over all their money. Hodžić joined the other prisoners kneeling in the hot sun.

Several hours later, Mladić arrived. "You are welcome here. No one will harm you," the Serb general bellowed across the field. "You should have given yourselves up earlier. You shouldn't have tried to go through the woods.

"Look what your Alija has done to you. He destroyed you," Mladić said. "You will be going to Bratunac and be spending the night there." Surrounded by his bodyguards, Mladić lumbered across the field to speak to Serbs who appeared to be officers. After a few minutes he left and trucks began arriving.[27]

At approximately 6:15 p.m., the truck Mladić had promised the elderly Muslims trapped in Srebrenica arrived. It was two hours late, but Zoran Radić's former teachers and the fifty women were ecstatic. The Serb driver helped the Muslims move the invalids—including Edhem Lućanin's mother—onto the truck. No one stopped them as they drove to Potočari.

In Potočari, Lućanin's improbable journey continued. His truck pulled up alongside one bound for central Bosnia. "Jump in that so you won't end up in a camp," said a Serb Lućanin had never seen before.

Lućanin, Mustafić and an elderly man who had been sleeping behind the couch when the Serbs rounded up the old men, hopped in the truck. Muslim women ordered them to lie down. The women filled the trucks, completely shielding the elderly men from potentially hostile Serb soldiers. The truck's engine rumbled to life. The convoy of refugees left Potočari with the men safely hidden.

Later that night, Serb policeman Radić returned to the house in Srebrenica to check on his teachers once again. It was empty. He was told the Muslims had been taken to Potočari. A wave of relief washed over him.

...

At approximately 6 p.m., a Serb officer appeared in the doorway of the Bratunac warehouse holding Hurem Suljić and the other Muslim men separated from their families. The prisoners recognized him immediately.

"Why are you holding us here? Why are you torturing us here?" the old men shouted. "Why are you dividing us from our families? We can't breathe in this warehouse."

"We had been unable to make an agreement with the Bosnian authorities earlier," General Mladić said. "But we have now arranged everything for an exchange in Kalesija." Mladić then asked one of the men in the warehouse to count the number of prisoners so he could provide transportation. There were 296 men.

"The buses will be from the Bosnian authorities," Mladić said before leaving. "You all will have enough places to sit in. Everything is going to be all right. You will not be hurt."

Suljić estimated that another forty men had been taken outside and beaten that day. Ten more men had also been chosen for another "volunteer" work crew and never returned. Roughly 400 of them must have been brought to the warehouse two days before. Now there were only 296. As Suljić scanned the sweat-covered faces around him, he realized that nearly all of the younger, healthier men were gone. At fifty-five, Suljić thought he was one of the youngest men left.

At 7 p.m., only 200 Muslim refugees remained inside the Dutch base. All three UN Military Observers told Hasan Nuhanović his family had to leave the base. Hasan was apoplectic. His mother sat in the Military Observers' office weeping. His father was pacing, trying to decide whether he would use his right as a Muslim negotiator to stay on the base or accompany his wife and youngest son.

One thought haunted the twenty-eight-year-old translator: I have killed my brother. When it was clear Srebrenica was falling, he, his family and his brother agreed that their best chance for survival was with the United Nations. The forty-mile trek to Tuzla would be hazardous and unpredictable. Even if the Dutch refused to concoct fake papers for Hasan's brother, Hasan had been sure they would not allow the Serbs to separate the men from their families.

The UN Military Observers, the aid workers from Médecins Sans Frontières and a representative of the UN High Commissioner for Refugees all said the same thing. Whether or not his brother stayed depended on the Dutch commanding officer. As the last groups departed, Hasan's father pulled him aside. "I'm going with your mother and brother," he said. Desperate, the translator decided to plead with Major Franken one last time.

"Please let him stay. Please put his name on the list," Nuhanović begged. "If he stays, my father will also, and I'm sure my mother will be all right on the buses."

The Serbs had told Franken they would be inspecting the base for Muslims after the last refugees departed.

"No," Franken said, clearly exasperated. The Dutch major felt he had no choice. He and his men were still surrounded and outgunned. He believed the Serbs wouldn't dare to kill the Muslims since he had a list of their names.[28]

Hasan stumbled back to his family in shock. The organization he had worked for over the last two years was sending his family to what he thought was their death. His mother sobbed. His twenty-year-old brother stood up.

"You're not coming with me!" he screamed at Hasan, fighting back tears. "You're not coming with me!"

As Hasan's mother and brother made their way to the front gate, Major Franken walked up to him and his father. "You can stay. You're on the list," Franken reminded Ibro. "You're a negotiator. It's your decision."

"I'm going with my wife and son," Ibro answered.

Franken turned to Hasan. "Go to the cantina with the other local staff," he said. "The Serbs are going to inspect the camp. They'll check your ID cards. We're not responsible for what happens."

Franken turned and walked with Hasan's father toward the gate. Hasan's brother and mother were waiting for them. Hasan lost sight of the group as they passed behind a fence.

At the gate of the Dutch base, Hasan's father tried to show

the Serbs that the Dutch considered him and his family important. He turned to Franken and kissed him on the cheek.

"Goodbye," Franken said.

"Goodbye," Hasan's father said.

Franken walked back into the UN base. Hasan's father,
mother and brother walked toward the Serbs.

A little over an hour after he left Potočari, Edhem Lućanin found
himself only four miles from Muslim-held central Bosnia. As the
truck emptied, he unfolded a blanket and gently lifted his ninety-
two-year-old mother and placed her in the center of it. Blind,
she also could not walk.

The retired schoolteacher, sixty-eight, and his wife, sixty-five,
braced themselves. Each grabbed two corners of the blanket and
lifted. They were going to carry her for four miles. As they departed, the Serb soldiers made no effort to stop them. For the
first mile, Lućanin felt well enough. But his arms began to tire
during the second mile. Sweat poured from him in the July heat.
He and his wife labored, alternating between carrying her on
their backs and carrying her in the blanket. By what he thought
was the third mile, he and his wife were reduced to taking a few
small steps and waiting.

"Leave me here," his mother begged him. "You're not going
to make it."

Lućanin and his wife ignored her. He started asking people
how much farther it was. None of the Muslim women around
him knew. Everyone was worried about stepping on mines. As
their grip on the blanket weakened and their arms burned, they
saw a Serb soldier sitting on a guardrail.

"Leave me!" his mother demanded again.

"Don't leave her," the Serb soldier said. "Go another three
hundred yards. After that, your people are waiting." Then, as
waves of relief washed over Lućanin, the Serb soldier looked at
the old man and woman struggling so mightily to save one life.

"Fuck Izetbegović, Milošević, Karadžić and Tudjman," the
Serb soldier said, referring to the Muslim, Serb and Croat na-

tionalist leaders that led Bosnia to war. "We are not guilty, the politicians are guilty."

The soldier told Lućanin that Serbs were also suffering in the war and reminded him to stay in the middle of the road to avoid mines. Filled with a final burst of energy, Lućanin and his wife crossed the front line five minutes later. The sixty-eight-year-old man's mother was still in his arms.

After his family departed and Hasan Nuhanović started walking toward the cantina, he stopped. André, a Russian who had worked for the UN High Commissioner for Refugees in Srebrenica for four to five months, was standing with other UN officials nearby. The Serbs had allowed the UN to send officials to monitor the "evacuation," but only after it was essentially completed.

"What's going to happen to my family?" Hasan asked. "What's going to happen to us?"

"As long as they didn't have anything to do with the BH they will be OK," André said.[29] Hasan turned and walked to the cantina. When he entered he gasped. It was filled with the faces of the UN's two dozen local workers. And there were other faces too. The mother, wife and small son of one of the Muslims who worked for Médecins Sans Frontières, as well as the two teenage sons of another MSF worker. The families hid inside the base, ignoring the Dutch instructions to leave. The Muslims were gambling that the Serbs would not thoroughly check for UN ID cards.

Nuhanović wanted to kill himself. He could have done the same thing with his brother. He left the cantina. Five minutes later, Franken returned from the gate. The Dutch major made a crack that Nuhanović would understand only later. "You know what just happened to me?" Franken told another Dutch officer. "For the first time in my life, I was kissed by a man!"

Approximately thirty minutes later, a handful of Serb soldiers conducted their long-awaited search. They looked over the empty factory hall quickly. When they got to the cantina, they opened the door, peered at the Muslims inside and left. Whether all of the Muslims had UN ID cards was never checked. If Hasan Nuhanović's brother had been allowed to stay on the base, he wouldn't have been discovered.

Energized and optimistic after finding each other in the chaos of the hillside, Mevludin Orić and Haris quickly caught up on what had happened during their separation. Mevludin asked if Haris had any idea where his father was. His cousin said no. Mevludin had no idea where any of Haris' relatives were either.

After the ambush in Kamenica, Haris had sprinted down the hill and gotten lost. That night, he joined a group heading toward Nova Kasaba. They were unsure where to go in the dark, so they slept in a grove of trees. Haris, explaining that his group had decided earlier to surrender, stood up.

"Where are you going?" Mevludin asked.

"We're going to surrender," Haris said.

"Don't fuck around," Mevludin warned. "Stay with me and we'll try to cross during the night."

Haris agreed to stay. Hunger crippled both of them. The only food Mevludin had eaten that day was a can of beef he had shared with all the other men. There didn't seem to be any apple orchards or vegetable gardens in the deserted area. The mundane was now invaluable.

Shrapnel suddenly tore through the trees around them.[30] The Serbs were spraying the hill with a Praga antiaircraft gun. Mevludin and Haris crouched beneath a tree for cover. Bedlam set in as it had in Kamenica, but with a twist.

The few Muslim men with rifles threatened to kill anyone who came near them. They fired wildly at what they thought were Serbs hiding in nearby trees. Others set off hand grenades that killed themselves and anyone who happened to be around them. Bursts of automatic rifle fire erupted across the hillside. Antiaircraft shells and hand grenades exploded at random. After fifteen minutes, there was no letup in the Serb shelling. Mevludin and Haris were convinced the Serbs were using some kind of poison gas. Men who had been rational only moments ago now threatened to kill them.

After half an hour, the shelling diminished to intermittent bursts. By 4:30 p.m. the dozen men Mevludin had been walking with that morning had gathered again on the hillside. Three men—the ones who knew the area best—set off at 5 p.m. to scout out the best place to cross the road. They never returned. At 7:30 p.m., Mevludin, Haris and the seven remaining men crept slowly down the hillside. Their plan was to get close to the road, but to wait until dark to cross. They advanced slowly through the forest. When they were 200 yards from the road, they ran into thick bushes covered with thorns. They shifted their direction and headed down a nearby path.

A man with a machine gun leapt out from behind a tree. "Stop! Surrender!" he shouted. A second man appeared from the opposite side. Mevludin realized he was surrounded and unarmed. He had lost his only weapon—a hand grenade—in Kamenica. "If you run, we'll shoot," the soldier warned.

The Muslims were led down the path at gunpoint for thirty yards until it widened. "Lie face down on the ground," the soldier said. Mevludin and the other men nervously complied. The Muslims were searched for weapons, then ordered to stand up. "Put your hands behind your head," the soldier demanded. The Muslims obeyed and were led to the asphalt road. Guarded at gunpoint, they walked to Konjević Polje. They filed into some form of storehouse, where they were ordered to put their hands against the wall and were searched again. Mevludin could not believe they had been caught. He prayed that the Serbs would give them some food.

An officer entered the room and began questioning them. Mevludin knew instantly from his accent that he was not a local Serb, but an officer from neighboring Serbia. His suspicions that Serbian President Slobodan Milošević's soldiers were involved in the attack were confirmed.

"Where are your guns?" the officer asked.

"We don't have any rifles. We are all civilians," Mevludin answered. Realizing he might be captured, Mevludin had changed out of the military uniform he was so proud of and into the civilian clothes he found in an abandoned bag in the forest.

"Why did you throw away your guns?" the officer asked, seemingly convinced the Muslims were well armed. The prisoners again said they had no rifles.

"What did you do in Srebrenica?" the officer pressed on.

"I delivered humanitarian aid," Mevludin said, lying. "I'm a civilian."

The officer promised to bring them food, but returned with only water. There was no food left, but he offered the Muslims precious cigarettes.

"There are more prisoners coming," the officer said. "Wait a while. A bus will come and take you to Bratunac."

The prisoners were left alone with one Serb guard. The Serb apologized to his prisoners. "I'd like to let you go, but I don't dare do it," he said. "I never wanted this war. I had Muslim neighbors. I told them I didn't want to fight, and I was beaten."

Two buses arrived from the direction of central Bosnia as the sun began to set. Mevludin thought of his mother, wife and daughter in Potočari. Maybe they were already in Tuzla. All of the Serb policemen on the bus wore a strange kind of flak jacket. They were light blue and carried the legend "civilian police" in English. As the bus sped to Bratunac, Mevludin realized the Serbs had stolen them from the peacekeepers his mother, wife and child now depended on.

When Lieutenant Egbers arrived in Nova Kasaba at 6 p.m., he was astounded by what he saw. He had caught up with his convoy that morning and spent the afternoon on the Serb side of the crossing point. But as he drove back to Potočari, he saw thirteen Dutch peacekeepers sheepishly sitting on the ground next to a Bosnian Serb checkpoint in Nova Kasaba. Only four jeeps were parked on the side of the road. Egbers, the ranking officer among the Dutch, got out of his jeep.

"What's going on here?" Egbers asked.

The Dutch said seven of their jeeps and almost all of their flak jackets and helmets had been stolen by the Serbs. Sergeant

Martyn Mülder, the commanding officer from Observation Post Mike, who had driven the Muslim officer's family to Potočari, had the most humiliating story. That afternoon, his jeep was first halted outside Konjević Polje by Serb soldiers who were members of the Drina Wolves. Mülder gave them his flak jacket. Two hundred yards later, his jeep was stolen.

A Serb policeman then walked the Dutch to Konjević Polje and promised them they would be given a ride back to the UN base in Potočari. But a group of Serb soldiers dressed in stolen Dutch uniforms driving a stolen Dutch APC arrived. One of the Serbs spoke a little English. The peacekeepers were ordered to come "Muslim hunting" with the Serbs. Mülder and the sergeant with him were handed rifles "for their own protection," the Serbs explained. "You shoot a Muslim if you see them," the Serb said.

The Dutch climbed onto the APC and sat silently as it roared down the road. The Serbs joked and laughed with each other. They briefly patrolled in the woods. Mülder prayed they would not find a Muslim. After ten minutes, the Dutch climbed inside the APC. The Serbs patrolled for a few more minutes and returned to Konjević Polje. Altogether, it was a twenty-minute "hunt."[31]

Egbers didn't know it but twenty miles away in Vlasenica, Corporal Hans Berkers, one of the APC drivers, had his Mercedes jeep stolen by a Serb policeman. Berkers was taken by two paramilitaries from Serbia to a hotel in town. As Berkers sat on the balcony and sipped beer while wearing his light blue UN baseball cap, busloads of Muslim women and children passed by.[32]

Exasperated, Egbers tried to find the ranking Serb officer. A young Serb major introduced himself as Zoran Divjak. A soldier who spoke excellent English translated for him.

"General Mladić told us to escort the women and children," Egbers said. "It's in your interest that we be able to tell the world that the women and children are OK. I cannot allow you to have Dutch hunting Muslims or have your soldiers steal our weapons and vehicles."

"We've got a big problem," Major Divjak explained. "There

are Muslims in the hills who want to surrender and there are other Muslims who don't want to surrender. They are fighting with each other."

The young major then confirmed Egbers' fears about the Serb soldiers lining the roads. "There are soldiers from all over the country on these roads and I can't guarantee your safety."

The Dutch were at the center of a massive mop-up operation referred to as "cleansing the terrain" by the Serbs. The Bosnian Serb Army had mounted such campaigns throughout the war, but this was by far the largest in two years. Mladić had pulled in army and police units from all across the country to capture as many Muslims from Srebrenica as possible.

The Dutch had also seen a handful of bodies scattered along the route to the crossing point. They assumed they were from the overcrowded trucks or Muslim men who had been killed in fighting or captured and shot.[33]

Mülder, who had been forced to "hunt" with the Serbs, insisted that the Dutch be allowed to drive to Potočari. "I want to go back," he said.

"I'm not sure if it's safe," Major Divjak warned.

"I want to try to go back because we need to get a jeep back to Potočari," Mülder said.

Egbers agreed, but said he would wait for one jeep that was headed toward Nova Kasaba from the crossing point. He was worried that they could have all their jeeps stolen and the Dutch would then have no radio contact with Potočari.

"OK," the young Serb major said. "I'll send one Serb officer with you to make sure you're safe." Three jeeps and twelve peacekeepers departed.

Ten minutes later, one jeep, packed with a dozen humiliated peacekeepers, returned. Two of the three jeeps had been stolen at gunpoint. Egbers radioed the UN base in Potočari. A jeep was sent to rescue the stranded peacekeepers, but it, too, was stolen.

Lieutenant Leen van Duijn, the Dutch peacekeeper who had agreed to have the Dutch help the Serbs control the refugees, went over to the house where the Muslim men were detained.

It was 7 p.m., and the evacuation was nearly complete. Van Duijn wanted to make sure the Serbs knew they were being watched.

The 250 to 300 Muslim men sitting outside the house were completely silent. They were obviously afraid of what was about to happen. Earlier, the Serb guards prevented the terrified Muslims from praying.[34]

Van Duijn peppered the Serb guards with questions about what the Serbs were going to do with the prisoners. He got the same answer he had heard over the last two days—the Serbs would check whether they were war criminals. As van Duijn left, he noticed a pile of papers lying near the house. Dozens of passports and identity cards that belonged to the Muslim men lay scattered across the ground. He walked up to Mane, the young Serb captain who had been outraged when he was called a Nazi.

"You're going to try to identify the people?" van Duijn asked.

"Yes," Mane said. "We have a list of war criminals."

"Then you'll need their passports to identify them," van Duijn said.

"I don't follow you," Mane said.

"Those passports," van Duijn said, pointing at the pile on the ground. "You're going to need them to identify the Muslims or they'll just give you false names."

"You're crazy," Mane said, shaking his head and laughing. "They don't need those passports anymore."

Van Duijn froze. The Serbs were going to kill all the men. Mane confirmed it. He walked away from the Serb officer and radioed the Dutch operations room. He reported what he had seen and been told. "We really need to escort the buses with the men," he radioed. "We need to escort the buses."

A few minutes later, the prisoners were being loaded onto a bus. Van Duijn tried to get on the bus, but a Serb soldier with a Kalashnikov assault rifle pushed him away from the door. Captain Mane was suddenly behind the peacekeeper. "Don't bother," the captain said.

Van Duijn radioed the operations room again. "Send a Mercedes out," he said. "We've got to follow this bus."

"We'll work on it," an officer replied.

A few minutes later, the bus full of Muslim prisoners departed. No Mercedes jeep appeared.

As nightfall approached, the young Serb major urged Lieutenant Egbers and the other Dutch to spend the night in Nova Kasaba for safety reasons. With fourteen men, only two jeeps left and Serb criminals lining the road, Egbers felt he had little choice. The Dutch moved into a local elementary school that the Serbs had converted into an army barracks.

The school was a half mile from the soccer field where the approximately 1,000 to 2,000 Muslim prisoners were gathered. The Dutch could not see the field from where they were, but prisoners were also being detained in a small building adjacent to the school. Explosions and gunfire intermittently erupted in the surrounding woods.

There were hundreds of Serb soldiers in the area, including men with dogs to track down Muslims. Many of them were Drina Wolves. The outline of a wolf's head was spray-painted on their green jeeps. Egbers had also seen Serbs drive by in one of the stolen Dutch APCs.

While the Dutch waited by the side of the road, the headquarters in Potočari suggested they set up a checkpoint to count the number of buses passing by. The Dutch did the best they could, but realized they had already missed numerous vehicles while their jeeps and personal belongings were being stolen.

A car from the International Committee of the Red Cross (ICRC) had also stopped at the Serb checkpoint in Nova Kasaba. Two men and two women who said they were from the ICRC office in Pale wanted to know if they could get through to the Serbian capital of Belgrade. The Dutch told the ICRC workers—whose organization specialized in monitoring and registering prisoners of war and was demanding access to the Muslims from Srebrenica—about the twenty Muslim prisoners seen in the building adjacent to the school. But the vehicle turned around and headed back to Pale.[35]

The Dutch were given bunks among the Serb soldiers in the

makeshift barracks. A Serb lieutenant[36] explained to the Dutch what was happening. "Muslims are blowing themselves up with hand grenades when they see the Serbs. There's a lot of fighting. Everyone is very nervous." At one point, a Muslim prisoner was brought into the barracks. Other Serbs complained that constant Muslim raids from Srebrenica had forced them to attack the safe area. They said Naser Orić had been allowed to leave the enclave after he bribed the Serbs, but had no specifics.

Chicken was served for dinner—the first hot meal the Dutch had enjoyed in weeks—and they had all the cigarettes they could smoke. An Austrian, apparently a mercenary who was fighting with the Serbs, introduced himself to the Dutch, and they started drinking plum brandy and vodka with the Serbs. Egbers was on the point of stopping them, but decided it was all right after everything the peacekeepers had endured in the enclave.

Major Divjak, the young Serb officer in charge, claimed he commanded three battalions. Officers and policemen from Milići and other towns were constantly checking with him. Major Divjak had his own office with a computerized chess game. Egbers started playing chess with him. The Dutch officer was again impressed with the Serbs' organization.

The young major explained why the Serbs attacked Srebrenica. "Naser Orić was constantly coming out of the enclave and killing our people," he said. "We had too many troops tied down guarding it. The Muslims were never fully disarmed."

Egbers had heard it all before. He was worried about getting his men back to Potočari safely. One of them was a Dutch Special Forces commando who had helped guide the NATO air attack on Srebrenica. The commando was terrified the Serbs would uncover his identity.

At 9 p.m., shouts were heard from the building where the prisoners were held. "Can I take a look?" asked one of the Dutch soldiers. Egbers and Sergeant Jos Vissiering tagged along.

They found thirty Muslim prisoners huddled in a single room. Two had black eyes and appeared to have been badly beaten. Another prisoner was suffering from a stomach wound. The look of terror was unmistakable.

When the Dutch returned, some Serbs pointed their guns at

the peacekeepers, but most were still friendly. Over the course of the evening, shots from hand-held weapons rang out from the soccer field and the woods to the north. Muslims fighting, the Serbs claimed, and they turned down Dutch requests to inspect the soccer field. It was too dangerous, they said. The Dutch might be shot by Muslims.

That night, a Dutch soldier was always on watch on thirty-minute rotations. At approximately 2:30 a.m., Sergeant Mülder, who had been forced to "hunt" Muslims earlier, heard a series of single shots—not gun battles—coming from the soccer field. They went on for an hour to an hour and a half.

He thought of the 1,000 to 2,000 prisoners he had seen on the field that afternoon and turned to one of his colleagues. "They're all going down," he said.

Mevludin Orić and his cousin Haris sat nervously on the hot, overcrowded bus. Seventy-five to a hundred prisoners were crammed onto vehicles that seated fifty. After leaving Konjević Polje, the two buses had stopped in Kravica. Thousands of Muslim prisoners, it seemed, were sitting in fields around the town. They could see Serb soldiers kicking men or hitting them with the butts of their rifles.

In Bratunac, the two buses parked in front of an elementary school.[37] Mevludin, Haris and the seven men with whom they had surrendered were jammed into the back seat. Serb soldiers told them they would be spending the night on the bus. Guards were on board at all times, constantly shouting at the Muslims to keep their hands on the backs of their heads. The prisoners were not allowed to sleep.

The Serb officer in charge, who said his first name was Ilija, had soldiers take groups of five to six Muslims into the school. Then shots would echo in the night air. "Don't worry," one of the Serb guards said. "It's only people celebrating. A recruit is joining the army." Mevludin tried desperately not to attract attention.

At one point, a retarded Muslim prisoner who was sitting near the front of the bus fell asleep. When a Serb tried to wake him, the Muslim woke up and grabbed the guard's flak jacket. The Serb slapped him. "Fuck your mother!" he roared. "Let's slaughter him." The prisoners tried to explain that he was retarded. It was too late. The young man was taken off the bus and shot. His body was dragged into the elementary school.

The school was only a few hundred yards from the agricultural warehouse which Hurem Suljić and 295 other elderly and crippled men had finally left after twenty-four hours. At approximately 8 p.m., six empty buses had arrived at the warehouse. Suljić quickly dug up his money and valuables from the floor and dutifully got on the bus. General Mladić watched the prisoners file on, gave instructions to the fifteen to twenty Serb soldiers standing nearby and disappeared. Each bus carried a soldier armed with an assault rifle.

"Why are we waiting?" one of the prisoners asked.

"I'm waiting for an order to leave," the driver said.

At 9 p.m., the convoy left Bratunac and drove north along the Drina River toward Zvornik. But halfway to Zvornik the buses halted. Suljić and the other prisoners waited. Suljić told himself he was on his way to a prisoner exchange.

In another part of Bratunac that night, Smail Hodžić and what he guessed were 600 Muslim prisoners who had sweltered through Mladić's speech on the Nova Kasaba soccer field were packed shoulder to shoulder in two sixty-foot-long, sixteen-wheel trucks. After Mladić's speech, some of the prisoners on the soccer field were forced onto the trucks. The cloth top had been pulled over the end of the truck and tied shut. Trapped in the darkness, the 300 Muslim men in each vehicle had no idea where they being taken. Hodžić's driver was kind. He told the Muslims they were being taken to Bratunac, and identified each village along the way. They had arrived at approximately 8 p.m..

For three hours, the men stood in the stifling trucks. At 11 p.m., guards finally lifted the top off the back entrance of the truck. Local Serb men and women from Bratunac were waiting. They asked if any Muslims from Bratunac or any old friends they knew were on board. "We brought you dinner," they said, or "We brought you cigarettes." About twenty Muslims got off the truck. They were asked questions briefly and then the Serbs began to beat them. The men in the truck listened to their cries, and then heard pistol fire. None of the twenty returned.

At 12:30 a.m., more people appeared at the back of Hodžić's truck, wanting to know if there were any Muslims from the villages of Kravica and Lolići on the truck. About twenty Muslim men, either deciding that they wanted to die or believing somehow that their friends would spare them, got off. They were immediately beaten. "Fuck your Gypsy mother!" one Serb shouted. Again, shots were heard. Again, none of the twenty returned.

As the night dragged on, the heat, the smell and the mosquitoes in the Muslim-filled truck and buses parked around Bratunac were overwhelming. Plagued by thirst, men drank their own urine.[38]

In Tišća, the crossing point, twenty-two men who have been caught trying to make it to central Bosnia are taken to a school. At one point their Serb guards bring a beautiful young Muslim woman before them. She knows one of the prisoners and is then led away. After two hours of beatings, during which men who tried to dress as women are singled out for the most brutal treatment, the group is driven to a nearby forest. Only one of them survives.

But nothing yet approached the depravity of the warehouse in Kravica. Still soaked in other people's blood, Hakija Husejnović lay in abject terror. Serb soldiers fired into the warehouse whenever they heard voices. Convinced he would be shot by Serbs outside if he tried to escape, he waited. As the hours passed, the two bodies on top of him seemed to grow heavier, the stench worsened and he tried to fight off nausea. His friends and neighbors were beginning to rot.

FRIDAY, JULY 14, 1995

COLUMN AND CONVOY ROUTES, JULY 14, 1995

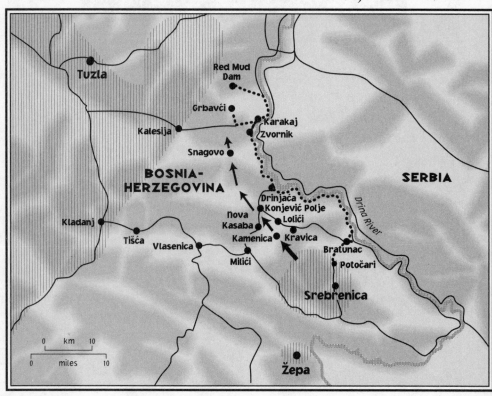

Muslim- and Croat-controlled ◄— Column of men •••••• Route of prisoners

The bus carrying Hurem Suljić and the other old men rumbled forward. The prisoners in the six-bus convoy had been waiting in the village of Drinjaća, halfway between the Bosnian Serb-held towns of Bratunac and Zvornik, for what Suljić thought was two to three hours. Questions about the delay were met with silence or vague answers from the driver.

They drove north toward Zvornik, in the direction of Kalesija—the town on the front line where Mladić had told them the prisoner exchange would take place. The half-mile-wide Drina River shimmered in the moonlight. The river was recognized by the international community as the border between the newly independent country of Bosnia and what was left of Yugoslavia—Serbia and Montenegro. But for Serb nationalists, the Drina did not mark the end of Serb lands, it marked the center of them. The Drina was "the spine" of Greater Serbia, they said, and the land on both sides of the river belonged to the Serbs. The fall of Srebrenica and the expulsion of Suljić, his fellow prisoners and 40,000 other Muslims was the culmination of the Serb nationalist agenda in eastern Bosnia.

They were driving through a region that before the war was 62 percent Muslim, but was now at best 1 percent Muslim. The Muslim-majority towns of Bratunac, Zvornik, Bijeljina and dozens of others had been "ethnically cleansed." The 150,000 Muslims who lived in the Drina Valley had been expelled or killed.

The Serb war effort there mirrored their tactics throughout mostly Muslim Bosnia; in essence, a brutally successful land grab.

The buses rolled north through Zvornik, where every mosque in a town that was once 59 percent Muslim had been blown up. Even the rubble from the mosques was carted away, leaving empty lots where mosques had stood for 500 years. In the next town, Karakaj, they turned left, again in the direction of the prisoner exchange.

But after ten minutes the convoy abruptly veered off the main road. At approximately 2 a.m. they pulled into what Suljić thought was a schoolyard. Serbs formed two lines on either side of the buses' front doors, creating a corridor of soldiers to a school gym. "Quickly! Quickly! Quickly!" Serbs bellowed as the elderly Muslims scurried by. Suljić didn't know it, but he was in the small, predominantly Serb village of Grbavći.

Once inside, he sat down with the other prisoners at the rear of the dilapidated gymnasium. It was slightly larger than a basketball court. All 296 prisoners filed in, occupying one-quarter of the gym. As Suljić surveyed his surroundings it hit him. They were far away from Kalesija. There wasn't going to be a prisoner exchange. Mladić had lied.

Lying on the floor of the corpse-filled warehouse, Hakija Husejnović heard voices. He had listened to the groans of the wounded and dying all night, but these were strong, clear voices coming from outside the warehouse. The sun had risen several hours before, but he had no idea what time it was.

"Is anyone alive in there?" a voice abruptly shouted from outside. There was silence in the warehouse. "Come out," the Serb said. "You're going to be loaded onto a truck and become part of our army."

To Husejnović's astonishment, he heard several men get up and walk out of the warehouse. What sounded like a truck departed.

The Serbs then returned. "Anyone who is wounded can come out," the voice said. "There is an ambulance here to take care of you." Again, men got up and left the warehouse. Gunshots erupted outside. Husejnović was sure the Serbs were killing the wounded. Silence settled over the warehouse.

An hour later a Muslim who must have been wounded started shouting someone's name. "Salko, Salko," the voice shouted in slow, drawn-out wails. "Salko, Salko . . ." The name was cried dozens of times.

"Are you alive?" a voice suddenly asked. "Fuck your Turkish mother!" the voice thundered. A single gunshot echoed through the warehouse. Silence again.

An hour and a half later another man cried out a woman's name. "Adila, give me water . . . Adila, give me water!"

"I fuck your Islamic tribe!" a voice roared, followed by a gunshot. Husejnović lay motionless beneath the two bodies. Paralyzed by fear, he waited.

In Nova Kasaba, Lieutenant Egbers woke up in the Bosnian Serb Army barracks feeling anxious. He had to get his men to Potočari, and he hadn't slept well. Gunfire had echoed up and down the road all night. Egbers thought the Serb soldiers were young and skittish, firing at any noise they heard in the forest. The men who tried to go through the woods weren't his responsibility anyway, he thought. If they had come to the Dutch base in Potočari it might be different, but they had chosen to walk through the woods.

Little had changed in his own predicament. Major Divjak insisted it wasn't safe for him to drive back to Potočari. The Serbs suggested again that he leave his two jeeps, they could give him a ride. Egbers declined, knowing that he would never see the jeeps again and that he would lose radio contact with his base. UN personnel were told to avoid riding in either army's vehicles.

Egbers radioed the Dutch base. After discussing the situation he decided to wait. The battalion didn't have enough weapons, let alone jeeps, to launch a "rescue mission" from Potočari to get them. Egbers and the thirteen peacekeepers were at the mercy of the Serbs.

...

The bus in which Mevludin Orić and Haris had been sitting for nearly fourteen hours finally roared to life at 10 a.m.

"There's fighting in the south," the guard said. "You're going to Kalesija to be exchanged." Three Serb soldiers stepped on board, replacing the three policemen who had kept an eye on them the night before. Mevludin's bus and five others full of prisoners moved north along the Drina River.

When they drove through the village of Drinjača, the Muslims were ordered to put their heads in their laps. Mevludin peeked through his fingers out the window. The convoy passed Zvornik, and then in Karakaj they turned left. The buses were headed toward Kalesija, but ten minutes later they veered off the road and followed a narrow asphalt track to a schoolyard. Mevludin Orić and his cousin Haris were herded into the same school gym where Hurem Suljić and the other elderly men and invalids were being held.

By now, the gym in Grbavći was packed with what looked like 1,000 to 1,500 men. A third of the men sat in other people's laps. The Muslims were ordered to take off their hats, shirts and jackets when they entered. A large pile of clothes sat at the front of the gym. Serbs searched it for valuables.[1]

The heat was overwhelming. Mevludin stretched his neck, tilted his face upward and desperately tried to breathe fresh air. Prisoners fainted around him. Suljić sat on another man's lap in the rear. Some of the prisoners tried to stand up or speak to each other. "Look what Alija has done," the guards shouted. "He fucked all your Turk mothers!"

After an hour, water was distributed by four prisoners who looked no older than fifteen. The Serbs made jokes as the prisoners fought over the plastic buckets of water. Some of the water spilled on the floor and the desperate men got nothing.

Haris kept asking his older cousin what was going to happen. Mevludin assured Haris that everything would be all right. When they had turned off the main road, he started to worry, but both he and Hurem Suljić relaxed when they saw how many men were in the gym. Mevludin had seen two of his neighbors from Lehovići in the crowd. There were simply too many men for anything to happen.

At 1 p.m., a hush fell across the gym. The square jaw, silver hair and piercing blue eyes of Ratko Mladić filled the doorway.[2] Mladić conferred briefly with his officers. He smiled and laughed as he spoke. Five minutes after arriving, Mladić left. Vehicles could be heard outside. The guards said they were taking them to work camps.[3] Thirty minutes later, the officer in charge, a tall Serb with short jet-black hair and sunglasses, led fifteen to twenty prisoners to a side room. Because Mevludin and his cousin were seated near the front of the gym, they had to wait another thirty minutes.

When he finally entered the side room, Mevludin was astounded. One of his neighbors from Lehovići, Nezir Gušić, was blindfolding prisoners. Another provided them with a sip of water before they were hustled out a side door. "What's going to happen to us?" Mevludin whispered as Gušić pulled a blindfold over his eyes. Gušić began to weep.

Mevludin, his cousin and two dozen other blindfolded men were led to the back of a small truck. After a three-minute ride, Serb soldiers pulled the disoriented prisoners from the vehicle.

"Mevlo," Haris called out. Mevludin walked toward his cousin's voice. He held his cousin's hand.

"They're going to kill us," Haris stammered.

"No," Mevludin said, trying to calm his cousin and himself. "They're not going to kill us."

Then the firing started.

At some point in what he thought was the afternoon, Hakija Husejnović heard the noise of several trucks outside the warehouse in Kravica. Serbs were cursing. An earthmover with a ten-foot-wide steel scoop on the front wouldn't fit through the warehouse door.[4] They were there to clean up the bodies.

The floor suddenly shook violently. An engine roared. Husejnović thought the walls were collapsing. The building was still. Then he heard the earthmover working in the next room.

After a few minutes, he realized that the Serbs had driven the earthmover through the wall of the warehouse. Bodies were being mangled as they were scooped up and dumped into trucks which departed in the direction of Bratunac. Husejnović tried to calm himself. One thought filled his mind—being thrown into the back of a truck and being smothered by corpses.

At the 11 a.m. briefing in Zagreb that day, General Janvier announced that he had ordered the Ukrainian peacekeepers in Žepa to withdraw from their observation posts immediately. The Muslims forced him to do it, he explained, not the attacking Serbs. The Ukrainians were to pull out to "avoid a situation as it was in Srebrenica where [the] BH wouldn't let us withdraw from OPs."

Žepa, which had only seventy-nine peacekeepers, was indefensible, according to the French general. "It is absolutely clear that we can't reinforce Žepa," Janvier said, referring to sending the still not fully deployed Rapid Reaction Force to the area. "We can't defend Žepa as a result." Janvier made no mention of defending the enclave's population of 15,000 with NATO air strikes.

UN and U.S. officials were also publicly predicting the town would fall within forty-eight hours. But Janvier went further and also ruled out defending Goražde, the third and largest enclave in eastern Bosnia, which was home to 60,000 people. "The BH has 6,000 soldiers [in Goražde]," Janvier said, using a slightly inflated figure. "They are perfectly capable of defending Goražde against the BSA. The Bosnian government can do something now if they want." The UN was only strong enough to act in Sarajevo.[5]

The French general was still pushing the proposal he had made to the UN Security Council in May: that the UN withdraw from Srebrenica, Žepa and Goražde. Unless Janvier was receiving secret instructions, he was apparently doing everything in his power to abandon the safe areas without the permission of the Security Council.

...

In thick forest twenty-five miles northwest of Srebrenica, Mido Salihović and Srebrenica's leaders stumbled upon their first piece of good luck since the attack began. Near the village of Snagovo, the lead column of Muslims from Srebrenica was ambushed by Serb soldiers, but there were only fifty of them. Salihović, Ejup Golić and their men quickly counterattacked with RPGs and machine guns, driving them back and overwhelming the disoriented Serbs. A Serb captain, twenty-nine-year-old Zoran Janković, surrendered with a half dozen of his men.

Janković and his fifty-man police unit were from Modriča, a town forty miles to the northwest. They knew little about the terrain in the area, had misjudged the column's size and had chosen a poor place for an ambush. The Serbs could only retreat through an open field. The tall, burly young officer expected to find a column of refugees, not Srebrenica's best soldiers.

After at first refusing,[6] Janković agreed to contact his superiors and ask Serb artillery in the area to cease firing and allow the column safe passage. Salihović promised to exchange the Serb officer only if the Muslims were allowed through. Janković's father was a general in the Bosnian Serb Army. His superiors agreed. Scouts from the lead section of the column slowly crossed the field a few minutes later. Serb guns were silent. The men from Srebrenica were thrilled. Salihović appeared to have captured a valuable piece of leverage they could use for the hardest part of the trek—crossing the front line.

Mevludin Orić hit the ground. He was sure he was dead. Haris gasped and squeezed his hand. A man lying near him struggled frantically as his lungs filled with blood, went into spasms and stopped breathing. Haris' hand went limp.

Mevludin waited to feel the burning sensations from bullet wounds. He waited to choke or suffocate. His mind raced, unable to grasp where or what he was. He could breathe, but he could barely hear anything. The roar of the assault rifles had deafened him. A heavy, limp body lay across his legs. Haris.

He slowly realized the Serbs took him for dead. He had to

remain completely still. From the sound of the firing, Mevludin figured out that the executioners were lining the Muslims up in neat rows and working left to right. After Mevludin's row was full, the executioners started a new one. Slowly, the firing approached again. He listened in horror as a group of prisoners was unloaded from the small truck directly behind him. One of the stray bullets was bound to kill him. The assault rifles thundered, bullets hit the ground near him. Mevludin felt a warm liquid spread across his back. The prisoners moaned, cried out. The Serbs moved on. He still felt no burning. The warm liquid was someone else's blood. The Serbs still thought he was dead.

He was afraid to open his eyes. He tried to grasp what was happening around him through sound only. He heard what seemed like a second execution squad working in a nearby field. Escape would be impossible. He lay motionless and lost track of time.

At one point, the Serbs suddenly began shouting and firing wildly. "Let's go kill him," one said. "He's behind that tree." One of the prisoners or a wounded man had tried to escape. A few seconds later, the Serbs apparently caught him. Mevludin heard a scream and a gunshot. A second commotion quickly erupted. "He's escaping!" one of the Serbs shouted, referring to another prisoner. "Fuck him!" said a Serb. Assault rifles blasted away for fifteen seconds. "We'll wait for him on the railroad tracks," a voice said. "We'll catch him." Mevludin's spirits rose. Someone had gotten away.

He panicked moments later. "You didn't finish your job!" roared a Serb who sounded like an officer. "Go and shoot each one again with a pistol." The end had come, Mevludin thought. A pistol bullet would soon be lodged in his head.

The first shot was only a few feet from his head. He flinched involuntarily. His heart pounded. A second shot rang out, closer. Mevludin's mind raced. The Serbs were finishing off wounded men. He felt something kick his foot—a boot. An executioner stood directly above him. A shot rang out close to his legs. The boot disappeared. The executioner moved on. The steady rhythm of shots echoed off the hills. Mevludin remained completely still. He felt something crawling on his back, then across his cheek. Ants. His cheek and back started to itch. He couldn't move. His cheek burned. The ants were biting him, but he couldn't move. Worse than the pain and itching was what the insects signified. Ants were the first to come and eat a dead body. Somehow, he remained still.

After what felt like two hours a bulldozer began working at the site. Mevludin nearly snapped. It was only fifty yards away. One thought filled his mind: he could be buried alive. Since he was a boy, he'd been frightened every time a dead animal or person was lowered into the ground. But he kept his composure. He was completely motionless.

As the afternoon crawled by, Mevludin listened to his executioners. "Fuck your Balje mother," one shouted, using a slur that meant roughly "dirty Muslim peasant." "We're safest after you're dead." Others seemed to relish their job. "You're never going to make a move," one executioner said before firing a bullet into an injured man. Some wounded were taunted. "Your leg is just fine," an executioner mocked. A shot rang out; a man screamed. "Your arm is just fine too." Another shot, another scream. They laughed sometimes as they reloaded their guns.

Back in Potočari, Dutch soldiers smoked their first cigarettes, ate their first chocolates and drank their first beer in months. The Serbs waited until all of the refugees had departed before allowing two UN resupply convoys to reach the base. A food convoy arrived Thursday night, and 30,000 liters of fuel, several tons of food and weeks' worth of medical supplies arrived Friday night.

Afraid the Serbs might not allow the Dutch to leave, the UN agreed to Mladić's demand that the Serbs be reimbursed for the fuel used to "evacuate" Srebrenica's Muslims. The fuel was handed over to the Serbs free of charge. In the end, the UN provided the gas for the expulsion of the 40,000 people it promised to safeguard.

With the Serb attack on the safe area of Žepa intensifying, 400 peacekeepers were still valuable leverage. A threat to kill the Dutch could halt the NATO air strikes needed to defend Žepa.

Inside the UN base, translator Hasan Nuhanović was convinced he had killed his father, brother and mother by urging
them to come to the base. Dutch doctors, worried about a suicide attempt, administered Valium.

Vahid Hodžić and the other translators were near panic. It
was far from certain whether the Serbs would let the UN staff
workers, or the Dutch themselves, leave. The Serbs could easily
seize all of the Muslim workers. Hodžić knew how much resistance he could count on from the Dutch.

Ćamila Omanović was under twenty-four-hour guard. Dutch
doctors and Médecins Sans Frontières staffers had heard about
her brother Abdulah's role in her suicide attempt. They ordered
him to stay away from her and placed peacekeepers at her bed-
side.[7] Ćamila was convinced that the two peacekeepers guarding
her were actually Serbs in Dutch uniforms. When they weren't
looking, she lunged at an extension cord running across the
room and tried to electrocute herself. She was stopped easily.

Marc Klaver, the lookout from OP Foxtrot, and most of the
other Dutch peacekeepers in Potočari spent much of the day
telling and listening to stories. Few of the Dutch spoke about
the old men who had been taken away. A handful didn't care
what had happened to them, they simply wanted to go home.
But other Dutch were already haunted by what they had been
unwillingly part of.

Five hours after Mevludin Orić left the school gym, Hurem Suljić
hobbled across the same gym floor. At first, Suljić and his friends
and relatives packed into the back of the gym worried that they
would be killed. Then Mladić's appearance[8] convinced them that
they would be exchanged or sent to a work camp. In Bratunac
the Serbs had chosen the 100 men they had wanted to kill, those
who were either young or well known. Elderly and invalided,
Suljić thought he and the other 295 were the lucky ones.

But as a blindfold was placed over his eyes, Suljić knew something was horribly wrong. Mladić had lied again. Suljić was the
last of twenty old men to be hustled into the truck. The guard

slammed the tailgate. Suljić pushed the blindfold up onto his forehead.

The truck was tiny, far too small for what was needed to take them to a remote work camp. "This isn't a vehicle for long distances," Suljić said to his fellow prisoners. None of them answered. Tears ran down the faces of some of the men.

The truck left the schoolyard and drove down a narrow asphalt road. A red car with two soldiers in it followed them. The passenger-side door was opened and a rifle was pointed at the men. "Don't talk!" the soldier barked.

The area seemed to be completely deserted. Suljić studied the wrinkled faces around him. His sixty-two-year-old friend, Jakup Mekanić, and his fifty-eight-year-old brother-in-law, Suljo Ejubović, sat just to his right. At fifty-five, Suljić was the youngest man in the truck.

The truck turned and Suljić's mind went blank as he stared out the back. Hundreds of dead Muslim prisoners lay in rows on the ground. Five Serb soldiers stood next to the corpses. A bulldozer was digging a mass grave.

It's over. It's over. For some reason, his mind fixated on his six-year-old granddaughter, whom he had last seen in Potočari. Merima, he thought, Merima, what's going to happen to you? He began to weep. Some of the other old men also called out the names of their grandchildren. His friend Jakup mumbled, "My Zlatka. Oh, my Zlatka."

The truck crossed a set of railroad tracks and stopped. A young Serb soldier swung the truck's tailgate down and yanked Suljić out by the arm. "Shut up and don't talk!" another shouted. "Shut up!" The prisoners hadn't said a word.

Suljić's numb leg crumpled as he hit the ground. He limped into place. Five Serb soldiers holding assault rifles were standing ten feet away from the old men. One of the executioners pointed with his foot to where the twenty grandfathers and cripples should stand. The spot was at the end of a row of dead bodies.

"Turn around!" the Serbs roared. "Don't look around!" Suljić felt a sense of resignation as he hobbled into place next to his brother-in-law and his friend. No great visions, no sense of well-being filled his mind. His thoughts were blank. Then the shooting started.

At 7 p.m., Lieutenant Egbers decided to give in to his Serb counterparts. He agreed to accept a ride along with the thirteen Dutch peacekeepers in a Bosnian Serb APC from Nova Kasaba to the Dutch base in Potočari. The two remaining UN jeeps were left for the Serbs. His orders from his superiors had been simple. Come back to Potočari when it was safe.

As the afternoon passed, a disturbing pattern had emerged. Two prisoners were led to the building adjacent to the school where prisoners were held. Two shots were heard. A single prisoner was led into the building. A single shot was heard. A small truck then appeared at the school and then left. When the Dutch were allowed to inspect the house, no bodies were found.[9]

The Dutch received gifts from their hosts as they departed. Egbers was given a World War II-era rifle, some wine and some clothes. As they left Nova Kasaba, Egbers and Sergeant Mülder made a point of sitting outside the APC so they could check the soccer field where the day before they had seen 1,000 to 2,000 Muslim prisoners. It was empty.

Ten miles from the gym in Grbavći where Hurem Suljić and Mevludin Orić had been taken, several hundred Muslim prisoners from Bratunac were forced into overcrowded classrooms in a school north of Karakaj in a village called Dulić. Most of them were men captured after the ambush in Kamenica or when they tried to cross the asphalt road between Konjević Polje and Nova Kasaba. Many had been on the soccer field in Nova Kasaba when General Ratko Mladić had promised they wouldn't be harmed.

At 8 p.m., two dozen prisoners were taken to a small classroom and forced to take off their shirts. Their hands were tied behind their backs. They were then loaded into a small truck.

As more prisoners filed onto other trucks, they knew what

was bound to happen; still, no one resisted. At times during the ride, men lifted their eyes and looked at the faces around them. No one spoke. What they felt was a secret to the living: how it feels to know that you are about to die.

The trucks stopped on a gravel plateau behind a large earthen dam—known as the Red Mud Dam. A half dozen Serb soldiers were waiting. The Muslims were forced to lie face down on the rocks and were shot. The trucks kept coming. The executions lasted for six hours.[10]

At 9 p.m., the Serbs stopped trying to clean up the warehouse where Hakija Husejnović still hid under two bodies. The Serb cleanup crew had not made it to his section of the building yet. He listened as an officer ordered the men to cover the bodies with hay, apparently to smother the rancid smell, and call it a night. The pavement outside the warehouse was washed down, there was so much blood on it.

Silence again enveloped the warehouse, but Husejnović was afraid to move. He thought he heard whispers. He couldn't tell if they were inside or outside. Desperate, he finally crawled out from underneath the two corpses. He had spent twenty-four hours lying under them. He crawled over decomposing bodies, following the whispers. He found two other men, somehow also alive and unscathed. One of them, whose name was Ramiz, was from Čerska. The other said he was from Lolići, the nearby village where Mladić had addressed the prisoners.

"Will you try to escape with me?" Husejnović whispered.

"We can't do it together," the man from Lolići said softly. "I'll go out the window. When you get to the asphalt road, turn left. You'll find a small watering hole. I'll meet you three hundred meters beyond that in the cornfield."

Stepping over corpses and body parts, Husejnović and Ramiz crept toward the front of the warehouse. It was littered with human remains. A Serb soldier was sitting on the other side of the road. Husejnović and Ramiz reached the hole in the warehouse wall made by the earthmover.

"Go ahead," Ramiz whispered. Husejnović froze. "Go,"

Ramiz whispered again. Husejnović couldn't move. "Go now," Ramiz whispered angrily. Husejnović stood totally upright for the first time in twenty-four hours and scrambled through the ten-foot-wide hole. Ramiz followed him.

"Stop!" the Serb soldier shouted.

Husejnović dove to the ground. He didn't hear anything. He didn't know where the Serb soldier was. He saw a hole in the fence that surrounded the compound. He jumped to his feet and sprinted toward it.

"Stop!" the Serb shouted again. "Stop!"

The two Muslims dashed through a tiny stream, slipped through the hole in the fence and melted into a cornfield. Husejnović didn't know why, but the Serb never fired.

Amazed to be alive, they waited anxiously for the man from Lolići. After fifteen minutes, shots rang out from the direction of the warehouse. Husejnović and Ramiz couldn't see what was happening. They waited another fifteen minutes. The man from Lolići never appeared. Their hair and clothes soaked with blood, they slipped into a cluster of trees and headed due west—toward Tuzla.

Hurem Suljić felt no pain. The Serbs had stopped firing. A man who had fallen across his legs was only wounded. He began to move. Suljić panicked. If the Serbs shot the wounded man again, the bullet would kill Suljić. The man went limp. Suljić relaxed.

He opened his eyes. There were no bodies to his right. He could see five executioners fifty feet away, reloading their guns. Piles of contorted bodies lay in rows. A bulldozer was digging a hole close to a row of trees bordering the field.

The truck had gone to collect more prisoners. It returned every ten to fifteen minutes. The execution squad worked quickly. As soon as the prisoners were away from the truck, the firing began. Most of the wounded were killed just as quickly. Some played jokes on the wounded before killing them. "Old man, talk to me, talk to me," one executioner urged. "If you're not feeling all right, I can put a bandage on your wound." Anyone who spoke or moaned in response to the Serb's plea was instantly shot.

At around 8 p.m., Hurem saw a red car drive onto the field and stop roughly forty feet away. Two officers got out of the car and Suljić recognized one of them immediately. General Ratko Mladić surveyed the killing field. His face was grim. Suljić could see that he was speaking, but he couldn't hear what Mladić was saying. Suljić heard the execution squad fire several volleys. The shooting stopped. Mladić and the officer departed.

When the sun set at 9 p.m., the Serbs used the lights from the bulldozers to illuminate the killing field. It had been almost two hours since Suljić's group had left the gym. The frail fifty-five-year-old was having trouble breathing. The bodies on top of him seemed to grow heavier and heavier. Suljić decided to try to crawl to what he thought were some nearby bushes.

Once a new group of prisoners arrived, he inched out from underneath the bodies. His heart was pounding. He flipped onto his back. Watching the execution squad thirty yards away, Suljić slowly moved backward. After ten seconds he was completely exposed. His pale white skin glowed in the moonlight. If any of the Serbs so much as glanced in his direction, they would see him. None did.

Twenty seconds passed, and he still had not reached the bushes. The Serbs had finished off the new group of prisoners. He didn't dare turn around to see what he was backing toward. He started to wonder whether he was going in the right direction. After thirty seconds, the back of his head hit a branch. He quickly slid his body behind two bushes. Somehow, the Serbs had not seen him.

Another man would have been in a perfect position to flee, but Suljić was trapped by his bad leg. Unable to run or even walk quickly, the fifty-five-year-old would be gunned down if he tried to escape. He told himself to stay calm and wait until the Serbs left for the night.

At 10 p.m., he guessed, the Serbs began to argue over who should finish off the wounded. None of them wanted to do it.

Finally the youngest soldier, a short man who looked as if his gun was too big for him, was ordered to do it by the older soldiers. After eight hours of machine-gunning blindfolded people in the back, the executioners were apparently beginning to lose their nerve.

In Washington, the number two and three officials on the National Security Council staff, Sandy Berger and Nancy E. Soderberg, briefed President Bill Clinton on the situation in Srebrenica. It was roughly 7 p.m. Washington time, 1 a.m. in Bosnia. The President was on the White House putting green.

The Bosnian government's policy of dumping Srebrenica's refugees was paying off. The UN regional headquarters in Tuzla was bursting with refugees, was running out of tents and was swarming with Western journalists. The airwaves, the front pages and the President's briefing were filled with tales of Srebrenica's women and old men being led away, women and children expelled. It was the largest act of Serb ethnic cleansing in Clinton's presidency. The UN and its Western backers were humiliated once again.

Clinton was furious, and flew into one of his celebrated rages. "Something has to be done to contain the situation."

Berger reminded Clinton that National Security Adviser Anthony Lake was developing an "endgame" strategy, but it was hardly consolation given the hammering Clinton was taking on the issue.[11]

Earlier that day, House Speaker Newt Gingrich had ridiculed the UN and the administration on Bosnia. Gingrich, speaking in Philadelphia, called for an end to international "whining" and "pathetic hand wringing" about Bosnia. "To whine in public while being impotent endangers everyone on the planet," Gingrich said. "Bosnia is the worst humiliation for the Western democracies since the 1930s.

"All the major industrial democracies look pathetically weak and incompetent," Gingrich added. "There are twenty ways to solve this problem without involving a single American directly in this thing."

Since Srebrenica's fall, even more members of Congress had been announcing their support for a Republican bill that would have the United States unilaterally lift the UN arms embargo against Bosnia and let the Muslim-led government get the arms it needed to defend itself. France and Britain vowed that if the embargo was lifted, they would withdraw their peacekeepers from Bosnia, triggering a bloody and ugly withdrawal of the entire UN mission which Clinton had promised 25,000 U.S. troops would lead.

The President had said he would veto any bill lifting the arms embargo, but one had passed the House with a veto-proof majority the previous month. Senate Majority Leader Bob Dole, the front-runner for the Republican presidential nomination, was pressuring Clinton on the issue and threatening to bring it up for a vote in the Senate.[12]

As he putted, Clinton complained to the two aides that he was in an impossible position. UN peacekeepers were being treated like dirt, the situation was unsustainable. As Clinton listed each option, he mentioned each downside. Lifting the embargo would lead to an ugly withdrawal, U.S. casualties and an even fiercer war in the long term. Adding U.S. troops to the unworkable UN mission would mean potentially going to war with the Serbs or having American peacekeepers humiliated.

It appeared that French President Chirac was getting under Clinton's skin with his bold but unrealistic proposals. That day, British Prime Minister John Major and the Dutch government had publicly opposed Chirac's proposal that the new Rapid Reaction Force retake Srebrenica. Major called for an international "crisis meeting" on Bosnia in London on July 21.

French Defense Minister Charles Millon responded by setting a Sunday deadline for allies to back Chirac's call for an offensive to retake the fallen safe area, reinforce UN troops in Goražde and punch through Serb lines to create a secure land corridor into Sarajevo. Chirac complained about the lack of support at a Bastille Day press conference. "I deplore that. For the moment we are alone," he said. The international community's reaction to Srebrenica's fall reminded him, he repeated, of efforts by Britain and France to appease Adolf Hitler at the 1938 Munich

conference, which resulted in the Sudeten region of Czechoslovakia being sacrificed to Nazi Germany.

Chirac accused the UN of "congenital impotence," but failed
to mention that the mission was headed by a French general,
Bernard Janvier. He urged the Western democracies to "pull
themselves together" and defend their honor. He hinted that
France, the largest troop contributor to the UN mission with
6,000 troops, would deal it a deathblow if it did not change.

"We can't imagine that the UN force will remain only to
observe, and to be, in a way, accomplices in the situation,"
Chirac said. "If that is the case, it is better to withdraw."

Clinton's aides, by contrast, had announced that the United
States would not commit ground troops to retake Srebrenica.
Instead, Clinton would send General John Shalikashvili, Chairman of the Joint Chiefs of Staff, to London on Sunday to "an-
alyze" the French proposals. Clinton's top foreign policy
advisers had met Friday and recommended that the United States
look for ways to aid the Rapid Reaction Force with "air support" only. The French President looked bold; Clinton and Major seemed cowed.

But to Clinton, Chirac's proposals, while they might make
people feel good, wouldn't solve the problem. He sounded as if
he was competing with the French President, as if Chirac had
him in a tight corner and knew it.

After forty-five minutes, the tirade on the putting green
ended.

Thirty miles north of Srebrenica, the truck carrying the prisoners
to the killing field finally returned to Grbavći at 11 p.m., empty.

"We're finished," one of the Serbs said. "The job's done.
We're not going to bury them all tonight."

"Do we have to guard this place overnight?" a soldier asked.

"If the truck comes to pick you up, then you don't have to
stay," said the soldier who seemed to be in charge. "If it doesn't,
you have to stand guard." The truck departed. The lights on the
bulldozer were turned off. The Serbs smoked cigarettes and

started arguing again. None of them wanted to stay and guard a field full of corpses all night.

Five minutes later the truck returned. The Serbs climbed on and left. After nine hours of bloody executions, the field was now filled with the sounds of a summer evening. Crickets chirped, mosquitoes buzzed. In the moonlight, Suljić stared at the dozens of nearby corpses and at his own blood-caked skin and clothes. A half dozen of his closest friends and relatives lay dead before him. None of it seemed real. He tried to stand up.

Thirty feet away from Suljić, Mevludin Orić listened intently. He had passed out at some point and regained consciousness an hour before the Serbs departed. It had been ten minutes since the Serbs left and he had heard nothing in that time. He finally decided to risk it. He opened his eyes for the first time in twelve hours and tried to crawl out from underneath Haris, but his legs wouldn't move. For a moment he panicked, until he realized they were simply numb. The weight of Haris' body had cut off his circulation.

As Mevludin rubbed his legs, he looked around. Dozens of shirtless corpses frozen in macabre poses surrounded him. Arms, feet and heads jutted in the air at jarring angles. A bulldozer sat silently next to a freshly dug mass grave. He wanted to run, to get away, to be as far away from the field as possible.

He turned around, and saw something moving. Ten yards away from him, a man was trying to stand up. He feared it was a Serb.[13]

"Come here," Hurem said. Mevludin realized it was another prisoner.

Before he walked toward Suljić, Mevludin glanced at his cousin's body. The executioner who had stepped on him and fired a shot near his legs had finished off his cousin. He picked his way across the corpses. "Are you wounded?" Mevludin asked hurriedly when the two met. "Are you wounded?" His voice shook.

"I lost my shoe," Hurem replied. While crawling free, the former carpenter had lost the thick orthopedic shoe that protected his numb right foot and kept his toes from curling. Walking without it would be dangerous. They put Hurem's left shoe on his numb right foot. Mevludin grabbed two shirts from nearby bodies. He put one on and wrapped the other around Suljić's good foot. "We have to hurry," Mevludin whispered.

Suddenly they heard moans coming from the corpses in the field. Another survivor had heard them. They scanned the area for Serbs. Mevludin found two other men who were still alive. One lay prone with a wound to his stomach. A second sat upright only a few feet away. His upper body was unscathed, but he had been shot in the legs several times.

"Run away," the man with the stomach wound whispered. "You can't help us."

Both men were doomed. Neither could walk.

"Please give me a shirt," the man with the stomach wound whispered. A chill had settled over the field as night fell. Mevludin found a shirt among the corpses, handed it to the man and said goodbye. The one with the wounded legs had still said nothing. Both were trapped.

He returned to Hurem and they decided to head uphill into the forest. They entered a thicket of trees and stumbled upon a concrete basin used by farmers to collect rainwater. As they tried to wash the blood from their bodies, the truck returned to the nearby field.

"We've got to find him by dawn," a Serb soldier said. Mevludin wasn't sure if he was referring to the man who ran into the woods in the middle of the execution or to them. Panicked, Mevludin turned and climbed up the hill. Hurem, hobbling, followed. Their clothes were tattered, their skin and hair were caked with blood. Once the sun rose a manhunt could be launched. They would be easy to spot. But the Serbs had chosen a poor execution site. Mevludin and Hurem didn't know it, but they were only one mile from Muslim-held central Bosnia.

Both men threaded their way through the trees in the moonlight. They weren't sure where they were going. They only wanted to get away from the field. Still in shock, only one thought filled their minds: survival.

SUNDAY, JULY 16, 1995

COLUMN AND CONVOY ROUTES, JULY 16, 1995

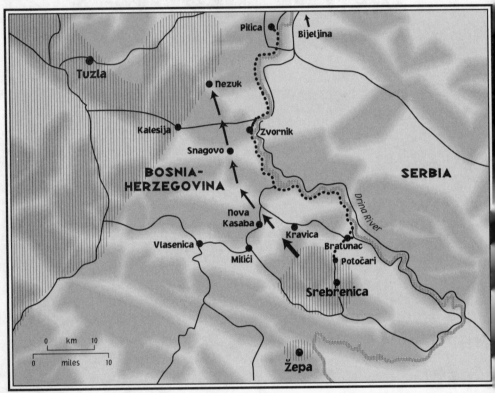

Sergeant Dražen Erdemović and the seven other men from his Bosnian Serb Army unit rode in the back of a small truck. They were on their way to Zvornik but had no idea why. That morning the unit had been called into the office of their commander, Lieutenant Milorad Pelemiš, in the Serb-held town of Bijeljina. They were told to drive to Zvornik. Pelemiš, the commander who had ordered the Muslim's throat cut in Srebrenica five days ago, said only that their orders came directly from the intelligence center of the Bosnian Serb Army headquarters in Han Pijesak.[1]

They arrived in Zvornik at 9 a.m. Sergeant Brano Gojković, the squad's commander, and the driver reported to a lieutenant colonel whom Erdemović didn't recognize. The lieutenant colonel and two military policemen got into a car.[2] Erdemović and the rest of his unit followed them. They headed north, back toward Bijeljina.

After entering Srebrenica on July 11, Erdemović and his unit had spent a day and a half in the town conducting mop-up operations. Erdemović then left for a funeral in Trebinje, a Serb-held town two hundred miles to the south. He'd returned to their base in Bijeljina only the day before. During his absence, the unit participated in a vast manhunt for Muslims fleeing through the woods, he was told. Gojković and a few other men in the unit had carried out a mass execution in a soccer field near a village called Nova Kasaba.

The car his unit was following turned left onto a dirt road which wound up a hill and through a lush green field of grass. They arrived at a state-run collective farm which consisted of four large red barns and a half dozen tractors and harvesters. An old red fire engine with "Zvornik Fire Department" painted on the door sat in the middle of the courtyard. Erdemović and the other soldiers got out of their truck to smoke a cigarette.

The farm was on a picturesque plateau. In every direction they could see rolling hills thick with cornstalks and dotted with terra-cotta-roofed farmhouses. The terrain was far gentler than the jagged hills ringing Srebrenica to the south. A pile of weapons had been delivered to the site. An M-84 .50 caliber machine gun sat next to wooden crates full of thousands of rounds of Kalashnikov assault rifle ammunition.

Erdemović overheard Gojković talking with the lieutenant colonel. Something about buses coming to the farm. The lieutenant colonel departed, and Gojković turned to his seven men. "Buses are arriving with Muslims from Srebrenica," he said. "We're going to shoot them."

Erdemović's suspicions were true. Gojković ordered them to bring the weapons and ammunition to a field 100 yards behind the complex of barns. The first bus came between 9:30 a.m. and 10 a.m. and parked about 100 yards away. Erdemović watched as two military policemen from the Drina Corps took ten Muslim men off the bus, ranging from teenagers to men in their sixties and seventies. They were blindfolded, and their hands were tied behind their backs.

Gojković showed Erdemović and the other soldiers how to line up. The military police walked the prisoners toward them, then Gojković and Vlastimir Golijan, one of the men in Erdemović's unit, placed the bewildered prisoners in front of Erdemović and the other five men.

Erdemović said he didn't want to participate. Gojković dismissed him with a threat. "If you feel sorry for them," he quipped, "why don't you line up with them."

The prisoners were thirty feet away from Erdemović. Their backs were turned to the execution squad. The Muslim civilians were silent. Erdemović faced a simple choice. Gojković's suggestion that he join the Muslims if he felt sorry for them was real. It was Erdemović's life or the lives of the Muslims.

The twenty-three-year-old raised his rifle to his shoulder. Erdemović aimed directly at one man's heart. The other executioners fired first, then he quickly joined in. It was over in seconds. Muslims quickly collapsed onto the rich brown soil. Erdemović reloaded.

Ten more men were led from the bus. Gojković lined them up in front of the corpses. The Muslims started to shriek. "Don't kill us," one man begged. "Our families in Austria will send you money!"

"Those who have deutsche marks will be saved!" joked one of the men in Erdemović's squad. Gojković interrupted him. "Don't bother, we stole everything from them in Zvornik!"

Erdemović and the other five men aimed and fired.

The Muslims were then finished off with a bullet to the head to make sure they were dead. Erdemović felt sorry for them. They had done nothing to him. He aimed directly at their hearts; it was kinder to kill them quickly.

Another group of ten were led from the bus. "Turk assholes! Naser really fucked you!" Gojković taunted. "Now you're going to pay for him." The civilians and old men were mowed down.

Before the last group were executed, Gojković entered the bus and handed a Kalashnikov to the driver. "You must each kill one," he said to the horrified driver. He didn't want anyone talking. Everyone would be guilty.

Twenty-four hours earlier, the senior leadership of the UN mission in the former Yugoslavia and two senior European special envoys had held a secret meeting with General Ratko Mladić and Serbian President Slobodan Milošević in Belgrade. The goal of the meeting was to negotiate the release of the 450 Dutch peacekeepers still trapped in Potočari and gain access for the

International Committee of the Red Cross (ICRC) to the estimated 6,500 Muslim prisoners. For the last five days, Mladić had refused to grant the ICRC access.

Yasushi Akashi, the civilian head of the UN mission, led the UN and European negotiating team. He was accompanied by Carl Bildt, the new European Union negotiator for the former Yugoslavia, and Thorvald Stoltenberg, the senior UN envoy to the former Yugoslavia.[3] British general Rupert Smith, the UN commander in Bosnia who favored using more force against the Serbs, was also present. Janvier, still under blistering public attack for failing to call in air strikes to save Srebrenica, was on leave.

The Bosnian Serb general who had so brazenly humiliated the international community for the last five days was the picture of cooperation at the meeting. Mladić signed an agreement stating that the 450 Dutch peacekeepers could leave Potočari by the end of the week with all of their equipment. The battalion could evacuate no more than thirty local staff workers with it, but Mladić promised that the remaining staff would receive fair and impartial treatment.

Mladić agreed that the ICRC could have access to the "reception points" the Serbs had established for the Muslim prisoners. The men from Srebrenica were being well treated, Mladić promised, and ICRC representatives would be free to visit all of them within the next seventy-two hours.

Dražen Erdemović watched a second bus arrive at the collective farm. This time, none of the men were blindfolded, nor were their hands tied behind their backs. No effort was made to hide from the prisoners what awaited them. Until it was their turn, they sat on the bus listening to the executions. The lucky ones waited for only a few torturous minutes. Others spent twenty minutes fighting off fear.

They faced death in their own ways. Some begged to be spared as they were lined up next to the fresh corpses. Others promised money from their families. A handful mustered the courage to curse their executioners. A few fell to their knees and prayed. Most said nothing.

At one point, a Muslim in his fifties being led to the field broke away from the group and begged Erdemović to save his life. At twenty-three, Erdemović looked boyish. He was only five feet eight and his face was covered with pimples.

"Please let me live," the man stammered. "I saved Serbs from Srebrenica. I smuggled them out. I have their telephone numbers in Serbia. You can call them."

For the next thirty minutes, Erdemović talked to the man and the executions went on without him. The Muslim had been a "human smuggler" in Srebrenica, just as Erdemović had been in Tuzla. He said he had smuggled Serbs trapped in the enclave across the front lines. After the fall of the enclave, the man fled to the UN base in Potočari for protection. He'd been separated from his family by Serb soldiers.

Erdemović approached Gojković. "Let him live," he said.

"I don't want any witnesses," the sergeant replied.

Vlastimir Golijan walked over and took the man by the arm. He lined him up next to a row of bodies. Thirty seconds after pleading with Erdemović, the Muslim lay dead.

Another bus arrived. Each one held approximately sixty men. As the morning passed, the execution squad kept having to move to new positions. Rows of dead bodies were slowly filling up the field.

Private Ynse Schellens and the fifty-four other Dutch peacekeepers were ecstatic. Captured by the Bosnian Serbs when their observation posts fell or their APCs were surrounded, they finally arrived in Zagreb at noon. Their release appeared to be a goodwill gesture by General Mladić. The fifty-five former hostages would be flying home the following day. The remainder of the Dutch battalion was expected to follow soon.

Schellens had found life as a Bosnian Serb hostage better than life as a peacekeeper. The food was an improvement, he could drink all the beer he wanted and he got to make longer phone calls home. He and nine other men from OP Kilo had spent most of their time playing soccer with local Serb children. They were totally unaware that Mladić had threatened to kill them if NATO strikes continued.

The Serbs got drunk and celebrated after the fall of Srebrenica. He'd watched in amazement as the convoys of Muslim women and children streamed through Milići. Some Serb women had thrown rocks at the buses, but what Schellens had seen the day before was still emblazoned in his mind.

As he and nineteen other hostages were driven through Nova Kasaba on a Serb bus, they saw dozens of small bags and knapsacks filling the soccer field. A tractor was pulling a cart with a dozen bodies stacked on it. An excavator was digging a hole—which looked like a mass grave—away from the road close to the Jadar River. The stench of rotting flesh made their stomachs turn. As they moved north, he saw two bodies lying in the road. Serb cleanup crews walked up and down it, wearing rubber gloves.

Schellens and the other peacekeepers were warmly greeted by top Dutch military officials when they entered Zagreb. They told senior Dutch military officials and UN investigators what they had seen, but there was no public announcement of the bodies, the Serb "cleanup" crews and the backhoe digging a mass grave.

At 3:30 p.m., ten Serb soldiers from Bratunac arrived in the killing field where Erdemović and his squad were working. There was only one remaining bus full of Muslims. The Serbs from Bratunac set about their work with glee. Muslims were pulled from the bus and beaten with iron bars. The Serbs knew some of their victims, but beat them anyway. Then they forced their prisoners to kneel on the ground and pray in the traditional Muslim position. As their captives bowed their heads, the Serbs fired.

Erdemović felt uneasy. At some point that afternoon, he had turned to another Croat in the unit. "God only knows how all this will fall back on us one day," he warned.

"Shut up," the soldier retorted. "If not, it will be our turn to die. We're only Croats."

The lieutenant colonel who had brought them to the farm that morning arrived after the last Muslims were killed. Erdemović thought his unit had executed between 1,000 and 1,200 people that day. The lieutenant colonel said machines would come to bury the bodies on the farm. "There are another five hundred in the village," the lieutenant colonel informed Erdemović and the other soldiers. "You've got to go and finish the job."

A half mile into Serb territory, Naser Orić greeted his decimated army with tears. As the lead section of the column finally streamed across the front line, his enormous chest and shoulders trembled. Naser Orić, Srebrenica's hope and curse, wept.

The ghostlike column of 3,500 men staggered into Muslim-held central Bosnia during the course of the afternoon. The gaunt, dazed and desperate men had not eaten or slept in a week. Shoes had disintegrated. Some marched only on the bloody soles of their feet. Others staunchly carried wounded relatives on tree limbs and blankets.[4]

The emotions of finally reaching safety after seven days were overwhelming. Most were furious. The 2nd Corps in Tuzla had made no major effort to help them. Naser and 170 volunteers had punched a hole through Serb lines near the village of Nezuk and created a corridor for them to cross. Salihović's soldiers wept when they heard Naser's voice over the walkie-talkie. After they arrived, many asked a simple question. "Why?" the survivors asked over and over again. "Why?"

"We were sold," Naser said. "We were sold."

Naser said that the United Nations and the Bosnian government had intentionally sacrificed Srebrenica. He told his fuming, exhausted soldiers that the Bosnian Army high command had blocked him from returning to Srebrenica. Some men believed him unconditionally. Others did not.

The last two days of their journey had been the worst. Mido

Salihović's gamble of holding the Serb officer hostage had partially backfired. The Serbs agreed to allow the Muslims to pass through their territory in exchange for the release of the officer. But while the Muslims passed through the Snagovo area safely, the Serbs prepared a new ambush farther north. Salihović never released the Serb officer.

The day before they reached the front line, ten scouts, including Salihović and Ejup Golić, were crossing a field when two concealed Serb tanks and an antiaircraft gun in front of them opened fire. A piece of shrapnel disemboweled the thirty-four-year-old Golić. After five days of leading the column through the woods, he died one mile from Muslim-held central Bosnia.

Serb tanks blocked the sole route to central Bosnia. The Muslims were armed with only rocket-propelled grenades. Naser and his men were too far away to attack the Serb armor. Fighting desperately, what remained of the enclave's elite units slowly closed in on the tanks for two hours. Veiz Šabić, another top Muslim commander, was wounded in the heavy shelling.

A heavy rain began to fall, which allowed the Muslims to creep closer to the tanks. Suddenly firing rocket-propelled grenades from only fifty yards away, the Muslims damaged one tank; the Serbs abandoned the other. Word passed through the column: the handful of Muslims who could operate tanks should move forward. The barrel was swung around and the Muslims gleefully pummeled Serb positions along the front line.

Under the combined pressure of Salihović's men pushing from the east and Naser and his volunteers advancing from the west, the Serb line finally broke that morning. Salihović fought on until 7 p.m., holding back Serbs attacking the flank of the narrow corridor the Muslims had opened in the front line.

When Naser was told of Ejup Golić's death, the giant fell to his knees. Throughout the afternoon, he sounded a simple theme over and over. "We'll get back at them," he said to his soldiers. "We'll do to them what they've done to us."

Surrounded by rows of dead bodies, Dražen Erdemović stared at the lieutenant colonel. He couldn't believe 500 more Muslims waited in the village, doomed. "No," Erdemović said. "I don't want to kill anyone. I'm not a robot for exterminating people." He waited anxiously for the other men in his unit to speak.

Three of them, Franc Kos, Marko Boskić and Zoran Goronja, supported him. Four others, Stanko Savanović, Aleksandar Cvetković, Vlastimir Golijan and Brano Gojković, said they would go. The ten soldiers from Bratunac appeared eager. The lieutenant colonel chose them.

Erdemović and the other members of his unit gathered their weapons. They would finally be leaving. But Gojković abruptly announced that he had a meeting with the lieutenant colonel in Pilica. They drove to the nearby village and entered a café across the street from the community center, which held the 500 Muslim prisoners.

Two bodies lay in the road. Gunshots and then a hand grenade explosion came from the community center. One Muslim broke out through the front door and sprinted down the street, only to be shot by one of the Serbs from Bratunac. The lieutenant colonel and Gojković finished their meeting in the café. Finally, the unit was allowed to leave.

As they drove, the other men in Erdemović's unit got drunk. Stanko Savanović bragged about how many Muslims he had executed. His seventeen-year-old brother died while fighting the Muslims in 1993, but he had killed 250 Muslims that day. Erdemović had killed seventy people.

The twenty-three-year-old sat silently as the other men in his unit began to sing.

AFTERMATH

FRONT LINES, MID-JULY 1995

Serbs   Muslim- and Croat-controlled

○ UN-designated Safe Areas

FRONT LINES, OCTOBER 1995

Serbs   Muslim- and Croat-controlled

Three months after the Bosnian Serb triumph in Srebrenica, General Ratko Mladić's forces were pummeled by a massive NATO bombing campaign and routed by a combined Muslim-Croat offensive. The attack on Srebrenica and the subsequent executions had emerged as the turning point of the war. By mid-September, the Serb attempt to end the war had backfired. The portion of Bosnia controlled by the Serbs would shrink from 70 percent to under 50 percent.

Days away from losing Banja Luka—the largest city held by the Bosnian Serbs—and the hundreds of square miles around it, Mladić's army was reeling. But he was saved by his longtime backer, Serbia, and an unlikely ally—the Clinton administration. The fall of Srebrenica and mass executions had changed the course of the war, but not Western priorities in Bosnia. The aftermath of Srebrenica's collapse would prove to be, in some ways, as dark as its fall.

With the Bosnian Serb attack on Žepa intensifying, pressure rose for an American or European response. On Monday, July 17, before a regular breakfast meeting of the administration's foreign policy team, Anthony Lake presented his "endgame strategy" of a new U.S. diplomatic initiative backed by a threat of air strikes against the Bosnian Serbs and a lifting of the arms embargo against Bosnia's Muslim-led government. Secretary of State Warren Christopher, Secretary of Defense William Perry, Chairman of the Joint Chiefs of Staff John Shalikashvili, U.S. ambassador to the UN Madeleine Albright and Deputy National Security Adviser Sandy Berger were present. An American troop presence in Bosnia seemed inevitable. The central issue was whether they would be enforcing a peace settlement or leading a humiliating UN withdrawal.

Usually the President did not attend such meetings, but Lake had secretly requested that he drop in on the meeting to empha-size his commitment to the new initiative. "I don't like where we are now," Clinton said. "The policy is doing enormous dam-age to the United States and our standing in the world. We look weak." He predicted more problems to come. "And it can only get worse down the road. The only time we've ever made pro-gress is when we geared up NATO to pose a real threat to the Serbs." But, Clinton added, "I'm not sure what we should do."[1]

That day Médecins Sans Frontières and the International Com-mittee of the Red Cross evacuated fifty-nine wounded Muslims from Potočari and Bratunac. Ćamila Omanović was safely taken to central Bosnia. But seventeen wounded Muslim men were sep-arated in various ways as "suspected war criminals" by the Bos-nian Serbs. One of them was the Muslim artillery officer who wrote "30 Dutch equals 30,000 Muslims" on Lieutenant Egbers' scrap of paper. Four men who were wounded after holding the Serb tanks in the Bibići trench with Ibran Malagić were also taken away.

The following day, July 18, Clinton and his senior foreign policy advisers gathered in the Oval Office. Vice President Gore spoke about Bosnia. "The worst solution would be to acquiesce to genocide and allow the rape of another city and more refugees," he said. "At the same time, we can't be driven by images, be-cause there's plenty of other places that aren't being photo-graphed where terrible things are going on, but we can't ignore the images either."[2] Gore referred to a front-page story in *The Washington Post* over the weekend that described a young Srebrenica rape victim who tied her belt and shawl together and hanged herself at the UN air base in Tuzla.

"My twenty-one-year-old daughter asked about that picture," he said. "What am I supposed to tell her? Why is this happening and we're not doing anything?"

Gore, who had a close relationship with Clinton, was openly challenging the President. "My daughter is surprised the world is allowing this to happen," Gore said. "I am too."

The President replied that the administration would take action.

Žepa could not be saved, Gore continued, "but we now can't watch sixty-five thousand people in Goražde be helplessly subjected to the same treatment."[3]

As for Chirac's proposal to retake Srebrenica, it was in the tradition of the grand French gesture. "Chirac now wants to roll the dice and keep his own record clear. We have to come up with something practical that makes real military sense," Gore said. "Acquiescence is not an option."

"I've been thinking along the same lines," the President replied. The status quo was no longer tenable, he said. "The situation underscores the need for robust airpower to be authorized," Clinton reportedly asserted. "The United States can't be a punching bag in the world anymore."

The following day, July 19, fighting dramatically escalated in Bosnia and neighboring Croatia. While Serbs in Bosnia pressed their attack on the UN safe area of Žepa in eastern Bosnia, Serbs in neighboring Croatia launched a major offensive against the surrounded UN safe area of Bihać on the other side of the country—in western Bosnia.[4] A sixty-square-mile chunk of the enclave fell in a single day.

For Serb nationalists, their own "endgame" was advancing smoothly. The goal appeared to be to seize the remaining Muslim enclaves and unite the 70 percent of Bosnia and 30 percent of Croatia that the Serbs had conquered and declare an ethnically pure "Greater Serbia." But they were gambling. Bihać was far more important strategically than Srebrenica to the West and, most importantly, to neighboring Croatia. Sandwiched between a chunk of Croatia and a piece of Bosnia controlled by Serb nationalists, the long front lines of the vast Bihać enclave of 180,000 people tied up thousands of Serb troops and dozens of Serb tanks and artillery. If the enclave fell, Serb soldiers and tanks would be free to swing around and blunt an offensive the Croatian Army was expected to launch that summer.

By threatening Bihać, the Serbs were giving the powerful Croatian Army an excuse to enter the war. For the last three years, the United States had tacitly allowed the Croatian government to violate the UN arms embargo and secretly import crucial tanks and heavy artillery. Retired U.S. generals openly trained Croatian Army officers in state-of-the-art NATO tactics. If Croatia joined the fighting, the war would widen and the Serbs would find themselves facing a real army—not outgunned Muslims.

But the Serb leadership pushed on. General Smith's analysis that the Serbs hoped to conclude the war that summer was proving correct.

As the Serbs attacked Bihać and Žepa, three Muslim men covered with blood and in tattered clothes staggered across the front line. Hurem Suljić, Mevludin Orić and Smail Hodžić—a third survivor of the execution whom they had met in the woods—were desperate to find their families. They were also eager to tell the world what they had survived.

The day after the execution, Suljić and Orić had glimpsed the nearby Drina River from a hilltop and realized how close they were to Muslim-held central Bosnia. Overwhelmed with hunger, Suljić dared to climb an apple tree later that day as Orić watched for Serbs. An unshaven elderly man in bloodstained clothes abruptly entered the clearing. As soon as they saw the blood, Hurem and Mevludin realized he too had survived an execution. The man was Smail Hodžić, the sixty-five-year-old Muslim who had heard General Mladić's speech on the Nova Kasaba soccer field. After spending the night in the back of a truck in Bratunac, Hodžić had been brought to the same school gym in Grbavći as Hurem and Mevludin. As the three talked, they realized that Hodžić had been taken to the killing field a few hundred yards from the one Mevludin and Hurem had escaped.[5]

The three forged on and later met another Muslim in the woods. Three days after the mass execution, they reached the front line but were unable to cross it. Two Serb bunkers with machine guns sat on either side of a stream leading to Muslim-held territory. Mevludin was convinced the stream was mined. The four waited until dark and crept down a path through the trees. The Serbs spotted them in the moonlight and fired. They retreated back into Serb territory.

The four men hid all the following day. Mevludin laughed for the first time since the execution when they found a pile of bags dumped by Muslims who had passed through the area. Hurem and Smail ate toothpaste to clean their mouths and satisfy their thirst. When darkness finally came, the four men crept up the stream on the night of July 18. They found no mines. At dawn, they were only a few hundred yards from Muslim territory but divided over what to do next.

They retreated to a nearby barn. Mevludin fell asleep. Desperately cold, Hurem started a fire. Mevludin woke and was furious. He was sure the smoke would lead to their capture. After four days of waiting patiently for slow-moving older men, the twenty-five-year-old abandoned them and set off up a steep hill. Two hours later, all four slipped across different parts of the front line. They were reunited that night in the village of Nezuk, amazed to be alive, and safe.

The following day, they were bused, along with other men who had emerged from the woods, to the UN air base in Tuzla. The first people to whom they told their story were stunned Bosnian police. Over the next few days, UN human rights investigators and journalists quickly descended upon them. The first credible survivors of the much-rumored mass executions had arrived.[6]

Akashi, who had failed to report the refugee accounts of atrocities to his superiors in New York, was under pressure to investigate. He had received a cable from Kofi Annan on July 18 asking him why New York had received no information to corroborate or contradict the accounts of Serb atrocities and UN passivity so widely reported in the press.

Even the three survivors didn't believe that the Serbs killed all of the men they captured. Many survivors hoped that the Bosnian Serbs still held thousands of prisoners and hundreds of men from Srebrenica still lurked in the woods. ICRC officials continued to demand that the Bosnian Serbs give them access to Muslim prisoners from Srebrenica, but were denied it. In Sarajevo, Muslim and Serb negotiators began talks about a massive prisoner exchange. Relatively few suspected or could believe that most of the thousands of missing were already dead.

The next day, July 21, American and European Defense and Foreign Ministers met in London to formulate a Western response to the Serb offensive that had begun fifteen days before with the attack on Observation Post Foxtrot. The conference produced the "London Declaration," which stated that "substantial and decisive" airpower would be used to defend Goražde. The U.S. delegation, led by Warren Christopher, William Perry and General John Shalikashvili, blocked a French proposal to have U.S. helicopters ferry 1,000 French reinforcements to Goražde. The United States warned of heavy casualties and argued that more Western soldiers in the enclave, which already had 280 British and 100 Ukrainian peacekeepers, would only create more potential hostages.

American, French and British officials hailed the declaration as a watershed; Srebrenica had galvanized the West. But it was bitterly denounced by the Bosnian government as another empty promise. Bosnian Prime Minister Haris Silajdžić called the conference "disgusting."[7] Western analysts dismissed the declaration as more meaningless American and European rhetoric. One of the most important aspects of the declaration was what it didn't say—an attack on only Goražde, not Žepa, would trigger the massive air strikes. Žepa, whose soldiers were still holding back

General Ratko Mladić's forces, was ignored.[8] The 15,000 Muslims who had resisted fierce Serb attacks and toiled in the isolated enclave for two years were abandoned to the same fate as Srebrenica's Muslims.

Almost from the outset of the Serb attack on Žepa, UN and Western intelligence and military assessments called the enclave "indefensible" and predicted it would fall within days. But Žepa, which was more mountainous than Srebrenica, was famous for frustrating attackers. In World War II, German forces occupied eastern Bosnia but were never able to gain full control of the jagged mountains, caves and ravines that surrounded Žepa.

The UN and NATO military assessment that getting reinforcements to the remote mountain enclave in the midst of the Serb attack would be dangerous was correct. But on July 21, UN reinforcements weren't needed. Žepa's own defenders were holding the town. Air strikes on attacking Serb tanks and artillery could have been attempted.

As Western leaders met in London, the Serbs seemed to try to weaken Western political will just as it was solidifying. The Dutch battalion and its Muslim staff workers received permission to leave Potočari. At 12:02 p.m. on July 21, a long caravan of UN trucks and jeeps began to stream out of the desolate Dutch compound. Before leaving, the peacekeepers had neatly stacked all of their weapons, flak jackets and helmets inside the base. General Mladić had reneged on the July 15 promise in Belgrade that permitted the Dutch to leave with all of their equipment. Food, medical equipment and supplies worth tens of thousands of dollars were left behind, but as the Dutch crossed the Drina River the Serbs lost 450 valuable potential hostages.

The Dutch convoy arrived at UN headquarters in Zagreb, Croatia, at 4 a.m. on July 22. Crown Prince Willem Alexander of the Netherlands, Defense Minister Joris Voorhoeve and the country's top military leadership gave the peacekeepers a heroes' welcome. A party, complete with a forty-two-piece brass band playing Glenn Miller songs, cases of beer and drunken Dutch soldiers dancing in a chorus line, was thrown that afternoon.

The following day, Dutch military officials allowed UN human rights investigators and staffers to interview seventeen peacekeepers chosen by the Dutch for only a five-hour period. A handful of peacekeepers agreed to speak with reporters about what they saw in Srebrenica and Potočari. One of them was Warrant Officer Be Oosterveen, the soldier who had taken the photos of the nine dead bodies.[9] Another was Ron Rutten, the peacekeeper who had called the Serbs "Nazis" and condemned other Dutch for working with them.

At a press conference, Voorhoeve announced that Dutch soldiers had seen Muslims being led away and then heard shooting. He also said Dutch soldiers had received a tip that 1,600 Muslims were reportedly killed in a local schoolyard. Rumors of rapes and other atrocities reported by survivors in Tuzla were too numerous and "too authentic" to be untrue, Voorhoeve said, and he complained that the International Committee of the Red Cross was still not being given access to the estimated 6,000 Muslim prisoners.[10]

The Dutch commander in Srebrenica, Colonel Karremans, then read a statement.[11] The attack on the enclave was an "excellently planned military operation," he said. Bosnian Serb military commander General Ratko Mladić was strategically very clever. "But he was a commander, not a gentleman. There are no gentlemen in this war." Karremans added: "We learned that the parties in Bosnia cannot be divided into 'the good guys' and 'the bad guys,' " apparently referring to Srebrenica's corrupt leaders.

He said nothing about the treatment of the enclave's civilians and failed to mention the beatings, one execution or nine bodies his soldiers had seen in Potočari. Egbers and thirteen other Dutch peacekeepers had told their superiors of gunshots coming from the Nova Kasaba soccer field on the night of July 13, but Karremans somehow failed to mention it. Nor did he bring up the fact that Dutch peacekeepers were disarmed, robbed and in one case forced to go "Muslim hunting" by Serbs.

He also omitted mention of a declaration the Serbs asked his deputy commander, Major Franken, to sign on July 17. It stated that the "evacuation" of Muslims was carried out according to

"international humanitarian law." Franken added one caveat:
"as far as it concerns convoys actually escorted by UN forces,"
and signed it.

The destruction of a videotape which showed the nine bodies
found near a stream and also showed the Forward Air Controllers at work before the town fell went unmentioned. The Dutch
feared that if the Serbs obtained the video they would harm the
Forward Air Controllers who guided the NATO attack. Not a
word was said of the 239 Muslim men forced to leave the Dutch
base or the list containing their names. Major Franken, who
promised to show the list to the world, turned it over to UN
officials in Zagreb that day. Assuming it was too late to do anything for the men, UN staffers made sure the ICRC had a copy
and then told no journalists of its existence.[12]

The battalion finally returned to a heroes' welcome in Holland on July 24. The Ministry of Defense granted them a one-
month vacation. The peacekeepers were instructed not to speak
to the media about what they saw before a debriefing scheduled
to begin in September.

After the Dutch departed, the hunt continued in the woods
around Srebrenica. Hundreds of men were still alive. Local Serb
military units carried out daily patrols to find them. Fear that
the Muslims would attack and kill Serb civilians was one mo-
tivation; revenge was another. Almost all Muslims captured were
executed.[13]

Three days after the London conference ignored them, Žepa's
defenders were still doggedly holding off General Mladić's
troops. But Janvier, incensed that Bosnian soldiers had taken
over UN positions and held Ukrainian peacekeepers hostage, opposed using airpower to defend Žepa. Before departing on a
two-day leave, Janvier stated in a July 14 letter to General Smith
that because Žepa could not be reinforced by land "CAS cannot
be considered." The letter also asked Smith to "propose possible
course of action" in Goražde and stated that "the option of immediately withdrawing the pointless forces would avoid being
placed in the same situation as in Srebrenica and Žepa."[14] In a

meeting, Admiral Leighton Smith asked Janvier what he wanted NATO to do to aid Žepa. Janvier stated that "I can't do anything" because "in order to get to Žepa I've got to fight my way through Serb territory and I'm not combat ready."[15] Janvier again appeared to be doing what he could to enact his proposal in May of withdrawing from Srebrenica, Žepa, Goražde, that the UN Security Council had rejected.

On July 24, the UN special rapporteur for human rights, former Polish Prime Minister Tadeusz Mazowiecki, completed a week of investigations into the fall of Srebrenica. Mazowiecki said 7,000 of Srebrenica's 40,000 residents seemed to have "disappeared." He urged Western leaders not to let the same fate befall Žepa's 15,000 inhabitants.[16]

More survivors emerged from the woods. The middle-aged man and teenage boy who suffered through the second mass execution of July 14, at the Red Mud Dam in Dulići north of Karakaj, were interviewed by UN investigators after they crossed the front lines. An investigator relayed the account of the older man to the U.S. ambassador to Croatia, Peter Galbraith, in Zagreb. Galbraith sent a highly classified "no distribution" cable directly to Secretary of State Christopher on July 25 using the survivor's tale to argue that many of the men from Srebrenica captured by the Serbs had been massacred. The ambassador urged Christopher to save Žepa's men from the same fate.

"The London Declaration implicitly writes off Žepa," Galbraith wrote. "In view of the numerous accounts of atrocities in Srebrenica and the possibility of a major massacre there, I urge reconsideration of air strikes to help Žepa." After giving a detailed account of the man's story, Galbraith continued: "Again, it is not too late to prevent a similar tragedy at Žepa. Žepa's defenders valiantly continue to hold on. Undoubtedly they realize the fate that awaits them. They should not be abandoned."[17] Galbraith's cable resulted in no change in the U.S. policy of defending only Goražde, but Christopher did order Assistant Secretary of State John Shattuck to travel to Tuzla and interview Srebrenica survivors.

That day, the International War Crimes Tribunal for the Former Yugoslavia charged General Mladić, Bosnian Serb President Radovan Karadžić and twenty-two other Bosnian and Croatian Serbs with committing crimes against humanity earlier in the war. The court, established with strong U.S. backing, by the UN Security Council in 1993, was the first of its kind since the Nuremberg and Far East war crimes trials following World War II.

The tribunal was essentially toothless. It had no power to arrest indicted war criminals and relied on the voluntary cooperation of countries to turn in people. In other words, the Bosnian Serbs or Serbia were expected to turn over Karadžić, Mladić and other indicted war criminals voluntarily.

The tribunal also suffered from severe budget problems. With the Republican-led U.S. Congress refusing to pay $1.1 billion in dues the United States owed the United Nations, Secretary General Boutros Boutros-Ghali cut spending across the board. At times, the number of trips war crimes investigators could take to Bosnia was limited.

The tribunal had still attracted top-notch talent. The United States seconded FBI investigators and Justice Department prosecutors to the court. Britain, France and other European countries also loaned top investigators to the Hague-based body. Eleven judges were chosen from eleven different nations and respected South African jurist Richard Goldstone became chief prosecutor.

Unlike Nuremberg, no trials in absentia could be held and the court could not inflict the death penalty. But supporters saw it as a crucial tool for bringing war criminals to justice and breaking the cycle of revenge that haunted the Balkans. If successful, supporters hoped, the tribunal, and a sister tribunal created to prosecute war criminals in Rwanda, could be turned into the world's first permanent war crimes tribunal.

The day he was indicted, Mladić flouted the tribunal by taking a second UN safe area. Žepa's civilian authorities finally surrendered. Serb soldiers took control of the town; two UN civilian negotiators also managed to reach it. But Žepa's military commander, the charismatic Avdo Palić, followed orders from Sarajevo and refused to abide by the surrender agreement. A rift had developed between the town's civilian and military leaders.

Over Palić's objections, the civilian leaders had met with Bosnian Serb commander General Mladić the previous week. After the meeting, Mladić was shown on Bosnian Serb television lifting weights near the front line.

The following day, July 26, thousands of Muslim civilians and soldiers still hid in the steep hills ringing Žepa. Mladić picked up a megaphone and began bellowing, "I am Ratko Mladić! I am Ratko Mladić!" His voice echoed throughout the valley. "Surrender! You will not be harmed!"[18] By the end of the day 2,500 of Žepa's estimated 15,000 inhabitants had been bused to Tišća and dumped at the border. Serb soldiers allowed one UN observer per bus. No attempt was made to separate old men from their families.

Mladić's confidence had apparently not been shaken by his indictment for war crimes the previous day. On boarding one of the buses, according to Muslims, the Serb commander said, "Not Allah, not the United Nations, not anything can help you. I am your God."[19]

In Washington, domestic politics increased the pressure on President Clinton. A measure supported by Senate Majority Leader and presidential candidate Bob Dole that would lift the arms embargo passed the Senate by a 69–29 vote. The measure had already been overwhelmingly passed by the House. The Senate vote was a direct repudiation of the White House's Bosnia policy. Clinton promised to veto it, but Dole, for now, appeared to have the votes for a humiliating override. With the summer recess ahead, it would be early September before an override vote could take place. With Clinton's approval, frantic efforts to launch the new diplomatic initiative envisioned in Lake's endgame strategy began.

On July 27, Žepa commander Avdo Palić met with General Mladić and two UN officials to negotiate the surrender and withdrawal of his approximately 3,000 men. Palić, though despised by the Serbs, had volunteered to come to the talks with no security guarantees. Following the meeting, the Muslim commander was led away by two of Mladić's bodyguards as UN officials stood nearby. The next morning, when the UN officials asked Mladić where Palić was, the general replied, "I shot him."[20]

When the UN negotiators returned to the area on July 29, most of the Bosnian Serb military units they had seen in the town were gone, even though Žepa's 3,000 men had not surrendered. Usually confident, Mladić seemed to be off balance.[21]

The Bosnian Serb general had been outmaneuvered. Thousands of Serb troops from across the country carried out the Srebrenica manhunt and Žepa attack, leaving Serb lines on the opposite side of Bosnia—the western front—desperately weak. More importantly, the powerful Croatian Army had carried out a lightning maneuver while Mladić laid siege to Žepa.[22]

In a classic flank attack that left Knin—the self-declared capital of Serb nationalists in Croatia—nearly surrounded, Croatian forces crossed into Bosnia and surged toward the Bihać enclave. By July 29, Glamoč and Bosansko Grahovo, strategic and traditionally Serb towns, had fallen and 10,000 Serb civilians fled toward Banja Luka, the largest Serb-held city in Bosnia. Over fifty square miles of Serb territory had been taken.

Croat forces were now to the east, south and west of Knin, only twenty miles away from Bihać, and could attack the portion of Croatia still in Serb hands from three directions. Western analysts noted that the Croat attack followed classic NATO strategy, not the Warsaw Pact strategy used by officers in the former Yugoslav National Army. The Croats were learning from the retired American generals advising them.

Two days later, the Serbs suffered a blow they would feel weeks later. On August 1, U.S. Assistant Secretary of State John Shattuck, on a mission prompted by Ambassador Galbraith's cable, finished two days of interviews with survivors from Srebrenica and Žepa. Shattuck spoke with Hurem Suljić, Smail Hodžić and the teenage boy from the mass execution at the Red Mud Dam.

When Shattuck returned to Washington, the State Department again asked the CIA to begin scanning aerial photos of the

Srebrenica area. The U.S. ambassador to the UN, Madeleine Albright, and the U.S. ambassador in Sarajevo, John Menzies, had turned over tips from Bosnian authorities of rumored mass executions in the Bratunac soccer stadium two weeks earlier, on July 13. But the CIA said they had no photographs that corroborated the claims. On July 17 the CIA's Bosnia Task Force wrote in its classified daily report that numerous refugee accounts "provide details that appear credible" but added that "we lack authoritative, detailed information to substantiate this information." Armed with the accounts Shattuck heard, an analyst began a new search on August 2.[23] The focus was on two towns—Nova Kasaba and Karakaj.

Over the next two days, the evacuation of Žepa's women, children and old men was completed, but Žepa's 3,000 men were trapped. Roughly 800 men opted to cross the Drina River and surrender in neighboring Serbia. The remaining 2,000 began a perilous fifty-mile journey to Muslim-held central Bosnia.

Among them were several dozen men from Srebrenica who had given up when they reached the Serb-filled asphalt road near Nova Kasaba. They returned to Srebrenica for food and then went on to Žepa, hoping that safe area would be defended. One of them was Hakija Husejnović, the survivor from the warehouse. He decided that crossing the road in Nova Kasaba was too dangerous. His fellow survivor, Ramiz, pushed on. Husejnović returned to Srebrenica, and then traveled the familiar route to Žepa. He believed that the UN would defend the safe area, but was cruelly disappointed once more. He didn't know it, but Ramiz—the only other warehouse survivor—had died in an ambush on the other side of the asphalt road. Husejnović was the only witness left.

On August 3, war spread to Croatia. The long-awaited Croatian Army offensive was launched. In a stunning rout, the Croats regained in only four days nearly all of the 400 square miles of territory Serb nationalists had seized in 1991 and 1992. Storming areas from which Croats had been brutally expelled in 1992, they exacted vengeance, burning houses and killing Serb civilians.

The Serb stronghold of Knin fell on August 5, and on August 6, after three years of siege, the Muslim enclave of Bihać was liberated. Serbs put up little resistance. In the largest single refugee crisis of the war, 120,000 Serbs from Croatia retreated into neighboring Bosnia. The retrained and rearmed Croatian Army had made Serb nationalist forces in Bosnia and Croatia look like paper tigers. Serbian President Milošević, who had urged Serbs in Croatia to rise up and declare their own state in 1991, now did nothing to aid them.[24] With his economy ruined by UN economic sanctions, Milošević was focused on cooperating with the West, ending the war, getting UN economic sanctions lifted and shoring up his own power base in Serbia.

European and UN officials harshly criticized the offensive, claiming a diplomatic solution was possible, but U.S. criticism of Croatia was muted. The fall of the Croatian Serbs helped create a balance of power in the region, and Bihać's liberation eliminated another enclave. Anthony Lake's endgame concept of a peace settlement based on simpler borders and no enclaves was moving forward.

On August 8, UN Special Representative Yasushi Akashi and Force Commander Janvier met with Serbian President Slobodan Milošević in Belgrade. The meeting focused on the UN's role in the one remaining piece of Croatia held by Serb nationalists— eastern Slavonia—an oil-rich strip of territory which bordered Milošević's Serbia. They feared a final Croat offensive to retake the area.

Near the end of the meeting, Akashi brought up Mladić's promise from the July 15 meeting, which he then gave in writing on July 17, to allow the International Committee of the Red Cross access to prisoners from Srebrenica. "The agreement was not implemented," Akashi said. "There are many questions regarding the missing. Mladić should give access to them."

"He must stick to his promises," replied the Serbian President, whose extensive state security apparatus was probably well aware that the prisoners were already dead. "I'll do everything I can to make him respect his promises."

Milošević then asked the UN to help provide supplies for the 800 Muslim men from Žepa who had crossed the Drina River and entered Serbia.[25] They were being well treated, he assured Akashi and Janvier. In truth, the imprisoned Muslims were being beaten and were rarely fed.

After the meeting, the group retired to a hunting lodge outside Belgrade where Milošević frequently took visiting dignitaries. They had lunch on a deck overlooking the forest and Milošević insisted everyone have a traditional sip of *šljivovica*, or plum brandy. Milošević, Akashi, Janvier and their senior aides filled the table.

"Do you see bear and deer from the deck we're on?" Akashi asked.

"Yes, from time to time," Milošević replied. "But there's no hunting next to the lodge. You have to go one or two kilometers away."

"A safe area for animals," Akashi joked. The entire table burst out laughing.

The following day, August 9, Clinton finalized Lake's diplomatic initiative and the National Security Adviser departed for a seven-country European tour. Lake was to present, not propose, the initiative. Clinton would be going ahead with or without European support.

The next day, the initiative received a crucial boost. The administration produced dramatic evidence of mass executions after the fall of Srebrenica. The CIA analyst had stayed up all night on August 2 poring over U.S. aerial photos of the Nova Kasaba area. He found what appeared to be mass graves. One spy photo showed several hundred prisoners gathered on the Nova Kasaba soccer field. Several days later, the prisoners were gone and four areas of fresh digging appeared conspicuously nearby.[26] The evidence was reported in the National Intelligence Daily on August 4 and Albright lobbied for its release. She unveiled the evidence at a closed session to the UN Security Council on August 10. The photos served a dual purpose. Powerful evidence of Serb atrocities, U.S. officials hoped they would convince Europeans, still skeptical that one side was worse than the other, that the Serbs should be bombed.

In Europe, Lake's initiative met with mixed reviews. The Europeans were thrilled to have Clinton put his personal prestige behind a new diplomatic initiative, but they opposed the plan's punitive measures—bombing the Serbs if they failed to cooperate and lifting the arms embargo.

On August 14, Assistant Secretary of State Richard Holbrooke took over for Lake. Holbrooke had a reputation for being overbearing, but he was also viewed as the one negotiator who might be able to outmaneuver the Serb, Croat and Muslim leaders who had frustrated so many past envoys.

Holbrooke was given an unusual degree of latitude in the negotiations and he quickly objected to one of the central tenets of Lake's proposal. The proposed settlement maps divided Bosnia between a Muslim-Croat federation that controlled 51 percent of the country and a Bosnian Serb "entity" that held 49 percent. The proposed borders were relatively simple and no enclaves existed. Goražde, the only remaining enclave in eastern Bosnia, was to be traded for the Serb-held suburbs around surrounded Sarajevo. Holbrooke said that after the fall of Srebrenica and Žepa it was immoral to ask Goražde's 65,000 people to abandon the town. The maps were later modified and the Goražde trade proposal dropped.

Holbrooke's first foray ended tragically on August 19. After visiting Belgrade and Zagreb, a French APC rolled off the narrow, winding dirt track that led into Sarajevo over UN-controlled Mount Igman. Three key members of Holbrooke's negotiating team died: Robert C. Frasure, a career diplomat who was Clinton's special representative for Bosnia and laid much of the groundwork for Holbrooke, Dr. Joseph Kruzel from the Pentagon's Balkan Task Force and Colonel S. Nelson Drew from Lake's National Security Council staff. Holbrooke's group had been forced to drive into the city because General Mladić refused to guarantee their plane's security if it flew into the then closed

Sarajevo airport. Mladić said he couldn't promise that the Muslims wouldn't shoot at the plane.

The cost of the war in Bosnia had been brought dramatically home to the White House.

After the funerals, Holbrooke began frenetically shuttling between Sarajevo, Belgrade and Zagreb.

In Holland, Srebrenica was quickly turning into a national scandal. The U.S. spy satellite photos confirmed suspicions of mass executions. There were damaging interviews with Dutch peacekeepers who said they saw dozens of bodies in Nova Kasaba and witnessed executions in Potočari. Other stories reported the Dutch dislike of the enclave's Muslim soldiers.

The Dutch Ministry of Defense then revealed that the roll of film containing photographs of the nine dead Muslim men found near the stream had been "accidentally" destroyed in a film-processing lab. Outraged members of the Dutch parliament accused the Defense Ministry of a cover-up.

Embarrassing information continued to leak. The statement the Dutch deputy commander, Major Robert Franken, had signed declaring that the evacuations accompanied by the Dutch were carried out according to international law was disclosed. A story then appeared that exposed the list of 239 men kicked off the Dutch base.[27] At an initial press conference responding to the story, Defense Minister Joris Voorhoeve denied that the list existed. One day later, Voorhoeve admitted there was a list, but said senior officers in the Dutch Army had not informed him of its existence.

The debriefing of Dutch peacekeepers finally began in September. More than six weeks had passed and the peacekeepers and their superiors in the Ministry of Defense failed to sound the alarm about the atrocities and evidence of mass executions witnessed by the Dutch. In hindsight, the Dutch failure to speak out after they left the enclave was as derelict as their conduct during the Serb offensive.

On October 30, the Dutch Ministry of Defense issued its final report on the debriefing. Dated October 4, it was an exercise in obfuscation. Much of what the Dutch saw was in the report, but what occurred was vastly played down or distorted. Throughout the report, references were made to UNPROFOR commanders turning down requests for Close Air Support. The reference appears at first glance to be to General Janvier—but was actually referring to UNPROFOR chief of staff Dutch general Nicolai, who turned down the first two requests.

Sergeant Mülder being forced to "hunt Muslims" was referred to as follows: "Both Dutchbat soldiers were ordered to go and sit on top of an [APC]. They were given hand-held weapons with the advice that, for their own safety, they would do well to shoot any BiH soldiers on sight. After a while, the Dutchbat soldiers turned back without a shot having been fired and without having seen any BiH soldiers." All of the captured Muslims were referred to as Bosnian "soldiers."[28]

The report exonerated the Dutch and blamed UN commanders hesitant to use NATO airpower for the fall of the enclave. Defense Minister Voorhoeve said only a public commitment by the international community to unleash massive air strikes could have saved Srebrenica. The blame for the fall of the enclave, Voorhoeve said, lay with the many nations that refused to contribute the 30,000 troops needed to defend the safe areas when they were created in 1993.

But the controversy refused to die. A play later debuted in Holland that portrayed the Dutch peacekeepers in Srebrenica as cowards and racist toward Srebrenica's Muslims. Other branches of the military and units in the Dutch Army privately criticized the 13th Air Mobile Battalion, the unit that served in Srebrenica, for hurting their reputation.

Embittered by their experience in Bosnia and their treatment after returning to Holland, some of the Dutch who served in Srebrenica left the Dutch Army. Many of the Dutch compared their experience to that of American soldiers who were sent to Vietnam. They were sent on an impossible mission, they said, and then blamed for its failure.

...

In Bosnia, the Serb attack on Goražde never materialized. With the London ultimatum and the 12,000-troop Rapid Reaction Force in place, the Serbs appeared to back off and wait for Western unity to dissolve again.

But on August 28 a shell landed near a Sarajevo open-air market, killing thirty-seven and wounding eighty-eight. The Serbs—as was their custom—accused the Muslims of firing the shell on their own people to create a pretext for NATO bombing. But a UN crater analysis ruled that the deadly shell and four others fired in the same volley all came from Serb positions.[29]

The UN commander in Sarajevo, British general Rupert Smith, now had the pretext he needed to launch air strikes. The London Declaration's earlier promise to defend Goražde had been extended to Sarajevo, Bihać and Tuzla. Neutralizing the hostage threat, peacekeepers had been steadily leaving Goražde over the last few weeks. After three and a half years of war, Washington, Paris and London unanimously supported intensive NATO air strikes against the Serbs. All pretense of neutrality was gone. Janvier, who could have blocked the strikes, was at his son's wedding. The last British peacekeepers leaving Goražde arrived safely in Serbia on August 28. At 2:10 a.m. on August 30 the ground began shaking in the Bosnian Serb stronghold of Pale. The first ammunition dump had been hit.

For the next three days, NATO planes and the new Rapid Reaction Force—which had positioned heavy artillery on Mount Igman above Sarajevo—pounded Serb positions around the besieged city. Janvier returned from leave and agreed to meet with General Mladić. Janvier's instructions were to stick to the pre-agreed UN–NATO ultimatum: the air strikes would halt only if Mladić withdrew his heavy weapons from around Sarajevo.[30]

Over the course of a grueling eleven-hour meeting in the town of Mali Zvornik, Mladić complained that withdrawing his weapons would leave the Serb-held suburbs of Sarajevo vulnerable to a Muslim attack. Janvier held firm at first but eventually compromised. At 4:08 a.m. Mladić signed a letter that did not meet the specific conditions of the UN–NATO ultimatum.[31] Because of the letter, a temporary pause in the bombing was extended.

The following day, NATO's governing body, the North Atlantic Council, ruled that Mladić's letter did not meet the ultimatum. Janvier argued that the halt in the bombing should be extended and the UN should force the Muslims to promise not to launch an offensive if the heavy weapons were withdrawn. But the rare consensus among Washington, London and Paris on the use of force prevailed. Mladić was given forty-eight hours to start withdrawing his weapons. Serb guns stayed in position. The bombing resumed on September 5.

Holbrooke continued his tireless shuttle diplomacy. The day before the bombing began, Holbrooke achieved a major breakthrough. On August 29, the Bosnian Serbs gave in to intense pressure from Serbian President Milošević and said he could represent them in negotiations. In the past, Milošević agreed to peace deals but the Bosnian Serbs refused to accept them.[32]

As NATO planes knocked out Serb communications systems, Bosnian and Croatian armies took advantage of it with the tacit approval of the United States.[33] A joint Muslim-Croat offensive swept across western Bosnia. Bosnian Serbs appeared to be in complete disarray. After two years of stalemate or Serb victories, over 100 square miles of Serb territory fell in a week.

On September 10, Janvier, under strict orders not to bend, met with Mladić in Belgrade. The Serb general demanded that the air strikes end before negotiations could begin. Janvier was instructed to leave. Minutes after Janvier's plane took off, thirteen Tomahawk missiles were fired from U.S. ships in the Adriatic at Serb SAM missile sites around Banja Luka. The NATO bombing and Muslim-Croat advances continued.

With their holdings in western Bosnia crumbling, Bosnian Serb President Radovan Karadžić and General Ratko Mladić signed an agreement drafted by Holbrooke's team on September 14. They promised to withdraw their weapons from around Sarajevo and begin peace talks immediately. There was a pause in the NATO attacks. Then Mladić conveniently entered a Belgrade military hospital for treatment of a kidney stone. The heavy weapons were finally withdrawn from around Sarajevo.

In the largest operation in NATO's history, planes had flown 3,400 sorties and 750 attack missions against 56 targets including ammunition bunkers, SAM missiles and communications centers. The Bosnian Serbs were capitulating. After three and a half years, the siege of Sarajevo was over. The use of large-scale NATO air strikes in Bosnia proved to be devastatingly effective once potential hostages were removed from Serb territory.

Holbrooke suddenly found himself confronted by another problem. Muslim and Croat forces were racing across western Bosnia—and they refused to stop. At one point, Holbrooke had color maps produced twice a day by the UN intelligence unit in Sarajevo showing the percentage of territory held by the Muslims and Croats versus the Serbs. When the balance of territory exceeded 51-49 percent on September 19, Holbrooke and other U.S. officials ordered the Muslims and Croats to halt. In a meeting with Bosnian President Izetbegović and Croatian President Tudjman, Holbrooke cited an intelligence assessment stating that Serb lines were solidifying and a counterattack was possible.[34]

But UN officials estimated that Croat tank columns were only seventy-two hours away from taking Banja Luka—the largest Serb-held city in Bosnia. If the city fell, the hundreds of square miles of flat plains around it in western Bosnia were expected to follow, which would leave the Bosnian Serbs with only their holdings in eastern Bosnia. The fall of Banja Luka would send over 200,000 Serbs fleeing toward Serbia, potentially threatening Milošević's power and derailing the U.S. peace initiative.[35]

Bosnian President Alija Izetbegović, whose forces were finally winning after three years, was less willing to relent. In the end, the Bosnians—who relied on the Croats' tanks and artillery for support—had little choice. On October 5, Holbrooke secured a sixty-day cease-fire. Fighting flared for another week. Two more towns fell to the Muslims and Croats, while the Serbs retook some territory near the Una River. On October 12, a country-wide cease-fire finally took hold. The Muslims, Croats and Serbs had "fought" to the lines more or less outlined in Lake's endgame strategy.

On November 1, Bosnian President Izetbegović, Croatian

DAYTON PEACE ACCORD

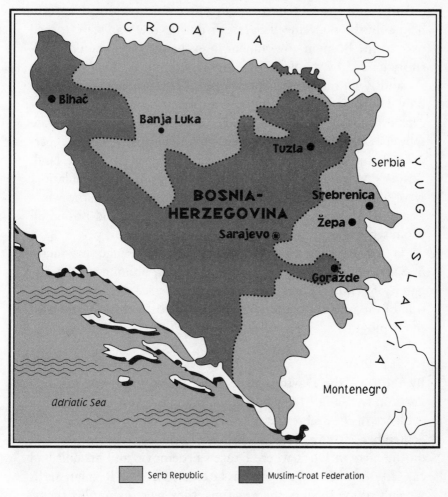

President Tudjman and Serbian President Milošević arrived in Dayton, Ohio, for peace talks. Twenty-one days of intense negotiations followed. Milošević, eager for a deal, made several concessions. Holbrooke and Secretary of State Christopher finally persuaded the deeply divided Bosnian government to accept the agreement on November 21, when the talks were on the verge of collapse.

Under the agreement, Goražde remained Bosnian government territory and was linked to Sarajevo by a thin corridor. The Serb-held suburbs that ringed Sarajevo during the war were turned over to the Bosnian government in exchange for a chunk of territory gained by the Bosnian Army in western Bosnia.[36] Srebrenica and Žepa remained in Serb hands. The Serbs, who made up only 31 percent of the country's population, would get 49 percent of Bosnia's land and the de facto "ethnically pure" state they had brutally created. Croats, who comprised only 17 percent of the population, received nearly 25 percent of the land. Bosnia's Muslims, who constituted 44 percent of the population, were allotted only 25 percent of the land, and were the war's clear losers. The governments of Serbia, Croatia and Bosnia all promised to hand over all indicted war criminals.

President Clinton, invoking images of marketplace massacres in Sarajevo and mass graves in Srebrenica, announced the dispatch of 25,000 American soldiers to oversee the implementation of the peace agreement. The majority of Americans opposed the deployment.[37]

By the time the Dayton peace accord was formally signed in Paris on December 14, a systematic effort by the Serbs to destroy evidence of the Srebrenica massacres was already under way. On September 29, spy planes had spotted heavy equipment at work on the farm in Pilica where Dražen Erdemović and his unit had carried out one of the final mass executions. The Bosnian Serbs weren't trying to bury their victims; they were exhuming them.

Apparently tipped off by the August 10 release of the Nova Kasaba satellite photos, the Serbs began unearthing bodies. My own trip to Nova Kasaba on August 16 may also have unintentionally prompted the Serbs to destroy evidence. After the Pilica farm, digging was then seen at an apparent mass grave in Glogova—three miles from the site of the Kravica warehouse massacre—on October 28.

Later that week, a Washington-based U.S. intelligence official leaked the locations of the suspected graves in Glogova, Grbavći and the Red Mud Dam to me.[38]

Entering Serb territory without permission, I reached Grbavći and the Red Mud Dam on October 29.[39] Everything matched exactly what Mevludin Orić, Hurem Suljić, Smail Hodžić and the two survivors told me. Both sites appeared not to have been tampered with. But a watchman at the dam arrested me and the documents I had found and pictures I had taken of the graves, civilian clothes, human bones and three old men's canes were seized.[40]

Over the next few months, the destruction of evidence would continue.

With peace and the onset of the harsh Balkan winter, hopes of more men emerging from the woods faded. Approximately 3,200 men crossed with the lead section of the column on July 16, 17 and 18. After that, only small groups, ranging from three to a few dozen, crossed at a time. Roughly 1,500 more men from Srebrenica emerged from the woods by late October.

Almost all of Žepa's men survived. In a testament to the importance of leadership, Avdo Palić's deputy commanders let civilians leave for Muslim-held central Bosnia only in groups of 300. Most groups were accompanied by soldiers and guides and traveled only through isolated territory. Special commando groups from Žepa made up of volunteers also ventured back into Serb territory to gather men hiding around the fallen enclave. One commando returned with 97 men in October.

But Žepa's men also had an enormous advantage over Srebrenica's—the Croatian Army. The Croat attack in western Bosnia forced General Mladić to send most of his units there instead of using them to hunt down men from Žepa.

In prisoner exchanges carried out as part of the Dayton peace accord, the 800 men from Žepa who had surrendered in Serbia were released. Several dozen men from Srebrenica were among them. The Serb prisoner-of-war camp in Batković also emptied, producing several dozen more Srebrenicans, including some of the wounded men who were seized in Bratunac. But the officer who wrote "30 Dutch equals 30,000 Muslims" and the four men who held off the Serb tank with Ibran Malagić were still missing.

The International Committee of the Red Cross collected a new list in February 1996—eight months after the enclave's fall. Over 6,600 men from Srebrenica were still missing.

The arrival of American troops in Bosnia in December 1995 raised expectations among Srebrenica's survivors. The Dayton peace accord called on all parties to turn over indicted war criminals to the War Crimes Tribunal. Bosnian Serb President Radovan Karadžić and General Ratko Mladić were indicted by the tribunal for the Srebrenica massacres on November 18 and hopes were high for an arrest. It was hoped, too, that much-rumored secret prison camps filled with the missing men would be found by American or NATO troops. On January 21, 1996, U.S. Assistant Secretary of State for Human Rights John Shattuck visited the warehouse Hakija Husejnović survived. Accompanied by investigators from the tribunal and a slew of reporters, Shattuck called for the exhumation of the apparent mass graves.

But almost from the outset of the mission, President Clinton and his advisers ruled out any attempt to arrest Karadžić or Mladić. With the administration still haunted by the disastrous experience in Somalia, hunting war criminals was ruled not to be part of the new NATO force's mandate. The White House had neutralized Bosnia as an election issue. American troops had a far safer mission than leading a UN withdrawal, but keeping casualties low remained a priority.

NATO troops were ordered to arrest indicted war criminals only if they ran into them by chance on patrol or at a checkpoint. If the troops felt it would be unsafe to arrest the indicted war criminals, they could, according to the policy, let them go. With Mladić and Karadžić constantly surrounded by heavily armed bodyguards, arrests were essentially precluded.

On February 2, survivors' hopes turned to frustration and then violence. Women from Srebrenica stormed the office of the International Committee of the Red Cross in Tuzla, shattering windows and occupying offices. They demanded that more efforts be made to find their missing sons, husbands and fathers. The ICRC had already inspected existing Bosnian Serb prisons as part of the peace settlement and found no men from Srebrenica. Rumors of slave labor on farms or in mines in Serbia persisted, but unannounced ICRC visits to mines produced no men or traces of men from Srebrenica.

In March, a panicked Dražen Erdemović had one of his friends call the U.S. embassy in Belgrade. Relations between Erdemović and some members of his unit had steadily deteriorated after the mass execution. His commanding officer, Lieutenant Milorad Pelemiš, threw him and his family out of his house in January 1996. The low point came in February when Erdemović got in an argument and was shot by Stanko Savanović—the member of his unit who bragged about how many Muslims he had killed in Pilica.

Erdemović's friend, twenty-nine-year-old Radislav Kremenović, told the U.S. embassy that Erdemović would be willing to testify before the War Crimes Tribunal in exchange for guarantees of safety for him and his family. An embassy switchboard operator thought it was a crank call and sent him a list of media organizations. Kremenović called ABC News. Serbian secret police were tapping ABC's lines. After an interview with ABC and the French newspaper Le Figaro, Erdemović was arrested and ABC's tapes were seized by Milošević's secret police. Under intense pressure from the United States, Milošević handed Erdemović over to the tribunal after one month.[41] CIA analysts checked old aerial photos of the Pilica area after Erdemović's story broke. Photographs showing bodies strewn across the ground and a grave being dug on July 21 corroborated his account. Albright visited Pilica with tribunal investigators in March.

In April 1996, Mevludin Orić's half brother Dašan was one of six men from Srebrenica to emerge from the woods nine months after Srebrenica's fall. After seeing that the road in Nova Kasaba was blocked, they had returned to Srebrenica and decided to wait. The group hid in the hills around Lehovići, sleeping and lighting fires in small caves they dug in a hillside. Food from the village's abandoned houses kept them alive. Serbs intermittently scavenging the area were avoided.

A second group of men from Srebrenica were less lucky. In May, they headed for central Bosnia after hiding in the caves around Žepa for the winter. Four miles from crossing into Muslim-held central Bosnia, they were spotted by Serbs. Fired on, they ran to a nearby American patrol and surrendered. Serb police quickly arrived. The Muslims were carrying two pistols, some hand grenades and a small amount of explosives. The Serb police insisted the men were Muslim commandos carrying out a raid from Tuzla. The American officer—after deliberating for two hours—turned the Muslims over to the Serb police. After being tortured by the Serbs, the Muslims signed confessions stating that they had killed four missing Serbs who were out cutting wood near Žepa.[42] As of January 1997, they were in a Serb jail waiting to be tried on murder charges.

When a team of investigators from the War Crimes Tribunal arrived for a three-week inspection of the massacre sites in April 1996, a bizarre arrangement was worked out with the U.S. forces patrolling the area. U.S. commanders—fearing "mission creep," or being slowly drawn into more and more duties—provided only "area security" for tribunal investigators and refused to clear mines from sites. No soldiers guarded the sites, so it was possible the Serbs had laid mines. Avoiding American casualities remained the Clinton administration's priority.

Investigators traveled to the sites anyway. I returned to Grbavći with them on April 2. Nearly 70 percent of the grave had been recently dug up. My October 29 trip had prompted the Serbs to destroy the evidence. Everything I had taken photos of—including the three canes—was gone.

But the cleanup had been sloppy. A decomposed body was found near the grave. A pile of identification cards from Srebrenica was found in the woods along with several dozen strips of cloth—the blindfolds Mevludin and Hurem had described.

Bureaucratic delays at the War Crimes Tribunal and the process of hiring a nonprofit mine-removal agency delayed the exhumation of the suspected mass graves until July. The first grave, near Čerska, produced 150 bodies—far more than expected. Most victims had their hands tied behind their backs and had been shot from behind.

After a group of mine-sniffing dogs were accidentally sent to Mozambique instead of Bosnia, the exhumation in Nova Kasaba began in late August 1996. Two of the four suspected graves were exhumed and only thirty-three bodies were discovered. There was no evidence of tampering. The CIA's loose estimate of 600 bodies, which was based on the surface area of the graves, appeared inaccurate.

The leg I had found jutting from the ground near the graves a year earlier was still there. One man, buried in a shallow grave, lay alone.

In early September, with winter approaching, investigators moved to Grbavći. They only dug up the grave Mevludin Orić and Hurem Suljić had eluded. The grave that Smail Hodžić survived would be dug in the spring of 1997. Investigators found 160 bodies, most with their hands tied behind their backs and wearing blindfolds, confirming Mevludin's and Hurem's stories.

But bodies were also clearly missing. The top nine feet of soil contained no corpses. Extra limbs and body parts were found mixed in with the topsoil, indicating that bodies had been removed and broken apart in the process.

In Pilica, 116 bodies as well as 14 extra body parts were found at the farm where Dražen Erdemović served as an executioner. As Erdemović said, they wore civilian clothes. Tribunal investigators believe that grave was also tampered with. Erdemović's rough estimate of 1,000 victims may also be high.

When the exhumations around Srebrenica were halted for the winter, more than one-third of the known graves had been dug up, but fewer than 550 corpses had been found. If bodies were to be found at roughly the same ratios next summer, approximately 1,650 victims of mass executions would be located, a fraction of the 7,079 men reported missing to the Red Cross. According to the ICRC, 2,935 of the missing were last seen in Serb custody.

The discrepancy can be attributed to two things—Serb tampering and inaccurate estimates from survivors. Considering the extent of the tampering, finding fewer than 2,943 bodies in the mass graves once the exhumations are completed is to be expected. Investigators said survivors experience severe stress and often unconsciously overestimate the size of crowds and number of bodies. In Rwanda, far fewer victims than survivors described were found in graves. Some exaggeration is conscious.

Several Muslim men interviewed for this book appeared to have made up their accounts of atrocities or exaggerated them. None of their stories were used. Hurem Suljić, Mevludin Orić and other survivors may have overestimated the number of victims, but the overwhelming amount of physical evidence found at the sites corroborated their account of a mass execution. Dražen Erdemović, an executioner, had little reason to exaggerate.

The Bosnian government claims that over 10,000 men from Srebrenica are missing, but the figure that appears most reliable is the ICRC total of 7,079 missing. The ICRC has gone through an exhaustive process of checking that the list is accurate. After the ICRC took an initial list of the missing when the women and children arrived from Srebrenica in July, the entire process was started over again and families were forced to submit a report of someone missing for a second time.

The updated ICRC list of missing was compiled eight months after Srebrenica's fall and did not come from the Bosnian government, which has been accused of inflating casualty figures in the past. For a listing to be accepted, a close relative had to submit an individual's full name, father's name, date of birth, place of birth and date and place they were last seen. The list was repeatedly cross-checked for redundancies.

Some of the reports may be false. But it is unlikely that the Bosnian government could convince or organize hundreds of people to submit thousands of detailed, nonredundant false reports of missing people that would wildly inflate the total. The ICRC, which has specialized in gathering accounts of missing persons during its 113-year history, stands by the figure of 7,079 missing.

The majority of the missing men—approximately 4,000—

appear to have been killed in lopsided firefights or ambushes. Only 30 percent of the fleeing Muslims were armed. Bosnian Serb police who were involved in "cleansing the terrain" operations told acquaintances that when they returned with small groups of prisoners, their commanding officers ordered them to take the prisoners into the woods and shoot them.[43] As part of an exchange of remains between Serbs and Muslims in the summer of 1996, Bosnian government investigators found over 150 bodies strewn across the hillside where the column was ambushed and split in two in Kamenica. Around the ambush site, bodies were intermittently scattered in the woods. Along the route men took to Tuzla, skeletons dotted the path.[44]

As many as 4,000 corpses are scattered across the forests and fields of eastern Bosnia. With UN, tribunal and Bosnian efforts to recover the bodies moving slowly, most of the bodies are already badly decomposed. The vast majority will never be identified.

As of January 1997, the fall of Srebrenica appeared to involve the largest single massacre in Europe since World War II. Barring secret labor camps and the Bosnian government massively inflating the ICRC missing figure, Bosnian Serb soldiers systematically slaughtered 7,079 mostly unarmed Muslim men in ambushes and mass executions between July 12 and July 16, 1995.

Based on the ICRC figure, the killing spree carried out by General Ratko Mladić's troops over the five-day period was the most systematic and intense of Europe's worst conflict since World War II. After nearly fifty years of superpower-imposed peace interrupted primarily by the Soviet invasions of Hungary and Czechoslovakia and Stalin's intermittent postwar purges, between 150,000 and 200,000 people are believed to have died in the war in Bosnia.

Other Bosnian Serb campaigns—such as the "ethnic cleansing" of northern and eastern Bosnia in 1992—involved larger numbers of people, but appear not to match Srebrenica in the intensity of the bloodletting. The number of victims in 1992 is also unclear, but thousands were beaten, tortured or killed and tens of thousands of Muslim prisoners were placed in concentration camps. Exactly how many perished during the campaigns or in the camps may never be known, but large numbers of prisoners were at least kept alive. In Srebrenica, virtually none was spared.

Srebrenica accounts for an astonishing percentage of the number of missing from the brutal conflict. Of the 18,406 Muslims, Serbs and Croats reported still missing to the ICRC as of January 1997, 7,079 are people who disappeared after the fall of Srebrenica. In other words, approximately 38 percent of the war's missing are from Srebrenica.

Based on the ICRC figure, nearly 3,000 men were summarily executed and over 4,000 hunted down like animals. But even if the number of victims proves to be no higher than the roughly 500 found so far at four execution sites and 150 found to date at one ambush site, what occurred in Srebrenica was unprecedented in postwar Europe. Srebrenica is unique because of the international community's role in the tragedy.

The international community partially disarmed thousands of men, promised them they would be safeguarded and then delivered them to their sworn enemies. Srebrenica was not simply a case of the international community standing by as a far-off atrocity was committed. The actions of the international community encouraged, aided and emboldened the executioners.

EPILOGUE

The fall of Srebrenica did not have to happen. There is no need for thousands of skeletons to be strewn across eastern Bosnia. There is no need for thousands of Muslim children to be raised on stories of their fathers, grandfathers, uncles and brothers slaughtered by Serbs. The fall of Srebrenica could have been prevented.

What was unusual about Srebrenica was the speed of its demise. The collective failure of the United States, France and Britain, NATO, the United Nations, the Bosnian government, the Dutch peacekeepers and the town's own Muslim defenders to effectively protect the town is one of the great controversies— and mysteries—of the war in Bosnia.

Serbs who captured the town are convinced that the Muslims defending it had secret orders from Sarajevo to abandon the enclave. Many Dutch are certain the Muslims had instructions from Sarajevo not to defend the town and that Janvier had secret orders from France to halt air strikes.

But French officers who are friends of Janvier see him as one of Srebrenica's victims, believe the Serbs and Muslims had a secret deal to trade the town, and that Janvier is being unfairly blamed for its fall.

The Bosnian government, meanwhile, denies there was any secret deal and holds Akashi and Janvier wholly responsible. Finally, Srebrenicans, in general, are convinced that the safe area was secretly traded for the Serb-held suburbs around Sarajevo in a deal brokered by the United States.

The reasons the town fell so quickly are clear: the lack of NATO Close Air Support and the absence of Naser Orić demoralized both the town's defenders and the Dutch peacekeepers. If NATO Close Air Support had been used earlier, or if Naser had been present, the 7,079 missing might still be alive today.

While the bombardment was intense, only four Serb tanks and several hundred infantry led the main attack up the narrow asphalt road, something NATO jets or well-organized defenders could have likely held off for several more days. The attack on Srebrenica should have taken the same pattern as attacks on the safe areas of Goražde in 1994, numerous attacks on Bihać in 1994 and 1995, the attack on Srebrenica in 1993 and the attack on Žepa only days later—large initial Serb gains slowed when confronted by entrenched Muslim defenders. Unwilling to engage in house-to-house fighting and suffer heavy casualties, the Serbs paused and tried to shell their opponents into submission. With the Muslims on the verge of collapse, the United Nations and Western powers were then finally embarrassed into taking some kind of action to stop the Serbs. Time was the key factor in Srebrenica. Close Air Support and Naser Orić would only have given the town a few more days at best, but that may have been enough.

Both the town's defenders and the UN failed in Srebrenica. Naser Orić's absence was slightly less responsible for the rapid fall of the town than the lack of NATO Close Air Support.

In peacetime, Naser Orić wears leather jackets, designer sunglasses and thick gold chains. He drives silver Audi and Mercedes coupes and tears out of parking lots—his tires spitting rocks and dust into the air. Just over six feet tall with a powerful, but compact frame, he looks like the weight lifter, bodyguard and nightclub bouncer that he once was. He asks foreigners to get him books about how American and British elite Special Forces units train—one of his main interests.

But Orić is far from the simple thug or small-time mafioso he may appear to be. At twenty-nine, he is already a *legenda*—

Serbo-Croatian for legend. Other men spend lifetimes trying to create the aura of fear and respect that now surrounds Naser in Tuzla. Both arrogant and charismatic, he has an intangible quality about him that is difficult to define. Naser is a leader.

The men who fought with him in Srebrenica still say his name with reverence. If Naser Orić and the enclave's fifteen best soldiers had been in Srebrenica, soldiers from Srebrenica insist, the town would have held for at least several more days. The UN, most likely, would have been forced to intervene. Srebrenica may have been peacefully traded as part of a peace settlement in the end, but 7,079 lives would have been saved.

Why Naser Orić was not in Srebrenica has become a bitter bone of contention. Naser insists the Bosnian government barred him from returning to the enclave. The Bosnian government insists that they ordered Naser to return, but he refused.

Rumors that Sarajevo intentionally sacrificed Srebrenica grew so persistent that it became a campaign issue in the September 1996 elections. On August 2, 1996, the Bosnian Army commander, General Rasim Delić, announced in a speech to the Bosnian parliament that Naser had been ordered to walk back to Srebrenica after the helicopter carrying Ramiz Bećirović was shot down on May 7. But Naser said he would return to Srebrenica only in an armored helicopter. A government-controlled newspaper then attacked a lakeside restaurant Naser had opened in Tuzla, citing it as evidence of his black-market activities.

In an interview, Naser said he would have been on the helicopter with Ramiz Bećirović that was shot down on May 7 but he was asked by General Delić to stay in central Bosnia until a weapons shipment for Srebrenica was arranged. After the helicopter was downed, Bosnian pilots refused to fly to Srebrenica or Žepa.[1] Naser said he and the fifteen officers opposed walking back to Srebrenica because in the past the Serbs were tipped off that such groups were departing, and they were then wiped out in ambushes. One of the fifteen officers who pulled out with Naser confirmed that the group had been given an order to reenter Srebrenica but had disobeyed it.

At the same time, Srebrenica's civilian leaders and military commanders sent a secret message to Sarajevo in mid-May stating that Naser and the fifteen officers should not be forced to walk back into the enclave, according to Zulfo Tursunović, one of the brigade commanders. It was too dangerous, they said; Naser and the officers should only fly back in an armored helicopter.[2] In May, it seemed, many officials—including Srebrenica's own leaders—had little sense of a pending Serb attack.

In June, Sarajevo's actions become more suspect. Either a decision was made to sacrifice Srebrenica or the government is guilty of ignoring the threat posed to the town. One month before the Serb attack, senior Bosnian Army officers in Tuzla began warning UN officials that the Serbs were preparing to seize Srebrenica.[3] At the same time, Bosnian Army headquarters then ordered the men in Srebrenica to carry out the largest raid ever from the safe area to aid the offensive to liberate Sarajevo. The raid clearly risked provoking the Serbs.

According to officials close to the ruling Party of Democratic Action, the Bosnian leadership was completely focused on the pending June 15 offensive to lift the siege of Sarajevo, which would involve over 20,000 troops from around the country. Throughout the war, Sarajevo was the center of national and international attention.

General Delić refused to be interviewed for this book but said in public speeches and interviews with the Bosnian press that he was confident that Srebrenica's defenders, with the weapons that had been secretly flown into the enclave by helicopter, could defend themselves from a Serb attack for at least thirty days. He also expected the UN to defend the safe area as promised and said he was surprised when it fell so quickly.[4]

But Naser Orić maintains that the enclave was deliberately sacrificed. He claims he was relieved of his command on May 29.[5] Then, when the town was on the verge of falling, he was ordered once again to walk to Srebrenica when commanders in Sarajevo knew it would be impossible. He says he asked for a written order to return to the town but was called back and told not to try to walk back. An attempt was made to get a helicopter pilot to fly him and the officers back to Srebrenica at the last minute, but this never materialized. By the time Srebrenica fell, Naser says, it was clear to him that the UN and officials in

Sarajevo had sacrificed it. His efforts during the attack to get the 2nd Corps in Tuzla to launch a major offensive in central Bosnia to relieve pressure on Srebrenica were rebuffed, according to Naser.

But senior officers from the 2nd Corps said in interviews that they did all they could to aid Srebrenica. Their best troops and equipment were still participating in the stalled offensive around Sarajevo and a major operation could not be mounted. Srebrenicans counter that the lack of aid from the 2nd Corps is proof that they were sacrificed.

Trading Srebrenica and Žepa for the Serb-held suburbs that encircled Sarajevo was proposed several times during the war. In the summer of 1993, Srebrenica's representative in Sarajevo, Murat Efendić, was asked by the Bosnian government whether the people of Srebrenica would accept. Naser Orić and Srebrenica's leaders refused. In the fall of 1993, the UN facilitated secret negotiations between the Muslim-led Bosnian government and the Serbs at the UN-controlled airport to discuss trading Srebrenica and Žepa for the suburbs of Sarajevo.

According to Bosnian Serb Vice President Nikola Koljević, the Bosnian Serb leadership supported the deal but could not get Serbs in the bitterly contested suburbs to agree to it. Former Bosnian Army commander Sefer Halilović and one senior former ruling party official say leaders in the Bosnian government also supported such a deal but couldn't persuade the people in Srebrenica to agree to it—a charge that Bosnian Vice President Ejup Ganić denied. But Halilović and the former ruling party official are convinced the United States or Europe brokered a secret deal in which Srebrenica and Žepa were abandoned by the Bosnian government in exchange for the suburbs, but the deal went wrong when General Mladić killed so many men.[6]

Richard Holbrooke and other U.S. and European officials vehemently deny making any secret agreements. There is also no concrete evidence of secret meetings between the Serbs and the Muslims. Most importantly, the failed Bosnian Army offensive in mid-June to capture the suburbs around Sarajevo cannot be explained by the conspiracy theory. If the Muslim-led government was to receive the suburbs in a deal, then the offensive should have succeeded. It is illogical that after the Sarajevo offensive failed the Bosnian government would still hand over Srebrenica to the Serbs.

Some UN military officers allege that the Bosnian government sacrificed Srebrenica to garner international sympathy. But giving up such a valuable bargaining chip without any certainty of a return would make little sense. Given the West's long record of passivity, there was no guarantee that the fall of a safe area would result in any substantive changes to the UN mission.

Another possible motive for the pullout is political. Naser Orić repeatedly thwarted attempts by the ruling Party of Democratic Action to gain control of Srebrenica's municipal government. The central government may have planned to replace him with a commander loyal to the party as they did in other parts of the country during the war. Bosnian Army officials also complained about Orić's corruption and said he organized the town's defenses poorly.

An officer who had pulled out with Naser presented a version of events that appears to be the most accurate. Naser and his officers received no new orders after they rebuffed the initial instructions to walk back to Srebrenica in May. The men from Srebrenica trusted neither officers in the Tuzla-based 2nd Corps nor those in the Bosnian Army headquarters in Sarajevo. They had still not forgiven them for failing to liberate the enclave in January 1993. The orders to reenter, they thought, were part of a plot to kill Naser.

Assuming the UN would defend the enclave, Naser and his men made no serious effort to return to it. There was last-minute talk of walking to the enclave or arranging a helicopter flight, but when the enclave actually fell, the officers from Srebrenica were as stunned as everyone else that the UN had not defended it with NATO air attacks, the officer said.

If one accepts that Naser Orić and his officers were simply stuck by accident or incompetence in central Bosnia after the downing of the helicopter on May 7, the onus then shifts to UN Special Representative Yasushi Akashi and French general Bernard Janvier, responsible for the UN's failure to protect the safe area.

...

Suspicions that Janvier cut a deal with General Ratko Mladić at the secret meeting they had in the midst of the hostage crisis on June 4, 1995, have steadily grown since the meeting was revealed roughly three weeks later.[7] Janvier turned down the requests for air strikes from Srebrenica, the theory goes, because he secretly gave assurances to Mladić of no further air strikes in exchange for the release of the 350 predominantly French peacekeepers.

In hindsight, a suspicious string of events followed the June 4 meeting. Two days later, French general Bertrand de Lapresle was sent directly from Paris to meet secretly with the Bosnian Serbs in Pale. The day after de Lapresle's meeting, the Serbs released 111 hostages.

On June 9, Yasushi Akashi held a meeting with Janvier and General Rupert Smith in the Croatian city of Split.[8] In a debate that struck at the core issue of the UN mission—peacekeeping versus peace enforcement, Smith argued that the Serbs needed to be confronted by force; he predicted they would soon try to create a crisis by attacking the eastern enclaves or cutting off Sarajevo to end the war. "I remain convinced that the Serbs want to conclude this year and will take every risk to accomplish this. As long as the [economic] sanctions remain on the Drina [River]," Smith said, referring to Serbia's alleged halt of military supplies to the Bosnian Serbs, "they risk getting weaker every week relative to their enemy."

Janvier completely disagreed, arguing that it was "essential to allow the political process" to begin and not confront the Serbs. He predicted the Serbs would not attack "unless there is a major provocation by the BH." "The Serbs need two things, international recognition and a softening of the blockade on the Drina," Janvier said. "I don't think they want to go to an extreme crisis. On the contrary, they want to modify their behavior, be good interlocutors."[9] After the meeting, Akashi stated that the UN would return to "strictly peacekeeping principles" or not use force or take sides in the conflict.

Four days later, on June 13, the Bosnian Serbs released 28

more hostages and their self-styled Foreign Minister, Aleksa Buha, said that Serbian President Milošević had received assurances of no further air strikes. "We understand that the international community will keep their promise to President Milošević that there will not be any more bombing," Buha said. Akashi denied any deal had been made.[10]

On June 17, Akashi met with Milošević in Belgrade. The Serbian President said he had been told by Chirac that Clinton agreed that air strikes would not occur without Paris' approval. On June 18, the remaining 26 UN hostages were released and 92 peacekeepers in surrounded weapons collection points allowed to withdraw to Sarajevo. Simultaneously, the UN released the four Bosnian Serb soldiers captured when French peacekeepers retook the Vrbanje Bridge in Sarajevo on May 27. Nikola Koljević, deputy leader of the Bosnian Serbs, said the Serbs had received the promises they wanted. "We got a commitment of no more air strikes," Koljević said. "No more hostile acts against the Serbs."

Three days later, two Bosnian Serb Super Galeb jet fighters took off from the Banja Luka airfield in violation of the NATO-imposed no-fly zone over Bosnia. NATO Southern Europe commander Admiral Smith, seeing the flight as a test of Western will, requested permission from Janvier to carry out air strikes against the airfield. Janvier flatly refused, saying an air strike would only lead to another confrontation.[11]

On June 30, a high-ranking French military officer then publicly criticized Smith's call for air strikes. "He is wrong to ask for those strikes against Banja Luka airfield," the officer said in a background briefing to reporters. "This would lead us to war with the Serbs."[12]

Janvier's secret June 4 meeting was exposed by Roger Cohen of *The New York Times* on June 23.[13] UN and French officials flatly denied any deal was struck but the rumors continued. The head of the UN's peacekeeping department, Kofi Annan, sent a cable to Akashi asking about Bosnian Serb statements that they had received assurances of no further air strikes. "You know well we have issued no such instruction," Annan wrote in the June 15 cable.

The strongest evidence came on May 29, 1996, a full year after the hostage crisis. An investigation by Roy Gutman of *Newsday* and Cabell Bruce of Reuters Television concluded that Janvier made a deal with Mladić and blocked the Close Air Support request as a result.[14] They quoted a close aide of Janvier's as saying, "We were the supplicants . . . Janvier proposed the meeting, Janvier proposed the deal." The aide said Janvier received no specific instructions from the UN in New York or the French government to speak with the Serbs, but felt under pressure to end the crisis. Janvier volunteered to secretly meet with Mladić. "He really thought he was doing the best he could. He was under pressure," the aide told Gutman. "Yes, he was naive to believe Mladić but what else could he do?"

But when contacted later by the author, the aide, who asked not to be named, backtracked. He said the story was accurate in terms of the sequence of events but he objected to the term "deal." The aide, who may have come under intense pressure not to speak after the *Newsday* story and Reuters Television documentary appeared, denied that even a vague understanding was reached between Janvier and Mladić about air strikes.

Unfortunately, the aide was not at the secret meeting. Those present—Janvier, a translator and two military aides—refuse to be interviewed. Janvier's report to the UN on the meeting, which wasn't filed until after Annan cabled Zagreb about rumored assurances, mentions no deal but states that Mladić prepared a letter stating: "1. The Army of the Republika Srpska will no longer use force to threaten the life of and safety of members of UNPROFOR. 2. UNPROFOR commits to no longer make use of any force which leads to the use of air strikes against targets and territory of the Republika Srpska. 3. The signing of this agreement will lead to the freeing of all prisoners of war." According to the report, Mladić asked Janvier to bring the document to Zagreb for "immediate ratification."

Without confirmation from Janvier's aide, there is no definitive proof of a deal. The French government denies Chirac or any other official ever gave assurance to Milošević or the Bosnian Serbs that there would be no further air strikes. General de Lapresle and an aide who attended the secret meeting on June 6 in Pale said in separate interviews that they only urged the Serbs to release the hostages and did not negotiate. UN Secretary General Boutros Boutros-Ghali refused to be interviewed, but Akashi said that he personally never agreed to a deal, nor had Janvier.[15]

Dutch Defense Minister Joris Voorhoeve, General Ton Kolsteren, the UN chief of staff in Zagreb, General Cees Nicolai, the UN chief of staff in Sarajevo, and Colonel Harm De Jonge, the operations chief in Zagreb, who came up with the idea for the blocking position, would appear to have no reason to spare Janvier after the debacle their countrymen suffered. All of them said in interviews that they do not believe Janvier made a deal with Mladić. The French general, they said, is at worst guilty of simply making a bad decision regarding Close Air Support. NATO Southern Europe commander Admiral Leighton Smith, an advocate of airpower, said in an interview that he asked Janvier after the fall of Srebrenica if he had made a deal.

"He said no, absolutely not," Smith said, "and I believe him."

Secret meetings in and of themselves were not unusual and occurred throughout the war. General Rupert Smith, whose aides said he opposed negotiating with the Serbs about the hostages, held secret phone conversations with General Ratko Mladić on May 28 and was told to "take a tranquilizer" by the Serb general, who rebuffed Smith's demand that the hostages be released and turned down an offer from Smith to meet.[16]

Nikola Koljević, who said he opposed taking the hostages, stated in an interview that he did not recall receiving any assurance that there would be no further air strikes from the UN or France. He only remembered Milošević putting intense pressure on the Bosnian Serbs to release the hostages through the frequent visits to Pale of Milošević's feared secret police chief, Jovica Stanišić.

Cutting a deal with the Serbs does not fit with Chirac's carefully crafted public image, at least, of his approach to the war in Bosnia. Chirac, a former cavalry officer, was reportedly furious at Lanxade and Janvier when he saw humiliated French peacekeepers surrendering with white flags. He criticized them for "cowardice and laxness" and reportedly ordered them to begin retaliating when attacked. Chirac's trademark (his nick-name was "the Bulldozer") was his bluntness, and U.S. officials say his arrival in office was a sea change in French policy toward Bosnia. Chirac publicly proposed the creation of the 12,000-man Rapid Reaction Force to British Prime Minister John Major and publicly proposed, even if it was a bluff, the recapture of Sre-brenica by force.

While Mitterrand saw the Serbs as France's allies from World War II, Chirac apparently dismissed them. At a European Union banquet on Friday, June 9, Chirac had just ended another phone call with Serbian President Milošević when Greek Prime Minister Andreas Papandreou began to defend the Serbs, saying they felt vulnerable spread out in different states and were only defending their Orthodox religious faith. Chirac cut him off, according to witnesses. "Don't speak to me about any religious war," Chirac said, fuming. "These are people without any faith, without any sense of law; they are terrorists."[17]

One Western diplomat with extensive experience in both Paris and the former Yugoslavia suggested the two most likely scenar-ios. Janvier may not have sensed the change in attitude in the new administration and brokered a deal with Mladić on his own, or Janvier had secret instructions from Paris to cut a deal for the re-lease of the hostages, the diplomat said, to solve the immediate problem of getting the hostages freed, not a long-term French conspiracy to sacrifice the enclaves launched only three weeks af-ter Chirac took office.

Whether the French, the UN and the Serbs are telling the truth is difficult to determine. For various reasons, none of the parties would want such a deal—if one in fact existed—to be revealed.

It's possible that language Chirac used during his phone calls to Milošević at the time or Akashi's "traditional peacekeeping" statement was interpreted by the Serbs as an assurance. It's also possible that an overt deal was, in fact, cut by French diplomats in Belgrade. The evidence, so far, is not conclusive.

But Milošević's claim that Chirac told him air strikes would not occur without French approval is not an assurance of no further air strikes. Milošević, desperate to curry favor with the

West and free the hostages, may have lied and told the Bosnian Serbs he received a verbal assurance when he did not. The response to the hostage crisis may simply have been the latest in the series of knee-jerk, short-term Western reactions to another crisis in Bosnia.

Intentionally or unintentionally, the very public halting of the May 29 air strikes as soon as the hostages were taken made it clear to the Bosnian Serbs that they could stop NATO air attacks by threatening peacekeepers. Deal or no deal, the hostage crisis reinforced the message the United States, France, Britain and the UN kept repeating to the Bosnian Serbs throughout the war: the West does not have the will to stand up to you.

The two individuals who bear the brunt of responsibility for the lack of NATO Close Air Support are Yasushi Akashi and Bernard Janvier. Akashi agreed to two lengthy interviews for this book. Janvier, who rarely spoke to the press before Srebrenica's fall, has never discussed the topic publicly, refused to be interviewed for this book and has turned down all interview requests from the media. The series of statements and proposals made by Janvier before, during and after Srebrenica's fall have fueled speculation that he intentionally allowed the safe area to fall.

In his May 24, 1995, address to the Security Council, Janvier urged the UN to withdraw from the safe areas, which he said the Bosnian government were abusing and using to launch raids. During his June 9 debate with General Smith in Split he talked about withdrawal again.

"What would be most acceptable to the Serbs would be to leave the enclaves," Janvier said. "It is the most realistic approach and it makes sense from a military point of view, but it is impossible for the international community to accept. . . . As long as the enclaves exist, we will be neutralized to an extent. In New York, I said the BH [Bosnians] should defend the safe areas. They are strong enough to do it. This was not well received at all."

But Janvier's statements and failure to approve Close Air Support in Srebrenica can be explained as vintage Janvier, not a decision to sacrifice Srebrenica. Except for the Close Air Support request he approved the day Srebrenica fell, he blocked every air strike or Close Air Support request he received. Akashi and Janvier consistently upheld the view that NATO airpower was a blunt, dangerous and generally ineffective tool that enraged Bosnian Serbs and put peacekeepers at risk. The new, restrictive May 29, 1995, guidelines issued by Janvier on the use of NATO Close Air Support were a reflection of this belief. Issued five days before Janvier's secret meeting with Mladić, they may indicate that there was no secret deal on air strikes—only Akashi and Janvier's unwillingness to use them.

Serb nationalists in Bosnia and Croatia were viewed as fierce and dangerously rash by both men, according to aides. In one meeting Akashi wondered aloud whether the Serbs had a "Masada complex"—referring to the fortress city whose Jewish inhabitants killed themselves rather than surrender to the Romans.

Western diplomats complained that both men bought into the notion of Serb invincibility and irrationality—an image Serb nationalist leaders cultivated in meetings. The ever-defiant "Serb spirit" could not be bombed into submission. The "Serb warrior" would simply withdraw to the hills to fight an endless guerrilla war. All sides were seen as equally bad. Aides in Zagreb who were seen as pro-Bosnian were viewed skeptically, according to staffers. General Rupert Smith, Janvier frequently said, was in *"le milieux Bošnjak"* or Bosnian Muslim world in Sarajevo and therefore couldn't see the war from the proper perspective.

The sixty-three-year-old Akashi dominated the relationship between the two men and strongly influenced General Janvier's view of the conflict, according to aides. A thirty-three-year UN veteran, Akashi was an adamant adherent of traditional peacekeeping. Any hint of taking sides or using force against one side was anathema to the bright, but single-minded Japanese diplomat with a dry sense of humor. One aide went so far as to call Akashi a "peacenik."

He was extremely uncomfortable with the enormous destructive power he wielded by controlling NATO air strikes. Akashi even had an eighteen-point checklist entitled "SRSG's criteria for use of Close Air Support of United Nations." The questions included "How is the reputation of UN likely to be affected by the use of Close Air Support?" and "What will be the impact of the use of Close Air Support on peacemaking efforts?" Playing for time, avoiding confrontation and constantly supporting more negotiations no matter how bad the situation were Akashi's hallmarks.

Conservative and cautious, Akashi was the opposite of the naive but bold former UN commander General Philippe Morillon, who had saved Srebrenica in 1993. The aggressive style of the astute British UN commander in Bosnia, General Rupert Smith, was an anomaly as well in the cautious, slow-moving UN culture. General Smith left Sarajevo two days before the attack on Srebrenica began, and aides say the rumors that Smith left because he knew Srebrenica was going to be sacrificed are untrue. The most influential proponent of the theory that the Serbs were going for broke in the summer of 1995 and needed to be confronted by force was on vacation.[18]

At times, Smith's and Morillon's boldness enabled them to embarrass or pressure Western capitals into giving the UN more of the political backing and military resources it needed to carry out its mission in Bosnia. Akashi's and Janvier's cautiousness, on the other hand, allowed Western governments to blame Akashi for the failures of the impossible UN mission, diverting responsibility from the countries themselves that lacked the political will to confront the Serbs and suffer politically unpopular casualties.

Janvier's May 24 address to the UN Security Council about the safe areas can be viewed as either Machiavellian or misguided. He was wrong when he stated that Bosnian government forces in Srebrenica and the other four isolated enclaves were strong enough to defend themselves. But he was correct in maintaining that the isolated peacekeepers in the enclaves were ready hostages the Serbs could use to cow the West at will.

Two months later, General Rupert Smith removed British peacekeepers from Goražde at the end of August and the strategy worked. It allowed NATO jets to pound Serb targets for two weeks without fear of UN hostages being taken. The difference was that Smith saw the Serbs as abusing their advantage in fire-power and had to be challenged. Janvier, on the other hand, viewed the Muslims as abusing the safe areas to draw the UN into fighting the war for them.

According to senior civilian UN staffers, Janvier was more in over his head than Machiavellian. He was generally considered the least competent of the four UN Force Commanders who served in the former Yugoslavia.[19]

A key element in Janvier's thinking was an apparent belief that he could do business with the Bosnian Serbs. Janvier may have turned down the crucial request for Close Air Support on the night before the town fell because he sincerely believed General Tolimir's promise the Serb attack had stopped. Janvier was quick to believe Serb propaganda and Mladić's complaints about Muslim provocations, according to aides. Janvier argued in the June 9 meeting in Split that the Serbs would no longer defy the UN if they were treated with respect.

Janvier's close aide and Yasushi Akashi both said there were no clear instructions from Paris or New York during the attack on Srebrenica. Akashi said Janvier was pressured by Paris several times—including during the hostage crisis—but Srebrenica was not one of them. Interviewed by Gutman, the aide said that the problem during Srebrenica was a lack of instructions. He described the situation as "chaotic." "When Srebrenica happened we were upset because of a lack of decisions and orders," the aide said. "Janvier was left out on a limb by himself."[20]

Akashi said that Janvier "agonized" over whether to use Close Air Support in Srebrenica during the final days of the attack. Janvier told him he could not understand why the Serbs would take the safe area, something Janvier also said during the Close Air Support deliberations the night before Srebrenica fell. Following the same logic of CIA analysts, Akashi said Janvier didn't think the Bosnian Serbs would want to risk provoking the international community.

Janvier, a longtime infantry commander, also advised Akashi that air strikes would not stop advancing troops in the Srebrenica area because of the terrain. Echoing the thinking of Colin Powell earlier in the war and the consensus among French commanders, Janvier said that air support would be totally ineffective. Janvier's military analysis of the effectiveness of air attacks may have simply been wrong.

Taking the extraordinary step of deciding to sacrifice a UN safe area on his own without the permission of his superiors does not fit into Janvier's character, according to supporters and detractors. "This was a man who should've been selling roasted chestnuts on the streets of Paris," said one former UNPROFOR official. "Not making these kinds of decisions."

Whether Janvier was cynical or misguided, he is more responsible than any other individual for the fall of Srebrenica. The restrictions on the use of airpower that he actively endorsed and his decision not to approve Close Air Support on Monday, July 10, had disastrous results. He did not take "the necessary measures, including the use of force" to deter attacks on the safe area as Resolution 836 charged him. He also consistently lobbied for and took actions that facilitated the UN's withdrawal from the eastern enclaves. What his motivations or actual instructions were will not be known until he volunteers, or is compelled, to explain his actions.

Supporters and detractors of Janvier agree on one point: he was a by-the-book general who closely followed orders. If Janvier were told to save or sacrifice Srebrenica, he would have done what he was told. But if there was an international conspiracy against Srebrenica, the Bosnian government, the Clinton administration and the new administration of French President Jacques Chirac would have had to agree on the plan. The Bosnians needed to neutralize the enclave's defense by pulling out Naser Orić, Janvier needed to block Close Air Support requests from UN officials not in on the conspiracy and the Clinton administration would have had to suppress intelligence on the Bosnian Serb buildup around the enclave.

Suspicions about what U.S. intelligence knew about the attack on Srebrenica and subsequent executions have been high. The CIA, the theory goes, knew of the pending attack and knew the town would fall. The United States then stood by as Srebrenica fell and an enclave that didn't fit into Anthony Lake's endgame strategy was eliminated. Aerial photos of suspected mass graves, according to the theory, were suppressed until after the executions were well over to avoid embarrassment and the United States being called on to stop the killing.

But senior officials in the National Security Council, State Department, Pentagon and CIA all deny intentionally or tacitly sacrificing Srebrenica. The United States underestimated the seriousness of what was occurring in Srebrenica, they say, due to an honest failure of the CIA to correctly assess Serb intentions. Like the UN, the CIA believed that the Serbs did not intend to take the entire safe area. On Sunday, July 9, the Serb attack was "most likely to punish the Bosnian government for offensives in Sarajevo and a means to press a cease-fire," according to the daily CIA intelligence brief circulated to senior U.S. officials in the National Intelligence Daily.[21] On Monday, July 10, the day before the town fell, the assessment was unchanged. The CIA believed that the Serbs would not take the town, in large part, because they did not want to deal with the tens of thousands of civilians inhabiting it.[22]

Officials in charge of monitoring Bosnia for the CIA, Pentagon and National Security Council say they believed until the day Srebrenica fell that General Mladić would never dare take a UN safe area and risk provoking the West.

The UN intelligence assessment in Zagreb matched and may have influenced the CIA's in Washington. But UN officials were missing crucial information. UN intelligence analysts knew little about the deep desire among Bosnian Serbs for revenge against Naser Orić. Through little fault of their own, they had minimal experience in Bosnia and knew little about Srebrenica's history. To make contributing peacekeepers more palatable to governments, the UN rotated most peacekeepers out of the former Yugoslavia after six months.

The gaps in the UN command chain were glaring. Officials in Zagreb never received reports of the mortars, the tank, the howitzer and the troops the Dutch hostages witnessed on the enclave's eastern front line en route to Bratunac on July 8 and July 9.[23] Somehow, the crucial reports were lost in the UN labyrinth that ran from the Dutch in Srebrenica to the UN's Sector Northeast command in Tuzla, to the UN's Bosnia-Herzegovina command in Sarajevo, to UN headquarters in Zagreb.

The disorganization was representative of a far larger problem. Intelligence operations were anathema to the traditional UN concept of peacekeeping. The UN prided itself on operating with complete "transparency," meaning that all parties it was dealing with were to be aware of all UN activities. Mounting any kind of covert intelligence-gathering operation was barred. The primary sources of information for the UN were Military Observers—officers who drove around the former Yugoslavia in white four-wheel-drive vehicles with "Military Observer" emblazoned on the side. Their access to certain areas was blocked whenever Croat, Serb or Muslim forces found it convenient.

The UN was also infamous for leaking information. NATO and national intelligence agencies, especially American ones, dreaded giving information to the UN because they feared it would quickly be leaked and made public and secret sources and methods would then be exposed. American officers occupied senior positions in the UN intelligence units in Zagreb and Sarajevo because they had access to sensitive U.S. intelligence, and could tightly control it. Private, informal meetings were sometimes held between the Americans and UN officers from other NATO nations—such as France, Britain or Holland—where sensitive information was discussed. But in larger group meetings attended by officers from other countries, such as Russia, the information was not mentioned, or it was deliberately kept vague.

The most potent form of American intelligence in Bosnia was aerial surveillance. U.S. satellites and spy planes photographed hundreds of miles of territory as they passed over the former Yugoslavia every few days, as Captain Groen in Srebrenica suspected.[24] In the spring of 1995, the United States had also begun deploying Unmanned Aerial Vehicles (UAVs), or drones, with high-tech surveillance equipment—including videotape cameras—over Bosnia. But the system was not operational in early July, according to Pentagon officials.[25]

U.S. spy planes and satellites, intelligence officials argue, do not see all. When a Serb missile shot down U.S. pilot Scott O'Grady on June 2, NATO and the Pentagon were stunned. The Bosnian Serbs had dismantled an existing SAM-6 missile in northern Bosnia and secretly transported it by truck to a new location a hundred miles away. U.S. intelligence spotted the system the day before O'Grady was shot down, but the information didn't get to O'Grady's commander. O'Grady did not know there were any missiles in the area. The Serbs had fired the missile first, and then turned on the radar that guides the missile to its target, giving O'Grady almost no warning his plane was locked on to.

Strict new rules for flights over Bosnia were subsequently established. One of them was that NATO planes were to fly over with an escort that could jam SAM missiles and avoid, when possible, areas where SAM missiles were. A SAM site was located near Han Pijesak southwest of Srebrenica. NATO Southern Europe commander Admiral Smith said reconnaissance missions would have to include electronic warfare planes but were still possible. Smith said he received no request from the Dutch military or the UN for the aerial photos Captain Groen so desperately wanted in Srebrenica.

But the deputy commander in Srebrenica, Major Robert Franken, said the Dutch requested UN and NATO intelligence on a suspected buildup in the area from his UN superiors in Sarajevo twice in June and for a third time in July only two days before the July 6 attack. After a UNHCR worker visiting Srebrenica on July 4 saw artillery moving toward Bratunac, Franken wanted to know what aerial photography of the region showed. Franken said he was told the June 3 attack on OP Echo was a local action, there were no indications of a large attack; and that flying within the SAM ring around Srebrenica, which included an active site in Sase only five miles outside the enclave, was judged not worth the risk.

"Someone had to have seen what was going on," said Franken. "That they didn't is fucking nonsense."

On the day the town fell, the reconnaissance photos made available to the UN[26] showed a potential attack coming from only four Serb tanks deployed to the south of the enclave. Possibly viewing the conflict on a NATO—not Bosnian—scale, UN intelligence officials concluded that there wasn't enough equipment to take the enclave. American satellites and spy planes should probably have spotted the artillery, tank and multiple rocket launcher to the east of the enclave and the multiple rocket launcher in Bratunac. According to intelligence officials in both Washington and Zagreb at the time, their honest assessment was that, despite the Serb build-up, it would be illogical for the Serbs to risk provoking the West by taking an entire safe area.

Warnings about the Serbs' intentions were ignored by the UN, the United States and NATO. In a March 1995 memorandum, the head of the UN intelligence unit in Sarajevo predicted that the Serbs would try to sweep across eastern Bosnia that summer and take all three enclaves. Each day, according to the analysis, the Bosnian Muslims were smuggling more weapons into the country and their army was becoming better armed and organized. The outnumbered Bosnian Serbs realized that time was against them. The analysis predicted that the Serbs would launch one final offensive in the summer of 1995, try to take the safe areas and sue for peace from a position of strength in the fall.

Four months later, the assessment—one of several produced by the UN—and other warnings sent in May and June had apparently been buried. Just before the attack on Srebrenica was launched, the UN intelligence analyst who wrote the report voluntarily went on vacation.

There is also no concrete evidence of the United States suppressing the aerial photos of suspected mass graves. Analysts involved in finding the graves insist they only began the time-consuming process of searching the hundreds of thousands of images of the Srebrenica area after the specific Nova Kasaba tip arrived. Madeleine Albright publicly distributed photos, she said in an interview, as quickly as possible.

U.S. diplomats deny they cut any secret deals involving the enclave. U.S. special envoy Robert Frasure did carry out talks with all three sides during the spring of 1995, but Richard Holbrooke and other U.S. officials say the talks focused on lifting UN economic sanctions on Serbia, not trading the enclaves.

It is unlikely that there was a vast, preplanned international conspiracy to sacrifice Srebrenica. It is unlikely that Muslim and

Serb leaders, after three years of merciless fighting, would trust their enemies to honor a trade. It is unlikely French President Chirac, who was inaugurated on May 17, could plan a conspiracy or would approve an inherited conspiracy only two months into office. It is also unlikely that the Clinton administration, focused on the 1996 elections, would see the war in Bosnia as a large enough political priority to risk being caught planning and carrying out an insidious scheme that would endanger the lives of 450 Dutch soldiers and 40,000 Bosnian Muslims.

France and the United States would have had to agree not to tell their closest ally—Britain—of a plan that would have a destabilizing impact in a country where 4,000 British peacekeepers were stationed. If the British were informed, then somehow the three nations who were so bitterly divided over what to do in the former Yugoslavia for three years would have miraculously agreed to a risky conspiracy to end the unpredictable war. Two factors—Bosnia not being important enough for a politically dangerous conspiracy to be launched and the West's inability to agree on what to do there—argue most powerfully against a premeditated plan.

That Srebrenica was tacitly sacrificed is the most likely possibility. The West, the Bosnian government and Akashi and Janvier let events run their course and a troublesome enclave was eliminated. Proving what key officials, like Janvier and Bosnian Army commander Delić, were thinking at the time is impossible. UN, American, European and Bosnian officials all vehemently denied tacitly sacrificing the town. "We are not that cynical," Akashi said.[27]

In the end, the most blame and the largest questions lie with the men who ordered the executions. Srebrenica's fall would have been largely ignored if it had not been so bloody.

On the night of Thursday, July 13, 1995, Bosnian Serb leader Radovan Karadžić and Bosnian Serb general Ratko Mladić held thousands of lives in their hands. Between 1,000 and 2,000 Muslim prisoners were crammed inside warehouses and buses around Bratunac that night. Serb soldiers, except those around the warehouse in Kravica, had clearly been given orders to gather prisoners but not kill them. What led the two leaders to make the decision is both simple and at the same time incomprehensible.

Both men appear to have been driven by a classic, deep-rooted racism that lay at the core of their nationalism. The Muslim prisoners around Bratunac that night were things that "bred" too quickly. The prisoners were also an opportunity for Mladić and Karadžić to make a dramatic historical statement.

For them, the fall of Srebrenica was part of the Serb people's centuries-old struggle against Islam and the Turks. It was an opportunity to avenge the Serbs killed in the Srebrenica area during World War II and an opportunity to wipe out several thousand soldiers whom the manpower-short Bosnian Serb Army would face again if they were exchanged.

One of Mladić's first statements when he entered Srebrenica—his vow to take revenge on the "Turks" for Serbs killed in the area in the 1804 "rebellion of the Dahijas"—appears to be self-explanatory. Mladić's father, who fought with Tito's Partisans, was killed by fascist Croats allied with Nazi Germany—Ustaša—during World War II. Mladić was only two years old at the time. The general's first name comes from the Serbo-Croatian word *rat*, or war. Ratko literally means "of the war" or "warlike." Karadžić's father survived a mass execution carried out by Tito's Partisans during World War II. Karadžić, a psychologist who lived and practiced in Sarajevo, later said he felt as if he had never been accepted in the multiethnic city. Nationalism brought him the success that had eluded him earlier in life.[28]

The years of haphazard and weak-kneed U.S. and European policy inflated Mladić's and Karadžić's real and imagined power. For the last three years, Radovan Karadžić had outthought, outmaneuvered and outnegotiated what he believed were the most sophisticated diplomats in the world. Time and again, Karadžić easily derailed or dismembered peace plans.

Mladić, a military commander who had a 400-to-50 advantage in tanks over his enemy, had twice halted the most powerful fighting force on earth—NATO—by taking 350 UN peacekeepers hostage in May 1995 and 55 Dutch peacekeepers hostage in July. Mladić was at the height of his military strength after the fall of Srebrenica. His delusional belief in his own power was at its zenith.

Karadžić and Mladić ordered the manhunt and mass execution of Srebrenica's men because they wanted to, because they could and because they were confident that no one would ever hold them accountable for it. In hindsight, they appear to have been right.

It would be comforting to think that the executions were a strategic mistake; that the massive manhunt Mladić launched to capture Srebrenica's men diverted his troops and allowed the Croatian Army to advance unchecked on the other side of the country. But the Bosnian Serbs still control 49 percent of Bosnia. Both Karadžić and Mladić have gotten away with Europe's worst massacre since World War II.

American, French and British policy in Bosnia has created twin cancers. Serb nationalists were taught that "ethnic cleansing" could succeed; Muslims learned that their lives didn't matter. Many survivors argue that if Srebrenica had been a Christian town surrounded by attacking Muslims, the West would have acted.

Most Muslims from Srebrenica do not ask that all Serbs be punished for what happened, only the leaders. They say they want to live with Serbs again. Supporters of the war crimes process say it is crucial because it relieves Muslim desires for revenge and makes one individual—not an entire ethnic group—guilty for what occurred. Equally important is the tribunal's potential effect on Serbs. By publicly airing what occurred, they say, Serbs will be forced to face what their leadership sanctioned.

Most importantly, an impartial, fiercely contested war crimes process allows some form of a historical record of what occurred—something desperately needed in the former Yugoslavia—to be thrashed out in the courtroom. If no accurate history emerges, Srebrenica is doomed to join the myriad of real and imagined atrocities that nationalist leaders can play on in five or fifty years to incite the next round of bloodletting. A young Ratko Mladić may have been born during the fall of Srebrenica.

This time, a Muslim will be brought up on tales of atrocities committed against his people.

The worst case is what is happening now. The court was created partially for political reasons—to show Western resolve in Bosnia. And the court is not allowed to be fully functional for political reasons—the West's unwillingness to arrest indicted war criminals due to the fear of casualties. The result is a still-born war crimes process. Serbs, Croats and Muslims dismiss most evidence as political and see indicted war criminals as demons or victims depending, of course, on their religion.

As long as war crimes prosecutions remain stunted, a new, fervent Muslim nationalism could rise in Bosnia. If another war breaks out, Western leaders may throw up their hands and try to dismiss it in terms of "ancient ethnic hatreds" in the Balkans. But they will be partially responsible for it. The cycle of revenge—enhanced by American and European policies—is now poised to flourish in Bosnia.

■

UNPROFOR   The United Nations Protection Force mission in Bosnia-Herzegovina officially ended on December 20, 1995. In a brief transfer-of-authority ceremony in Sarajevo, UN Force Commander Bernard Janvier turned over the responsibility for peacekeeping in Bosnia to Admiral Leighton Smith of the United States, the commander of the U.S.-led NATO Implementation Force. Smaller UN peacekeeping operations would continue in neighboring Croatia and nearby Macedonia, but the UN's largest, most expensive and most deadly peacekeeping operation was over.

In all, 210 peacekeepers died during the mission's nearly four-year deployment. Supporters argued that the UN mission saved the lives of over one million Muslims by facilitating the delivery of humanitarian aid when possible. Critics held that it prolonged the war and in some cases—such as Srebrenica—facilitated the deaths of thousands of Muslims.

As of January 1997, the UN had launched no investigation into the conduct of its officials. The Dutch parliament has asked the independent body that investigated conduct in Holland during the Nazi occupation to investigate Srebrenica over the objections of the Dutch Ministry of Defense. Eighteen months after Srebrenica's fall, no Bosnian, UN or Dutch official has been reprimanded for what occurred.

■

YASUSHI AKASHI   The UN Special Representative for the former Yugoslavia returned to UN headquarters in New York in October 1995 and was promoted to Under Secretary General for Humanitarian Affairs.

In an interview for this book, the Japanese diplomat blamed the UN Security Council for giving the UN mission in Bosnia a safe-areas mandate without the soldiers needed to enforce it. He argued that even if Close Air Support had been approved several days earlier in Srebrenica, it would not have halted a determined Bosnian Serb attack on the safe area. Akashi has repeatedly said that he and General Janvier made no major mistakes during the fall of Srebrenica.

■

GENERAL BERNARD JANVIER   The UN Force Commander in the former Yugoslavia returned to France in February 1996 and was named director of the Ecole des Hautes Etudes Militaires—a prestigious government think tank. The new position was, at best, a lateral move. Janvier hoped to win the prestigious post of commander of the French Land Army, but President Jacques Chirac—reportedly unhappy with Janvier's performance in Bosnia—rejected him. Janvier's actual instructions from Paris during the fall of Srebrenica remain unknown.

■

DUTCH DEFENSE MINISTER JORIS VOORHOEVE Voorhoeve somehow survived the scandal surrounding the fall of Srebrenica. As of January 1997, he remained the Dutch Defense Minister. His reputation for personal integrity appeared to have saved him. Fairly or unfairly, Voorhoeve was able to shift much of the blame for the appearance of a cover-up to senior commanders in the Dutch Army.

■

LIEUTENANT COLONEL THOMAS KARREMANS While Dutch Defense Minister Joris Voorhoeve was on vacation in the fall of 1995, the Dutch Army promoted Karremans from lieutenant colonel to full colonel. He was transferred to the Dutch embassy in Washington and participated in a training program in Virginia. Karremans refused to speak to journalists, including the author, about Srebrenica.

One year after the fall of Srebrenica, Karremans again sparked controversy. In testimony before the International War Crimes Tribunal for the Former Yugoslavia in July 1996, Karremans failed to mention his initial opposition to the use of Close Air Support, confusion in the mostly Dutch UN command chain over Close Air Support versus air strikes and his statements to Srebrenica's leaders that they should withdraw their troops from the "zone of death" that was going to be created by NATO south of Srebrenica town.

Under follow-up questioning from Judge Fouad Riad of Egypt, Karremans stated that he held another meeting with General Mladić on Friday, July 14. But in the meeting, Karremans failed to ask about the elderly Muslim men who were separated from their families in Potočari. "To be frank," Karremans told Riad, Judge Odio Benito of Italy and Judge Claude Jorda of France, "I [had] not thought about the idea of asking him what happened with the refugees."

■

MAJOR ROBERT FRANKEN The deputy UN commander in Srebrenica now commands his own unit in Holland. After turning down all requests for one year, he gave his first interview regarding the fall of Srebrenica to Dutch television in July 1996. He maintained that the outgunned Dutch could have done nothing more to halt the Serb attack or protect the enclave's civilians. He faxed the list of the 239 men to the Dutch government from Potočari, and blamed the UN and Dutch officials for failing to publicize the list of men forced to leave the UN base. All 239 men on the list are missing. The Dutch major points out that his soldiers identified at least thirty-eight Serb tank, artillery or troop encampments around the enclave. Franken, who was told by Serbs that 6,000 soldiers participated in the attack, believes U.S. spy satellites must have seen the buildup around the town.

■

CAPTAIN JELTE GROEN One of the first people the commander of the southern half of the safe area spoke to when he arrived back in Holland was the mother of Raviv van Renssen. He assured her that the peacekeeper killed by a Muslim hand grenade was one of the finest men in his company.

As of January 1997, Captain Groen was still an officer in the 13th Air Mobile Battalion and planned to stay in the Dutch military for the remainder of his career. He still believed that trying to fight the Serbs would have been hopeless. Not firing directly at the Serbs prevented an even worse massacre in Srebrenica, he said, one that could have involved more of the enclave's women and children.

■

LIEUTENANT VINCENT EGBERS Shortly after he arrived in Zagreb on July 21, the Dutch officer was interviewed by Dutch journalists. Lieutenant Egbers failed to mention the prisoners on the Nova Kasaba soccer field, the shots heard by the Dutch during the night and the abused prisoners he had seen. Egbers said he assumed his commanders would mention them in their press conference.

In the summer of 1996, Egbers left the Dutch Army, which was drastically cutting back its size, to study for a master's degree. He hopes to join the Dutch Air Force after graduation. He vehemently argued that there was nothing more the Dutch could have done in Srebrenica. The politicians who put the peacekeepers in the hopeless situation were to blame, not the soldiers.

■

LIEUTENANT LEEN VAN DUIJN The Dutch peacekeeper who agreed to work with the Serbs to control the crowd of Muslims in Potočari is still in the Dutch Army and intends to stay.

He rejects charges that making an agreement with the Serbs to control the crowd was "collaborating"; it would have been worse if the Dutch simply retreated to their base, he argues, and watched the Serbs abuse Muslim civilians as they were expelled. What he did was not aiding the Serbs, van Duijn believes, but saving lives.

■

LIEUTENANT EELCO KOSTER   The pictures he and the other peacekeepers took of the nine bodies, including the one of Koster posing next to them, were on the roll of film that the Ministry of Defense "accidentally" destroyed. Koster, who believes he risked his life by taking the photos, is convinced the Dutch government intentionally destroyed the film to cover up the scandal.

■

PRIVATE MARC KLAVER   The lookout in OP Foxtrot and one of the peacekeepers who formed the human wall in Potočari returned to Holland with the rest of the battalion on July 24. His brother Tonny, who suffered from cystic fibrosis, died the day before his arrival.

Klaver, who is now a sergeant, pointed out that the much-maligned 13th Air Mobile Battalion, still consisting of many men who were in Srebrenica, beat an elite American armored unit in a war game in the summer of 1996. Klaver plans to stay in the army, but has nothing but resentment against the Muslim who killed his fellow lookout Raviv van Renssen, who Klaver still believes died a pointless and meaningless death in Bosnia.

Depressed by the criticism aimed at the Dutch battalion by his peers in the military and by the public, he feels it would have been better if the seven peacekeepers in OP Foxtrot had fought the Serb tanks closing in on them and been killed. "Maybe if more Dutch boys died defending the town," he says, "it wouldn't have been so easy for them [the politicians] to sacrifice Srebrenica."

■

PRIVATE RAVIV VAN RENSSEN   The soldier killed by Muslims after the fall of OP Foxtrot, was buried in the Dutch National Military Cemetery in Arnhem. Defense Minister Voorhoeve and every member of Captain Groen's Bravo Company attended a memorial service for him on July 26.

His mother, Magda Prins, is divorced and lives alone in the small town van Renssen grew up in, Sgraveland. On the wall of her living room is a large photograph of the peacekeepers from

OP Foxtrot carrying her son's coffin draped in the light blue flag of the United Nations.

When she thinks of the women from Srebrenica who have lost their sons, fathers and husbands she is overwhelmed by the scope of their anguish. She tries to "cradle" her pain and not let it make her bitter. She said she doesn't let herself think about whether her son's death was meaningless or not.

■

BOSNIAN PRESIDENT ALIJA IZETBEGOVIĆ The Muslim nationalist leader who portrayed himself to the West during the war as a believer in a multiethnic Bosnia where Muslims, Serbs and Croats could live together, ran an overtly nationalist reelection campaign in September 1996. One of the main campaign slogans of his nationalist Party of Democratic Action (SDA) was "Croats know who they're going to vote for, Serbs know who they're going to vote for . . . And you?"

Playing on Muslim fears, Izetbegović's Party of Democratic Action was reelected. His ruling party systematically removed many Serbs and Croats from top positions in the government and from state-owned companies, even if they had remained loyal to the Muslim-led government.

■

NASER ORIĆ In June 1996, Orić and several business partners opened a floating restaurant on the shores of a lake just outside of Tuzla, located at a prime spot on a stretch of beaches and restaurants. It was rumored that Orić's profits from black marketeering in Srebrenica paid for the construction of the floating platform of two dozen tables and a bar.

Orić denied ever being involved in black marketeering, saying that he was "just a small businessman." When asked whether he had a message for General Milenko Živanović, the commander of the Bosnian Serb Drina Corps, which led the attack on Srebrenica, Orić replied, "Tell him the score is one to nothing."

■

RAMIZ BEĆIROVIĆ Srebrenica's acting commander during the attack, Bećirović works in a training school for officers. Bećirović and four of Srebrenica's five brigade commanders survived the walk through the woods. Many of the officers also reached central Bosnia. He denies that he or his wife absconded with any of the $20,000 in charity money for orphans that had not yet been distributed when Srebrenica fell. He claims that his wife, who fled to Potočari, threw the $20,000 in a dumpster outside the Dutch base when she heard the Serbs were searching people.

∎

FAHRUDIN SALIHOVIĆ AND OSMAN SULJIĆ Salihović, the town's mayor, and Suljić, the war president, at first took over aid distribution for Srebrenica's refugees in Tuzla and were rumored to again be pilfering aid money. Neither of them was planning to run for a post in Srebrenica's municipal government in exile in local elections scheduled to be held in the spring of 1997.

∎

MIDO SALIHOVIĆ AND IBRAN MALAGIĆ The two men who helped lead the fight to defend Srebrenica survived, but their fathers did not. Ibran Malagić and his brothers believe they are the only three brothers from one family to have survived the walk to Tuzla. Their father went to Potočari, was seized by the Serbs and is still missing. Two of Mido Salihović's brothers survived, but his youngest brother—who was last seen near the Kamenica ambush—has never been seen since. Salihović's father went to the Dutch base in Potočari, was taken away by the Serbs and remains missing.

∎

EDHEM LUĆANIN AND HAŠIM MUSTAFIĆ The two former teachers of Bosnian Serb police officer Zoran Radić survived and are living in Tuzla. Mustafić lives with his family, and Lućanin with his wife and ninety-four-year-old mother. Following Radić's instructions not to identify him, Lućanin refused to name the Serb who saved his life. A prisoner whom Radić helped earlier in the war led the author to the compassionate policeman.

Lućanin works part-time for a Bosnian aid agency and stays

in touch with many refugees from Srebrenica. He knows of only three other cases in which a Serb saved a former Muslim friend and helped him escape.

■

VAHID HODŽIĆ The translator who narrowly escaped his run-in with General Mladić outside the Dutch base, left Po-točari with the Dutch and reached Zagreb. As of January 1997, Hodžić was a college student in Sarajevo. His mother lives alone in a formerly Serb town now so full of people from the fallen safe area that refugees have renamed it "Srebrenica." The trans-lator's father and fifteen-year-old brother are missing.

■

HASAN NUHANOVIĆ The entire family of the transla-tor, whose brother, father and mother were forced to leave the Dutch base, is missing. According to eyewitnesses, Nuhanović's brother and father were immediately separated from his mother after they left the base. Nuhanović's father, who was one of the civilian negotiators,[29] is rumored to have been killed as soon as the truck full of men crossed into Serb-held Bratunac. His brother's fate is unknown.

His mother was last seen in Tišća, where the buses carrying women and children dropped people off for the four-mile walk to Muslim-held central Bosnia. Babbling incoherently about Hasan's brother, she was last seen walking back into Serb territory. As of January 1997, Hasan refuses to accept that his family is dead. To abandon them now would be "like burying them alive," he says. He works as a translator for the UN in Tuzla and spends most of his free time trying to verify rumors of prison camps.

■

HAKIJA HUSEJNOVIĆ The man who survived the mas-sacre in the warehouse has settled with his family in central Bos-nia. After a flurry of interviews after he crossed into central Bosnia, interest in his story died out.

He was elated when American troops arrived in Bosnia, but bitterly disappointed when they made no effort to arrest General Ratko Mladić. He believes Mladić will never be arrested and he believes this book will do nothing to change the situations.

■

ĆAMILA OMANOVIĆ   Evacuated from Potočari with the
wounded on July 17, Ćamila found her children the following
day by telephoning a house where she was told they were staying. When she heard their voices, she was unable to speak.

For three months she received psychological counseling and
withdrew into a circle of close friends and family. In October
1995, she finally gave her first interview, to *The Boston Globe*.
She then refused to speak to journalists for another three
months.

Ćamila's daughter, her husband and their son Naser—like
thousands of other refugees from Srebrenica—moved into an
apartment abandoned by Serbs when the suburbs around Sarajevo were turned over to the Muslim-led government as part of
the peace settlement. Ćamila and her son Đermin settled outside
Tuzla. Every household in her neighborhood has a man who is
missing.

Ćamila's husband, Ahmet, never emerged from the forest.
She clings to the idea that maybe one of Ahmet's former Serb
co-workers spared him and that he is being held in a secret
prison camp. She tells herself he will be used to rebuild the zinc
factory in Potočari. Killing such a gifted engineer, she says,
would be senseless.

■

HUREM SULJIĆ   Of the hundreds of mostly elderly men
separated from their families in Potočari, Hurem Suljić is the
only known survivor.

After arriving in Tuzla and telling the police his story, Suljić
got a ride to the nearby town where he heard his family was
staying. When he hobbled into the house, his wife and daughter
wept. His granddaughter Merima was the most excited. She sat
next to him on the couch for hours, refusing to let go of his arm.

Men who turned back at the blocked asphalt road and returned to Suljić's village said they found his paralyzed cousin
still alive in mid-July. But the family has no idea what has happened to him since.

After seeing that NATO troops were not enforcing the guarantee that people be allowed to return to their homes, Suljić

moved to a home abandoned by Serbs outside Sarajevo. Suljić, who was religious before the war, still finds solace in Islam. He is remarkably calm, considering what he has endured, and makes no calls for revenge. He blames Serb nationalists for Srebrenica, and says he is willing to live with "good Serbs" again. When asked what he would do if his Serb executioners were lined up in front of him and he was handed a gun, he said he would be unable to pull the trigger. Hurem said he has seen enough killing. He only asks that General Ratko Mladić be tried.

■

MEVLUDIN ORIĆ   Orić quickly found his mother, wife and daughter on the UN base in Tuzla. He broke down as he told them his story, but he cried the hardest when he located the young wife of his cousin Haris and his infant daughter Lejla.

Mevludin went about the grim task of informing the relatives of the other neighbors he had seen in the Grbavći gym. One was Haso Hasanović, the sixteen-year-old from Lehovići who was captured near the Kravica warehouse and escaped when he was sent to fetch water. Haso had been captured again in Konjević Polje but spared with three other young boys when a Serb officer arrived and said the children should be separated.[30] Haso's father had not been so lucky. Mevludin had seen him in the Grbavći gym. Haso accepted that his fifty-nine-year-old father was gone, but his mother refused to believe it, arguing that he might somehow still be alive.[31]

In Tuzla, Mevludin lived like most of Srebrenica's 30,000 other impoverished refugees. He and his family moved into an overcrowded elementary school turned refugee camp. For the next year, he, his wife, mother, daughter and a newborn daughter shared a chemistry classroom with thirty-five other people. The 120 refugees who lived in the school shared one bathroom.

Mevludin grudgingly gave up his hopes of returning to Lehovići and moved in the summer of 1996 to a house abandoned by Serbs outside Sarajevo. His former village lies in ruins. Makso Zekić, the Serb who vowed to burn Mevludin's house to the ground, apparently kept his word. Journalists who visited Lehovići found all twenty-five houses burned or dynamited. Bricks, wiring and anything else of value had been looted.[32]

Of the forty-five men from Lehovići who set off with Mevludin and his father on July 12, only fifteen survived. Four out of five of the village's men are missing. One woman and one boy are unaccounted for.

The male sides of entire families were wiped out. Fifty-six-year old Sevko Hasanović and his twenty-five-year-old son Sefik are missing.

Osman Hasanović, fifty-four, the former Yugoslav National Army officer, survived. But his brothers, Ismet, fifty-two, and Nusret, forty-three, are missing. Ismet's son Jusuf, eighteen, is also missing. Redzep Hasanović, the village giant with the basketball hoop, is missing. His wife and two teenage children wait for him in Tuzla.

Mevlida Hasanović is typical of women from Lehovići and Srebrenica. Her two sons and husband are missing. Her daughter-in-law's husband, father and brother are missing. Her grandson has no father, no uncles and no grandfathers.[33]

For months, Mevludin Orić had a secret plan. When called before the International War Crimes Tribunal to testify at the trial of General Ratko Mladić, he would remain calm and get as close to Mladić as possible. When the opportunity came, he would lunge for Mladić's throat and avenge his cousin Haris' death. But Mevludin has given up on the plan. He thinks Mladić will never be tried.

Like Hurem Suljić, Mevludin believes that Serb nationalists are responsible for what happened in Srebrenica, not all Serbs. He too says he is willing to live with Serbs again and even scolds neighbors who criticize Serbs as a group.

During one drunken evening in March 1996, he sat down between two men he had become friends with since arriving in Tuzla. "This man, this man," Mevludin said, putting his arm around the man to his left. "This man is my greatest friend and he is a Croat."

Putting his arm around the man to his right, he said, "This man is my greatest friend and he is a Serb."

Mevludin pulled each man's face close to his.

"This is my Bosnia," he said. "This is my Bosnia."

Mevludin Orić's father is missing.

■

ZORAN RADIĆ   A broad grin spread across Zoran Radić's face when he was told in June 1996 that his old high school teacher—Edhem Lućanin—was alive and well in Tuzla. Radić, who quit being a policeman shortly after the war ended, wanted Lućanin to know that his former student was now a cook at the hotel where Lućanin once instructed him.

After the war ended, Radić moved back to Srebrenica, but he knew few people. Serb refugees from Sarajevo neighborhoods turned over to the Muslim-led government under the peace accord filled most of the town's abandoned houses. The cash-short Bosnian Serb government struggled to repair the town's damaged infrastructure. Eighteen months after the "liberation" of Srebrenica, the town had no telephone service and running water only every other day.

Radić said he still doesn't view people by what they were; he judges them by what they did. But echoing state-controlled television, he said he believes the war was a good thing. If it wasn't for Radovan Karadžić's Serbian Democratic Party, he said, Serbs probably would have been forced by Muslims to leave eastern Bosnia.

The Bosnian Serbs won the war, he believes, but lost the peace. Under the Dayton peace accord, the Bosnian Serb Republic, the Republika Srpska, is an "entity" within Bosnia. On paper at least, the Bosnian Serbs do not have a fully independent state. Again echoing state-controlled TV, he said the Serbs had been unfairly demonized by the international media, and accounts of mass executions—especially those involving General Mladić—are totally untrue.

Still amazed by the lack of Muslim resistance during the attack on the safe area, he is convinced that Srebrenica and Žepa were traded in some kind of a secret deal that ended the war.

Radić said he believed Bosnia's people could never live together again. There was too much bitterness left from the war. Muslims, Serbs and Croats would never trust each other. "We will be better friends if we stay apart," he said.

■

DRAŽEN ERDEMOVIĆ   The reluctant executioner pled guilty to crimes against humanity before the International War Crimes Tribunal in June 1996. He then testified in hearings to issue arrest warrants against Bosnian Serb President Karadžić and General Mladić in July. He detailed the executions and said he was told the unit's orders came directly from Bosnian Serb Army headquarters in Han Pijesak.

Repeatedly breaking down on the witness stand, Erdemović begged the judges to be lenient. He said he had killed the prisoners because he was sure that if he resisted he himself would be killed and the prisoners would die anyway. The executions had destroyed his life, he said. Whether Erdemović was playing to the judges and cameras is unknown. He agreed to be interviewed for this book, but the tribunal bars interviews with suspects in its custody.

As of January 1997, the tribunal had indicted 74 Serbs, Croats and Muslims for war crimes, but only seven of them were in custody. The rest live freely in Serbia, Bosnia and Croatia, with little fear of being arrested and extradited by their own leaders or NATO. In November 1996, Erdemović was sentenced to ten years in jail with time off for good behavior for killing seventy people. Eighteen months after the Srebrenica massacres, Dražen Erdemović was the only person brought to justice for the massacre of as many as 7,079 men.

■

SLOBODAN MILOŠEVIĆ   With the signing of the Dayton peace accord, the President of Serbia had come full circle. The man who was most responsible for cultivating Serb nationalism, riding it to power and bringing war to the former Yugoslavia was portrayed as the West's new peacemaker in the Balkans. Whether he has completely given up on the goal of achieving a Greater Serbia remains to be seen.

Milošević at least tacitly approved of the attack on Srebrenica. Volunteers and possibly whole units from the Milošević-controlled Yugoslav Army were seen participating in the attack on Srebrenica by Dutch and Muslim eyewitnesses. The fuel-short Bosnian Serb Army must have also received large amounts of gasoline from Serbia to be able to carry out the expulsion of Srebrenica's Muslims.

General Ratko Mladić was close to Milošević and was repeatedly seen in the Yugoslav Army headquarters in Belgrade before the attack.[34] Milošević's secret police supported or at least tolerated the activities of Serbia-based ultranationalist paramilitary groups like the Arkan Tigers. His government paid the salaries of the Bosnian Serb Army officer corps. In short, without Milošević's approval, the Bosnian Serbs would not have received the fuel and supplies they needed for the attack on Srebrenica.

Milošević's link to the executions is less clear. There is no direct evidence that Milošević explicitly approved the executions, but he was most likely aware that they were taking place. If they weren't involved, his secret police had extensive knowledge of what occurred in Bosnian Serb territory. They probably knew of or quickly heard about the first round of mass executions on July 14. Milošević then attended the July 15 meeting at which General Mladić promised the ICRC access to the prisoners. The following day, July 16, the remaining prisoners were executed by Dražen Erdemović and his unit.

With Serbia's economy in shambles and nationalists criticizing him for selling out Serbs in Croatia and Bosnia, Milošević's party was soundly defeated in municipal elections in November 1996. His Socialist Party, dogged by charges of corruption, lost control of the local governments in the capital of Belgrade and dozens of other large cities and towns. The Serbian President immediately declared the election results "invalid" and refused to give up control of the city governments.

As of January 1997, the Serbian President, who was careful to avoid direct links between himself and ultranationalist paramilitary groups like the Arkan Tigers, had not been indicted by the International War Crimes Tribunal. Milošević, whom both Karadžić and Mladić could probably implicate if they were turned over to the War Crimes Tribunal, has made no moves to arrest either man, as called for in the Dayton peace accord.

■

RADOVAN KARADŽIĆ   With the Dayton peace accord mandating that no indicted war criminal could hold public office, Karadžić resigned from the presidency of the Republika Srpska in July 1996 under intense international pressure. But Karadžić appointed a loyal deputy and hard-line nationalist, Biljana Plavšić, to replace him. He is believed to control the government from behind the scenes. Surrounded by bodyguards at all times, he lives comfortably in the Bosnian Serb capital of Pale.

Karadžić promised his people that the Republika Srpska would be a "new Switzerland" in Europe. Instead, it is an impoverished nation dominated by corrupt former nationalists and secret police loyal to Karadžić. Bosnian Serbs are discouraged from doing business with Muslims or Croats, their historic trading partners, while few foreign companies are interested in investing in the Republika Srpska.

Karadžić, who called himself the commander in chief of the Bosnian Serb Army, flatly denies that any executions occurred after the fall of Srebrenica. In an interview with *The Times* of London on February 12, 1996, he said: "In connection with these so-called massacres of Muslims in Srebrenica, there was no order to kill them. Nobody under my command would dare kill those who were arrested or captured as prisoners of war. I am absolutely fully involved. Everything concerning the Serb Republic is in my hands."[35]

The accounts of atrocities are part of an international conspiracy against the Serbs, nationalists say, led by Middle Eastern countries who, through oil, control the West and CNN. Karadžić-controlled state television showed war crimes investigators arriving in the Srebrenica area, but reported that no evidence of executions was found. The bodies were Muslim soldiers killed in legitimate fighting. Many ordinary Serbs like Zoran Radić, sincerely believe the theme harped on by Karadžić and state-controlled television throughout the war: the Serbs were the war in Bosnia's true victims.

As of January 1997, Karadžić and Serb nationalists had won the war in Bosnia. Attempts by Muslims to return to their homes were repeatedly blocked by crowds of angry Serb civilians organized by police loyal to Karadžić. His Serbian Democratic Party swept September 1996 elections mandated by the Dayton peace accord that were designed to oust nationalists from power.

No attempt has been made to arrest Karadžić, who is constantly surrounded by bodyguards. Only four of the more than forty Serbs indicted by the War Crimes Tribunal are in custody.

Karadžić and the Bosnian Serb nationalists have achieved their goal. A de facto ethnically pure Bosnian Serb state has been brutally carved out of once multiethnic Bosnia.

■

GENERAL RATKO MLADIĆ General Mladić still has an almost mythic following among Bosnian Serbs. Most Bosnian Serbs interviewed do not believe any mass executions occurred after the fall of Srebrenica. If they admit some killings occurred, they say it is impossible that Mladić, with his reputation for professionalism and decency, was involved. Their primary source of information is a video aired repeatedly on Bosnian Serb television showing General Mladić in Potočari promising that no one would be hurt and Serb soldiers doling out bread and chocolate to Muslim women and children.

Mladić resigned as commander of the Bosnian Serb Army in November 1996, but he remains hugely popular among Serb soldiers and is believed to still tacitly control the Bosnian Serb Army.

He lives with his wife, Bosa, in a vacation house inside the Bosnian Serb Army headquarters near Han Pijesak. The sprawling complex, built by Tito as a final stronghold in case of invasion, includes miles of underground shelters that allegedly can withstand a nuclear attack. Mladić is constantly surrounded by bodyguards. During 1996, an American military base was set up only twelve miles away. U.S. troops announced their visits to the headquarters complex, making it painfully clear that they would not try to arrest Mladić.

A journalist who met with Mladić said the retired general fills his days tending a bee colony and caring for a small herd of goats he is raising.[36] The goats are named after the former UN commanders in Bosnia and the leaders of the Western world.

POSTSCRIPT

Three years after the fall of Srebrenica, efforts to implement the Dayton peace accord and bring war criminals to justice progressed slowly in other parts of Bosnia, but were deadlocked in Srebrenica.

In the summer and fall of 1997, Western governments launched a series of aggressive new tactics in Bosnia designed to undermine Bosnian Serb and Bosnian Croat nationalists. First UN investigators, then British, then Dutch, and finally American commandos arrested three Serbs and two Croats wanted for war crimes. One Bosnian Serb who resisted arrest was killed by British troops. The Croatian government turned over six Croats indicted for war crimes in October 1997, and a Bosnian Serb voluntarily surrendered to the tribunal in March 1998.

NATO troops also intermittently seized police stations and television transmitters controlled by hardline Serbs allied with Radovan Karadžić and handed them over to forces loyal to newly moderate Bosnian Serb President Biljana Plavšić. Karadžić's allies retaliated with firebombings, grenade attacks and brick-throwing mobs. The attacks injured NATO troops, but killed no one.

In January 1998, Milorad Dodik, a moderate with strong Western backing and protection from NATO troops, was elected Bosnian Serb Prime Minister. Serb public opinion was difficult to gauge, but sentiment appeared to be turning against Karadžić, who was increasingly viewed as corrupt. Karadžić circulated a 144-page book that outlined his defense at a potential war crimes trial and blamed General Mladić for any massacres in Srebrenica. But as of June 1998, Karadžić remained free. U.S. officials complained that French officials were dragging their feet on launching a raid to arrest the wartime leader. The French denied the charge.

While Karadžić remained the focus of international attention, General Mladić skillfully stayed out of the public eye. Alternately reported to be living quietly in retirement in Han Pijesak, Montenegro or Serbia, the general kept Bosnian Serb Army units loyal to him from threatening NATO troops. It appeared unlikely in May 1998 that Mladić, still popular among Bosnian Serbs and seeming to have reached a tacit agreement with Western officials to keep a low profile, would ever stand trial for crimes committed around Srebrenica.

As of June 1998, only twenty-one of the more than seventy people indicted for committing war crimes in the former Yugoslavia had been arrested or surrendered to the tribunal. More than fifty others, including an unknown number whose indictments are secret, remain free.

Only one individual involved in the Srebrenica massacres has been brought to justice—Dražen Erdemović. The Bosnian Croat who had pled guilty to the charge of executing seventy prisoners on the farm in Pilica appealed the ten-year sentence he received in November 1997 and received a new, five-year sentence in March 1998. He will serve twenty-six days for each of the seventy people he admits killing. Having already been in tribunal custody for two years, Erdemović will be released from jail in 2001, free to start a new life. Tribunal officials said his sentence was designed to encourage other indicted war criminals to surrender voluntarily to the tribunal.

Although small numbers of refugees on all sides began to return to their prewar homes under the terms of the Dayton peace accord, no Muslims were able to return to Srebrenica. Many survivors of the town's fall still say they want to return. Mevludin Orić and Hurem Suljić, both still living in homes abandoned by

Serbs around Sarajevo in June 1998, say they want to return to Srebrenica. Ćamila Omanović, who still lives near Tuzla, also wants to return, but has heard no news of her husband.

Efforts by Bosnian Muslims to reclaim control of Srebrenica through elections failed. In municipal voting held in October 1997, Srebrenica was the only town in Bosnia where Muslims, voting by absentee ballot, won control of a municipal government in Bosnian Serb–controlled territory. Most of the town's wartime Muslim leaders were not reelected to office. But Serb hard-liners refused to allow the new municipal government to meet. In January 1998, a crowd of stone-throwing Serb nationalists turned back a busload of the town's newly elected Muslim leaders, accompanied by American troops, when they tried to enter the town. An American helicopter escorting the Muslims accidentally crashed, seriously injuring one of its pilots.

In March, the town's new Muslim leaders, including Nesib Mandžić, the high school director who was a negotiator in Potočari, safely entered Srebrenica. But they stormed out of a meeting when local Serbs played a Serb national anthem. In June 1998, Serb public opinion in Srebrenica appeared divided. Serbs from Sarajevo living in Srebrenica appeared to be embittered by the poverty and rural isolation they live in. They said in interviews that Muslims could return to Srebrenica if Serbs were allowed to return to Sarajevo. But Serbs who grew up in Srebrenica—including Zoran Radić, the policeman who had saved his two former schoolteachers—said they would never allow Srebrenica's Muslims to return.

As of June 1998, an American diplomat was serving as the town's interim mayor. U.S. diplomats and military leaders struggled with how to solve what was increasingly viewed as the most intractable problem in Bosnia—returning Muslims to Srebrenica peacefully.

Scant progress was also made on finding Srebrenica's missing. Nearly three years after its fall, most of the roughly 7,000 men reported missing to the International Red Cross remain unaccounted for. New reports of missing men continued to filter into the ICRC between January 1997 and May 1998, raising the total number of men reported missing during the fall of

Srebrenica to 7,373. The total number missing from Žepa stands at 104.

Exhumations of mass graves progressed at a haphazard pace. A lack of funds from the United States, Britain and France and other backers, as well as bureaucratic delays at the International War Crimes Tribunal, led to no exhumations of mass graves around Srebrenica in summer 1997. But Western governments provided sufficient funds for exhumation in spring 1998 when a breakthrough occured.

After receiving tips from Bosnian Serbs, tribunal investigators located more than ten additional mass graves near Srebrenica. A NATO work crew widening a road near Karakaj also accidentally discovered a mass grave. The Serbs, investigators said, had systematically exhumed nearly all of the original mass graves around Srebrenica, including the one Mevludin and Hurem had narrowly escaped, and moved the bodies to remote locations in an effort to hide the evidence. As of June 1998, 160 more bodies had been exhumed from two of the new graves.

Little progress was made on identifying the bodies that have been found. A project by the group Physicians for Human Rights positively identified only 15 of the roughly 650 bodies exhumed from mass graves and 500 bodies collected in the woods around Kravica. The group lacked sufficient funding to identify the bodies through DNA testing.

Rumors of men from Srebrenica being secretly held in Serb prisons continued to circulate. But Serbian and Bosnian Serb government officials continued to deny secretly holding any prisoners. As part of an international effort, headed by former U.S. Senator Bob Dole, to locate the missing from all the three sides in the war, Bosnian Serb officials provided the Red Cross with the names of 314 people from Srebrenica they said died near Kravica. The Red Cross did not require the Bosnian Serbs to explain how the men died.

A handful of families from Srebrenica reportedly paid thousands of dollars to Bosnian Serbs who claimed to be holding their missing relatives. But the Serbs, who appeared to be simply defrauding the Muslims, never turned over any prisoners.

The only men from Srebrenica known to still be in a Serb prison are the group of men turned over to Bosnian Serb police in Zvornik by American soldiers in May 1996. Four of the seven men were freed, but three remain in a Serb jail awaiting trial.

Frustrated by the West's failure to identify the missing or to make arrests, women from Srebrenica intensified their protests. A group of women from Srebrenica tried to march back to Srebrenica in July 1997 to mark the two-year anniversary of the town's fall, but were blocked by NATO troops, who said violence could ensue.

Other survivors, including Hasan Nuhanović—the translator whose family the Dutch forced to leave the UN base—traveled to the United States and Britain to garner support for arrests and identification. And in fall 1997 and winter 1997–1998, women from Srebrenica began holding monthly protests in Sarajevo and Tuzla.

Many survivors from Srebrenica and many Dutch peacekeepers continued to believe the town was sacrificed as part of an international conspiracy. But no definitive proof of a conspiracy had emerged by June 1998.

In meetings with survivors, Bosnian President Alija Izetbegović continued to deny striking any deal to sacrifice Srebrenica and blamed the international community for its fall. An inquiry by the Dutch institute that had exposed Dutch collaboration during the Nazi occupation in World War II continues, but no Dutch officials or soldiers have been punished to date. Colonel Karremans is still serving in a Dutch Army posting in Virginia and is writing a book about Srebrenica. Joris Voorhoeve remains Dutch Defense Minister. Sergeant Marc Klaver, Captain Jelte Groen, and Major Robert Franken are still in the Dutch Army, and Brigadier General Cees Nicolai was promoted to major general. Vincent Egbers is a captain in the Dutch air force.

The United Nations refused requests for a formal inquiry into the conduct of UN personnel during the fall of Srebrenica and Žepa, and refused to release internal documents pertaining to it. Two members of the Security Council, France and the Netherlands, reportedly blocked any inquiry.

Yasushi Akashi retired from the United Nations in December 1997 to head a nuclear disarmament institute in Hiroshima, Japan, and still says he did nothing wrong in Srebrenica. General Bernard Janvier, living in seclusion, is still barred by the French government, or refuses himself, to speak about the fall of Srebrenica. The Janvier aide who told journalist Roy Gutman that Janvier did make a deal with General Mladić—and then denied it to the author—now also refuses to be interviewed.

American officials, for their part, continue to deny any culpability in Srebrenica or Žepa. William Perry, in a June 1997 interview, said he called for air attacks to defend Srebrenica as the town fell, but European officials blocked him. Perry said it was the Pentagon's military judgment that Žepa could not be defended by air attacks in July 1995 and said Žepa was not intentionally sacrificed to make negotiating a peace agreement easier.

Richard Holbrooke, in a book published in May 1998 on the Dayton peace accord, said the United States did not sacrifice the enclave and that the Dutch government had blocked his request for air attacks to save Srebrenica. He said American officials are still unsure whether France or Janvier had made a secret deal with the Serbs in June 1995.

American activists who believe there was a conspiracy to sacrifice Srebrenica filed a Freedom of Information Act request with the U.S. government in August 1995 for all documents and intelligence photos relating to Srebrenica. Government officials released several thousand pages of documents, but the vast majority revealed little or no new information.

One of the most telling documents released was a cable sent from the U.S. embassy in Sarajevo to Washington at 6:11 p.m. on the day Srebrenica fell. The cable describes a 2:00 p.m. meeting in which Bosnian Prime Minister Haris Silajdžić warns a massacre would ensue if Srebrenica fell. It concludes by stating, "No consensus has formed among government and diplomatic contacts here as to the ultimate Serb military strategy. But most think it is interactive—that is, the BSA probes resistance and pushes until it locates opportunity." The cable then reiterates Silajdžić's warning. The final two sentences were blacked out for security reasons, State Department officials said. According to the cable, U.S. officials were still not sure whether Bosnian Serbs intended to take Srebrenica two hours after the town had already fallen.

In hindsight, the fall of the town was neither a terrible mistake that resulted simply from incompetence and poor policy making nor the result of a vast international conspiracy agreed upon by Clinton, Major, Chirac, Izetbegović and Milošević. Instead, the most likely explanation for the fall of Srebrenica and Žepa is that the tacit sacrifice of the two safe areas was in the interests of all the parties. The conspiracy was a passive one. No leader wanted to be seen openly sacrificing the two enclaves. Instead, each sat back on his own, and for his own reasons, paid little attention to events in Srebrenica and Žepa or intentionally misread them and did not intervene.

The French brokered a tacit deal to halt air strikes in exchange for the release of hostages in June 1995 in order to free their peacekeepers. The deal endangered Srebrenica and Žepa, the two smallest and weakest enclaves, but the two enclaves held no French peacekeepers and were not a French priority. U.S. officials grossly misread the situation in Srebrenica and Žepa or paid little attention to them because the two enclaves, unlike Bihać, were not strategic priorities, and their continued existence complicated efforts to end the war through a de facto partitioning of Bosnia.

Bosnian government officials had the Bosnian Army do little to aid Srebrenica and Žepa because they had already decided the two enclaves should be traded but knew exchanging the two enclaves in a peace settlement would be politically difficult. Akashi and Janvier did little to defend the towns because avoiding peacekeeper casualties was their top priority and the loss of two enclaves simplified the UN's troubled mission.

After Srebrenica and Žepa fell, each leader or official could claim that he did all he could to save the town and blame others for the town's fall. The loss of the two enclaves reflected the dynamic of Western policy in Bosnia and were emblematic of policy making in an age of plausible deniability. Like gardeners who never water a plant and declare dismay when it dies, Western leaders and the UN officials carried out a passive conspiracy against the two safe areas.

What they each, for their own reasons, did not do—not what they agreed to together in a secret backroom conspiracy—doomed Srebrenica and Žepa. There are no fingerprints—except for the 7,300 missing.

NOTES

PREFACE

1. When the central characters are first introduced, their views of the war and Bosnia are described to give context to events, but the individual may not have necessarily been thinking those thoughts at the exact time portrayed. Where I do express an individual's views or thoughts, I am repeating direct statements they made to me. Sections containing the central characters' thoughts or emotions were double-checked in follow-up interviews where they confirmed their recollections.
2. In 1987, Slobodan Milošević rose to power in Serbia. In April 1990, Slovene nationalist Milan Kućan defeated the Communists and was elected President of Slovenia. The following month, Croat nationalist Franjo Tudjman was elected President of Croatia. And in November 1990, nationalist Muslim, Serb and Croat parties defeated the Communists in Bosnia.
3. Laura Silber and Allan Little, *The Death of Yugoslavia* (London: Penguin Books/BBC Books, 1995–96), p. 72.
4. Ibid., pp. 220–21.
5. Nesib Mandžić, the director of Srebrenica's high school during the war, told the legend. Other residents confirmed its existence. Srebrenica's history is from Mandžić and Noel Malcolm, *Bosnia: A Short History* (New York: New York University Press, 1994–96), pp. 2, 6–8, 53–55.
6. The description was taken from a brochure produced by the Crni Guber spa before the war.
7. Villages surrounding Srebrenica and households that were poorer had a lower standard of living.
8. On May 6, 1993, the Security Council passed Resolution 824 and declared Sarajevo, Tuzla, Bihać, Goražde and Žepa also safe areas. On June 4, 1993, the Security Council passed Resolution 836, which formally extended the

mandate of the UN mission to the safe areas. Chapter Seven of the UN charter, which allows "peace enforcement" was cited and the use of force was authorized. The problematic nature of Resolution 836 will be discussed later.

9. Boutros-Ghali warned regarding the "light option" that "this cannot . . . completely guarantee the defense of the safe areas, it relies on the threat of air action . . . and it assumes the consent and cooperation of both parties," according to the Report Based on the Debriefing on Srebrenica, Dutch Ministry of Defense, Assen, October 4, 1995, p. 9.

THURSDAY, JULY 6, 1995

1. Klaver was unable to remember who was on duty in the operations room that morning.

2. Throughout the book, Srebrenica's residents are referred to as the Muslims. Unlike many other parts of Bosnia controlled by the Muslim-led Bosnian government, Srebrenica had almost no Serbs or Croats who remained loyal to the government. The population of the enclave was almost entirely Muslim.

3. Zoran Radić is a false name. The individual asked that his real name not be used. In interviews between June and September 1996, Radić repeatedly denied having any knowledge of the attack or seeing any soldiers move from Skelani or Serbia toward Srebrenica.

4. A three-way guerrilla conflict was fought in Yugoslavia during World War II. The region was occupied by both German and Italian troops and some of the most brutal fighting occurred in eastern Bosnia. Serbs, Muslims and Croats fighting with Tito's Communist guerrillas were known as Partisans. The Fascist, Nazi Germany-allied forces of the Independent State of Croatia were primarily Croats and to a lesser extent Muslims and were known as Ustaša. Serb nationalists fighting for the reestablishment of the Serb-dominated Kingdom of Yugoslavia were known as Chetniks.

5. The allegations of discrimination are direct statements by Radić. Bosnian Muslims deny that there was any discrimination against Serbs in Srebrenica and say it was actually an advantage to be a Serb. Tito's government is generally believed to have aggressively combated discrimination and used methods such as strict quotas to ensure that members of ethnic groups who were in the minority in a certain area were guaranteed jobs. Tito's government did openly discriminate against individuals of any nationality who were not members of the Communist Party.

6. No forced conversions have been reported in territory controlled by Bosnian Muslims. The charge was generally viewed as baseless and a tool used by Serb nationalists to frighten Bosnian Serbs.

7. There is no evidence of UN personnel in Srebrenica selling combat weapons to Bosnian Muslims. Raids were carried out from the safe area. In an Oc-

tober 1996 interview, Serb officials in Srebrenica said 50 to 60 Serbs died since Srebrenica became a safe area.

8. Whether Bratunac had the second-highest casualty rate could not be confirmed. The figure of 2,000 dead was given by officials in the new Serb-run municipal government in Srebrenica who were interviewed in September 1996 but asked not to be named. Bosnian Serb general Milenko Živanović, a native of Srebrenica, told Stacy Sullivan of *Newsweek* that Serbs died in the Srebrenica area during the war, in an October 1996 interview that was not published. As of January 1997, Sullivan had not published the interview. The allegations of torture could not be confirmed but were widely believed by Serbs.

9. Bosnian Muslims who were once Radić's prisoners described the kind treatment they received from him before he was interviewed. Without knowing his former prisoners had already described his behavior, Radić corroborated the prisoners' accounts.

SATURDAY, JULY 8, 1995

1. Klaver and other Dutch peacekeepers were unable to remember who was on duty at the time.

2. Reconstructed conversations and radio communications are based on interviews with Groen, van Rossum, Klaver and recordings made by Sergeant Frank Struik at the time.

3. Interviews, General Cees Nicolai, June and July 1996, and Report Based on the Debriefing on Srebrenica, Dutch Ministry of Defense, Assen, October 4, 1995, p. 22. Former Swedish Prime Minister Carl Bildt, the new European Union peace envoy, was carrying on negotiations at the time. Nicolai described the guidelines and a copy of them was printed in Leonard Ornstein, "Dutchbat werd gepiepeld" ("Dutchbat Was Screwed"), *Vrij Nederland*, July 13, 1996, p. 7.

4. The cliché of "ancient ethnic hatreds" driving the conflict in Bosnia was accepted by some British, French and American officials as an explanation of the war. The region's Serbs, Muslims and Croats had fought for centuries and would fight for centuries, they argued, so why should French, British or American soldiers die trying to halt it?

5. Only by sending thousands more ground troops to Bosnia would the UN be able to enforce peace and take on the Serbs, French and British officials argued, something the British and French public did not widely support.

6. President Bush followed the recommendations of the Chairman of the Joint Chiefs of Staff, General Colin Powell, in 1991 and backed away from threatening the Serbs with NATO bombing. Critics, including presidential candidate Bill Clinton, contended that a strong use of U.S. airpower in 1991 or 1992 could have cowed the Serbs and prevented four years of war. But once Clinton took office himself in January 1993, he backed away from the

conflict after only one major effort failed. U.S. Secretary of State Warren Christopher toured European capitals in the spring of 1993 and proposed a lifting of the UN arms embargo against Bosnia's Muslims, combined with air strikes against the Bosnian Serbs. The "lift and strike" proposal was rejected by the Europeans as naive and counterproductive.

7. Two forms of air attacks were created by the UN. There was Close Air Support, which was designed for self-defense. Any UN unit being attacked on the ground could ask Akashi to call in NATO jets to destroy a tank, an artillery piece or—if it could be firmly identified—an infantry position that was attacking them. A second, much more powerful attack was a request for NATO air strikes. An air strike involved a larger number of NATO planes attacking Bosnian Serb ammunition bunkers, headquarters or communication relays as a punitive measure for actions taken by the Serbs in some other area. NATO air strikes were first authorized by the Security Council in August 1993 and approved by NATO's governing body, the North Atlantic Council, on February 22, 1994. Akashi took over as civilian head of the UN mission in January 1994.

8. Sarajevo was declared a safe area in May 1993. After a shell killed 69 people in a Sarajevo marketplace in February 1994, NATO established a twelve-and-a-half-mile heavy weapons exclusion zone around Sarajevo. Serb weapons were placed in UN-monitored storage sites. The Serbs gradually began violating the exclusion zone and by May 1995 were entering the UN storage sites and firing the weapons as peacekeepers stood by. An exclusion zone was established around Goražde after an April 1994 Serb attack. Srebrenica, Žepa, Tuzla and Bihać were never declared exclusion zones.

9. Akashi and Janvier had turned down a request for air strikes by Smith on May 8, 1995. Smith later agreed that this request was a mistake. Eleven people in Sarajevo had been killed in a shelling attack. Most of the victims were manning a tunnel the Bosnian government used to smuggle food and weapons into Sarajevo.

10. According to interviews with administration officials and a White House document listing Bosnia-related meetings issued to *The New York Times* and Laura Silber and Allan Little, *The Death of Yugoslavia* (London: Penguin Books/BBC Books, 1995–96), p. 351, and Woodward, pp. 260–61.

11. Željko Ražnjatović.

12. Ibro Dudić did not survive the fall of Srebrenica. Exactly what weapons he had is unclear. They may have had mortars and RPGs like other units in the enclave.

13. According to Bećirović, Karremans said that he had received two different orders. UN headquarters in Sarajevo had recommended he withdraw from all of his observation posts after the Serbs seized the 350 UN hostages at the end of May. The vulnerable OP teams of eight to ten men were hostages ready for the taking. But the Dutch government had urged Karre-

mans to stay in the OPs. If the OPs were abandoned, they'd have no idea how large a Serb attack was. It would also appear as if the Dutch were abandoning the enclave and making no effort to protect it. In the end, according to the Dutch debriefing report, Karremans decided to keep his men in the OPs, but to prepare plans for a rapid withdrawal in case of attack.

14. According to Bećirović and other Bosnian soldiers, the Serb soldiers seen arriving in Zeleni Jadar and in Zalazje were seen coming from the direction of Serbia. The Bosnians believe these soldiers were members of the Yugoslav Army and were coming from Serbia, but it was not possible to verify where they came from.

15. The account of the conversation is based on a UN Military Observer report filed from Srebrenica on July 8, 1995, and an interview with Bećirović. Exactly who the UN officer was is unclear. Major Piet Booring was the battalion's chief liaison officer, but Major Bert Rave was also a liaison.

16. Karremans refused to be interviewed but an assessment of the Serb attack written by Karremans and faxed to the UN at 1 p.m. on July 9 predicts that the Serb attack will move west to secure the road, not north to take Srebrenica town and the rest of the enclave.

17. Serb accounts of atrocities committed by Naser Orić will be discussed again later in the text.

18. Silber, p. 266.

19. Interview, Sefer Halilović, September 1996.

20. Interview, General Philippe Morillon, July 1996.

21. Interview, Murat Efendić, September 1996.

22. Interview, General Philippe Morillon, July 1996.

23. Silber, p. 268.

24. Ibid.

25. Interview, Sefer Halilović, September 1996, and Silber, pp. 269–74.

26. Interview, Shashi Tharoor, UN, and Silber, p. 274.

27. The safe areas were part of the Washington agreement announced by the United States, France, Britain, Spain and Russia on May 22, 1993. The vague compromise called for the creation of the safe areas as an interim measure until the Bosnian Serbs could be pressured into accepting the Vance-Owen peace plan. The creation of a war crimes tribunal and the dispatch of monitors to verify whether Serbia had cut off all but humanitarian aid to the Bosnian Serbs was also approved. Interview, Diego Arilla, and Silber, pp. 274–75. Elaine Sciolino, "Allies Announce Strategy to Curb Fighting in Bosnia," May 23, 1993, *The New York Times*, p. A6. Paul Lewis, "Hostility to Allies New Plan for Bosnia Increases Around UN," *The New York Times*, May 25, 1993, p. A1.

1. The figure comes from Srebrenica UN Military Observer reports, July 9 and 10, 1995.

2. Nada Krsmanović was not interviewed. The statement is based solely on Omanović, whose accounts proved to be accurate when they could be verified and who was judged a reliable source.

3. Ljubica Đurić was not interviewed. The anecdote is based solely on Omanović.

4. Novica was not interviewed. Omanović was the sole source.

5. Simić was not interviewed. Omanović was the sole source.

6. A brief search yielded three Muslims who were aided by their Serb neighbors after the Arkan Tigers entered the town.

7. Report Based on the Debriefing on Srebrenica, Dutch Ministry of Defense, Assen, October 4, 1995, p. 25. Egbers was unable to remember when the APC arrived.

8. Interviews, Zulfo Tursunović, March and September 1996.

9. The sequence of events is inexact. Egbers was unable to remember when the jeep arrived.

10. The sequence is inexact. Egbers was unable to remember precisely when he discovered the Bosnian position.

11. The accounts of Egbers and a Bosnian soldier who was at the site differed over whether the Bosnians and Dutch were speaking before the gun was located. The account here is a combination of the two.

12. Bećirović and other Bosnian officers confirmed the missile was fired Sunday morning but were unsure at exactly what time. The soldier who fired the missile said he needed permission from his current commanding officer to speak about the incident but the commanding officer could not be located.

13. Bosnian pilots stated in interviews with a Bosnian reporter that they refused to fly to Žepa after a helicopter was shot down on May 6. The interviews were never published. The pilots would not speak with the author, but the Bosnian journalist was judged to be reliable. In interviews in September 1996, Naser Orić and one of the fifteen officers trapped in central Bosnia confirmed that the pilots refused to fly. The officer asked not to be named. There is no evidence of a secret order from Sarajevo barring pilots from flying to Žepa as part of a conspiracy to sacrifice Srebrenica. Bosnian Army commanders apparently ordered the pilots to fly to Žepa but the orders were disobeyed. The issue will be discussed further in the Epilogue.

14. The men who fired the missile later told friends that they had destroyed a Serb tank. Ramiz Bećirović said he received conflicting reports—some stated that a tank had been destroyed and others did not. Lieutenant Vincent Egbers, who was observing the tank in Pribičevac all day, said no tank was destroyed.

15. By mid-May 1995, the heavy weapons exclusion zone that had been established in February 1994 and barred Serb tanks and artillery from within twelve and a half miles of Sarajevo, existed in name only. Violations of the zone went unpunished by the UN, which was authorized to call in NATO air strikes to enforce it. Serbs routinely shelled the city, brazenly entering UN "weapons collection points," and firing weapons while UN peacekeepers stood by.

16. From an internal UN document describing the meeting. The document is not described in detail in order to protect sources.

17. A French officer based in Sarajevo stated that only one sniping incident had been linked to the Bosnian government. It is not known whether Janvier intentionally lied or had bad information. Numerous French officers and soldiers believed that the Bosnian government killed peacekeepers and its own people and then blamed the Serbs to generate international sympathy. Other than a handful of sniping cases, the allegation of the government targeting its own people was never proven.

18. This is a false name. The individual asked that his real name not be used in case he still had relatives in Serb custody.

19. Malagić stated that Ramiz Bećirović ordered the soldiers, including his group, not to fire even rifles at the advancing Serbs. Bećirović denies that he issued such an order, and two separate sources say Bećirović ordered Ibro Dudić to hold his position by force after OP Foxtrot fell the previous day. Bećirović said it is possible that his order not to fire the artillery piece was exaggerated into an order against firing all weapons as it passed from soldier to soldier.

20. Karremans declined to be interviewed. A copy of the July 9 assessment was obtained.

21. Interviews, General Cees Nicolai, May and July 1996. Boutros-Ghali had returned the authority to approve Close Air Support attacks to Janvier and Akashi on June 22. Elaine Sciolino, "U.S. and France Are Split on Role of UN in Bosnia," The New York Times, May 25, 1993, p. A7. Paul Lewis, "UN Is Authorizing Allied Air Attacks Against the Serbs," The New York Times, June 5, 1993, p. A1. Michael R. Gordon, "Pentagon Is Wary of Role in Bosnia," The New York Times, March 15, 1994, p. A6.

22. Interview, Major Robert Franken.

23. The account of the conversation is based on a report filed by Nicolai's military aide at the time.

24. Interviews, General Cees Nicolai, May and July 1996, General Ton Kolsteren, June 1996, Colonel Charles Brantz, July and September 1996, Major Robert Franken, September 1996, Lieutenant Colonel Andrew de Ruiter, July 1996, and Colonel Harm De Jonge, June 1996. All described confusion over what kind of air attack was going to occur. Franken and Brantz say they may have been misled. There is no concrete evidence of a

Dutch conspiracy to sacrifice Srebrenica—and risk the lives of their own peacekeepers.

25. There were conflicting accounts given by people present. Some said 200 deutsche marks ($130) were offered, others said 300 deutsche marks ($200).

26. Bećirović denied there was a difference of opinion, in spite of what others said.

27. Both Izetbegović and Silajdžić turned down interview requests. Srebrenica's war president, Osman Suljić, said he proposed that Srebrenica surrender and the land be traded to the Serbs on July 9. "Call the international community. Call Karadžić," Suljić allegedly said. "Give up the land and save the people." Suljić said that after he made the proposal President Izetbegović was silent. Suljić was judged not to be a reliable source and the account could not be confirmed.

28. Mido Salihović said Ramiz Bećirović opposed the counterattack because it was too risky. Bećirović said he supported it but could not get any volunteers. It is unclear who is telling the truth.

MONDAY, JULY 10, 1995

1. Salihović said Yugoslav Army identification papers were found on the dead Serb soldiers. The papers indicated the soldiers were based in Valjevo. Salihović said he carried the papers with him to central Bosnia, but Bosnian Army officials failed to produce them. The existence of the papers could not be confirmed.

2. The officers and men had been handpicked for the original mission, but Dutch commanders still found themselves struggling to equip the blocking position with infantrymen, and not cooks. The reason is that after the Serbs blocked the 180 peacekeepers who had gone on leave from reentering, only 430 were left in the enclave. Roughly 200 of them were infantrymen trained to fight. But 140 of the infantrymen were then deployed in groups of eight to ten so they could man the enclave's fourteen observation posts. The Dutch could muster a fighting force of only sixty infantrymen.

3. From interviews with Mido Salihović in June and September 1996. A man interviewed who was present at Živkovo Brdo asked not to be named.

4. The account comes from an internal UN document describing the meeting. The document is not described in detail in order to protect sources.

5. Approximately 100 refugees from Srebrenica—soldiers who had apparently left the enclave five days before when Serb troops first appeared around the enclave—crossed into central Bosnia.

6. It is not known where the report came from. It is unlikely that Janvier,

who was described by his supporters and enemies as a "by the book" officer, would fabricate the account.

7. Interview, Major Robert Franken, September 1996. Franken could not recall exactly what time he spoke to Tuzla.

8. Orić was rumored to run a prostitution ring and to feed sugar to racehorses he had in the enclave, a commodity the enclave's poorest residents desperately needed. No proof of the allegations was found.

9. The practice was common throughout Bosnia during the war.

10. Interviews, Ramiz Bećirović, March and September 1996.

11. Interviews, Ramiz Bećirović, March and September 1996.

12. Various residents made the allegations in interviews between March and September 1996. They asked not to be named, apparently due to fear of retaliation from Orić.

13. There is no credible evidence that Mustafić was working for the Serbs.

14. Other reports of intimidation were heard, but the individuals asked that the accounts not be published, apparently out of fear of retaliation from Orić.

15. What actually occurred is unclear. Bećirović said he sent 200 reinforcements south that morning. Mido Salihović said no reinforcements had arrived by noon. A soldier on Živkovo Brdo in the south, who asked not to be named, said no reinforcements had arrived by 3 p.m.

16. A soldier who was present insists the gun was not fired. Egbers said he has no proof it was. According to Dutch sergeant Frank Struik, a Dutch Special Forces lieutenant who was stationed at OP Hotel with him on the evening of Monday, July 10, also panicked. Struik said the lieutenant cowered in a ditch after a period of intense shelling and kept on repeating that he had to go. The lieutenant, who was also trained to be a Forward Air Controller, insisted on leaving the OP with British SAS commandos when they were ordered to return to Potočari that evening. The lieutenant had no specific orders to leave and departed even though Struik asked him to stay. Struik is believed to be credible, but the account does not appear in the main text because a second eyewitness was not located.

17. Dutch soldiers were not given vacations for capturing rifles, but this was widely believed by Muslims—illustrating the deep distrust between the two sides.

18. The account is approximate. A soldier who was on Živkovo Brdo and asked to not be named was interviewed, but no second source could be located. Many men who fought in the south appear to have not survived.

19. Interviews, Mido Salihović, June and September 1996.

20. This is an estimation of what occurred. Malagić's position and the market where the Dutch were was a half mile apart and they could not see each other. The Dutch later complained that the Muslims put up no resistance in the town while the Muslims complained about the Dutch putting up

no resistance. On the evening of July 10 it appears that they did not see each other.

21. The account of the meeting is based on interviews between February and September 1996 with five of the participants. Only General Ton Kolsteren agreed to be identified. The account is also based on an internal UN document describing the meeting. The document is not described in detail to protect sources.

22. Both Janvier and Moné refused interview requests. It is not known where the call came from. One individual's notes from the meeting state that the call was from Paris, but that was speculation. Others present remember Janvier speaking in French, but he always spoke in his native tongue. It is possible that the call was from Paris and Janvier was receiving instructions on Srebrenica, but it could also have been "Janvier's stockbroker" as one participant put it.

23. One source, who was judged to be highly credible, remembers Janvier making this final statement. Others present remember him saying that he spoke with General Tolimir but could not recall exactly what Janvier said.

24. Rod Nordland, "The Snitch," *Newsweek*, September 9, 1996, pp. 22–24, and testimony of Dražen Erdemović before the International War Crimes Tribunal for the Former Yugoslavia, July 5, 1996; Garrick Utley, *ABC News World News Tonight*, "Srebrenica: The Confession," March 7, 1996, and Renaud Gérard, "Bosnia: A Criminal's Confession," *Le Figaro*, March 8, 1996.

25. Ibid.

26. UNPROFOR Civil Affairs, BH TV News Summary, July 10, 1995, 1930 hours.

27. UNPROFOR Civil Affairs, Bosnian Serb Radio News Summary, July 10, 1995, 1900 hours.

28. Ibid.

29. Ibid.

30. I briefly left Bosnia in late June, expecting a lull in the fighting, and I made no requests to visit Srebrenica during the eight months I spent in the region before it fell.

31. The account is based on interviews with participants Ramiz Bećirović in March and September 1996; Osman Suljić and Fahrudin Salihović in March 1996; an individual who was present and asked not to be named; and on a UN Military Observer report, July 11, 1995.

TUESDAY, JULY 11, 1995

1. Mido Salihović and 100 men would have again tried to push the Serbs back, according to Bećirović, but he wanted to keep Salihović out of the "zone of death" the NATO planes would be creating.

2. Silajdžić refused to be interviewed. The account of the conversation given by several sources in Srebrenica at the time was deemed to be credible.

3. The individual asked that a false name be used, but was judged to be a reliable source.

4. The individual was not interviewed or asked whether his name could be used. A false name is used here. Srebrenicans tend to fear that their missing relatives will be retaliated against if they are being held in secret Serb prisons.

5. It is unclear exactly how many UN soldiers were present. Ramiz Bećirović said only two British were present but the translator stated that two British and three Dutch were present. Dutch sources said two British and three Dutch were present. The Dutch and British either could not be located or declined to be interviewed.

6. Dutch peacekeepers interviewed denied ever seeing such a thing occur. But similar incidents were described by other Muslims who were judged to be credible. The incidents probably occurred, but only rarely.

7. The figure comes from Ramiz Bećirović and was judged to be credible.

8. Nicolai said he heard nothing from Srebrenica all morning and assumed the situation had stabilized.

9. Zagreb-based UN intelligence officials confirmed their assessment that morning that the Serbs did not want to take the entire enclave. They were interviewed between March and May 1996 and asked not to be named.

10. According to Akashi's code cable Z-1130, "Situation in Srebrenica," July 11, 1995. The six requests for Close Air Support were: (1) July 6 (afternoon), turned down by General Nicolai; (2) July 8 (1500 hours), turned down by Nicolai; (3) July 10 (1900 hours), turned down by Janvier; (4) July 10 (2200 hours), target site for following morning; (5) July 11 (0800 hours), stopped in Tuzla due to incorrect form; (6) July 11 (1000 hours), approved.

11. Both reliable Dutch and Muslim sources reported that elderly people were abandoned or pushed out of trucks going to Potočari.

12. Malagić could not remember the individual's name.

13. President Clinton's Remarks Before a Meeting with Congressional Leaders, Federal News Service, July 11, 1995.

14. Interviews, Corporal Hans Berkers, May and July 1996.

15. Before departing, the group tuned in to the 3:05 p.m. Bosnian government news hoping for a miracle, according to Malagić. The newscaster reported that the air attack had been carried out and said the situation was improving in Srebrenica. According to the UN officials quoted on Bosnian radio, Malagić said, Muslim families were returning to the Swedish Shelter Project in the southern edge of the enclave. State-controlled Bosnian radio and TV denied access to their archives. The existence of such a broadcast could not be confirmed.

16. The following account from Ferid Malagić, Ibran's brother, could not be

confirmed. No Dutch remembered such an incident occurring. The Bosnian soldiers turned and started walking toward the northwestern corner of the enclave and Tuzla. They walked toward the two Dutch APCs that had slowly been withdrawing since 1:30 p.m. The APCs were parked on a dirt road 300 yards south of the post office. As the Muslims passed by, one of the Dutch in the APC with a headset motioned to the Bosnian soldiers as they approached. The peacekeeper was making a swooping motion with his hand. He was signaling that more NATO planes would soon be bombing the Serbs.

Ferid was furious. Didn't the Dutch understand it was too late? How stupid did they think the Bosnians were? During the withdrawal, the Muslims had stayed 100 yards in front of the Dutch when it was the UN that was supposed to be defending the town. Ferid was sure the peacekeeper was listening to the latest news or some music on his headset. None of the Dutch cared, he thought. They had let Srebrenica fall.

Ferid aimed his gun at the chest of the Dutch soldier. The peacekeeper froze. Ferid wanted to kill him. "Don't do it," Sanel Begić said. Malagić's brother also ordered him to stop.

Ferid turned his rifle around and held the barrel in his hands. He stepped forward and swung it like a club. The butt slammed into the peacekeeper's head. The impact nearly knocked his headset off. Dazed, the peacekeeper disappeared into the APC and pulled the hatch. Ferid thought they were all greedy bastards. They had taken their guns and betrayed them. He wished he had killed him.

17. *Dutchbat in Vredersnamm* ("Dutchbat in the Name of Peace") (Ryswyki: Debut Press, 1996).

18. Interviews, Corporal Hans Berkers, May and July 1996. Other peacekeepers deny ever seeing the body, but Berkers insists the accident occurred. It is unlikely he would make up an incident that puts him in such a bad light.

19. The account of the SDA meeting is from a reliable source who was present and asked not to be named. The account is also based on a document describing the meeting. It is not described in detail to protect sources.

20. Delić again warned that morale in the enclave was low. Over the last three months, he said, more than thirty soldiers had been arrested and disarmed after they fled to Tuzla. "We have enough fighters, and now also enough arms," Delić claimed. "At places where the Serbs have met resistance, there was no movement."

21. "Across the Bosnian battlefield we have the advantage, so it is possible that Srebrenica is an experiment by the Chetniks to see if international forces are willing to do anything for Bosnia," Delić said. "The other enclaves," he warned, "could also meet Srebrenica's fate."

22. Whether Delić was covering up his own mistakes or intentionally sacrificing the town will be discussed in the Epilogue.

23. This is an approximation. Golić did not survive and none of the men who were with him were interviewed. The account is from soldiers who say they were later told by Golić what happened.

24. At 4:30 p.m., Bosnian Serb radio reported the Bosnian Serb Army had "liberated" Srebrenica in a "counterattack." A new Serb mayor was appointed.

25. Whether France cut a secret deal and gave assurances of no further air strikes to win the release of the hostages will be discussed in the Epilogue.

26. "Dutchbat-III," p. 240.

27. The account is based on an internal UN document. A more detailed description is not given to protect sources.

28. Janvier described the situation in Potočari and the Serb threat to kill the hostages and shell the Dutch compound and civilians. The NATO liaison, Air Commodore Mike Rudd of Great Britain, pointed out that no reconnaissance had been done to assess bomb damage, according to the internal UN document.

29. He said an estimated 1,500 to 1,800 Serbs were involved in the attack and perhaps a company of twelve Serb tanks. The Dutch had been vulnerable from several directions; two shells had impacted in the garden of the headquarters compound.

30. They should prepare for attacks on the other eastern enclaves and review the ability of the Rapid Reaction Force to respond, he said, according to the internal UN document.

31. Political pressure had to be brought on the Serbs to allow the Dutch and the refugees to withdraw, he said, according to the internal UN document.

32. The account comes from Karremans' testimony to the International War Crimes Tribunal for the Former Yugoslavia, July 1996.

33. The information was relayed in an inaccurate cable from Zagreb (Z-1138) July 11, 1995.

34. White House Special Briefing Re: U.S. Recognition of Vietnam, Federal News Service, July 11, 1995.

35. The conventions established norms for how prisoners of war should be treated. Prisoners were to be free from torture, fed and given medical treatment along with other basic rights.

36. Bećirović is not sure which officer he was communicating with in Tuzla. The communication system involved typing and receiving messages and he could not identify individuals.

WEDNESDAY, JULY 12, 1995

1. According to Omanović, Mladić also stated, "If I catch any of Naser Orić's people, I'll roast them here on the spit of the Hotel Fontana." The quote could not be confirmed. Nesib Mandžić and Colonel Karremans did not

remember hearing Mladić say such a thing. The general could have said it during his brief private conversation with Omanović.

2. The account of the meeting is approximate and based on Colonel Karremans' testimony to the International War Crimes Tribunal on July 3–4, 1996, and interviews with Mandžić and Omanović, who were both also present.

3. In separate interviews, the two Muslim negotiators remember Karremans saying, "I don't have much fuel, but I can give you some." They said that Karremans was not as assertive with Mladić as he portrayed himself in his July 3–4, 1996, testimony before the War Crimes Tribunal.

4. The Muslims again stated that Karremans seemed cowed by Mladić and only suggested his men should escort every convoy.

5. It appears the Bosnian Serbs and their backers in Belgrade adopted this strategy. General Živanović, the commander of the Bosnian Serb Drina Corps, said the decision to attack Srebrenica was made after Višnjica was burned on June 26. But it is highly unlikely that the Serbs would be able to organize the attack on Srebrenica and have the dozens of buses they used to expel Muslims ready in such a short period. UN analysts speculated that the Bosnian Serbs may have adopted the strategy at a meeting of their senior leadership in March. The attack may have been delayed by the Bosnian Army offensive to break the siege of Sarajevo in June.

6. According to Karremans' July 3–4, 1996, testimony at the War Crimes Tribunal, Mladić then stated that he would like to question all of the men in Potočari between seventeen and sixty to screen for potential war criminals. Both Omanović and Mandžić said that Mladić made no mention of the men being separated and wished they had been warned beforehand. Mladić may have informed Karremans privately about his intentions to separate the men. Karremans said in his testimony that he protested the separation of the men, but there was little he could do.

7. This is a combination of Karremans', Mandžić's and Omanović's descriptions. According to Omanović, Mladić claimed that the Muslim representatives were able to contact the soldiers but Karremans and Mandžić did not remember such a statement being made.

8. The account here is again a combination of the descriptions given by Karremans in his July 3–4, 1996, tribunal testimony and Omanović and Mandžić in interviews between April and September 1996. The most credible descriptions are used.

9. Rod Nordland, "Death of a Village," *Newsweek*, April 15, 1996, pp. 52–56.

10. According to Mevludin Orić, who was interviewed repeatedly between September 1995 and September 1996.

11. Nordland, pp. 52–56, and "Missing Persons in the Territory of Bosnia and Herzegovina," International Committee of the Red Cross, August 10, 1996.

12. According to Omanović, she interrupted Mladić and said, "One should welcome every victory, but since you conquered my town I cannot congratulate you. I grew up there." Karremans and Mandžić did not remember her saying that.

13. The previous day's developments and Mladić's demands at the meetings the night before were announced by Colonel De Jonge, chief of operations. "It's evident that in Mladić's mind the BH must lay down their weapons," Janvier said. "We have no information regarding the BH army in the area. We don't know what the BH could have done or did do for the defense of Srebrenica—but it is obvious that they did not show much combativeness." Janvier reported that the chief of staff of the Dutch Army, General Hans Couzy, had said the Dutch government would like to see their peacekeepers withdraw within a few days. Janvier replied that, for humanitarian reasons, that would be impossible. The Dutch had to stay and provide assistance, though he agreed that the use of force would be "unrealistic." The account is based on an internal UN document. It is not described in detail in order to protect sources.

14. "I spoke with Bildt two times yesterday," Akashi said, referring to Carl Bildt, the new European Union peace envoy who had been shuttling through the region. "He said negotiations he's involved in will suffer negative consequences from the use of CAS, but realized there were factors to counterbalance and accepted our decision."

"I don't want to be misunderstood," Rudd explained. "Smith does not want to get into a debate, because if he does, he believes CAS was too late."

"That's his opinion," Janvier retorted. "I hope he won't commit himself to that path. I don't know what it's based on. I don't agree at all."

An aide pointed out that there were two misnomers regarding the press line. UNPROFOR was viewed as a "protection force" because of its name and "viewers will want to know why the UN is not protecting safe areas." The account is based on the internal UN document.

15. A copy of the letter was obtained by the author.

16. Of the six safe areas Srebrenica was the most demilitarized. Sarajevo, Goražde, Tuzla and Bihać were never demilitarized and Žepa was only partially demilitarized.

17. Koster was unable to remember the Serb officer's name. He was interviewed in December 1996.

18. Whether the better-organized soldiers were from Serbia will be discussed in the Epilogue.

19. Klaver, Hodžić and Groen were unsure who actually spoke to the Serbs first. All were interviewed between June and November 1996.

20. The description comes from separate interviews with Hodžić, Groen and Klaver between June and November 1996.

21. State-controlled Bosnian TV and radio denied the author access to copies

or transcripts of their broadcasts made at the time. It is not known whether Izetbegović actually made the statement or if his words were exaggerated.

22. Koster's translator told him what the Serbs were saying.

23. Koster described slightly different versions of the conversation in an interview and in testimony before the War Crimes Tribunal. The account here uses the central points Koster mentioned in the descriptions.

24. According to UN code cable Z-1142, July 12, 1995, Muratović told UN officials in a meeting at 7:45 that morning that all civilians should stay in Srebrenica and the safe area should be reestablished. Only those suffering from medical emergencies were to be evacuated. They were to be sent to foreign countries because Bosnian hospitals, Muratović said, did not have the capacity to treat them. According to critics of the government, Bosnian officials were again using their people as cattle.

25. According to an interview with van Duijn, December 1996.

26. Edited diary of Kristina Schmidt, Médecins Sans Frontières coordinator in Srebrenica, released by Médecins Sans Frontières, Paris, p. 5.

27. UNPROFOR code cable Z-1142. To Annan, UN, NY, from Akashi, UNPF HQ, Zagreb, July 12, 1995.

28. Van Duijn said that not all of the men were taken away by the Serbs. He estimated that 50 men were taken away the first day and 250 to 300 the second day. But other Dutch said that hundreds of Muslim men were taken away. The ICRC received over 2,935 reports of men from Srebrenica last seen when they were arrested by the Serbs. The majority of those reports would appear to be from Potočari, where women saw men taken away, versus the chaos of the woods.

29. Laura Silber and Allan Little, *The Death of Yugoslavia* (London: Penguin Books/BBC Books, 1995–96), p. 349.

30. Some women later reported seeing several bodies strewn along the road, including men with their throats cut. Others reported not seeing any bodies. The accounts could not be confirmed.

31. According to translator Vahid Hodžić, who was interviewed in July and October 1996.

32. Silber, p. 286.

33. Eastern Bosnia was home to extremists of all three sides that fought in Bosnia in World War II—Croat and Muslim Ustaša fighting with the German Nazis; Tito's Serb, Muslim and Croat Partisans fighting for a multiethnic Communist Yugoslavia; and Serb nationalist Chetniks fighting for a Greater Serbia. The leader of the Chetniks, Dražen Mihailović, was hidden by local Serb nationalists in the town of Šehovići in eastern Bosnia until he was finally arrested by Tito's police months after the war ended.

34. I could not obtain a copy of the book. The descriptions were from Zoran Radić, the Bosnian Serb police officer, whom I judged to be a reliable source.

35. A list of those killed produced by General Milenko Živanović in a November 1996 interview with Stacy Sullivan of *Newsweek* magazine appeared to contain the names of mostly young men who were apparently soldiers. As of June 1998, the interview had not been published.

36. It is impossible to verify the Serb claims. But Muslims confirmed that Naser Orić adopted a tit-for-tat strategy. Burned-down Serb villages can be seen in the vicinity of Srebrenica, and the author found Serb headstones that had been knocked over in a graveyard in Srebrenica.

37. A funeral for the people killed in the Ratkovići attack produced what Serbs cited as their clearest evidence of the international media's anti-Serb bias. Video of a Serb mother kissing her son's coffin was shot at the funeral; when it was aired, the footage was described as a Muslim mother kissing her son's coffin. When or if the footage was actually aired is not known, but the story was common among Serbs.

38. A Serb who gave a credible account of his elderly parents being burned alive in their house was interviewed. It is unclear exactly how many Serbs died in the attack. Muslims denied that any civilians were killed.

39. Accounts of both were heard. It is not known which is true.

40. The story was confirmed by numerous Srebrenica residents.

41. John Pomfret, "Weapons, Cash and Chaos Lend Clout to Srebrenica's Tough Guy," *The Washington Post*, February 16, 1994, p. A14.

42. The account was heard by so many different Muslim and Dutch sources that it was judged to be credible.

43. General Milenko Živanović, the commander of the Bosnian Serb Drina Corps, referred to Srebrenica as the "epicenter of genocide" in a November 1996 interview with Stacy Sullivan of *Newsweek*.

44. Dutch Debriefing Report, Dutch Ministry of Defense, Assen, October 4, 1995, pp. 46–51.

45. Ibid.

46. Ibid.

47. Paul Groenewegen, testimony before the International War Crimes Tribunal for the Former Yugoslavia, July 4, 1996.

48. According to Hodžić, Mladić then distributed bread again to the people. The story could not be confirmed and could be a reference to the bread distribution earlier in the day.

49. Hodžić did not remember the officer's identity. Van Duijn confirmed it was he.

50. Separate interviews with van Duijn and Hodžić in June and December 1996 produced accounts that corroborated each other.

51. Lieutenant Leen van Duijn had demanded the Serbs give back the ID and the Serbs complied. He then gave it to Rave.

52. Lieutenant Leen van Duijn, who said he was always present during the expulsions, stated that he saw only 50 old men depart for Bratunac that day. They were loaded onto the small truck that had brought the bread.

It is possible that van Duijn did not see Suljić's group of approximately 300 old men being led to the two buses. Suljić said no Dutch saw them or escorted them while they were loaded onto the buses.

53. UNPROFOR Civil Affairs, Bosnian Serb Radio News Summary, July 12, 1995, 1900 hours.

54. Oslobedjenje News Agency, Morning, Afternoon and Evening Services, Sarajevo, July 12, 1995.

55. UNPROFOR Civil Affairs, BH TV News Summary, July 12, 1995, 1930 hours. Izetbegović also said he had met with the Bosnian Army commander outside Sarajevo the previous day to discuss the offensive around Sarajevo and agreed that Sarajevo "has to be liberated [in] either a political or military way. The army is ready to do its job."

56. UNPROFOR Civil Affairs, Bosnian Serb Radio News Summary, July 12, 1995, 1900 hours.

57. Bosnian war crimes investigators recovered 125 bodies from the site in the spring of 1996. More bodies may have been removed by the Serbs.

58. From the Dutch Debriefing Report, p. 56.

59. It is unclear exactly how many women were raped in Potočari. Dutch peacekeepers interviewed said they saw no Serb soldiers in the area that night, but Muslims say there were. Rape carries a large stigma in rural Bosnian society and women may not have reported all of the attacks. The accounts are from Stephen Kinzer, "Bosnian Refugees' Accounts Appear to Verify Atrocities," *The New York Times*, July 17, 1995; and Snejžara Vukić, "Refugees Tell of Women Singled Out for Rape," *The Independent* (London), July 18, 1995; as summarized in "The Fall of Srebrenica and the Failure of UN Peacekeeping," Human Rights Watch/Helsinki, New York, October 1995, pp. 26–27.

60. The Dutch who stayed outside at night, including Marc Klaver and Lieutenant Eelco Koster, said they saw no Serb soldiers dressed in Dutch or Serb uniforms moving in the crowd. The Muslims insisted there were Serbs and the Dutch said it is possible that some Serbs may have slipped into the area in the darkness.

61. Ćamila had heard a story earlier in the afternoon. A pregnant woman who thought she was going into labor and a woman who had an asthma attack asked two Dutch soldiers to help them. The soldiers rudely pushed them away. The women decided they were Serbs dressed in stolen UN uniforms.

62. The Dutch who were interviewed said the disturbances and the screaming were caused by the mentally ill patients from the abandoned hospital. The Dutch said they did evacuate several mentally ill people. Klaver and Koster said they saw no soldiers in Dutch uniforms whom they did not recognize. But other soldiers reported seeing Serbs in Dutch uniforms in the area, in Report Based on the Debriefing on Srebrenica, Dutch Ministry of Defense, Assen , October 4, 1995, p. 45.

63. The Dutch said they heard few screams and that any panic or disturbance was caused by mental patients from the abandoned town hospital. They said there were no reports and no evidence of any kind of poison gas being used.

64. Both Lućanin and Radić were interviewed repeatedly between April and September 1995.

65. "The Fall of Srebrenica and the Failure of UN Peacekeeping," Human Rights Watch/Helsinki, New York, October 1995, p. 26.

THURSDAY, JULY 13, 1995

1. Of the men Omanović said she saw taken away only Purković is not listed as missing on ICRC lists. His family may have failed to report that he was missing.

2. It appears that two separate suicides are being described. Omanović said the construction worker hanged himself with a belt from a truck, but heard the information secondhand and did not find the body herself. Van Duijn said only one man was found who had hanged himself with a rope in a factory building on the other side of the street. Koster also stated that the victim's brother identified him and buried him, while the man Ćamila knew was alone. The bodies of at least two old men were also found that morning by the Dutch. It is possible that suicide victims were found by Muslims and not seen by the Dutch before burial.

3. Interview, Lieutenant Eelco Koster, December 1996, and Report Based on the Debriefing on Srebrenica, Dutch Ministry of Defense, Assen, October 4, 1995, p. 56.

4. Stephen Kinzer, "Bosnian Refugees' Accounts Appear to Verify Atrocities," *The New York Times*, July 17, 1995. According to the Dutch, only the Muslim man who hanged himself in the factory was found. No girl who hanged herself was found, but the Dutch did report that a "young girl" was one of the people they buried behind the base. It is also possible that the family found the body and buried it themselves.

5. Report Based on the Debriefing on Srebrenica, October 4, 1995, p. 87.

6. Omanović said Mladić's threat to "roast" anyone connected to Naser Orić on the spit of the Hotel Fontana also filled her mind, but the Mladić statement could not be confirmed. None of the other Dutch or Muslims present at the Hotel Fontana remember the comment from Mladić.

7. Omanović was the primary source for the story and she gave a slightly different account to investigators from the War Crimes Tribunal. Exaggeration is possible due to her state of mind, but her son gave a detailed account of the Serbs making threats about Bratunac when interviewed separately.

8. Both Lućanin and Radić were interviewed between June and September 1996. Each man's account differed slightly.

9. The description is based on a videotape shot by a Serb journalist, which was repeatedly shown on Dutch television and used in the British Broadcasting Corporation documentary series "The Death of Yugoslavia," produced by Brian Lapping, 1996.

10. Ibid.

11. The columns of buses and trucks were stopped in Bratunac. Serbs entered the buses and demanded money, jewelry and other valuables from the Muslims. No one approached the truck Omanović's children were in and they arrived safely in Tišća, the crossing point.

12. At some point during the day, Egbers ran into General Ratko Mladić. The general told him, "Join my army, I'll make you a lieutenant." Egbers replied, "That's OK, I'll stay with mine." When Egbers pointed at Mladić's stomach—trying to ask why the general didn't wear a flak jacket—his bodyguards thought the peacekeeper was making fun of Mladić's waist. The conversation quickly ended.

13. Charles Lane, "The Fall of Srebrenica," *The New Republic*, August 16, 1995, pp. 14–18. Ron Rutten is part Jewish, but is not religious, according to friends.

14. Many Serbs also fought with the Serb royalist and nationalist Chetniks, the other faction that fought in the three-way conflict that devastated Yugoslavia in World War II.

15. Bob Woodward, *The Choice* (New York: Simon & Schuster, 1996), pp. 259–60, and interviews with a senior administration official in August 1996 and January 1997 who asked not to be identified. The official corroborated Woodward's account.

16. Several individuals who marched in the lead section of the column were interviewed, but asked not to be named.

17. The description of the conversation is approximate. Mandžić was interviewed, as was the translator at the meeting, but Franken agreed only to be briefly interviewed. The interviews were conducted between September 1995 and September 1996.

18. According to Lieutenant Eelco Koster, the photos of the bodies in the town were on the same roll of film as the nine bodies found near the stream.

19. According to an edited version of Kristina Schmidt's diary made available through Médecins Sans Frontières, Paris.

20. Report Based on the Debriefing on Srebrenica, p. 47.

21. According to Hasan Nuhanović, Major Franken was skeptical of the dangers the men faced. Franken was not asked about this point in a brief interview that focused on Close Air Support requests.

22. The exact number of prisoners at the site is not known. Throughout the book, the estimates given by survivors—which can be inaccurate—are presented. The Epilogue details how many bodies were found at each site. At the time of publication, most mass graves around Srebrenica had not been

exhumed or had been tampered with and it was extremely difficult to determine exact numbers of victims.

23. Rod Nordland, "Death of a Village," *Newsweek*, April 15, 1996, pp. 52–56. Nordland did not name the third man from Lehovići who was seen in the group of prisoners.

24. Ibid. Haso Hasanović was not interviewed. According to Nordland, he stated that the girl was a thirteen-year-old, and a Serb with a Mohawk haircut carrying a long knife was seen leaving the area.

25. Each room measured approximately 180 feet by 35 feet.

26. Smail Hodžić is the lone source of the alleged incidents. He was deemed credible because of evidence found that corroborated his story of a later mass execution in Grbavci.

27. Smail Hodžić and a second man who was present on the soccer field and asked not to be named were interviewed in September 1995. Their accounts were credible and corroborated each other. The account given here is a combination of their recollections.

28. Franken was not asked specifically about this point. He said in a brief interview that focused on the requests for Close Air Support that he did not believe the Serbs would kill all of the Muslim men and that the Dutch had no choice but to obey the Serbs and have them leave.

29. The UNHCR worker was not interviewed. The story was credible and Nuhanović was judged to be a reliable source.

30. Mevludin Orić was unsure what time the sequence of events on the hill above Konjević Polje occurred. It was over the course of the afternoon and the heavy shelling may have happened at approximately 3 p.m.

31. Interview, Martyn Mülder, September 1996.

32. Berkers was interviewed in July 1996.

33. Report Based on the Debriefing on Srebrenica, Dutch Ministry of Defense, Assen, October 4, 1995, p. 50.

34. Ibid., p. 47.

35. Ibid., p. 51.

36. The lieutenant said he was a Croat fighting in the Bosnian Serb Army, according to Egbers.

37. Prisoners were taken to a building behind the Vuk Karadžić school in the center of Bratunac, according to Orić.

38. Smail Hodžić, Mevludin Orić and two men who were also prisoners on trucks were interviewed in September 1995. Their accounts were consistent and judged to be credible.

FRIDAY, JULY 14, 1995

1. Suljić recalls the following occurring, Orić did not: As the gym filled, a tall Serb officer with jet-black hair and sunglasses kept screaming, "Back up!

Back up! I'm going to kill you all." He fired bullets over the heads of the prisoners to make his point.

2. What happened next is unclear. Hurem Suljić says that Mladić then addressed the prisoners. Mevludin remembers seeing the general, but says only the Serb officer in charge spoke and he did so after Mladić left.

   According to Suljić, a prisoner began shouting questions. "General Mladić. Why are you treating us this way?" he asked. "Why don't you take us somewhere?"

   "Your government doesn't want to accept you, so I must take care of you," Mladić replied. "In a few hours you will be sent to work camps in Bijeljina and Velika Kladuša."

3. The guards said the men would be taken to Batković, a Serb prison about forty miles north. Other guards said they were being taken to Velika Kladuša, the stronghold of Fikret Abdić, a Muslim businessman who had rebelled against the government in Sarajevo and was fighting with the Serbs.

4. Husejnović never saw the machine, but the type of earthmover he believes was used is common throughout the former Yugoslavia. The size of the hole that was punched in the wall, which was later found in the warehouse, indicated the width of the shovel.

5. Janvier then said the only place the UN and the Rapid Reaction Force could defend was Sarajevo. "What we can [do] is for Sarajevo," he said. "There we're surely able to carry out some actions." Later in the same meeting, Akashi stated: "[We] need to pay attention to the situation of the Dutch—would be bad for them to leave in current circumstances when civilians are in that predicament. I spoke with the Force Commander [Janvier] who spoke with [General Rupert] Smith. The Dutch will stay for now and eventually leave with dignity and their equipment to [whatever] extent possible. It's embarrassing to go to Milošević all the time, ask his help. He says he's never compensated."

6. Accounts of what got Janković to agree to cooperate vary widely. Mido Salihović said he quickly agreed. Other soldiers said Janković agreed to cooperate when the Muslims said they would kill him or his soldiers. One soldier said Janković agreed to cooperate after three of his soldiers were beheaded in front of him. The account could not be confirmed. Attempts to reach Janković were unsuccessful.

7. According to Omanović, she and her brother decided to carry out a double suicide on Friday morning. They tied two nooses, but he was told by his Médecins Sans Frontières supervisor that they would leave the enclave with the UN. Abdulah gave Ćamila two fake suicide pills and was able to talk her out of making another suicide attempt.

8. Both Suljić and Orić say Mladić appeared in the gym but Suljic says Mladić spoke to the prisoners; see note 2 above.

9. Based on interviews with Lieutenant Vincent Egbers, Sergeant Martyn

Mülder and the Dutch Debriefing Report, Dutch Ministry of Defense, Assen, October 4, 1996, pp. 50–51.

10. The scene is based on interviews with two men who survived the mass execution but asked not to be named. The thoughts about what the men must have been feeling were expressed by Vahid Hodžić, the Muslim translator, who also spoke to one of the survivors.

11. Stephen Engelberg, "How Events Drew U.S. into Balkans," *The New York Times*, August 19, 1995, p. A1, and Bob Woodward, *The Choice* (New York: Simon & Schuster, 1996), pp. 280–81. Richard Holbrooke stated that Clinton's realization of the need for a new policy came after a June 15 dinner with French President Chirac, according to Michael Dobbs, "Holbrooke's Parting Shot—For Now," *The Washington Post*, March 3, 1996, p. C1. Clinton's push for a new policy appears to be first driven by the prospect of U.S. troops inevitably going to Bosnia and accelerated by Srebrenica.

12. Woodward, pp. 270–95.

13. Hurem Suljić's and Mevludin Orić's account of what occurred differ. Suljić says he called out across the field, "Is anyone here alive?" Orić says the two simply saw each other.

SUNDAY, JULY 16, 1995

1. The head of the military intelligence unit in Han Pijesak was Colonel Petar Salapura. Salapura was in direct control of Erdemović's unit and frequently issued it orders, according to a transcript of Erdemović's testimony before the International War Crimes Tribunal for the Former Yugoslavia on July 5, 1996, Garrick Utley, *ABC News World News Tonight*, "Srebrenica: The Confession," March 7, 1996, and Renaud Gérard, "Bosnia: A Criminal's Confession," *Le Figaro*, March 8, 1996.

2. The two military policemen were from the Drina Corps, the Bosnian Serb military unit responsible for the Drina Valley region.

3. Stoltenberg's post was created after an international peace conference held in London in 1991.

4. John Pomfret, "Bosnian Soldiers Evade Serbs in Trudge to Safety," *The Washington Post*, July 18, 1995, p. A1.

AFTERMATH

1. The President went on to say, "We're in the worst possible situation. The Europeans could bring force to bear but they prefer to whine at us." He described Chirac's proposal and said it had not been thought through, but welcomed the new attitude. "We have war by CNN. Our position is unsustainable, it's killing the U.S. position of strength in the world." From Bob Woodward, *The Choice* (New York: Simon & Schuster, 1996), pp.

261–62. A senior administration official who asked not to be named corroborated the account in a January 1996 interview.

2. According to Woodward, Gore was referring to U.S. aerial spy photos showing suspected mass graves around Srebrenica, but a senior administration official said he was not, in a January 1996 interview. Some UN officials suspect that the administration may have had photographs indicating mass executions were taking place but waited until the executions were over to release them. The administration has repeatedly said CIA analysts did not begin scanning the thousands of images of the Srebrenica area for mass graves until survivors described Nova Kasaba to Assistant Secretary of State John Shattuck between July 30 and August 1. Dutch peacekeepers saw the graves being dug on July 14 and 15. The Oval Office meeting was four to five days later. Whether the United States intentionally suppressed evidence of mass executions will be discussed later in the Epilogue.

3. According to Woodward, Gore then cited reports that women related to the local commanders were singled out for gang rapes. Where he got the information is unclear. One nurse in the medical convoy was accused of being Naser Orić's sister, but it could not be confirmed that any of his relatives were actually raped. "The cost of this is going to cascade over several decades," Gore also said. "It goes to what kind of people we are. Acquiescence is the worst alternative."

4. The Serbs attacking Bihać fought alongside Muslims loyal to Fikret Abdić, a Muslim businessman who was elected a member of Bosnia's rotating presidency and rebelled against the government in Sarajevo when Bosnian President Alija Izetbegović did not turn the post over to him as scheduled.

5. It is possible that the three men met in the woods and made up the execution story, but the discovery of a mass grave in the location they described confirmed their accounts.

6. While other men claimed to have survived mass executions or to have seen large numbers of bodies, the three survivors from Grbavći appear to have been the first actual survivors of a mass execution to emerge from the woods. Others would soon follow. The Bosnian journalist who first broke the story could not be located, but worked for "Radio Zvornik"—a program apparently run by Muslims expelled from Zvornik by Serbs in 1993. Alexandra Stiglmayer of *Time* magazine was the first Western journalist to speak with Smail Hodžić. Hurem Suljić could not remember who was the first journalist with whom he spoke.

7. UNPROFOR Civil Affairs, BH TV News, July 22, 1995.

8. U.S. officials argued that massive air strikes would stop the Serbs in Goražde, but it was too late to save Žepa.

9. Roy Gutman, "Dutch Reveal Horrors of Mission Impossible," *New York Newsday*, July 24, 1995, p. A7.

10. Ibid.

11. Lieutenant Vincent Egbers and Private Marc Klaver said the statement was

written for Karremans by a Dutch officer from the Ministry of Defense. Karremans refused to be interviewed.

12. Interviews with Major Robert Franken and the UN official who received the list, January 1997.

13. A Serb soldier interviewed by the author in the Nova Kasaba area on August 12, 1995, stated, "We just talk to them and kill them."

14. A copy of the UN document was obtained by the author.

15. Interview with Admiral Leighton Smith, January 1997.

16. Roy Gutman, "An Appeal for Žepa," *New York Newsday,* July 25, 1995, p. A6.

17. A copy of the cable was obtained by the author.

18. According to a UN official involved in the Žepa negotiations who was interviewed in June 1996 but asked not to be named.

19. John Pomfret, "Serbs Drive Thousands from Žepa Enclave," *The Washington Post*, July 27, 1995, p. A1.

20. According to a UN official involved in the Žepa negotiations interviewed in June 1996 who asked not to be named.

21. Ibid.

22. With the pressure on Bihać mounting, the Presidents of Bosnia and Croatia, Alija Izetbegović and Franjo Tudjman, met in the Croatian city of Split on July 23 and signed a joint defense pact. The alliance the United States had been trying to foster between Muslims and Croats was finally materializing. The United States negotiated a cease-fire that ended a year of fighting between Muslims and Croats in Bosnia in March 1993 and created a Muslim-Croat federation. Until the summer of 1995, the federation and alliance had existed in name only and efforts to get the Muslims and Croats to fight together against the Serbs had failed.

23. Michael Dobbs and R. Jeffrey Smith, "New Proof Offered of Serb Atrocities," *The Washington Post*, October 29, 1995, p. A1, and Roy Gutman, "UN's Deadly Deal," *Newsday*, May 29, 1996, pp. A7, A24, A25, A31.

24. Fears were high at the time that Milošević would send Serbia's powerful army to defend the Serbs in Croatia and full-scale war would break out between Croatia and Serbia—the former Yugoslavia's two most powerful republics.

25. Akashi's response to Milošević's request is unknown.

26. State Department spokesman Nicholas Burns and CIA and National Security Council officials say they produced the photos as soon as possible and the release of the photos was not timed to achieve the maximum political effect. Dobbs and Smith, p. A1; Gutman, p. A31.

27. The story stated that the list was never turned over to the UN by Major Franken. The story was inaccurate. Major Franken did turn over the list to the UN in Zagreb on July 23.

28. Report Based on the Debriefing on Srebrenica, Dutch Ministry of Defense, Assen, October 4, 1995, p. 58.

29. According to UN officials, General Smith was ready to go ahead with the bombings before the analysis had been completed. The investigation was viewed as largely a formality, but they insisted it did show that the shell was fired by the Serbs.

30. NATO had issued the same ultimatum two years earlier in February 1994 but violations were largely unpunished.

31. According to an official who was present at the meeting but asked not to be named when interviewed in July 1996.

32. On September 6, the Foreign Ministers of Serbia, Bosnia and Croatia agreed in Geneva to the 51-49 percent division of Bosnia envisioned in Lake's initiative.

33. In separate interviews, two UN officials said Holbrooke had the language in the ultimatum changed to state that the Bosnian government would not take advantage of the NATO bombing "around Sarajevo"; the rest of the country was not mentioned. Holbrooke denied the charge.

34. Holbrooke said allegations he invented the intelligence assessment are untrue. Holbrooke then brokered a "further agreed principles" agreement in New York on September 26 with the Bosnian, Serbian and Croatian Foreign Ministers.

35. Two UN officials confirmed the production of the maps and a U.S. official confirmed the effort to halt the offensive. Croat tanks had cleared the last ridge separating them from Banja Luka. The U.S. assessment at the time that the Serbs had formed a strong defense wall around Banja Luka was later discounted as exaggerated by UN officials. A senior U.S. official interviewed in January 1996 said Milošević hinted he might intervene if Banja Luka fell, but did not threaten to do so. Holbrooke said Milošević never threatened or hinted he would send the Yugoslav Army into Bosnia to save Banja Luka.

36. The future of Brčko, the Serb-held town that lay in the center of the strategic Posavina corridor, the one Bosnian commanders chose to attack instead of liberating Srebrenica in 1992, was to be decided by arbitration.

37. The public opinion polls fluctuated.

38. The official also informed me of the tampering. I chose not to go to Glogova because it would be too dangerous.

39. I had been blacklisted after visiting the grave in Nova Kasaba, changing the date on an expired Bosnian Serb press pass, and entering Serb territory without permission.

40. The evidence found at the graves by the author was removed.

41. Utley, March 7, 1996, and Gérard, March 8, 1996. Erdemović's account, while possibly exaggerated, was judged to be credible by the author.

42. Where the men were actually from remains the subject of debate. U.S. military officials insisted at the time they appeared too well-fed to have been living in the woods for the previous nine months. U.S. officers speculated that the Bosnian Army had a secret elite commando unit of men

from Srebrenica and Žepa. But Red Cross and UN officials say they are from Srebrenica and were on lists of those reported missing. As of January 1997, they were awaiting trial. Mike O'Connor, "7 Dead Bosnians Alive," *The New York Times*, May 27, 1995, p. 2.

43. The Bosnian Serb source said he was told the story by policemen involved in the operation. He was judged to be a reliable source and did not want to be named. The story is plausible, but it was not possible to confirm if the Serb police were telling the truth.

44. The author and another journalist inspected the area around Kamenica in April 1996. With some local Serbs hostile toward foreign journalists, only a limited search could be carried out.

EPILOGUE

1. In interviews in September 1996, Naser Orić and an officer from Srebrenica who asked not to be named confirmed that Bosnian pilots refused on their own to fly to Žepa. A reliable Bosnian journalist who asked not to be named interviewed helicopter pilots who confirmed that they refused to fly into the enclave because it was too dangerous.

2. According to Zulfo Tursunović, Ramiz Bećirović confirmed that the message was sent.

3. From an interview with a senior officer in the Tuzla-based 2nd Corps in March 1996. Hasan Muratović, the Bosnian government's minister for relations, during the August 2, 1996, session of the Bosnian Assembly complained that the UN ignored warnings of an attack and accused Janvier of sacrificing the town. He did not mention that the government had pulled out the town's top defenders.

4. Delić's statements are from his August 2, 1996, speech to the Bosnian Assembly in Zenica.

5. Orić did not produce a copy of the order. He said a copy of the order was shown on a BBC documentary. A copy of the order for Naser to leave the enclave was shown, not his removal from his command.

6. No officials were able to produce proof of a deal.

7. Roger Cohen, "France Held Secret Talks with Serbs," *The New York Times*, June 22, 1995, and Roy Gutman, "UN's Deadly Deal," *New York Newsday*, May 29, 1996, pp. A7, A24–A25, A31. Janvier also stated in a July 28, 1995, morning briefing that the last time he saw Mladić was June 13. Janvier may have had another secret meeting with Mladić on June 13. It could not be confirmed.

8. On June 9, Akashi, Janvier and Smith met in the Croatian coastal city of Split to discuss the ongoing hostage crisis and how the new 12,000-man Rapid Reaction Force would be used. What follows is abridged.

Smith opened the meeting by stating that he refused to negotiate with the Serbs over the hostages. "To all intents and purposes we have been neutralized," he said. "The exclusion zones and weapons collection points are ignored; the safe areas are under increasing threat. . . The BSA will continue to engage the international community and show that they cannot be controlled. This will lead to a further squeezing of Sarajevo or an attack on the eastern enclaves, creating a crisis that short of air strikes we will have difficulty responding to. . ."

Janvier agreed that the Serbs were in control of the situation but countered: "What is essential is to allow the political process [peace negotiations] to begin. As long as the situation is such, we cannot go toward confrontation. What would be the most acceptable to the Serbs would be to leave the enclaves. It is the most realistic approach and it makes sense from a military point of view, but is impossible for the international community to accept."

Smith predicted that further negotiations would be a waste of time. The Serbs would mount an offensive that summer to settle the war on their own terms. "I remain convinced that the Serbs want to conclude this year and will take every risk to accomplish this. As long as the sanctions remain on the Drina [River], they risk getting weaker every week relative to their enemy. . . . I agree that a stabilization period is good for political talks, but believe the pot will boil over before the political process can work."

Janvier said all that the UN and the new Rapid Reaction Force or "Theater Reaction Force," as Janvier called it, could do was "help us with defense, but [it] will not help us open a corridor to Srebrenica, Goražde or even Sarajevo." He said the Serbs' right to create an independent state should be recognized and UN economic sanctions should be lifted.

"The Serbs need two things," Janvier explained, "international recognition, and a softening of the blockade on the Drina . . . I don't think that they want to go to an extreme crisis. On the contrary, they want to modify their behavior, be good interlocutors. It is for this that we must speak to them—not to negotiate but to show them how important it is to have a normal attitude."

Akashi then cautioned that the Rapid Reaction Force's mission of protecting peacekeepers fit under the rubric of traditional peacekeeping, but opening up corridors to the enclaves by force ventured into peace enforcement or taking sides. Akashi predicted it would be difficult to get the Serbs to release the hostages unless they received assurances of no further air strikes, "which is impossible," he said. "This combination brings us to the edge of the Mogadishu line," Akashi said, using a term coined by Smith's predecessor in Bosnia, British general Sir Michael Rose, that referred to the disastrous U.S.-led 1993 effort to arrest Somali warlord Mohammed Farah Aidid. General Rose, who became increasingly suspicious of the Bosnains during his tour, suspected them of pulling back their troops around Goražde in the spring of 1994 to trick him into carrying out Close Air Support.

"If we do not cross it, we will be accused of being timid and pro-Serb," said Akashi. "If we cross it, we will be accused of being reckless and abandoning chances for peace," he added. "As peacekeepers, we must talk to all parties; the small gains that we achieve from doing so are better than the losses from the combative approach. We remain vulnerable, but our vulnerability provides for a modicum of support from the parties."

Smith then warned that they must get clear instructions from the Security Council and nations contributing troops to the Rapid Reaction Force on how it should be used. He said the only use he saw of the force was the establishment of aid corridors into the enclaves similar to the ones established for Berlin during the Cold War. "Are we going to use the [Rapid Reaction Force] to fight?" Smith asked. "If not, I am not sure I want them— they will just be more mouths to feed and create expectations that I cannot meet."

Janvier again disagreed. "It is clear we cannot impose a solution, such as a corridor," he said. "We can only achieve that through political negotiation."

"I see no prospects of the parties agreeing to such routes. It would be a waste of time to negotiate," Smith answered. "If we are not prepared to fight, we will always be stared down by the BSA. We are already over the Mogadishu line. The Serbs do not view us as peacekeepers."

"Can we return?" Akashi asked, referring to crossing back over the Mogadishu line.

"Only by either doing nothing or showing an absolute readiness to fight, including going over the top," Smith said. "That is possible because the BSA have their hands full with the BH [Bosnian Army]."

"I insist we will never have the possibility of combat, of imposing our will on the Serbs," Janvier asserted. "The only possible way is to go through political negotiations. That is the only way we can fulfill our mandate." But Smith predicted a crisis involving the Sarajevo heavy weapons exclusion zone, or the safe areas, that in turn could lead to the UN being forced to request airpower. There could be a crisis, he warned, even before the Rapid Reaction Force was in place.

The potential crisis was exactly why more negotiations were needed, Janvier averred. "It is just for this that we must establish contact with the Serbs, to show, to explain to them that there are just some things that they cannot do."

"My judgment is that they will not listen," Smith replied.

"I have a different approach," Janvier insisted. "Once again the Serbs are in a very favorable political position and that is something they will not want to compromise. The external political situation is such that the Serbs will understand the benefits of cooperation. Unless there is a major provocation by the BH, the Serbs will not act."

"Either we fail [to carry out our mission] or we act and we will be the enemy of the Serbs," Smith said. "I think we will be forced to make a decision within one month."

After discussing briefly the UN escorting convoys into Sarajevo, Janvier stated that whatever new firepower the Rapid Reaction Force gave them would be counteracted by having peacekeepers in Srebrenica, Žepa and Goražde who could be quickly taken hostage. "With the Reaction Force, we would be able to impose tactical superiority in Sarajevo if we had a conflict," Janvier said. "As long as the enclaves exist, we will be neutralized to an extent. In New York I said that the BH [Bosnians] should defend the safe areas, they are strong enough to do it. This was not well received at all."

After the meeting Akashi publicly announced that the UN mission would be returning to "traditional peacekeeping principles."

9. An internal UN document describing the meeting was obtained by the author.

10. Roger Cohen, "Serbs Free More UN Captives," *The New York Times*, June 13, 1995, p. A1.

11. John Pomfret, "UN Rejects NATO Request to Bomb Serb Airfield After No-Fly Violations," *The Washington Post*, June 22, 1995, p. A25.

12. Bernard Edinger, "French Aide Sees Euro-U.S. Confrontation on Bosnia," Reuters, June 30, 1995. The June 20, 1995, *Glasgow Herald*, citing Reuters/AP, quoted Russian President Boris Yeltsin as saying before he left the G-7 summit in Halifax, "Russia has a common stand with France and other members of the UN Security Council on this issue and we intend to not allow further air strikes." Whether "we" refers to Russia or the members of the Security Council is not clear. French and American officials denied any agreement regarding air strikes was made at the G-7 summit.

13. Roger Cohen, "France Held Secret Talks with Serbs," *The New York Times*, June 23, 1995, p. A7.

14. Roy Gutman, "UN's Deadly Deal," *Newsday*, May 29, 1996, pp. A7, A24, A25, A31.

15. Akashi was interviewed in May 1996 and January 1997.

16. From UN internal document, "Telephone Conversation, Gen. Smith/Gen. Mladić: 28 May 95."

17. William Drozdiak, "Bulldozer Heads for Halifax; French Leader Chirac Brings Reputation for Frank Talk to Summit," *The Washington Post*, June 14, 1995, p. A7.

18. Smith was at the home of Fitzroy Maclean, the British military intelligence agent and SAS commando who served in Yugoslavia during World War II and was the basis for Ian Fleming's James Bond character. Maclean's home is on an island off the coast of Croatia, and Smith was in regular contact with his subordinates in Sarajevo during the attack on Srebrenica.

19. General Raymond Germanos, chief of the French Military Cabinet, said in an interview in July 1996 that Janvier was not to blame for the fall of

Srebrenica; the problem was that the Dutch did not fight and defend the blocking position. He also said they were on drugs, an apparent reference to the legality of marijuana in Holland.

20. Gutman. Gutman read his notes from the interview to the author.
21. A U.S. official read the daily briefs to the author and other journalists.
22. Ibid.
23. Several members of the UN intelligence units in both Zagreb and Sarajevo were interviewed. Colonel Harm De Jonge, the Dutch officer who was chief of UN operations in Zagreb, said he did not know about the reports until he returned to Holland after the fall of Srebrenica. In separate interviews, two other UN officers serving in Zagreb confirmed that the information was never received.
24. From interviews with current and former U.S. intelligence officials specializing in Bosnia, who asked not to be named.
25. From a transcript of a background briefing by a senior Defense Department official, Federal News Service, July 11, 1995.
26. Americans who ran the UN intelligence units were completely dependent on their colleagues in the United States. Washington could have had more information on the attack but not released it to the UN. The availability of satellites, spy planes and Unmanned Aerial Vehicles depended on Washington. Which of the thousands of aerial photographs and communications intercepts captured by the United States in Bosnia were thoroughly examined and analyzed was also at Washington's discretion.
27. In interviews between December 1995 and January 1997 former U.S. Assistant Secretary of State Richard Holbrooke and officials specializing in Bosnia or intelligence in the State Department, National Security Council and Pentagon all consistently denied Srebrenica or Žepa was overtly or tacitly sacrificed.
28. Bruce W. Nelan, "Seeds of Evil," *Time*, July 29, 1996, pp. 56–58, and Stacy Sullivan, "To His Hometown, Serb Karadžić Is a Local Hero Who Made Good," *The Washington Post*, August 21, 1996, p. A20.
29. Nuhanović was also reportedly on a list of war criminals issued earlier in the war. He was never in the army and was apparently wanted for political reasons.
30. Rod Nordland, "Death of a Village," *Newsweek*, April 15, 1996, pp. 52–56. Haso Hasanović told Nordland that after he was captured the second time he was taken to a large field with 500 other Muslim men with their hands tied behind their backs. The prisoners were forced to lie down on dead bodies that were already in the field. The Serbs told the men they would be executed, but they shot over their heads and laughed. A Serb officer then arrived and separated Haso and the three other boys. Haso said the men he knew who were in the group of prisoners are all missing. Haso's account was not included in this book because he was not interviewed by the author and his account could not be confirmed.

31. Ibid.
32. Ibid.
33. Ibid.
34. Reports of General Momcilo Perišić, the commander of the Yugoslav Army, in charge of the attack on Srebrenica from a mountain on the other side of the Drina, could not be confirmed. But there is little doubt that Perišić supplied the Bosnian Serbs with the fuel and supplies they needed. At the time, Milošević said he was no longer supplying the Bosnian Serbs militarily.
35. Jean-René Ruez, testimony before the International War Crimes Tribunal for the Former Yugoslavia, July 3, 1996.
36. Jadran Pandurević, Associated Press, June 28, 1996.

ACKNOWLEDGMENTS

I owe the largest debt to my family and my editors. My parents, stepparents, brothers Lee and Erik, sister Laura, sister-in-law Beth, Uncles Carl, Tom and Sig and Aunts Ruthie, Wanda and Mary pushed tirelessly for my release in November 1995. Clayton Jones and Faye Bowers, the foreign and Balkans editors at *The Christian Science Monitor*, and eleven members of my family flew to the peace talks in Dayton, Ohio, and won my release. I am also indebted to the Clinton administration and the Committee to Protect Journalists for making my release a priority. Richard Holbrooke, John Menzies and Kati Marton have my deepest thanks and gratitude.

The Christian Science Monitor is and will always be responsible for this work. David Cook and John Dillin, editor and managing editor at the *Monitor*, gave a young reporter an opportunity to cover Bosnia. Clayton Jones and Faye Bowers encouraged and supported pursuing rumors of mass executions to the end and were friends as well as superiors.

I owe the characters in this book a tremendous debt. They sat through hours of draining interviews, reliving traumas best forgotten. Captain Jelte Groen's decision to cooperate led nearly a dozen other Dutch to agree to speak with me after months of silence. Several UN and Dutch officials also helped bring facts to light that would never have been known. They asked not to be named and have my thanks. Zoran Radić, the Bosnian Serb who asked not to be named, was especially brave to speak when so many other Serbs refused.

This book could not have been written without the support, advice and friendship of Alexandra Stiglmayer, a friend and outstanding journalist who sat through endless deliberations on conspiracy theories and generously shared apartments and cars.

I owe thanks to Stacy Sullivan for reporting and help long after Srebrenica had faded from interest; Samantha Power for eloquence in November 1995 and friendship in Zagreb and Sarajevo; Kathleen Reen for friendship and encouragement; John Pomfret, Julian Borger and Jonathan Landay for teaching me how to report and work in the former Yugoslavia; Roy Gutman for making me dig deeper; and Kit Roane for friendship and support even when it was not deserved.

In Tuzla, Sanel Hadziahmetović was both a translator and a friend. Tamara Trbojević and Alma Ahmedbegović endured endless searches for survivors and even several arrests. In Zagreb, Duro Novaković and Ljubica Babić have my thanks. In Belgrade, several people have my deepest thanks.

Esther van Osselen helped a stranger in Holland, Lotte Liecht was a generous host and valuable sounding board in Brussels, Gail and Rob Chaddock were supportive and generous through two weeks of frustration and Jonathan Randal and Roger Cohen gave valuable advice and contacts in Paris.

David Herring of *The Christian Science Monitor* turned Srebrenica's complexities into clear, detailed maps that were crucial to making what occurred understandable. John Glusman and Rebecca Kurson put up with late manuscripts, brought passive prose to life and, most importantly, supported making this a book focused on the right thing. The generous support of the Open Society Institute and Aryeh Neier made initial research possible. Gail Ross and Howard Yoon had faith in this project when no one else did and made it a reality.

Finally, Robyn Smith listened, edited and understood. This book would never have been possible without her patience and support.

INDEX